LIVING OPTIONS IN PROTESTANT THEOLOGY

A Survey of Methods

by

JOHN B. COBB, JR.

THE WESTMINSTER PRESS
Philadelphia

LIBRARY OF CONGRESS CATALOG CARD NO. 62-10568

PRINTED IN THE UNITED STATES OF AMERICA

Contents

Preface

THIS BOOK IS WRITTEN IN THE HOPE THAT IT CONSTITUTES A RESPONSIBLE survey of the present situation in Protestant theology. Only on the basis of some such survey can one intelligently define his own position. But a survey can lead to responsible decision only if it points up the bases on which such decision must ultimately rest. Since it is my judgment that these bases must be understood in terms of *methodology,* this survey is oriented to the critical study of the methods employed by major theologians.

A critical comparison of theological methods in the contemporary scene must appear to the average Christian and even to the average student of theology to be quite remote from the vital concerns of faith and of the church. Yet it is undertaken here from personal necessity and from the conviction that it is urgent because it is a means toward the revitalization of faith in our day. In this preface I want to indicate briefly the reasons for my judgment of the importance of methodology.

Usually when a man sets out to present his theological position, he takes as given his own imaginative insights, his traditional convictions, and his intuitive reactions to the ideas of others. Undoubtedly much of the most significant theological writing in every age is formed in this way. It bears the imprint of the living personality of the thinker, and in this lies its power. But in this lies also its weakness.

Theologies of this sort can be endlessly proliferated, and there is little reason to hope that they can ever be reconciled. For those who follow rather than lead the theological movement, only chance or personal inclination can determine who will be accepted as a guide.

Both Roman Catholicism and Protestant orthodoxy have known how to keep the creative individuality of their thinkers within bounds. Both have asserted the authority of Scripture and of tradition, differing, of course, between themselves in the interpretation of each and of their mutual relations. The appeal to authority by no means stifles imaginative originality among the faithful, and the variety of tolerated opinion usually exceeds the expectations of the outside observer. Nevertheless, the body of established doctrine provides a secure springboard for pioneering thought and a sufficient grounding for the life of the church.

Even in liberal Protestantism during much of its history, the real consensus of the church has been sufficiently secure to allow wide diversities among theologians without serious danger and at the same time to hold these diversities within bounds. Hence, the often strange and radical ideas of leading thinkers could be tolerated by the church and eventually, in moderated form, even assimilated. But today in many of our larger American denominations the sustaining consensus of faith is largely dissipated. Divergences of attitude and conviction go so deeply into the heart of the inherited faith that agreement is more easily achieved on questions of mores or social action than on the issue of the fundamental purpose and mission of the church.

In this situation two courses seem to be possible. We can continue to drift with the secular currents of our time, measuring our achievements by our institutional success; or we can undertake the study of theology with radical seriousness to attempt to recover a sense of direction that will enable the church authentically to be the church. In the face of the existing chaos in theology the latter course is fraught with the utmost danger. It cannot but bring to the center of attention existing differences within the church that have been largely concealed for purposes of amicable co-operation on practical and institutional goals. To these differences it must add whole new ranges of issues of which most churchmen are not even aware. Finally, it will reveal for all to see the insecurity of our faith and our pitiable vagueness as to what it is or should be.

Such a course can be recommended in the face of such dangers only because the other alternative seems to lead to the death of the church. The church can be itself only in so far as it has a clear commitment that sets it off from the secular values of its time. During the past century the presence of such a commitment has been increasingly threatened at the conscious level, but the church has survived because of the great reservoir of unquestioned self-understanding left it by centuries of believers. In many critical areas that reservoir is nearly exhausted. It cannot be refilled by anything less than heroic efforts and profound suffering.

The twentieth century has witnessed a theological revival within the liberal context that seemed to offer hope for a line of movement between the two extremes I have identified. In many different ways we have been called to a return to the Bible as read through the eyes of those great Protestant leaders from whose work our denominations sprang. We have been assured that we can thereby recapture the vitality of early Protestant faith without the intellectual obscurantism and arbitrary authoritarianism of some of the orthodox and fundamentalists. In one way or another most of the leading Protestant thinkers of our time have supported this program.

However, as a response to the need of the church in our time, this program, for all its admirable achievements, must be pronounced a failure. That is, it has not in fact brought us closer to real clarity of real conviction. It cannot do so for two reasons. First, as I have tried to show in *Varieties of Protestantism,* the living faith from which we still draw such virility as we have is itself deeply divided. This did not weaken its power in the past, when men could take their stand unequivocally in one tradition or another. But today, at least in America, the traditions have so intermingled that most of us cannot return to a pure affirmation of any one tradition without felt arbitrariness. Second, the challenge of secular thought is far too profound to be met by a return to a purified form of earlier Protestant theology. Western man's spiritual situation has been radically altered by the rise of the new sciences and their interpretation in philosophy. Secularism rather than Christian faith seems now the " natural " stance in a way that was utterly alien to the experience of earlier generations of Protestants. Even the idea that we can solve our problems by a *return* to their thought expresses the gulf that separates us from them.

The leaders of the theological revival of our century have increasingly recognized the complexity of the theological task. They have perceived the need for thorough exposition of the content of faith as they see it. They have seen also the necessity of explaining fully the principles that guide them in their affirmations. This means they are self-consciously concerning themselves not only with systematic theology as doctrine but also with the *method* of systematic theology. In the process of articulating their teaching and their method it has become clear both that their divergences from each other are very serious and also that these divergences arise largely from differences in method.

Typically, in the past, explicit concern for method has arisen only late in the life history of theologians. First they develop their distinctive emphases on the basis of intuitive insight and conviction. Later they consider how these insights may be systematized and justified. The process of systematization and justification often brings about alterations in the doctrines, but it is not surprising that sometimes affirmations are retained that are incongruent with the explicit discussion of method.

Today the church's need for theology is too acute to allow this approach to dominate. The man who utters his personal opinions in an oracular fashion does not help the church in the sober task of articulating its faith. Whoever wishes a hearing must be prepared to explain the grounds on which he affirms whatever he affirms. Only then can others judge intelligently the worth of his statements. If we are to develop responsible theology, doctrines must be accepted or rejected not on the basis of our spontaneous liking or disliking of them but rather on the basis of our judgment of the grounds on which they are affirmed.

There are, of course, many assertions in any given work on theology that can be accepted or rejected on grounds other than that of the theological method employed. A large part of the content of most works consists in interpretation of history, summary or criticism of the opinions of others, and comment on the present situation of man. To some degree we must recognize that even here basic theological assumptions color much of what is said, but accuracy of description and profundity of interpretation are partly independent of such perspectival influences.

However, our present concern is with what is affirmed as essential Christian truth. Here method is all-important. Is the affirmation made on the basis of personal experience? If so, it has just the authority that we attribute to the experiences of the writer. Is it intended to express the consensus of the Christian community or some branch of it? If so, we must determine what authority to attribute to the community in question. Is it an appeal to the message of Jesus or Paul or the New Testament generally? If so, we are turned to the prior question of the locus and extent of the authority of Scripture. Or does the writer justify his assertions in terms of philosophy, modern psychology, or the insight of great artists? If so, we are confronted by the basic issue of the relation of all these authorities to the Christian faith.

In all these instances we are given a second criterion of judgment. That is, is the author's position actually supported by the norms to which he appeals? Has he accurately interpreted his own experience or is he seeing his experience through distorting assumptions? Is there really a churchly consensus of the sort he affirms, or is he reading his own prejudices into the minds of others? Do Jesus and Paul in fact teach what the writer asserts, or is he insufficiently alert to the results of the great body of scholarship that should guide him in such difficult judgments? Is the doctrine in question in fact supported by secular disciplines, or is he selecting dubious conclusions of second-rate thinkers because they bolster his own preferences?

The point here, however, is that the latter type of criticism is secondary to the former. If a writer claims that certain doctrines are true on the authority of Paul and only incidentally points to aspects of modern psychology that agree, there is little point in arguing against him on psychological grounds. If he is shown to have completely misunderstood psychology, his position is not really affected, for its validity depends on the authority of Paul. We must decide first whether we agree as to the authority of Paul and then, if we do, whether he has interpreted Paul aright. If we do not ourselves accept Paul's authority, we may still investigate the accuracy of the writer's interpretation, but this will not have for us the basic theological significance it has for him.

The above suggestions of possible authorities for theology are of course altogether oversimplified. Most serious thinkers are concerned about the relations of a variety of authorities rather than simply the selection of one. A position would not be Christian at all if it did not accept *some* authority of at least *some* aspect of the Bible. At the same time it would not be theological at all if it consisted entirely of Biblical texts unselectively assembled. Any serious statement of Christian theology must have *some* concern for the present cultural-intellectual-spiritual situation of man as well as *some* concern for the Bible.

The real question is, then, *how* the Bible is to be used and *how* the contemporary situation is related to it. Here the greatest variety of possibilities present themselves. One question, however, stands out with special importance for the whole history of theology. It is in philosophy that man's present situation achieves its clearest and most explicit expression. How then should Christian theology relate philosophy to the Biblical affirmations? Should we take philosophy as the starting point and interpret the Bible as supplementing the knowledge we derive therefrom? Or should we oppose the Biblical faith to all philosophy? Or should we distinguish within philosophy areas that are authoritative for us from those which are not? In any case, what philosophy should we employ in this age of philosophical relativism? Or, by much the same token, what aspect of the Biblical teaching shall we take as normative for us?

If the question of theological method is as important as I am arguing, it might seem best simply to treat it systematically. We might then ask, in abstraction from what is in fact being done, just what role philosophy *ought* to play and just how we *ought* to use the Bible. Such studies are entirely legitimate and indeed I have attempted them myself. But to be really significant in a situation where there are already many competing theologies, a study must be related to the actual practice of living theologians. The question of what *is* cannot settle the question of what *ought to be,* but history has shown the danger of attempts to determine what ought to be in abstraction from what is.

For this reason I am attempting in this book to present the positions of a cross section of leading Protestant theologians in terms of the methods that they employ. By their methods I mean here, as above, to point to the question of the authorities to which they appeal or the grounds on which their affirmations can best be justified. One might call this a "logical analysis" of the positions investigated if one understands this as an analysis of the principles of verification that are operative.

It is important to distinguish this analysis from biographical or psychological study of the authors and their ideas. No attempt is made to trace the development of a man's thought, or to determine his indebtedness to various teachers. These are interesting questions but they provide only indirect light on the value or adequacy of the ideas as such. In cases in which there are important shifts in a man's thought, I have concentrated on what I take to be the more systematically developed position, which is generally also the last. I have omitted biographical information almost entirely.

In one sense, therefore, this is a quite specialized study of contemporary theology. It focuses on the single question of the methods employed in theological formulation. However, I take this approach because of my conviction that any developed position is understood best when it is grasped in terms of its essential structure. This structure in turn can be understood only as the immediate embodiment of the controlling principles of a man's thought.

The discussion of each man is divided into two sections, the first being expository and the second critical. Readers interested in an introductory presentation of the position can omit the criticisms. Others, already familiar with the theologians treated, may be chiefly interested in my critical comments. To aid both types of readers ◈◈ separates the exposition from the criticism.

I have kept in mind also that some readers will be interested only in selected chapters. For this reason I have kept cross references to a minimum. Most of the material in any chapter will be intelligible apart from its context in the whole volume. Nevertheless, I need hardly say that the book is written primarily to be read as a unity.

Even when I am attempting only to present and clarify the structure of a theologian's position, I have avoided all quotations and close paraphrases. It has seemed best to present the ideas only in the form in which I am able to assimilate them into my own thinking. Thereby I can minimize the shift in vocabulary from chapter to chapter and greatly reduce the number of technical terms that are used. Thereby, also, I assume full responsibility for the interpretation of every position. The footnotes indicate passages that in my opinion support my formulation and interpretation. In many cases, however, the understanding that I express derives from an over-all view and cannot be precisely documented.

In any such volume as this the selection of positions to be critically investigated is a major problem. Few readers will approve the list exactly as it stands. I myself recognize that inclusion and exclusion are sometimes determined by such arbitrary considerations as accessibility of materials and personal familiarity. At the same time, I hope that most readers will agree that most of the major types of contemporary theology are represented.

This claim can be made, however, only within the limits I have adopted for this project. In the first place, as indicated in the title, the theology studied is limited to Protestantism. This in no way disparages the excellence of contemporary Roman Catholic theology, but such theology has special assumptions and problems that interfere with its direct accessibility to Protestants.

In the second place, no pretense is made of giving a fair representation to conservative and orthodox Protestant theologians. A brief treatment of one representative is included in Chapter 5, but again there are special assumptions and problems operative in orthodox Protestantism that render it also not directly accessible to those who have been nurtured in the atmosphere of liberalism.

In the third place, the perspective of this volume must be frankly American. As an American with very limited linguistic skills and inadequate familiarity even with the literature available in translation, I can make no useful judgments with respect to most of the work that has been going on in such areas as Scandinavia and the Netherlands. My view of the Swiss and German scenes, too, is undoubtedly distorted by special factors that have governed it. For example, the major role of Brunner in this volume reflects his importance in the American scene rather than his position in the German-speaking world. The neglect of theologians from the British Isles reflects the historic ties of American theology to the Continent rather than to the British Isles, despite the greater accessibility of the latter. I have undoubtedly chosen American theologians when men of other countries of equal or greater stature have been omitted.

I should add that I have been guided in my selections also by the explicitness with which theologians have raised and dealt with methodological problems and by a concern to display a wide variety of proposed methods. Chapters 2 and 11, in both of which more than one man is treated, should be understood as efforts to display — without, I hope, serious distortion of the thought of the men taken as illustrating these methods — systematic possibilities that would otherwise be neglected. Finally, I have limited myself to living theologians who have published major works since World War II. It is interesting to note that despite this criterion most of the men discussed are around seventy years of age or older.

The classification of theological positions under three headings is based intentionally on *apparent* groupings rather than on my own final judgment as to the real options that are offered. In view of the importance for theological method of the status and role of philosophy, the distinction between Parts I and II is based on the positive or negative attitude adopted toward the use of philosophy as a constitutive part of theological work. Since existentialism is a philosophy that is itself hostile to traditional philosophy, those theologians who relate themselves chiefly to existentialism are treated as a third group in Part III. Whether they can really distinguish their approach from those approaches studied in Parts I and II can be decided only in the process of exposition and criticism.

The first chapter in each Part is an attempt to orient the material treated in that Part both historically and systematically. In these chapters, I have in some instances relied heavily on secondhand sources.

The body of the work in its intention of responsible analysis and criticism lies in the other eight chapters. Although I cannot claim to have done exhaustive research on any one of the men treated, I have worked extensively with primary sources, checking my interpretation against that of others wherever possible.

The criticisms made of each position are intended as *internal* criticisms only. By this I mean that they are intended to expose the actual situation in the theology in question and not to judge it by any standard of orthodoxy or personal preference. They deal with the relation of the actual procedure employed to the avowed method, the internal consistency of the method, the apparent implications of taking the method seriously, and the kinds of ultimate assumptions upon which the whole position rests. This kind of analysis should help to expose apparent theological methods that leave crucial questions unsettled. It should thereby enable us to limit the range of real possibilities to those which are capable of being carried through with consistency to intelligible conclusions.

In my " Personal Conclusions " I state what seem to me to be the genuinely living options and also my personal choice among them. The task of working out constructively the problems of theological method to which this choice leads is indicated but not undertaken. My original intention had been to devote a considerable portion of this volume to this constructive task, but the book grew beyond reasonable bounds. Whatever contribution I may be able to make must be postponed until I have more time and more mature insight.

This book is almost exclusively concerned with the thought of others. For the most part these others are men who appeared on the theological scene in the twenties and thirties. The implication may seem to be that I regard their achievements as setting the limits for the work of the generation to which I myself belong.

Actually, my judgment is almost at the opposite extreme from this view. The positions presented are those which are most effectively offered to today's student, in or out of seminary. In this sense they are the living options that he faces. Personally, however, I deplore, rather than accept, this situation. The total spiritual climate both in Europe and America has changed greatly in the past thirty years, and the tempo of change is even now accelerating. The magnificent response to the situation faced immediately after World War I is not in itself adequate to the situation that will be faced in the sixties and seventies. The great men treated in this book have adjusted to some degree to the changing times, but it is too much to expect dynamically new approaches from men now retiring from professional life. The younger generation must imitate the creative power of these men, not reproduce their systematic conclusions.

My concern for finding fresh approaches to our rapidly changing situation is expressed in my co-editorship with James M. Robinson of a new series of volumes on emerging trends in German theology. It is our hope not only to identify important new developments as they occur but also to encourage full and fruitful interchange between younger American and German theologians. It is in such undertakings that we may look for real theological progress.

But we cannot progress in theology by ignoring the achievements of our teachers. There must be a real coming to terms with their thought before a meaningful advance is possible. It is to facilitate such a "coming to terms" that this book provides these schematic critical presentations of some of the major accomplishments of the older generation.

◈ ◈

My first extended attempt to confront the problems of theological method was in my doctoral dissertation at the University of Chicago. A few pages of what I wrote then have found their way into this volume. My first systematic attempt to come to terms with the range of theological proposals that confront us today was in lectures delivered to the Southern California-Arizona Conference (Methodist) Pastors' School, in September, 1959. The present book began as a revision of these lectures, but in fact it is an almost totally different work.

The writing of this book was made possible by the combined generosity of the Southern California School of Theology at Claremont and the American Association of Theological Schools. To both I am deeply and permanently indebted. I did most of the writing while living at Drew University. At the kindness of Drew in not only allowing me use of the library but also providing me with an office in the library building I am gratefully amazed. I can imagine no more favorable situation for a year of concentrated study than was provided me at Drew. To the administration and faculty of both seminary and graduate school as well as to the library staff both collectively and individually I am profoundly grateful.

Profs. L. Harold DeWolf, Henry Nelson Wieman, and H. Richard Niebuhr graciously read and commented on the chapters dealing with their thought in substantially their present form. Prof. Reinhold Niebuhr read an earlier essay of mine on his thought similar in content and thesis to what I have written here. I do not, of course, claim their agreement with all that I have said, but I have tried to take some account of their criticisms and have been reassured as to the general accuracy of my accounts of their thought. In the case of Wieman, I have avoided, in the text of my chapter, substantive changes based on his response, since that response has taken the form of an essay, "In Defense of My Faith," that he intends to publish. I have, however, made some references to this response in footnotes.

Among other persons who have been especially helpful, thanks are due to Profs. Thomas J. J. Altizer, John Dillenberger, Edward Dowey, Robert Funk, John Godsey, Ray Hart, George Lindbeck, Schubert Ogden, Donald Rhoades, James Robinson, and Thomas Trotter. Each of these men gave me the benefit of his encouragement and advice, and in some instances enabled me to correct serious errors of interpretation. No one has read more than a small fraction of the whole, and for all remaining errors and confusions I remain, of course, solely responsible.

Mrs. Frances Baker typed the entire manuscript with conscientious care. Frederic Fost has worked over the entire manuscript, improving clarity and accuracy of expression. He has also corrected the proof and prepared the indexes. Without his intensive work and frequent counsel the book would have been much poorer.

Finally, my greatest debt is to my wife, whose co-operation and assistance in countless ways cannot be itemized.

J. B. C., Jr.

Part I
NATURAL THEOLOGY

1: The Historic Role of Natural Theology

WHAT MOST STRUCK THE EARLY CHRISTIANS ABOUT THEIR NEW FAITH was precisely its newness. Nevertheless, both then and now we are also aware that those who became Christians did not leave altogether behind the ways of thought by which they had lived in their pre-Christian days. Jewish Christians understood their faith quite differently from Greek Christians, and among the Greeks other differences emerged reflecting backgrounds, for example, in the mystery religions on the one hand and classical philosophy on the other.

In the long run, it was Greek and not Jewish Christianity that triumphed; hence, it was the problems of relating Greek thought to Christian faith that determined much of the intellectual history of Christendom. Furthermore, among the thinkers of the church the problem understandably focused specifically upon the relation of Greek philosophy to Christian revelation. The entire history of Christian thought may be studied in these terms, and the present book is guided in its presentation of contemporary Protestant theologies by the kinds of problems that have emerged.

From the earliest days to the present, many Christians have stressed the opposition between the conclusions of philosophy and theology. On the basis of this view some have simply turned away from philosophy and have encouraged others to do so. They have held that since God has granted us in Christ all that we need to know, concern with rational speculation can be only a detriment to faith and a source of heresy. Tertullian is the classical exponent of this view. For him, revelation decisively displaces philosophy.[1]

Others who have recognized the antithesis of Christian faith and phi-

[1] Etienne Gilson, *Reason and Revelation in the Middle Ages,* pp. 5–10.

losophy, however, have believed that the problem lay not in reason as such but in a reason that refused the guidance of revelation. Man's reason is seen as corrupted by his self-centeredness but as capable of serving a very useful function when man repents and receives the grace of God. Indeed, reason illuminated by revelation can explain that revelation and give intelligibility to the whole of reality. The real opposition is not between faith and reason but between Christian thinking and pagan thinking. The former, whether called Christian philosophy or Christian theology, is an eminently worthy task. Some such view as this has characterized the otherwise widely varying positions that may be loosely called Augustinian.[2]

Still others who have seen philosophy and faith as opposing each other have found that they must accept both and simply live with this opposition. They have believed, for example, that philosophy must begin with data that are universally acceptable and not depend upon revelation. They have believed that when this is honestly done the conclusions to which one is led are at odds with important Christian teachings. Usually some one philosopher such as Aristotle is taken as having shown once and for all what philosophy in its pure form must conclude. In the Middle Ages the interpretation of Aristotle by Averroës was widely held to have this authoritative status. Those who, despite their interest in a philosophy that contradicted the teaching of the church, continued sincerely to accept the Catholic faith, were forced to the conclusion that the results of philosophic demonstrations, though rational and necessary, are untrue. Others who overtly accepted this position were no doubt really mockers of the faith.[3]

As long as faith and autonomous speculative reason are seen as arriving at incompatible conclusions, there can be no such thing as natural theology. This consists in those theologically important conclusions of reason from generally accessible data which are confirmed by, or at least compatible with, Christian doctrine. But such conclusions constitute a natural theology in distinction from a philosophy only when they are brought into constructive relationship with other beliefs derived from revelation. The idea of natural theology presupposes a Christian revelation that essentially confirms and supplements reason, rather than either displacing it or functioning as its ground. This supplementary relationship is at least implicit in much early Christian thinking, wherever, for example, the convert assumes that the one God of whom he has learned in Greek philosophy is he who has revealed himself in Jesus Christ. Actually, certain aspects of Greek thinking about God had a considerable in-

[2] *Ibid.*, pp. 15–22.

[3] *Ibid.*, pp. 37–66.

fluence upon the formulation even of the official creeds of the church. Hence, it must be said that natural theology has existed from the earliest days.

However, it was the special problems faced in coming to terms with Aristotle as interpreted by Averroës that led to the first and still normative definition of natural theology. On the one hand, Thomas Aquinas could not accept the view that the great achievements of Greek rationality should simply be ignored by Christians or assumed to be fundamentally distorted by sin. Philosophy appeared to him as having its own proper integrity of data and method which the Christian, too, should respect. On the other hand, Thomas could not accept the view that the conclusions of philosophy should either replace the content of revelation or be regarded as untrue. Truth is one. Mutually contradictory propositions cannot both be true. God has not deceived us in his revelation, but neither does he deceive us in the proper functioning of our reason.

On these assumptions we must suppose that the conclusions of philosophy are compatible with those of theology. The former begins with generally accessible data and employs reason in deriving conclusions. The latter begins with the act of will in which God's revelation is believed and also employs reason in its understanding. If theology and philosophy seem to conflict, rational error has been made somewhere. This error is to be found and remedied by rational reflection.

The position of Thomas entails creative philosophic work on the part of the theologian. He can no longer simply identify the position of a particular philosopher as the necessary conclusion of reason itself. Since in his day Aristotle was the authoritative philosopher, Thomas devoted great energy and philosophical genius to his reinterpretation. But in principle he did not commit himself to agreement with Aristotle's philosophy. He committed himself only to showing that where he disagreed with Aristotle he did so on responsible philosophic grounds. His natural theology is an *improved* Aristotelian philosophy. We may judge historically that he was guided in his improvements by his commitment to Christian faith, but he would have us judge his work on purely rational grounds. In this way we can distinguish his natural theology from the Christian philosophy of the Augustinians.[4]

Thomas' philosophical work enabled him to conclude that some of the

[4] Some modern Thomists have so emphasized the distinctively Christian character of Thomas' philosophy as to put in question any distinction between his natural theology and a Christian philosophy. Gilson entitles his important work on Thomas *The Christian Philosophy of St. Thomas Aquinas.* The question as to theological method that follows when this view is pressed will be considered in the criticism of Mascall in Chapter 2.

doctrines that were given in revelation are also susceptible of philosophical demonstration. Hence he distinguished three types of convictions. The highest is that which, while compatible with reason, could be known only by revelation. The second is that which, although actually revealed for the benefit of those who have neither time nor capacity for philosophic speculation, is also subject to such knowledge. The third is that which is left undetermined by revelation and is the proper province of philosophy alone.[5]

In the later Middle Ages this magnificent synthesis of faith and reason began to crumble, but the basic distinction between natural theology and revealed theology remained. In general, we may say, confidence in the purely rational character of philosophical conclusions declined in the face of the actual variety of belief among philosophers. Philosophy became more technical and abstract while the need of popular piety became more urgent. The view that autonomous reason has a proper sphere of operations remained, but there was less confidence that it included much that had theological value. Hence, a greater burden was placed upon faith in revelation and a widespread reaction against philosophical subtleties set in. Both Reformation and Renaissance express this mood in their quite different ways.[6]

Nevertheless, philosophy did not lose its theological importance. Leading Renaissance thinkers sought a synthesis of New Testament faith and Platonic thought in a new Christian philosophy.[7] Even Luther, despite his hostility to Scholasticism, made use of philosophic categories and of the Aristotelian logic.[8] In later life, he allowed a place to natural theology in the sense of a knowledge of God that leads men to despair.[9] His chosen spokesman, Melanchthon, returned to Aristotle the place of honor and gave to his *Physics,* which Luther had rejected, the role of a positive natural theology hardly distinguishable in form from its role in Thomism.[10] Since Melanchthon was also responsible for the education of the Lutheran ministry, his reinstatement of Aristotle into the curriculum had far-reaching consequences for the whole history of Lutheran theological debate in the following century.[11] The developments in Calvinist circles were not dissimilar.

[5] For a much fuller discussion of Thomas along the lines of this presentation, see Gilson, *Reason and Revelation in the Middle Ages,* pp. 69–84.

[6] *Ibid.,* pp. 85–95.

[7] Jaroslav Pelikan, *From Luther to Kierkegaard: A Study in the History of Theology,* p. 8.

[8] *Ibid.,* pp. 12–14.

[9] *Ibid.,* pp. 22–23.

[10] *Ibid.,* pp. 33–35.

[11] *Ibid.,* p. 48 and Ch. 3.

The elaborate systematic theology of the schools was largely unaffected by the rise of modern science, whereas just this new movement was rapidly becoming decisive for Western thinking generally. Already in the seventeenth century the most sensitive thinkers had come to see their world in terms of matter whose motion is governed by mathematical laws. Since the nature of matter as such could in no wise account for the perfect order of its movements, there was almost unanimous agreement that the laws of nature must be understood as imposed by a supreme intelligence. To this intelligence it seemed natural to attribute the creation of matter as well.

For most thinkers, the success of the human mind in discussing the divine order showed an indubitable separation of man in his rationality from matter. Hence, the existence of man must be understood as a further creative act of God. Since man's activity is then in the moral rather than the natural category, God is understood to have provided for him a moral law. This is comparable to the natural law except that its enforcement is by rewards and punishments rather than by necessity. These are incompletely distributed in the course of this life, but man's radically nonnatural status enables us to suppose that he can survive natural death and receive full justice in another life. To the God who is the author of our being we owe gratitude, praise, and obedience.[12]

From our twentieth-century perspective, it is clear that these beliefs represented a rationalization of inherited Christian faith, but to most men of the seventeenth and eighteenth centuries they appeared as no more than the rudiments of common sense. Christians and enemies of Christianity agreed to this extent. Many supposed that the natural religion of all mankind consisted in this ethical monotheism. Those who limited their beliefs to this natural religion we may call deists.

Given agreement on this body of religiously important beliefs understood as the product of pure reason or common sense, the theological debates centered on the relation of Christian faith to these beliefs. Several possibilities were exemplified. One might regard Christianity as in opposition to them, in which case its corruption and superstition should be exposed.[13] One might regard Christianity as essentially identical with them, in which case its additional elements should be rejected or minimized.[14] One might recognize that Christianity entails something more than these common-sense ideas but believe that its additional elements can be shown

[12] For a summary of the rationalistic creed, see Neve, *A History of Christian Thought,* Vol. II, p. 57.

[13] Voltaire, Paine.

[14] Herbert of Cherbury, Tindal, Toland, Chubb.

to be reasonable extensions of them, because of the corruption which had infected history.[15]

In one usage of the terms, all these positions accept a natural theology. However, we are using the term "natural theology" in this book in distinction from philosophy or philosophy of religion to refer to a use of rational conclusions in constructive relation to another source of belief found in revelation. In this sense only the last can be understood as embodying a natural theology. Even here the line between natural theology and Christian theology is blurred. Many orthodox thinkers in England, however, did accept the deistic view as a natural theology that is both confirmed and supplemented by Christian revelation.[16] Thus the formal pattern of relation between revealed theology and natural theology as expounded by Thomas received new expression in the "age of reason."

Whereas Thomas justified the acceptance of revelation as a supplementary source of truth by the miracle of the church, the later orthodoxy appealed to the fulfillment of prophecy and the miracles of Jesus as evidence of the supernatural authentication of the Biblical revelation. Against this view thoroughgoing deists argued that belief in miracles is a superstition.[17]

The debate between deism and rationalistic orthodoxy was ended by the defeat of both. Historically, this defeat was occasioned by the gradual erosion of the Newtonian understanding of the world, which both had accepted. Systematically, it was achieved much earlier by the work of David Hume. Hume has unusual importance for this study because he foreshadowed the emergence of a now widespread self-understanding of philosophy in which it abandons all cosmological and metaphysical pretensions. This means that it ceases to deal with those topics which it has had in common with theology in the past. In so far as this orientation is accepted, the possibility of a natural theology is undermined in a quite new way. At this point, therefore, we will summarize just those aspects of Hume's thought which are relevant to the deist and orthodox rationalist positions.

A miracle was understood in the eighteenth century as an event that contradicted the universal laws of nature.[18] Few Protestants supposed that such events had occurred after Biblical times. Hence, Hume could appeal to uniformity of present experience against the occurrence of miracles. Although Hume himself clearly disbelieved that any miracle had ever

[15] Locke.

[16] For a list of such writers, see Neve, *op. cit.,* Vol. II, pp. 62–63.

[17] Arthur Cushman McGiffert, *Protestant Thought Before Kant,* pp. 194–210, 216–219.

[18] David Hume, "An Enquiry Concerning Human Understanding," *The English Philosophers from Bacon to Mill,* Edwin Arthur Burtt, ed., p. 656.

occurred,[19] he was too shrewd to argue from present experience to such a conclusion.[20] He argues instead that a rational man must employ his own experience as a guide to the credibility of assertions about what he has not experienced. Since our experience consistently confirms that every event occurs according to natural law, we are properly suspicious of assertions that events have occurred that contradict natural law. Indeed, we could reasonably accept such assertions only if their error would be more contrary to our experience than the occurrence of the events they report. In other words, we should believe that a miracle has occurred only if the reliability of the testimony is so great that we would regard its error as more miraculous, that is, in greater conflict with rational expectation, than the supposed event.[21] This means that the evidence required for belief in a miracle is as great as the evidence required for belief in the idea that the miracle is supposed to authenticate. That no miracle has ever occurred could never be proved, but the probability against the occurrence of any particular miracle is so great that the supposition of its occurrence could never serve as evidence for anything else.[22] In recent years few have attempted to revive the argument for Christianity from miracles.

Against deists and the orthodox alike Hume argues that the supposed self-evidence of a supreme and moral intelligence is illusory. If we wish to speculate as to the source of the ordered universe we know, we cannot exclude chance. In an infinite length of time every pattern of order and chaos may have occurred any number of times. Any one arrangement is exceedingly improbable, but one such improbable arrangement must obtain.[23] Therefore, we can hardly argue from the present arrangement against the theory of chance.

But even if we acknowledge a cause of the universe beyond the universe, what can we know of it? The deists argue from the mechanical nature of the universe that its author must be like a machine maker—intelligent and purposeful. But Hume points out that an argument from the similarity of the whole to one of its parts allows equally for arguments from its similarity to others of its parts. The universe is also like an animal—therefore its author must resemble another animal; and like a plant—therefore its origin must be sought in a seed.[24]

Again Hume is satisfied to show the weakness of the analogy without pressing the argument. Suppose that we do allow that in some vague way

[19] *Ibid.,* p. 663.
[20] *Ibid.,* p. 665.
[21] *Ibid.,* p. 657.
[22] *Ibid.,* p. 665.
[23] David Hume, "Dialogues Concerning Natural Religion," Burtt, *op. cit.,* p. 729.
[24] *Ibid.,* p. 725.

the analogy with a machine is better, what follows? If a mind is demanded, why stop with that? We are aware of bodies without minds, hence, we might simply take the universe as it is, but we have never experienced a mind without a body. Hence, we should provide God with a body. Then we must ask as to his origin, which presumably must be in parents who originated from their parents and so forth.[25]

Once again, Hume shows the weakness of the deist position but allows the possibility that it might be adopted. What, then, should we say of the divine mind? Essential to the deist's view is the idea that God is good. But what is the evidence for God's goodness? Surely nothing else than his creation. But the deist agrees that there is much evil in this world. Hence, how can he suppose that God, who is known only as its author, is perfectly good? The question is not whether the idea of God's goodness can be made *consistent* with the evil in the world granted certain other assumptions such as God's finitude. The question is whether the mixture of good and evil in the world as such can provide the basis for supposing its maker to be absolutely good. And to this, the answer must be negative.[26]

At the level of common-sense rationalism, Hume's arguments could be ignored but hardly refuted. The general sensibility since Hume has been less and less inclined to regard belief in a powerful and good God as unequivocally supported by common sense. If God's existence is to be believed at all, we require a far more elaborate and technical argument—or else an acknowledged leap of faith.

Since Thomism offers this more elaborate argument, it has survived the critique of Hume much more successfully than has deistic natural theology. However, we should note that Hume raised an objection to theology that applies also to Thomism and that will play a role in the following chapter. Thomism escapes the difficulties of arguing from the particular nature of the universe to a cause that explains its form by asserting that any existence whatsoever requires a ground in a different order of being. Hume had little appreciation for this kind of thinking, but he did see that the argument could not provide any concept of God. We may affirm that there is a "cause" of the world, but we can say nothing else whatever about it. In this case, Hume thinks, little of religious or even philosophic importance has been affirmed.[27]

Modern philosophy also had developed more technical arguments for the existence of God that could not be so lightly brushed aside. Descartes employed the ontological argument to the effect that the idea of God en-

[25] *Ibid.*, p. 728. [26] *Ibid.*, pp. 742–746. [27] *Ibid.*, pp. 734–735, 744, 756–757.

tails his existence.[28] Spinoza developed a rigorous metaphysical scheme in which God could be identified as the one substance underlying or constituting all other reality.[29] Berkeley formulated an ontology and epistemology that required God as the source of all experience of the nonmental world.[30] Although none of these philosophies was incorporated into an important theological tradition as its natural theology, they were open in varying degrees to this use.[31]

German rationalistic philosophy was developed by Leibniz and Wolff in still closer relation with Christian theology. However, the union of theology and philosophy that they developed is too intimate to allow a clear distinction between natural and revealed theology.[32]

Against these philosophic positions also, Hume posed crucial objections. All of them made use of the concepts of substance and causality, and in every case the doctrine of God depended on these concepts. Hume argued that the concept of substance is meaningless, and that causality is intelligible only as regularity of succession. This argument is so important for the critical evaluation of contemporary natural theologies that it must be elaborated briefly.

Hume begins with the empirical doctrine that all knowledge of fact and law arises in experience.[33] There are no innate ideas and no special source of ideas in a mysterious intuition. This view had been accepted by Locke and Berkeley also. But Locke had supposed that the qualities given in sense experience required the positing of a substance in which they inhered.[34] Thus a certain brownness and a certain rectangularity both inhere in a substance that with its qualities constitutes our idea of a table. Likewise, our thoughts inhere in a substantial mind.

Berkeley says that if we take seriously the empirical principle, we cannot pretend to have any idea of a material substance. All we experience of the physical world are qualities, so we can form no idea of anything beyond the conjunction of such qualities.[35] He held, however, that we do have a " notion " of mind or spirit as the active cause and locus of ideas.

28 Etienne Gilson, *God and Philosophy,* pp. 81–82.
29 *Ibid.,* p. 101.
30 James Daniel Collins, *God in Modern Philosophy,* p. 110.
31 Surprisingly enough, Spinoza's philosophy serves almost this function in Schleiermacher's theology.
32 Pelikan, *op. cit.,* pp. 85–87.
33 Hume, " An Enquiry Concerning Human Understanding," Burtt, *op. cit.,* pp. 595–596, 600–601.
34 John Locke, " An Essay Concerning Human Understanding," Burtt, *op. cit.,* pp. 294–295.
35 George Berkeley, " The Principles of Human Knowledge," Burtt, *op. cit.,* pp. 523–531.

On the basis of this we may meaningfully posit a divine mind that causes us to have our regular and reliable sensory experience.[36]

Hume examined his own experience and found no substantial mind or active cause underlying or effecting the qualitative flow that constituted his experience.[37] Since no idea of such a power can be constituted out of qualities, he rejected the idea of substance altogether. Furthermore, among the qualities he observed in his experience he could find only spatial and temporal relations. The necessitation of one occurrence by another was unobservable. Hence, the idea of causality can be nothing other than that of a particular kind of spatiotemporal relation.[38] Clearly, then, it must be irrelevant to any such relationship as that between God and the world.

Hume's phenomenalism was so radical that it was largely ignored in Great Britain during the following century.[39] However, in our own time it has revived and largely triumphed in the English-speaking world. It can be identified by its rejection of substance, of causality as other than a descriptive term, and of the subject-object duality. Basically, the position of Wieman, presented in Chapter 4, belongs to the phenomenalist orientation. Those who today continue to accept the categories of thought undermined by Hume cannot ignore his objections with impunity.

In the eighteenth and nineteenth centuries Hume's greatest historical importance lay in his influence upon Kant and through Kant on the whole German development. Kant recognized that Hume's attack on such categories as substance and causality was a radical threat not only to metaphysics and theology but also to science and morality. He accepted Hume's challenge and created the most original and influential system of modern times.

A summary of Kant's philosophy would be out of place here, but its implications for natural theology must be noted. Kant introduced a sharp dichotomy between appearance and reality, which he distinguished as phenomena and noumena. In contrast to almost all earlier modern thought, he argued that science dealt only with the world of phenomena. As Hume had shown, this world consists entirely of the flow of experienced qualities that cannot in themselves explain or justify our ideas of substance and causality. Indeed, Hume should have seen that our ideas of space and time are equally underivable from this process. However, space,

[36] *Ibid.*, pp. 532–533. For Berkeley, a "notion" in distinction from an "idea" need not arise from an impression.

[37] Hume, "An Enquiry Concerning Human Understanding," Burtt, *op. cit.*, pp. 623 ff.

[38] *Ibid.*, pp. 632–633.

[39] Note, however, the arguments against it by the Scottish realists. Collins, *op. cit.*, pp. 122–125.

time, causality, and many other categories do function, and necessarily so, in our experience. Since they cannot derive from the flow of experiential qualities, they must be understood as functions of mind. Although Hume is right that the mind is never qualitatively experienced, its noumenal reality must be assumed. Likewise, a noumenal objective source of sensation must be posited. But of noumenal reality nothing can be known except its existence, and to it the categories of thought appropriate to phenomena cannot be applied. Metaphysics and cosmology, therefore, are almost wholly eliminated, and their relevance to belief in God is ended.[40]

Since natural theology has always consisted in metaphysical or cosmological arguments for the existence and nature of God, the Kantian argument confirmed the Humean refutation of it. The greatest consequence of Kant's thought for the history of theology was its separation of the sphere of distinctively human existence—the moral, spiritual, and historical—from the sphere of the phenomenal world in which scientific thinking is relevant. With natural theology eliminated and the study of the human divorced from the natural sciences, theology received a quite new understanding of its role and function. For the first time it became possible to suppose that natural philosophy was simply irrelevant to systematic theology.[41] Parts II and III of this book treat the history and contemporary exposition of this theological orientation.

Kant himself did not understand the theological implications of his work in this way. On the contrary, he developed an elaborate justification for rational belief in God on the basis of ethical experience and worked out the religious implications of his understanding of God and man. Although the basis and content of his beliefs differed from those of the deists, he resembled them in his view that the only acceptable religion is that which is rationally justified. For Kant, too, reason defines the content and limits of authentic religion.[42]

The immediate and most revolutionary impact of Kant on his philosophical successors lay in his attribution of a creative role to the mind. Kant severely restricted this role by positing an objective noumenal source of the content of experience. But just as Berkeley had rejected the material substances of Locke, so Kant's successors rejected the objective noumena of Kant. Berkeley had assumed that the objectivity of sensory stimulation must still be explained and hence had argued for God as its cause. But the

40 The "Prolegomena to Any Future Metaphysics" is Kant's attempt to state these aspects of his thought in a simple way. *Kant's Prolegomena to Any Future Metaphysics,* Carus, ed., pp. 8–9.

41 Luther had approached this position on very different grounds but had not reached it. See Pelikan, *op. cit.,* pp. 10–15.

42 Immanuel Kant, *Religion Within the Limits of Pure Reason.*

idealist successors of Kant could regard creative mind as the source of the whole of its experience.

They did not mean that the conscious intention of the individual could create the content of his experience. Quite the contrary, the creative mind was understood as altogether suprapersonal. Individual minds only embodied it to a greater or lesser degree. The whole movement of nature and history was to be understood as the self-manifestation or self-actualization of absolute mind.[43]

This absolute idealism received its superlative expression at the hands of Hegel. Its implications for the work of theology differed radically from those of Kantian philosophy. Whereas Kant separated the realms of the noumenal and the phenomenal, Hegel regarded the phenomenal as an embodiment of the pure rationality of the noumenal. The philosophic ideal was to explain the flow of observable events from the perspective of the structure of pure thought. Metaphysics in a quite new form is restored as the queen of all thought. From it and from it alone we can comprehend the truth in each of the particular fields of human inquiry. This process is embodied in such disciplines as philosophy of law, of history, of nature, and of religion. Philosophy of religion provides the norm by which the kernel of truth in theology can be distinguished from its mythical expressions.[44]

Philosophy of religion as developed under the influence of Hegel introduced a quite new conception of the relation of philosophy and theology. During the Middle Ages and early modern period, theological assertions were taken seriously as embodying literal meanings. They were either true or false; as assertions about the nature of reality they were of the same order as philosophic statements. The question was that of the compatibility of the two sets of assertions, or of the justification of one or another statement. The deists and Kant rejected revelation as a source of knowledge. Christian orthodoxy typically accepted both philosophy and revelation and argued for their compatibility.

Now, however, theology is taken as expressive of a dim intuition of a truth that philosophy can grasp directly and clearly. Divergences between the two are recognized, but they are not seen as contradictions. The spiritual experience to which theology gives expression is vindicated, and even the theological expression is appreciated as a kind of poetry, but the real task of interpretation is taken over by philosophy.

[43] For a very brief summary statement of major idealists between Kant and Hegel, see Neve, *op. cit.*, Vol. II, pp. 101, 119. For a somewhat fuller discussion of this development, see Moore, *The History of Christian Thought Since Kant*, pp. 56–66.

[44] A brief exposition of relevant aspects of Hegel's thought is found in Mackintosh, *Types of Modern Theology*, pp. 101–117.

Hegelian philosophy of religion as such cannot be understood as a natural theology, since it sought to supersede theology rather than to provide it a basis. However, like all philosophies that lead to conclusions about the reality of God, it could be regarded as susceptible of use as a natural theology. Such theologians as Biedermann and Dorner expended great ingenuity in this attempt.[45]

Critics of natural theology argue that it always tyrannizes over the revealed theologies of those who use it. The doctrine of God and his relation to the world is so fixed by the philosophy employed that the revealed truth about God is distorted and foreshortened. Whether or not this is true of every use of natural theology, few doubt that the Hegelian philosophy resists Christianization and that the efforts of the theologians failed. Since the decline of Hegelianism, few Protestant Continental theologians have favored the use of natural theology.

The relations of philosophy and theology have had a very different history in the English-speaking world. Hume's radical ideas were not taken seriously, and Kant's influence was far from decisive. Bishop Butler was able to justify Christian orthodoxy by arguing that it offered no more obstacles to rational credence than did the natural religion of the deists.[46] In America, it was the religious inadequacy of deism rather than its philosophic difficulties that caused its downfall. Fundamentally, the view that the orderliness of the world pointed to God as its source and sustainer remained a part of Anglo-Saxon common sense. Reason continued to supply the natural theology that the church supplemented by revealed truths.

For this reason, the great shock to Anglo-American natural theology was Darwinian science rather than critical philosophy. The argument centered around the view that man has an animal ancestry, but a more fundamental issue was at stake.[47]

The wider implication of Darwin's evolutionism was that blind forces immanent in nature account for the complex order that we now observe. In the context of the Newtonian world view, this meant that God, if posited at all as the cause of the world, was only the initiator of a much simpler and less impressive world than ours. It also meant that man was a part of the mechanical world of matter in motion, with only the remotest relations to God. No wonder that Darwinism appeared as synonymous with atheism to many sensitive Christians!

The response to Darwin dominated Anglo-Saxon thought for half a

[45] See the discussion of their work, *ibid.*, pp. 130–134.

[46] Joseph Butler, *The Analogy of Religion, Natural and Revealed, to the Constitution and Course of Nature.*

[47] A brief discussion is found in Moore, *op. cit.*, pp. 151–175.

century or more. Apart from sheer rejection, which rapidly lost all color of justification, and sheer acceptance, which led in fact to atheism or agnosticism, three major alternatives emerged. It is interesting that they are fundamentally reappraisals of the Newtonian-deistic vision more than of evolution as such.

First, Kantian philosophy was now seen as saving morality and religion from the imperialistic claims of a hostile science. The whole Newtonian world was reduced to the phenomenal realm, and ethics and religion were vindicated in the superior sphere of the noumenal. In the less technical language of much theology, the realms of fact and value were distinguished and the Newtonian-Darwinian world was limited to the former.[48]

Second, absolute idealism could be used to show the ultimate unreality of matter. The whole notion of matter in motion producing mind could be reversed to show that in fact it is absolute mind alone that is the source of the real and that what we call matter in motion is only its self-manifestation.[49]

Third, the fundamental naturalism of the Newtonian-Darwinian world could be maintained while rejecting the mechanistic images that dominated it. If nature contained the power of producing life, intelligence, and spirit, then clearly it was not merely an inanimate machine. The persistent thrust toward spiritual being that dominates the evolutionary process could not be understood as a mechanical necessity. There is a force at work within nature that transcends all Newtonian natural categories.[50]

Different interpretations of the relation of this creative force to God are possible. The least disturbing view of the situation to the Anglo-Saxon mind is that we have simply learned more about the way in which God creates. We had supposed he did so in a moment of time, and now we see that he is constantly creatively at work.[51] The religious implications of such a view are far from disturbing.

Others have thought the inference from creativity in nature to a transcendent God to be a weak one and have simply identified this creativity or some aspect of it with God. The implications of such a view may be much more disturbing to traditional Christianity, but they must not be confused with those of an earlier mechanistic naturalism.[52]

Whereas the Kantian and Hegelian solution to the Darwinian threat to theology tended to displace natural theology with philosophy of religion,

48 This is the line taken by the Anglo-American Ritschlians.
49 Bradley, Royce.
50 Fiske, Alexander, Bergson, Tennant.
51 Lyman Abbott.
52 Neo-naturalism. See Chapter 4.

the creative evolutionism of English and American thinkers revived natural theology in a new form. In quite different ways, roughly comparable to those indicated in the two preceding paragraphs, Bertocci and Wieman offer contemporary formulations of this kind of modern natural theology.

This historical survey of the fortunes of natural theology has focused attention on four of the forms that it has taken in Christian history. The first is that of a modified Aristotelian philosophy as employed by Roman Catholic and Protestant Scholasticism. The second is that of the rational religious beliefs of the deists. The third is Hegelian philosophy as adopted by theologically conservative thinkers. The fourth is some form of creative evolution. Since we have noted that many other types of philosophy are susceptible of the formal relation to Christian theology that defines natural theology, it is not necessary to stress that the foregoing list is in no sense exhaustive. In the thought of Brightman as presented in Chapter 3, a different type can be seen. Nevertheless, the four types on which we have focused attention do seem to have played the more prominent roles in the history of Christian theology.

Of these four, the second and third are not now widely regarded as serious possibilities. Hence, it is not surprising that the three positions treated in the following chapters represent primarily the first and fourth views. Further, we have seen that after the abortive attempt to employ Hegelian philosophy as a natural theology, Continental Protestant theologians turned against natural theology as a whole. Hence, it is also not surprising that, whereas Parts II and III are dominated by treatment of Continental thinkers, Part I treats only English and American theologians.

Special difficulties have attached to the selections of contemporary theologians who employ natural theology. The inclusion of a Thomist was clearly demanded, but the most famous Thomists are Roman Catholic. Stretching the definition of Protestant, I have included the Anglo-Catholic, E. L. Mascall.

In many ways at the opposite pole of the theological spectrum we find the radical empiricism of Neo-naturalism. Its clearest systematic exponent is Henry Nelson Wieman. Wieman's work is primarily philosophy of religion rather than systematic theology, and for this reason his inclusion, too, raises questions. However, he does provide us with some clear indication of the way in which his philosophy can function as a natural theology in relation to specifically Christian theology.

The great body of American thought that still looks to natural theology stands between these polar positions: the Thomist, which thinks of God as transcendent and supernatural; and that of Wieman, which presents God as a process immanent in nature. It finds expression in many books, but few recent writers have treated it systematically and extensively. Generally, the philosophers of religion have been left by the theologians to go their own way, with relatively little interchange.

The place at which close co-operation between theology and a philosophy of religion falling in this middle area has been kept most vitally and viably alive is in Boston Personalism. Even here, no one contemporary has developed philosophy of religion as a natural theology in the context of a total theology, but the materials for the task are readily at hand.

The theological position of L. Harold DeWolf will be the basis of the chapter on Boston Personalism, but it would be unfair to criticize the natural theology of which he makes use only in terms of the limited development it receives at his hands. Hence, the arguments for the existence of a personal God developed in two recent books by Personalist philosophers will be used as illustrating the kind of philosophical thinking that can support DeWolf's position. These books are Bertocci's *Introduction to the Philosophy of Religion* and Brightman's *Person and Reality,* edited posthumously by Bertocci.

Despite the fact that the discussions in the three following chapters will leave many other possible approaches uncriticized, most of the basic issues with respect to the viability of an approach to Christian thought through natural theology should be clearly raised. The fundamental questions that should be kept in mind are as follows. First, can we escape philosophical relativism sufficiently to justify any constructive doctrine as an objectively rational basis for understanding revelation? Second, can any doctrine of God arrived at philosophically be compatible with the distinctively Christian understanding of God? Unless both these questions can be answered positively, natural theology as understood in this chapter must be rejected.

2: The Thomism of E. L. Mascall

WHEN WE THINK OF NATURAL THEOLOGY, WE THINK FIRST AND FOREmost of Thomism. Natural theology existed before the time of Thomas, and many new forms have appeared since his time, but it was he who gave classic statement both to the relation of natural theology to Christian revelation and also to the content of natural theology itself. The semiofficial adoption of his basic formulations by the Roman Catholic Church has guaranteed a historical importance to his work that is commensurate with its intrinsic interest.

Our own century has witnessed a revival of Thomism that has had great influence even beyond the bounds of the Roman Catholic Church. For many Protestants, as well as Roman Catholics, much of Thomas' position appears to be viable despite the lapse of centuries since its formulation. Hence, even though this book limits itself to Protestant theology, it is fitting that it begin with a serious discussion of Thomism.

Unfortunately, despite the very real respect with which many Protestants regard contemporary Thomism, they have left its exposition and development largely in the hands of Roman Catholics. The names of Etienne Gilson, Jacques Maritain, R. Garrigou-Lagrange, and E. Przywara come readily to mind, but as Roman Catholics they are not available for use here. However, E. L. Mascall, a contemporary Anglican theologian, drawing heavily upon the writings especially of the French Thomists,[1] has done impressive work in interpreting and developing Thomism in a non-Roman Catholic context.

Even Mascall can be called a Protestant only by the very loosest use of the term. He thinks of himself as a Catholic, and the detailed formulation

[1] E. L. Mascall, *He Who Is: A Study in Traditional Theism,* p. x.

of his theology gives clear expression to this fact. In the following exposition, predominant attention will be given to his natural theology which, as such, would be quite compatible with non-Catholic doctrines. Mascall's Catholic theological position, which presupposes an understanding of the church alien to Protestantism generally, is barely sketched. His extensive discussions of the liturgy, orders, and sacraments of the church are almost wholly neglected.[2]

Contemporary Thomists are not concerned with slavishly reproducing the ideas of Thomas Aquinas. They recognize that much of what he said was conditioned by the naïve science of his day and by his excessive commitment to Aristotelian philosophy.[3] But they do believe that the basic principles and structure of his system provide the basis for solving both the philosophical and the theological problems of our own time. It will not be our concern in this chapter to judge whether Thomas in fact intended all the ideas that Mascall and other Thomists derive from him. Our concern will be only to formulate these ideas as clearly as possible in a brief compass and to evaluate the adequacy of the evidence to which appeal is made for the conclusions that are drawn from it.

It is sometimes supposed that natural theology intends to embody only those ideas upon which all reasonable men in fact agree. Since today there are no ideas of religious importance upon which such agreement can be claimed, there clearly could be no natural theology in this sense. Since this is self-evident, we may assume that the practitioners of natural theology do not claim universal acceptance for their views. On the other hand, if they affirmed only that their natural theologies constitute one among a plurality of equally rational systems of thought, they would be left with a relativism that would be alien to the concept of natural theology.

Mascall is fully aware of this difficulty, but he does not think that it destroys the case for natural theology in its traditional Christian form. The argument is not that all men capable of rationality reach the same conclusions but that those who are willing to be attentive to the right data and open to the correct interpretation can be led to see that certain conclusions follow necessarily.[4] The obstacles to the acceptance of traditional natural theology are indifference, habit, prejudice, blindness, and laziness.[5] Our whole urban way of life with its artificiality and emphasis on distractions militates against the kind of concern, sensitivity, and patience that is required for natural theology. Hence, it is not surprising that the arguments

[2] For these aspects of Mascall's work, see especially *Corpus Christi; The Recovery of Unity;* and *Christ, the Christian and the Church,* Chs. 9 to 11.

[3] E. L. Mascall, *Existence and Analogy,* pp. xvii, 73, 77, 84–85.

[4] *Ibid.,* p. 75.

[5] *Ibid.,* p. 90.

of natural theology seem strange and irrelevant to many moderns. But it is clear also that this understandable response does not imply the falsity or inadequacy of the doctrines themselves.[6]

The foregoing might seem to suggest that natural theology could be found adequately developed among pre-Christian thinkers who devoted themselves with requisite patience and concern to the discovery of ultimate truth. But history shows us that this is not the case. Does this not invalidate the claim of natural theology to be the reasoned knowledge of God that is systematically independent of revelation?

Again Mascall is fully aware of the problem. Indeed, he places considerable emphasis upon the difference between the philosophy of the Greeks and the natural theology of the Scholastics.[7] He recognizes the role of revelation in making possible the achievement of this natural theology. He does *not* claim, therefore, that natural theology was factually possible apart from revelation.[8] He *does* claim that the ideas and arguments developed in Christian natural theology are intelligible to those who do not accept the claims of revelation and that if they are sufficiently open and interested they can be led to see the decisive cogency of the reason that is employed. Presumably one might compare the situation with that which occurs with respect to a new discovery in mathematics. It is not factually the case that reasonable men acknowledged this truth prior to the time of its discovery. It is not factually the case that all reasonable men acknowledge it after its discovery. Nevertheless, what has been discovered is in principle rational, and those who have sufficient patience and interest can be shown that this is so.

In this way Mascall clears away the most obvious objections to natural theology as such. The factual relativism and historical conditionedness of every systematic position, he argues, do not imply the systematic relativism of every position. The systematic claims of a philosophical argument must be taken at face value and judged on the basis of rational examination. If this is done, Mascall believes, the traditional Christian natural theology that is given classical expression by Thomas Aquinas can be shown to be true.

In our time, the objections to natural theology have come not only from philosophers but also from theologians. These have argued that our attempts to gain an understanding of God by reason are a betrayal of the God who has revealed himself to us. The God of reason is an idol of the mind and not the living God of revelation. Faith is not faith unless it is a

[6] *He Who Is*, pp. 80–81.
[7] *Existence and Analogy*, pp. 1–10, 15–17.
[8] *Ibid.*, p. 11.

leap beyond all reason and all calculations of probability.[9]

Once again Mascall is quite aware of this attack by Protestant theologians upon the enterprise that he advocates. He agrees that there is a real difference between the philosophic apprehension of God and the understanding of God given in revelation and worship, and that the former is poor and barren beside the latter.[10] But he is quite sure that the God who is apprehended in these two different ways is the same God. We cannot meaningfully affirm that Christ is the incarnation or revelation of God unless we can explain what we mean by God,[11] and although the most valuable part of our knowledge of God comes from the revelation in Jesus Christ, that part which reason provides is a necessary basis on which the rest can be built.[12] The value of faith stems not from the irrationality of its object but from the humility that is required to see the truth which is accepted, and the courage required to act upon it.[13]

Of course, it is not necessary for each individual to study natural theology before he is prepared to accept revelation. Those who grow up in the Christian church normally follow no such order. But we must be concerned also for those whose thought is not formed in a Christian environment and who quite reasonably ask what faith is all about. To them we must be prepared to explain what we mean by God and to show that he exists, in order that they may be prepared to consider seriously the claim that he is revealed in Jesus Christ.[14]

What has just been said indicates that special revelation cannot constitute the sole basis of our knowledge of God. Unless our total understanding includes belief in something that can reveal itself, we cannot apprehend any occurrence as a revelation. Revelation reveals more about that which is already known to be. Faith cannot dispense with this prior knowledge.

For this reason there are only two real alternatives to natural theology as a basis for Christian faith and theology. One might affirm that the required general knowledge of God is given in religious experience, that is, in direct consciousness of him.[15] One might also affirm that God's existence is strictly self-evident, so that no reasoning is required to arrive at this knowledge.[16] Mascall considers both these alternatives to show their inadequacies.

Many Protestants reject the view that God is known by argument or inference in favor of the view that he is immediately experienced. Apart from such experience, they suppose, argument is unconvincing. With this

[9] *He Who Is,* p. 76.
[10] *Ibid.,* p. 81.
[11] *Ibid.,* p. 2.
[12] *Ibid.,* p. 24.
[13] *Ibid.,* p. 77.
[14] *Ibid.,* pp. 26–27.
[15] *Ibid.,* p. 16.
[16] *Ibid.,* p. 30.

experience, argument is unnecessary.

Mascall does not deny that there is such a thing as authentic, immediate experience of God, but he does deny that this is the normal or general basis for believing in God. By far the larger part of the experiences to which men appeal can be explained from a psychological viewpoint without recourse to the hypothesis of God's reality.[17] Only the greatest mystics have attained that purer experience which radically transcends these natural categories. Even with respect to them, we must acknowledge a diversity of interpretation as to the immediateness of their awareness of God in himself,[18] and these interpretations will depend in part upon some other knowledge of God than that given in the experience itself. Mascall, therefore, does not disparage religious experience, but he emphatically insists that it cannot become a substitute for natural theology.[19]

Some who acknowledge the inadequacy of both revelation and religious experience as bases for belief in God affirm that God's existence is self-evident. The classical formulation of this position is the ontological argument of Anselm of Canterbury. According to Anselm, the concept of God implies his existence. This is because the concept of God is the concept of that than which nothing greater can be thought, and lack of existence would contradict this concept.[20]

Mascall agrees that in the sphere of being, the essence of God is unique in that it includes his existence. Thus Anselm's argument may be accepted as showing that if God exists, his existence is necessary. But the fact that God's essence includes his existence does not imply that our concept of God implies his existence. Our concept of God's essence only proves that we cannot form a concept of God that does not include the idea of his existence. But the idea of God's existence is not the same as his actual existence.[21]

Having cleared away the objections to the enterprise of natural theology and having shown that we cannot regard its conclusions as self-evident, we must turn to the enterprise itself. Its heart and core consists in displaying the rational necessity of acknowledging the existence of God and the implications that are given in this argument with respect to God's nature.

Thomas Aquinas developed five arguments for the existence of God. The first argument, and that upon which he relied most heavily, is the

[17] *Ibid.*, pp. 17 ff.

[18] *Ibid.*, p. 21. See also his discussion of mysticism in *Words and Images: A Study in Theological Discourse*, pp. 42–45.

[19] *He Who Is*, p. 29.

[20] *Ibid.*, p. 31. For further discussion of essence and existence, see Gilson, *The Christian Philosophy of St. Thomas Aquinas*, pp. 29–45.

[21] Mascall, *He Who Is*, p. 34.

familiar argument from motion or change. Change is understood in Aristotelian terms as the actualization of a potentiality. This actualization requires an explanation in terms of a cause that cannot lie either in the potentiality as such or in that which is actualized. Hence, change points to a cause beyond that which changes. This cause may be some other changing entity, but we cannot conceive of this succession of causes as infinite. Hence, a cause must be acknowledged that causes change without itself changing. This cause is God.[22]

The second argument is that not only change but the being or preservation of entities requires causal explanation. Once again the being of one entity may be explained by the act of another, but an infinite series cannot be admitted. Hence, a first cause of being must be affirmed.[23]

The third argument is based on the categories of contingency and necessity. The fact that the entities we encounter around us are subject to generation and decay indicates that they are contingent, that is, that they are capable of not being. But if there had ever been a time when nothing existed, then nothing could ever have come to exist. Hence, it is necessary that there be something that is not contingent, therefore, necessary. This necessary being either has its necessity in itself or receives it from another necessary being. To avoid an infinite regress we must affirm a being that is the cause of its own necessity.[24]

The fourth argument is from the degrees of excellence perceptible in things. These degrees of excellence can be understood only as degrees of approximation to an absolute norm by which they are judged. One thing is better than another if it more nearly approaches that which is ideally good in itself. Hence, the presence of degrees of excellence in things demands as its cause that which is perfect in itself, namely, God.[25]

The fifth and final argument is that from purpose. Just as every entity requires an explanation of its being in terms of an efficient cause of being (the second argument), so also it requires an explanation in terms of final cause or purpose. In this case also, the final cause, the goal at which all purposes aim, is God.[26]

All five arguments depend for their force upon the idea of causality. Mascall recognizes that this idea has been banished from modern physics, although it seems to continue to play a role in such sciences as biology and psychology. Even if it were wholly removed from science, however, this would not affect the force of the arguments. Causality as treated in these arguments is a purely metaphysical idea that is not dependent for its validity upon its relevance in the special sciences.[27]

[22] *Ibid.*, pp. 40–45.
[23] *Ibid.*, pp. 45–46.
[24] *Ibid.*, pp. 46–49.
[25] *Ibid.*, pp. 52–54.
[26] *Ibid.*, pp. 54–56.
[27] *Ibid.*, p. 45.

It will be clear to even the casual reader, however, that the formulations above are vulnerable to many other objections. This is due partly to their very brief and vague formulation here, but even in the more adequate statements of Thomas and in Mascall's account of Thomas' arguments, they remain vulnerable. Mascall, like most contemporary Thomists, fully recognizes that these arguments require extensive elaboration if they are to be rendered defensible in our day. This elaboration consists in the end in presenting the five arguments as five aspects of a single argument that Thomists find implicit but unclearly expressed in all of them.[28] It is this single fundamental argument rather than the explanations of the five arguments in its terms that is important to us in understanding contemporary Thomist natural theology.

This one argument can be formulated very simply.[29] Every entity that we encounter in the world is finite. This finitude consists among other things in a lack of the power to cause or sustain its own being. Thus the cause of the being of all things lies outside of them. That which can give being to everything that is cannot be understood as one finite entity among others, or as merely the first in a long series of causal agents. Since Thomas did not believe that the denial of the eternity of the world could be established by reason, his argument to a first cause should not be construed as an argument for a first member of a temporal sequence.[30] The first cause must belong to an entirely different order of reality. Furthermore, it must differ from all finite entities in having the ground or power of its being in itself, for otherwise we would have to posit an infinite regression of beings deriving their being from other beings.

From this perspective we can see clearly what is valid in Thomas' arguments. Each of them points to some aspect of finitude and insufficiency on the part of the entities in our world, on the basis of which we are driven to recognize a self-sufficient cause of a wholly different order. The first argument points to the lack of self-sufficiency of change; the second, to that of endurance in being. The third shows that the totality of finite beings must still remain contingent and hence dependent for its being on that which possesses being in itself and by necessity. The fourth and fifth show that the perfections and purposes of finite things share in their finitude and lack of self-sufficiency.

They are all so many expressions of the fact that when our eyes are opened to the finitude, insufficiency, or contingency of ourselves and the environing entities, we perceive every aspect of these entities as pointing

28 *Ibid.*, p. 40; *Existence and Analogy*, p. 79.

29 Formulations are found in *He Who Is*, pp. 37–39, 65, 95; *Existence and Analogy*, pp. 68–69, 85, 89–90.

30 *Existence and Analogy*, pp. 72–76.

directly to a supernatural cause.[31] This does not deny that there is also a natural order of causation, but the fullest explanation in natural terms does not in any way affect the need for understanding the whole network of natural causes as wholly dependent for its being and preservation upon a supernatural cause. The whole network of natural causes, even if it is supposed to have no temporal beginning or ending, remains radically finite, insufficient, and contingent.

Once we see clearly the fundamental conception underlying Thomas' sometimes unclear formulations, we can also see the fundamental requirement for the acceptance of the argument. It is the simple recognition that there are finite entities and subsequent reflection on what this means.[32] Philosophically this may be stated as the fact that the essence of finite entities does not imply their existence.[33] But many ordinary people recognize all this immediately, and while knowing nothing of the philosophical concepts in which it is expressed, live by the knowledge of God which they have.[34] On the other hand, many sophisticated intellectuals are prevented by their theories from recognizing the simple fact that there are finite entities.

Mascall sees that if he is to establish his case for natural theology in the context of modern philosophy, he must refute those epistemological views that lead to the denial of the existence of finite entities.[35] In this sense, like all Thomists, he defends existentialism.[36] He sees also that in our own day many find that human existence, rather than the existence of things objective to man, is the natural starting point, and he has no serious objection to this. So long as the existence of any finite entity is acknowledged, the basic argument follows from its insufficiency to a self-sufficient existent.[37]

Nevertheless, Mascall's own procedure is to argue first for the existence of objective finite entities. Their existence is obscured by essentialism because the radical uniqueness of existence is not recognized. Against essentialists, therefore, the task is simply to call attention to the difference between essence and existence. In our day the more acute threat comes from those persons who deny objectivity to essences as well as to individual existents.[38] Their position must be understood and refuted.

[31] *Ibid.*, pp. 71, 78.
[32] *He Who Is*, p. 73.
[33] *Existence and Analogy*, pp. 68–69.
[34] *He Who Is*, p. 137.
[35] He does this most systematically in *Via Media*, Ch. 1.
[36] E.g., *Existence and Analogy*, Ch. 3.
[37] *Ibid.*, pp. 167–169.
[38] *He Who Is*, p. 83.

If we take the primitive givens of experience as sense data, we seem to be forced to recognize that from their givenness we cannot infer the existence of any entity whatsoever. The argument that these qualities must inhere in an underlying substance can be disposed of by the simple fact that if all our ideas or concepts arise in sense experience, we can have no idea or concept of substance. Hence, it would be absolutely meaningless to affirm a substance even if evidence could be adduced. All that can be spoken or thought of is an endless flow of qualities. All distinction of subject and object and all discrimination of discrete entities evaporates into the one ongoing process. The organization of sense data into objects is the creative and distorting act of mind.[39]

The Thomistic objection to this philosophic development must not be confused with that of idealism. There is no tendency to assign a prior ontological status to either finite minds or to impersonal reason. The primacy of experience as the normal starting point for all knowledge is fully recognized, but the Thomist insists that along with sense experience man has the equally primary faculty of judgment, whose object is the existence of the entities that are sensuously apprehended. We do not in fact know only patches of brown and green. We know existent entities that are of definite shape and color. This knowledge is a work of the mind that can never occur apart from sense experience but that is not limited to the mere reception of that experience.[40] The mind may, of course, be in error in its judgments, but this does not mean that it is always or usually in error in attributing existence to things.[41]

It must be stressed that we do not first recognize finite existents when we have understood the epistemological theory that explains how we recognize them as such. The theory is a description of a fact of common experience. The fact and not the theory is the basis for the natural knowledge of God. The theory is needed only to refute those who suppose that common experience must be illusory because it cannot be explained philosophically.

Thus far we have considered only the basis on which the existence of God is rationally affirmed. It is constituted essentially by the immediate implication of the awareness of the world as it is in its finite existence. We must ask next what it is that is implied in this argument.

First of all, and most essentially, we know that God possesses precisely those characteristics the absence of which in finite things causes us to perceive that God is their cause. That is, God is self-existent, infinite, self-

[39] *Ibid.*, pp. 83–84.
[40] *Ibid.*, p. 65; *Existence and Analogy*, pp. 53–57; *Words and Images*, pp. 30 ff., 63.
[41] *He Who Is*, pp. 84–85.

sufficient, and necessary.[42] This is clear to anyone who considers what is involved in finitude, since to attribute finitude to what one called God would simply postpone the real question of God. We can also say that God is the cause of all that is finite as well as the cause of his own being, for it is just as the self-causing cause of all things that we have come to know his existence. Furthermore, God is changeless, for we have seen that whatever changes must be subject to a source of change and that ultimately this must be a source of change that does not itself change.

At this point, however, we confront an acute problem. It seems that if we are to speak of God as cause of the world we must mean something more by the term "God" than that he is cause. Hume showed that if all we affirm is that an absolutely mysterious X is responsible for all that is, agnostics will have little reason to object. Certainly as Christians we must affirm much more of God than this purely causal relation to the world. But every term or concept that we employ has arisen and received its meaning in our relations with finite things. Since we know that God is not finite, else he would not be God, how can we apply to him ideas that belong properly only to the finite sphere? [43]

One answer is that we cannot apply any terms to God except by way of negation. According to this view we cannot know what God is; we can only know what God is not. But this position does not escape the objection of Hume and is entirely inadequate in relation to the Christian revelation of God as living and loving and acting in history.

If we are to speak affirmatively about God, as we must, we seem to have two choices.[44] On the one hand, we could assert that the meaning of terms as applied to the finite and to God is univocal. This would mean that God's life and love are in specifiable respects identical with finite life and love. But to assert this would necessarily imply that in some respect God is finite, contingent, and lacking in self-sufficiency. This, in turn, would run counter to the whole basis of constructing the natural theology.

On the other hand, we could state that terms as applied to God are purely equivocal. This would imply that no aspect of their meaning in one context could be carried over to the other. Since the meaning of life and love as we use these terms is necessarily derived from the finite sphere, we would be forced to acknowledge that our use of these terms with respect to God could only be ejaculatory — in no way cognitive. We would be left claiming the existence of that about which nothing whatsoever could be said or thought.

[42] *Ibid.*, p. 96.
[43] *Existence and Analogy*, pp. 86–87, 92–93, 96.
[44] *Ibid.*, p. 97.

Either of these alternatives would leave us in the impossible position of abandoning or contradicting the foundations of the argument to which it is supposed to give expression. The only possibility of maintaining the general Thomist position is to develop a third way between the univocal and the equivocal. This third way is formulated in the doctrine of analogy to which Mascall devotes considerable attention.[45]

Mascall's careful analysis does not persuade him that a clear and convincing doctrine of analogy can be formulated that is free from mystery and logical difficulties.[46] On the contrary, he appeals to a kind of intuition of general intelligibility rather than claiming a logically unexceptionable statement. This would be a serious weakness in Mascall's total position except for the fact that he does not believe that the reality of intelligible analogical discourse depends upon its adequate explanation.

The case here is parallel to that with respect to our knowledge of finite existents as such. This knowledge occurs first, and our account of how it occurs follows. One need not have an impregnable doctrine of how it occurs to see that it does occur. Similarly, it is clear to Mascall that Christians do talk meaningfully about God without applying terms to him univocally. Hence, analogical discourse about God does occur. The task of the philosopher is not to prove this fact, but only to describe and explain it as far as possible. It is only when we know that infinite being exists and that we can think meaningfully about it that we approach the problem of analogy properly.[47]

Mascall shows, then, that discourse about God employs two kinds of analogies in close interconnection: the analogy of attribution and the analogy of proportionality.[48] The analogy of attribution is that of attributing to God as cause whatever perfection is found in the world as effect. But taken in itself this tells us nothing about God except that he is cause of this effect, that is, in Scholastic terminology it tells us nothing formally about God.[49] Hence, we need to supplement this with the analogy of proportionality, which asserts that the relation of such perfections of God as life and love to God's existence resembles the relation of finite perfections to the finite existents that participate in them. In this way we do speak formally of God, but we must recognize that the resemblance between the two pairs of terms is by no means one of equality. We cannot say that God's life or goodness is related to his existence just as our life or goodness is related to our existence, for his life and goodness *are* his exist-

[45] *Ibid.*, pp. 98 ff.
[46] *Ibid.*, pp. 116, 121.
[47] *Ibid.*, pp. 94, 121; *Words and Images*, p. 103.
[48] *Existence and Analogy*, p. 101.
[49] *Ibid.*, p. 102.

ence.[50] This means that by itself the analogy of proportionality provides us with no knowledge about God and is compatible with agnosticism.[51] Mascall believes, however, that when this analogy is held in closest relation to the analogy of attribution, we are enabled to speak of God both meaningfully and formally.

The real conclusion of this crucial discussion of analogy is that at the level of concept we have no real alternative to the univocal and equivocal modes of discourse, but that our thought about God consists in judgments about existence rather than concepts. Since God is He Who Is, that is, pure being, every attribute of God is only a way of speaking of his one act of existing. With respect to God, unlike all other beings, we can have no knowledge of essence apart from existence.[52]

In terms of his natural theology, Mascall does not hesitate to deal with one of the most controversial of traditional doctrines about God, namely the doctrine that God is impassible. Mascall notes that in our century many theologians have surrendered this doctrine, and he recognizes that there is an apparent difficulty in reconciling it with God's love.[53] Nevertheless, Mascall argues that the doctrine follows from the basic position and that it is also religiously important.

Those who have abandoned the doctrine of the impassibility of God have generally been those who have lost the sense of the divine transcendence.[54] Once we think of God essentially in the immanent order, we cannot think of him as free from the change and suffering of that order. But then we have lost sight of the Biblical God, He Who Is, the author of all being.

This is not to say, however, that a problem does not exist for those who do understand the divine transcendence.[55] They, too, are concerned to affirm God's compassion for his creatures as an essential part of the Christian message. But compassion does seem to imply that the one who feels it is affected by the fortunes of the one for whom it is felt. If so, then God's impassibility is incompatible with his love.

Mascall's solution is highly interesting. God does know and love the world as well as himself. If we conceived of God and the world as two entities that could be added together to make a whole larger than either one, then it would follow that God's love for the world implied passibility in God. But this addition is illegitimate. God and the world are not commensurate entities in this sense, since God is infinite and the world finite. Hence God's real knowledge and love of the world neither add nor subtract from his being in himself. In his own being he enjoys perfect beati-

[50] *Ibid.*, pp. 103–112.
[51] *Ibid.*, p. 113.
[52] *Ibid.*, pp. 88, 117–120.
[53] *Ibid.*, pp. 134–135.
[54] *Ibid.*, pp. 135–137.
[55] *Ibid.*, p. 135.

tude. His knowledge and love of the world do not affect this beatitude.[56]

Clearly this means that God's knowledge and love are quite different from that which is operative in the finite sphere. But just this is what we must expect. We have already seen that we do not attribute such qualities to God univocally but analogically. We have seen also that they are thereby understood as ways of talking about the one wholly mysterious act of existing by which God eternally constitutes himself. Hence, the proper analogical predication of love and knowledge to God does not contradict his impassibility as would be the case if predication were univocal.

Mascall is aware that this subtle philosophical argument will leave the plain man unsatisfied. If God's compassion for him does not affect God, he cannot take much satisfaction from that compassion. But Mascall thinks that what men really need is not sympathy in the sense of feelings but help of a practical kind. God's compassion expresses itself as the gift of all good things to his creatures.[57]

Furthermore, what is religiously important to us is not that we believe that God is involved in our problems and suffering. It is far better to know that there is one who is altogether free from and victorious over all evil and who offers to us the ultimate privilege of sharing with him in his blessedness.[58] Since it is in this context that we are primarily to understand the work of Christ, this will provide a suitable point for transition from a discussion of God and creation primarily based upon natural theology to a very brief statement about Christ and salvation primarily based upon revelation.

It has already been made clear that this transition is not a sharp one. Mascall, like Thomas, moves back and forth in his discussion between natural and revealed theology. He is much clearer than is Thomas that the actual practice of natural theology depends historically upon revelation.[59] Indeed, only as nature is healed by grace can reason function properly.[60] Furthermore, many of the discussions in which philosophy plays the primary role consist in developing distinctions or new concepts that make possible the intelligent affirmation of doctrines that are believed strictly on the grounds of revelation. Hence, natural and revealed theology are quite inseparable. Nevertheless, Mascall insists that a systematic difference between natural theology and revealed theology exists and has great importance.[61]

[56] *Ibid.*, p. 141. Cf. also pp. 132–133.
[57] *Ibid.*, p. 142.
[58] *Ibid.*, p. 143.
[59] *Via Media,* p. 1.
[60] *Christ, the Christian and the Church,* p. 233.
[61] *Ibid.*, pp. 234 ff.

Natural theology is that part of our religious thinking which does not appeal for its warrant to revelation, unless we speak of nature itself as general revelation. It consists entirely in the rational reflection upon the universal nature of finite things and the implication of this nature for our thought about God. By contrast, revealed theology takes as its starting point the whole richness of the existing faith of the church. Its task is to make explicit the revelation that is committed to the church.[62]

The task of the theologian can be fulfilled only to the degree that he participates actually in the life of the church.[63] Theology does not consist of the describing of beliefs held about God by a designated group of persons but of the affirming about God and creatures in their relation to God of that which it has been given to the church to know.[64] For this purpose Scripture and its ecclesiastical interpretation in their indissoluble unity are both necessary.[65]

The revelation consists first and foremost in the person of Jesus Christ himself, but this can become material for theological use only as it is given in human language. This is done in the words of Jesus and in the Bible. But the Bible does not itself provide us with systematic theological formulations. It is rather like a mine from which the greatest variety of materials can be quarried. Therefore, inspiration is needed for its correct interpretation just as for its writing. This inspiration occurs not through individuals but through the whole church, through whose total life and particular decisions dogma are formulated. The theologian works with these dogma that are taken as inspired interpretations of the inspired Scripture.[66]

Clearly, this account of the method by which the theologian works has substantive presuppositions as to the content of theology. For example, if one understood by the church simply the historically given communities with their multiplicity of beliefs and practices, the view of theology as the articulation of the church's faith would lead to a plurality of theologies that could hardly escape the recognition of their relativity with respect to historical factors. Mascall, on the contrary, assumes that theology is concerned only with the truth itself and that the received dogma embodies that truth. This presupposes an understanding of the church as a supernatural community in which truth is authenticated. In concluding this exposition of Mascall's theological position, therefore, we will survey the history of God's acts for man as these in turn explain the situation of the theologian.

Mascall believes, first, that although the body of man may have evolved,

62 *Ibid.*, p. 241.
63 *Ibid.*, p. 239.
64 *Ibid.*, pp. 228–229.
65 *Ibid.*, p. 242.
66 *Ibid.*, pp. 230–232.

the immortal soul of man was directly created by God and conjoined to his body at some point in the evolutionary ascent.[67] The first union of human soul and body was in Adam.[68] Adam's sin against God lost for himself and for his descendants the union with God that had been granted to him [69] and that profoundly affected their human nature as well.[70] The temptation that led to this sin as well as to the other evil in the created order is to be explained by the previous rebellion of angels.[71]

Although the very great seriousness of the consequences of the Fall of man is not to be denied, we must not go to the extreme of supposing that all capacities for good were lost. Even fallen man is the suitable object of God's supernatural grace, a grace that has operated even apart from any knowledge of God's new act of creation in Christ.[72] This act, however, by which God created a new manhood out of the material of fallen humanity, is his supreme work.[73]

In Christ, God himself took the form of flesh. This act is supremely mysterious, but Mascall shows that considerable clarity can be attained in its exposition. He affirms that the personal subject is the second person of the Trinity, who unites to his divine nature an impersonal and unfallen human nature consisting of both body and soul.[74] The union is to be understood as the taking up of human nature into the divine rather than of the lowering of the divine nature to the conditions of the human.[75] Hence, we are not to think of the divine nature as abandoning its divine powers and knowledge in the incarnation. Rather we are to think of Jesus' human nature as informed and transformed by its union with this divine nature without in any way ceasing to be human.[76]

By this act of recreating human nature, God mysteriously created the new possibility of individual man's divinization through incorporation into that glorified nature.[77] This incorporation occurs through baptism and continues through the process of sanctification.[78] The church is the continuing body of which Christ is the head.[79] Through participation in

[67] E. L. Mascall, *The Importance of Being Human: Some Aspects of the Christian Doctrine of Man,* p. 14.
[68] *Christ, the Christian and the Church,* pp. 154–157.
[69] *Ibid.,* pp. 139–140.
[70] *Ibid.,* p. 233.
[71] *The Importance of Being Human,* pp. 77–83.
[72] *Christ, the Christian and the Church,* p. 150.
[73] *Ibid.,* p. 73.
[74] *Ibid.,* pp. 2 ff.
[75] *Ibid.,* p. 48.
[76] *Ibid.,* pp. 53–56.
[77] *Ibid.,* p. 78.
[78] *Ibid.,* pp. 83–84.
[79] *Ibid.,* pp. 109 ff.

Christ's body we participate in his union with God.[80] The Eucharist is primarily the cause and secondarily the expression of the unity in the church and with God.[81]

◈ ◈

At this juncture we turn from a primarily expository to a primarily critical presentation of Mascall's position. This criticism has considerable importance in view of the fact that, on the one hand, Thomism has had a long and impressive history, maintaining its intellectual authority over a large portion of responsible Christian thought and, on the other hand, it is radically rejected by most Protestant theologians, including all those treated in the following chapters. If we are to understand why Protestant thinkers today accept the peculiar difficulties that confront them when they reject the kind of natural theology that Thomism represents, we must understand the systematic difficulties that Thomism itself encounters.

In the first place, we must return to the peculiar situation in which Mascall finds himself in claiming rational necessity for a position that most rational people reject. He explains this situation by showing that a certain habit of mind is required in order that the data of natural theology be allowed to present themselves to the viewer. Once these data are presented, the argument follows by necessity.[82] Does this account provide the escape from the relativism of philosophic positions that is essential for Thomistic natural theology?

It seems to me that it does not, or rather, that an additional and doubtful assumption is required for it to do so. If we first assume that the perception of things as finite existents is the natural perception for man, then we may assert with Mascall that what inhibits this vision blinds us to what is as it is. Then we may argue with him that the philosophy that follows from this vision is the one true philosophy. But according to Mascall's own account, few if any thinkers had understood their experience in this way prior to the time of the great Scholastics, and they did so under the influence of Hebraic modes of thought. Can we say that what we learned to see only under the influence of revelation is in fact the one natural way of seeing things?

It might be argued that the failure of thinkers to accept the data as they really are has been due to special factors such as their preoccupation with forms or essences and that common people have always viewed things as finite existents. But again, by Mascall's own account, such a vision apart

[80] *Ibid.*, p. 211.
[81] *Ibid.*, p. 193.
[82] *Existence and Analogy*, p. xi; *He Who Is*, p. 75.

from philosophic sophistication leads to a fundamental understanding of God that was absent apart from the special historical influence of revelation. Hence, the absence of the Christian understanding of God in pre-Christian religion indicates that the vision of things as finite existents was virtually absent for common sense as well as for philosophy until the impact of Biblical thought caused it to prevail.

The point of the foregoing is that the distinction which is made by Mascall between the historic and the systematic dependence of natural theology on revelation has an even smaller relevance than he seems to suppose. The distinction would be important if the vision of things as finite existents were in fact universal but had been brought to clear consciousness only by revelation. But if in fact in the common vision of reality apart from revelation this element has been subordinate to other elements or entirely lacking, then we must acknowledge that revelation creates the data on the basis of which natural theology reasons. These data may be created for some who do not acknowledge the revelation as authoritative, and for this reason natural theology may have a wider basis of acceptance than revealed theology. But we must recognize that natural theology receives a basis on which to operate only as a gift from revelation.

This criticism of Mascall does not have serious consequences for the content of his position. Although he tends at times to obscure the dependence of natural theology upon revelation, he is not unaware of it, and his arguments do not depend on the occasional oversight. However, the relation between theology and philosophy is markedly altered once we fully recognize that the starting point of philosophy, that is, the fundamental vision with which the thinker begins, is historically conditioned and that Christian faith has played a major role in the formation of the Western vision.

Systematically, it seems that a fundamental decision must be made. If the data of philosophical reason are natural, that is, if they are given for human experience independently of historical conditions, then natural theology as commonly understood becomes a major possibility. If, however, the data for human experience are historically conditioned, and if the Christian arguments from philosophy presuppose distinctively Christian data, then it seems less misleading to call the philosophy in question Christian philosophy rather than natural theology. In this case, we seem led to the Augustinian view, in which reason plays its role in interpreting and developing the starting point given in faith.

Mascall's actual position seems to fall between these two alternatives. He sees that the vision of existence from which his natural theology arises depends historically on Christian revelation, but he does not think that it is simply a part of the truth that is given in revelation. It remains a separate starting point for thought from that which God has directly revealed in Jesus Christ. This starting point, although historically formed, has a much wider acceptance than has special revelation, being acceptable to many who consciously reject that revelation. Hence, a clear distinction should be kept between natural theology and revealed theology.

This intermediate position appears eminently sensible. To continue to call the philosophy conditioned by revelation simply natural theology may, however, perpetuate a confusion that is manifest even in Mascall's own thought. I suggest that the term "*Christian* natural theology" might be used.[83] It should then be recognized that as an apologetic device its sphere of relevance is limited to those whose vision has been consciously or unconsciously already modified by Christian faith. It cannot provide a basis for justifying the Christian doctrine of God to one who stands radically outside the Christian circle.

Emphasizing more consistently than Mascall the historical relativity and conditionedness of the data upon which he builds his thought, let us still acknowledge that for many of us such data are nonetheless very real and important. Let us further acknowledge that, although this vision has dimmed considerably from the Western mentality, much of it remains latent in such a way that a vivid presentation of its importance still has widespread effectiveness. We can then consider whether the implications that a Thomist like Mascall draws from these data actually follow with the necessity that he claims.

The fundamental characteristic of finite entities on the basis of which the whole system of thought is constructed is their contingency, which may otherwise be expressed as the separability of existence from essence. It is because there is nothing in the nature of the finite thing to afford it existence that we must posit a source of being that does contain its own ground of existence. That is, we recognize that there must be some being

[83] There are no clearly established distinctions between Christian philosophy, Christian natural theology, and natural theology. I am using "natural theology" to refer to conclusions of philosophical inquiry supportive of some Christian teaching from data that are understood to be factually and logically independent of Christian revelation. I am suggesting here that when the data are recognized as historically dependent on Christian revelation, we should call the rational conclusions from these data "Christian philosophy" or "Christian natural theology." By Christian philosophy I mean any attempt to build a comprehensive scheme of ideas on the basis of distinctively Christian data. By Christian natural theology I mean the attempt to justify certain Christian beliefs rationally on the basis of data that, though historically conditioned by Christian revelation, are widely held by persons who are not self-consciously Christian. In these terms Christian philosophy and Christian natural theology, though distinct, are intimately related and fully compatible with each other.

whose essence does imply or contain its existence. This being is then self-sufficient or necessary. Thus far, given the original vision of finite existents as contingent, reason seems necessarily to carry us. We cannot understand how there can be existent things at all unless there is somewhere a being that is the cause both of their existence and its own.

From this, however, Mascall draws conclusions that seem to be in considerable tension with the Biblical view of God. The Bible seems to present God as one who is in loving interaction with his creatures in such a way that he is affected by what happens to them. Mascall, loyal to the Thomist natural theology, argues that God is strictly changeless and, therefore, unmoved by our suffering. His love is pure act without shadow of passivity. Thus he sets himself sharply against all those who have stated that Jesus reveals God as suffering for and with man.

We must ask here whether the conclusion that God cannot be affected by events within his creation in fact follows from the fundamental argument from contingent to necessary being. Mascall thinks that it does, and indeed he seems to regard this as so evident as to require little explanation. However, recent philosophers, especially Charles Hartshorne, have proposed other interpretations of God that combine the doctrine of his necessity with the view that he is capable of being affected by the course of events.[84]

The central issue is whether the necessity of God implies absolute immutability. The argument for this implication seems to be that if God is necessary being there can be nothing contingent about him. A being that is partly necessary and partly contingent would seem to be in its totality and wholeness not necessary, and hence, according to the argument, not God. But if everything about God is necessary, then nothing could ever have come to be in or for him; that is, he is strictly immutable. Phrased in this way the argument seems quite convincing.

However, the proper starting point as established by the original argument from the contingent to the necessary is not "necessary being" as such, but a being whose existence is necessary. This is all that the argument warrants. There is then no contradiction in supposing that a being whose existence is necessary may nevertheless alter in some respects in the mode of that existence. *That* God is must be necessary, hence altogether free from contingency or change; but *what* God is, beyond the basic fact that he is the ground of his own existence and of all other existents, may without any contradiction contain contingent elements and, therefore, change.

[84] See especially Hartshorne's *Man's Vision of God* and *Philosophers Speak of God*, pp. 499–514.

The Thomist objection to this suggestion is that it neglects the crucial categories of essence and existence in terms of which the argument is most rigorously formulated. The lack of self-sufficiency in finite things consists in the separability of essence and existence. That is, it is not of the essence of finite things to exist. In a necessary being, in contrast, it must be of its essence to exist. Hence, in God essence and existence are identical. If so, *what* God is can only be his *is-ness,* and all contingency or change is strictly excluded.

I do not believe, however, that this form of the argument affects the possibility of drawing different conclusions. In these terms it must indeed be *of* the essence of God to exist, but this need not imply the strict identity of essence and existence in God. The assertion that it is *of* God's essence to exist does not imply that nothing other than existing can be of God's essence. It does not exclude the possibility that it is also of the essence of God to be affected by what occurs in the experience of his creatures. This would imply again that it is of God's essence to include contingent elements.

The upholders of the view that there are contingent elements in God are not arguing that his behavior or character is vacillating and unpredictable. Their major religious concern is to show that we may take seriously the Biblical doctrine of God's love for his creation without contradicting the necessity of God's being. If we mean anything at all by asserting that God loves his creatures, we must surely mean that God is not indifferent to the events in their lives. But if God cares, then to some degree the total experience that is God is affected by contingent events and is itself contingent.

A second line of argument against the presence of any contingent element in God stems from the doctrine that God is Being. This doctrine has two foundations: the first, Biblical; the second, philosophical. The first can be summarized as follows. At the one point in the Bible where God reveals his name he affirms himself as He Who Is, thus as pure being or existence. Therefore, the philosophical doctrine of God as Being is demanded by revelation. However, Mascall himself recognizes that the interpretation of the passage in question in these terms is highly doubtful. He wishes to base the doctrine of God as pure Being upon the teaching of the Bible as a whole.[85] But it is difficult to see that such implications of this doctrine as that God is strictly impassible are admitted in the Bible. If the doctrine itself is not explicit in the Bible, and if its implications are not admitted in the Bible, it is hard to see how the doctrine can be defended on the basis of Biblical revelation.

[85] *Existence and Analogy,* pp. 11–14.

Mascall's view is that philosophy demands that we maintain the traditional view of the immutability and impassibility of God and that this view is in full harmony with the basic witness of the Bible. I am assuming that this view is in serious tension with the Bible and am arguing that it is not logically required by the philosophical argument. I would go further and say that there are positive philosophic reasons for the alternative suggested, namely, that there are both necessary and contingent elements in God.[86] However, this would exceed the proper scope of the present critique. All that is needed here is to show that Mascall's typical Thomist conclusions do not necessarily follow from his starting point. It is my belief that a still wider hearing could be secured for the starting point if it were clearly seen that it did not entail these traditional consequences.

We are now prepared to discuss Mascall's doctrine of analogy. The discussion will be somewhat more extensive than otherwise appropriate to this context because this doctrine is crucial to other theological positions as well as to that of Thomism. Among those treated in this volume we find Bultmann explicitly appealing to it. Since he provides virtually no explanation or justification of the doctrine, the present critique will have to be regarded as applicable also to him. Tillich's symbolic use of terms also seems vulnerable to much the same criticism.

Mascall acknowledges the limitations of his account of analogy, but the problem seems to be even more acute than he recognizes in his defense. In his presentation, the argument that God exists as self-existent cause of all finite being is established first, and the problem of analogical predication follows. In this situation, since God's existence as cause of things is known, the objection that nothing further can be said or thought about God univocally might appear as a quibble. It does seem that God must be known somehow from his effects. In this connection Mascall appeals to the analogy of attribution as an essential part of the explanation of how we can speak meaningfully about God.

But all this seems to assume that it is already clear that the terms "cause" and "existence" can be applied to God univocally, whereas I take it that Mascall holds that they are themselves applicable only analogically. If there is no univocal element in the assertion that God is cause of the world, on what basis can one say that the perfection of the world is even virtually (that is, as cause) present in God? This would seem possible only if we understood what was meant by attributing cause to God univocally, at least in so far as our idea of cause tells us that the power of producing the effect must be in the cause. But this would imply some

[86] Hartshorne's works, including those listed in n. 84, develop these reasons in detail.

element of univocal meaning in the application of the term "cause" to God's relation to the world. Apart from this, the whole basis of the analogy of attribution would seem to be pure equivocation.

Similarly, the analogy of proportionality is formulated in terms of the relation of God's attributes to his existence. But if we cannot first affirm his existence univocally, it is hard to see that there is any escape here too from pure equivocation. In this situation the combining of the two analogies cannot improve matters. Christian natural theology as Mascall understands it would seem to be impossible.

The fact is that although Mascall quite explicitly affirms the purely analogical character of even causality and existence as applied to God,[87] he elsewhere seems to assume that these terms are quite clear and definite in their application to God.[88] Hence, we should consider the possibility that causality and existence are affirmed univocally of God. This would at least introduce the possibility of approaching the doctrine of analogy without sheer bewilderment, but before reconsidering the argument in these terms, we must first note that the acknowledgment that some terms can be applied to God univocally has very significant consequences.

In the first place, if we may speak univocally of God as cause and existing, there seems no reason to doubt that other metaphysical terms have equally univocal application. The whole language of self-sufficiency, necessity, simplicity, immutability, and infinity turns out to be quite univocal.[89] It appears in the end to be that the doctrine of analogy is required only for the preservation of the Biblical language about God. One need not be surprised if in the conflict between the apparent implications of Biblical concepts, understood to be analogical, with metaphysical concepts, understood to be univocal, it is the implications of the Biblical concepts that give way.

In the second place, this throws quite a different light upon the situation to which Mascall appeals as the real warrant for a doctrine of analogy. This situation, it will be recalled, is that there is in fact meaningful discourse about God. This fact means that the task of the doctrine of analogy is not to justify such discourse but simply to describe and explain it. On this basis, Mascall can recognize the logical inadequacy of his account and still insist that it is sufficient for its purposes.

But if Mascall's own assumptions explain that the meaningfulness of a

[87] *Existence and Analogy,* p. 87.

[88] *Ibid.,* p. 96.

[89] If Thomists acknowledge these terms to be literal, they must also understand them as negations, since only negative statements about God are literal. This does not affect the fact that whereas metaphysical terms can be literal, Biblical terms are typically analogical.

good deal of discourse about God can be understood in terms of the univocal use of metaphysical concepts, then it is only the use of the apparently incongruent religious language that requires special explanation. On the two hypotheses that this language is meaningful and that his philosophy is correct, the fact of analogical discourse, defined as meaningful, nonunivocal discourse, follows. But this argument is unusually weak in view of the fact that both hypotheses are doubtful, and the conclusion may not be meaningful at all.

The first hypothesis will be denied not only by positivists but also by philosophers who take seriously the religious implications of a doctrine of God as infinite, immutable, simple, and necessary. They will hold that popular religion attempts to think about this God in terms that actually do not apply at all.

Others, such as Brunner, will agree that the tension between the two sets of categories implies their strict incompatibility but will understand that this means that the Biblical categories, based on revelation, must altogether supersede the philosophic categories, based on corrupted reason. Although this position does not deny Mascall's first hypothesis and does not philosophically dispute the second, it places them on such different levels as to destroy their force.

The second hypothesis can also be directly attacked philosophically. This can be done from many points of view, but I have suggested above that the crucial attack is that which accepts the same data and then shows that the argument does not exclude the presence of contingent elements in God's total nature. Like all the other criticisms, this makes it possible to avoid the doctrine of analogy. Hence, it is clear that the meaningfulness of religious language can be accepted without entailing any doctrine of analogy. Religious language, however much it may be poetically elaborated, can be seen to have, at its base, affirmations that, whether they are true or false, have univocal meaning.

This may be illustrated briefly. Mascall affirms that the assertion that God is living is neither univocal nor equivocal, but analogical. If Mascall's philosophic doctrine that God is absolutely immutable is accepted, we must agree that we cannot assert life of God univocally. As an alternative approach, we may take certain possible definitions of life and ask whether or not they *might* apply univocally to God. If we define life in terms of generation and decay, it is quite clear that we must deny that God is characterized by life, since these characteristics are incompatible with the necessity of his being. If, however, we define life in terms of the capacity to respond selectively to events, a conception of God that allows some contingent elements in his experience will permit us to apply the term " life " to God univocally. It may, of course, not be factually the case that God responds selectively to events, but that he might do so quite literally is not ruled out by our knowledge that God's being is necessary. Furthermore, if we quite univocally call God living in this way, this does not imply that God's life is in other respects like ours. Indeed, we may be able quite univocally to show ways in which his life necessarily differs from ours. Finally, a great deal about God must surely remain wholly unknown to us. But nowhere are we forced to introduce a kind of meaning that is neither univocal nor equivocal.

I have not tried in these comments to prove in detail the ambiguity and inadequacy of Mascall's account of analogy. His own commendable clarity and frankness cause him to display and acknowledge these limitations himself. He poses the issue as that of explaining what he supposes manifestly occurs, that is, meaningful but nonunivocal discourse about God. He knows that he has not fully succeeded in explaining this possibility. Hence, to say that he has not done so is not an argument against him. Therefore, I have confined myself to showing that the existence of meaningful discourse about God as a necessary being does not imply that there is meaningful nonunivocal discourse. From this it follows that there may well be no such thing as analogical discourse.

Thus far the criticism of Mascall has been that his data are even more radically conditioned than he has recognized and that they do not necessarily lead to all the conclusions that he draws from them. The alternative set of conclusions has the advantage of being in less tension with the Bible and also of not requiring the confusing doctrine of analogical discourse as a third way between the univocal and the equivocal. We must now ask, granted that Mascall's Thomist conclusions do not follow necessarily from these data in all respects, whether they constitute an intelligible and self-consistent position that does account for the data.

In this volume, I am not undertaking to criticize philosophical ideas philosophically. I am not asking here whether Thomism as a philosophy can survive systematic analysis and criticism. Indeed, I am assuming that in general it can do so. Our question is, instead, whether the theological affirmations made by the Thomist are intelligible within the context of his philosophical doctrines.

I have already indicated that I perceive a tension between the Thomist doctrines and the thought patterns of the Bible. The point was made in terms of the tension between God's compassionate love and his impassibility. However, there can be no question that the theological doctrine of God's impassibility is compatible with, and indeed demanded by, the philosophical doctrine. We must now ask whether the Thomist is willing to tailor all of his theological doctrines to fit the demands of his philosophy. If so, we might deny that the total position is Biblical, but we would also recognize its internal consistency.

A crucial question concerns the understanding of God as personal. Thomism certainly intends to make this affirmation. It speaks of God in terms of intellect, will, and memory, and it attributes acts and purposes to him. Does this make sense in the light of the doctrine that in God there is no element of contingency or change?

Clearly, all of this language about God must be understood as analogical discourse. What we humans know as intellect, will, memory, activity, and purpose involves contingency and change. But even if we allowed the possibility of analogical discourse, could we attribute even the vaguest meaning to these terms when they are applied to infinite, necessary, simple Being? Or, if the demand for intelligibility is illegitimate, can we see any reason whatever for attributing the terms to God? According to Mascall's own account of the " life " of God it seems clear that all these terms can be only so many ways of referring to the pure act of existing that is God. In God's own being, presumably, the distinctions suggested by these terms have no place. But if all these terms when applied to God refer ultimately to the one act that we can more accurately call existing, I am unable to see how we can regard the use of terms like these as analogical rather than simply equivocal.

Mascall's argument, we have seen, is that in fact we do discuss meaningfully about God in these terms without claiming that our use is univocal. I argued above that it is quite possible that the meaningful portion of our discussion about God does use terms univocally. I wish to argue now that it seems likely that the appearance of meaningful nonunivocal discourse about God is due to historical factors, and that when these are understood, the appearance is destroyed.

I have already indicated that I believe the data on which Thomist theology bases its affirmation of God are derived historically from Christian revelation. Hence, in an important sense the Thomist philosophical doctrine of God is Christian. Nevertheless, its original formulation was profoundly influenced also by Aristotelian philosophy and took over much of what Aristotle had said about a self-sufficient prime mover.[90] The doctrines of God derived from this influence have stood through the centuries in marked tension with Biblical personalism. Theological discourse has been caught in this tension and has included assertions that, when taken univocally, must be regarded as mutually contradictory.

[90] Pre-Thomist thought about God also involved a synthesis of Biblical and Greek categories and, therefore, posed much the same problems.

The ecclesiastical sanctioning of this way of thought has forced generations of thinkers to expend great ingenuity on the acute rational problems that are involved. They have certainly carried on meaningful discourse with one another about the problems. Furthermore, the ordinary Christians who acknowledge the situation as defined by the approved theologians have found meaning within this context. In this situation the doctrine of analogy, namely that meaningful language need not be univocal, necessarily played a large role.

However, none of this proves that, in fact, meaningful discourse about God takes place that does not use terms univocally. It would seem, therefore, that we can understand historically why persons find themselves talking in this context without supposing that they are forced to do so by the nature of things or by their apprehension of God as the cause of finite beings. Since this is so, and since no satisfactory doctrine of analogy exists,[91] we must declare that the attribution to God by Thomists both of immutability and of personal characteristics is an inconsistency. More specifically, since it is the personal characteristics rather than the immutability that are held to be analogical, we must declare that Thomists have not yet shown us that, given their philosophical doctrine of God, the attribution of personal characteristics to him is not pure equivocation.

This point has been pressed not only for the systematic reason that it appears to be a real weakness in the Thomist position but also because much of modern Protestant thought can be understood only against the background assumption that philosophical theology of the Thomist type must necessarily lead to conclusions that diverge from the Biblical understanding of God. Some have held that this must follow from the use of any philosophy whatsoever. Others have identified this consequence with the use of metaphysical, in contradistinction to cosmological, philosophy. Still others accept the implication that God is not properly understood as personal.

This rather lengthy criticism of Mascall's Christian natural theology, however, is not intended to show the necessity of its radical rejection. Quite the contrary, its purpose is to argue that the fundamental Thomist vision of finite existence as pointing to its self-sufficient cause is fully compatible with a doctrine of God that can embody the real strengths of the Thomist position without entailing its religiously and logically unsatisfactory conclusions. This has been shown in the philosophical work of Charles Hartshorne.

[91] Perhaps the most promising discussion is that of Austin Farrer, much of which is summarized appreciatively by Mascall in *Existence and Analogy,* pp. 158–175; and *Words and Images,* pp. 109–120.

In conclusion, the same problem of the relation of Mascall's philosophy and Biblical thought should be stated in a distinctively Protestant way. I have repeatedly affirmed that there appeared to be serious tensions between the Biblical understanding of God and that which emerges in Thomist natural theology. The Catholic basis for denying this tension lies in the argument that Scripture must be read as interpreted in the ecclesiastical tradition. If this principle is followed, it must be granted that one will not find in the Bible the univocally personalistic thinking about God that many Protestants suppose they see. That is to say, the church has in fact interpreted the Bible since early times in terms of some of those ideas about God which Thomism embodies in its natural theology.

The Protestant objection is that we can in fact gain a more objective view of the Bible by direct study and can criticize the traditional interpretation from this point of view. To this Mascall has replied that the Bible can be used in favor of an indefinite number of systematic positions and that it cannot be used fairly to support one such position against others. Systematic theology must depend upon the inspired interpretation of the Scripture. If it is to do more than organize the private interpretation of one person, it must assume that God's Spirit has been at work in the whole church. The theologian must take the Catholic tradition that has resulted from the guidance of the Spirit as his authoritative guide.

We must ask two questions of decisive importance. First, is it true that the Bible is open to a virtually unlimited number of systematic interpretations? The Reformers thought that its message was quite clear and needed little or no interpretation, but the history of Protestantism seems to support the Catholic claim. Nevertheless, the Protestant cannot admit total relativity of interpretation. If one cannot say definitively what the Biblical teaching *is,* one can at least specify some things that it is *not.*

This much a Catholic may also acknowledge. Hence, the real issue is the second. Is the Catholic traditional interpretation of the Bible one of those which can be known on the basis of our present study of the Bible to be in serious error? If not, then the assertion that there are important tensions between some of the approved philosophical doctrines of Thomism and the Bible is unsubstantiated. If it is, then the Reformers were right in demanding a choice between the Bible and Catholic tradition, and we will be right today in reaffirming that demand. An answer to this question can be approximated only by open and scholarly investigation.

3: Boston Personalism

AMONG EUROPEAN THEOLOGIANS, IT IS OFTEN ASSUMED THAT ANY USE OF philosophy must lead to a doctrine of God which is in sharp tension with the personal God revealed in the Bible. I have argued that this tension does in fact exist in Thomism, and we will note similar problems in other theologians.[1] However, there is another kind of philosophy available for use as a natural theology that takes the category of person as decisive for the strictest thinking about God. Many of the usual objections do not apply against this kind of natural theology.

In this approach, as in Thomism, the idea of analogy plays an important role. However, the objections raised in the preceding chapter are not relevant. When the deists argued that the resemblance of the world to a machine meant that its maker must be like a mind, they did not mean that the likeness must be altogether unspecifiable. On the contrary, they meant quite literally that the maker of the world had a knowledge of mathematical principles and physical laws, that he had purposes which he undertook to realize in time, and that he had a concern for his creation. The deists were not prevented from meaning these things by a prior commitment to God's simplicity and nontemporality. Analogy meant likeness of a specifiable sort, although it also pointed to the vast differences between a mind capable of producing and sustaining our world and our minds.

The rather static conception of God as creator, sustainer, and lawgiver, which characterized what we call deism, gave way under the impact of evolutionary theory to a more dynamic mode of thinking in which the immanence, as well as the transcendence, of God is stressed. In a general way, the fact of order and the adaptation of the world to man is now, as it has been for centuries, the mainstay of much popular religious thinking.

[1] See especially the discussion of Paul Tillich in Chapter 10.

That this order and adaptation have been achieved gradually through evolutionary processes affects the understanding of the way in which God works, but it does not alter the evidence for purposive creation. At least in the English-speaking world a common-sense natural theology of this sort predominates in lay thinking and underlies much preaching. Nowhere is the gulf between the dominant forms of contemporary theology and the theology of the folk church more apparent than in the attitude toward this kind of natural theology.

The popular convictions could not sustain themselves indefinitely if they were not supported by serious intellectual leadership. The most widely influential leadership of this sort in America has come from Boston University, where for several generations a recognized school of thought has dominated both philosophy and theology. This chapter includes a presentation and criticism of the theological method advocated and practiced by the leading contemporary theologian teaching at this institution, L. Harold DeWolf. It includes also a discussion of philosophical arguments for the existence of a personal God as developed by E. S. Brightman and his successor in the Bowne professorship at Boston University, Peter Bertocci.

Grouping these philosophers together with the theologian DeWolf in a single chapter under the heading of " Boston Personalism " suggests a unanimity and self-consciousness as a school of thought that does not in fact exist. In personal correspondence, DeWolf has protested this impression, which is given by both the title and the content I have chosen for this chapter. He prefers to classify himself as an evangelical liberal, and he stresses that theological orientations should not be labeled according to the philosophical elements or methods employed.

I wish here to acknowledge the justice of DeWolf's objections to this grouping and classification of his theology. However, throughout this volume attention is focused upon the theological methods employed and especially upon the relation of theology to philosophy. In Part I the concern is specifically with the alternative ways of formulating and justifying natural theology and of relating distinctively Christian theology to it. In these respects, despite DeWolf's increasing emphasis on the Bible and traditional theology,[2] his position is not seriously misrepresented when correlated with the positions of the Boston philosophers.

DeWolf is clear and emphatic in his conviction that theology should not dispense with natural theology.[3] Christian faith assumes the existence of

[2] L. Harold DeWolf, " Biblical, Liberal, Catholic," Article X in the series How My Mind Has Changed, *The Christian Century,* Vol. 77, 1960, pp. 1303–1307.

[3] L. Harold DeWolf, *The Case for Theology in Liberal Perspective,* pp. 31–41.

God.[4] Not only so, but it presupposes the existence of God as creator of the world and as concerned for his creation. All these basic Christian convictions are to be accepted on the basis of philosophy, as well as on the basis of specifically Christian revelation.

Since the case for Christian theology depends largely upon philosophical arguments for the existence of the Christian God, we must turn directly to these arguments. DeWolf lists six types of evidence for his rational belief. The first type is the evidence of the objectivity of abstract truth. This argument may be summarized as follows. Truths exist unchangingly prior to, and independently of, human knowledge of them. On the other hand, we cannot think of a truth as existing except as it is thought. Hence there must be a suprahuman mind that thinks these truths eternally.[5]

The second argument is called " evidence from causal law." Causal laws are systems of meanings describing the patterns exemplified in physical events, but as such they do not explain the occurrences. In man's mind, the conjunction of will with ideas explains the expression in action of these ideas. The only reasonable explanation of the operation of causal law in nature is the belief in a supreme intelligence that combines idea and will.[6]

The third argument is called " evidence from apparent purpose in nature." The virtually universal adjustment of means to ends in the organic world indicates a purposefulness in the structures and relations of plants and animals. The long directional movement of evolution cannot be accounted for by the principle of survival of the fittest, for at certain stages of evolution the presence of an evolving organ did not at that time render the organism more fit to survive.[7]

The fourth argument, " evidence from human adaptation," follows much the same line as the third; and the fifth, " the objectivity of moral ideals," resembles the first.[8] The sixth evidence for theism is religious experience, which DeWolf recognizes as having limited force except for those who have enjoyed this experience.[9]

DeWolf does not claim that these arguments singly or in conjunction establish beyond possibility of doubt the existence of a personal God. This kind of certainty is an illusory ideal.[10] What is achieved is the demonstration of the superior reasonableness of theism in relation to any other in-

[4] L. Harold DeWolf, *A Theology of the Living Church*, p. 46.
[5] *Ibid.*, pp. 48–49.
[6] *Ibid.*, pp. 49–50.
[7] *Ibid.*, pp. 50–51.
[8] *Ibid.*, pp. 52–58. The fourth argument is the one most fully developed by DeWolf, but I have chosen to treat it in the still fuller form of Bertocci's exposition.
[9] *Ibid.*, pp. 58–59.
[10] *Ibid.*, p. 32.

terpretation of experience and its world.

Since certainty with regard to life-determining questions is impossible, we can choose only between complete skepticism and the acceptance of the guide of probability. But the permanent suspension of judgment that is the essence of skepticism is, in fact, just as impossible as rational certainty.[11] Life must be lived in terms of decisions, and decisions must be made in terms of reasonable consideration of evidence. The only question is whether we live vigorously and committedly in terms of what we believe to be true or use our lack of certainty as an excuse for timidity and halfheartedness.

It is in this context that we must understand faith. Faith is commitment of the will to that which it is reasonable to believe is worthy of that commitment despite the lack of objective certainty that always remains.[12] In relation to religious belief, faith is the decision to live as if given ideas were definitely known to be true. Our effectiveness depends upon the courage and vigor with which we act on our faith.[13] But there is no justification for closing our minds to new evidence that may alter the content or object of our faith.[14]

Since philosophic considerations show the reasonableness of belief in God, this belief should play the central role in a rational faith. In itself this appeal is independent of any further commitment to a particular religious tradition. On the other hand, the understanding of God that emerges from these considerations as reasonable is a norm in terms of which the beliefs of different religions can be judged. Whatever else these traditions affirm should be in harmony with what is thus rationally given.

Despite the extreme importance that attaches to the arguments for the existence of God in DeWolf's thought, he himself has given them only brief exposition. Of the six listed, all except the first are considered more thoroughly by Peter Bertocci in *An Introduction to the Philosophy of Religion*. His presentation of the case, like that of DeWolf, is intended to establish belief in a personal God as the most reasonable view. His argument takes the form of what he calls "the wider teleological argument," which he develops in seven steps or links.[15]

11 *Ibid.*
12 *Ibid.*, p. 37.
13 *Ibid.*, pp. 41–42.
14 *Ibid.*, pp. 43–45.
15 DeWolf lists Bertocci among those whose work in philosophy should be appreciated by theologians and refers with approval to Tennant's use of "the wider teleological argument" (*The Case for Theology in Liberal Perspective*, pp. 36, 19). However, this may not imply an unqualified acceptance of Bertocci's formulation of this argument. Indeed, DeWolf's personal preference is for the formu-

The first link arises in a consideration of the evolutionary process in which life appeared from the inorganic world and achieved new levels of organization. Bertocci examines a variety of theories developed by scientific and philosophic thinkers and shows that the effort to understand this process in mechanistic terms breaks down.[16] Some kind of directionality is apparent which points to a goal rather than to a blind force. Movement in the required direction demands complex conditions, which do not appear now and again as if by chance but continuously as the stable environment of life. The best way of explaining this fact is by recognizing it as the work of some kind of purposive intelligence.[17]

The second link is constituted by reflection upon the relation of human thought to the world. Here again we take for granted a measure of adaptation that we cannot understand in terms of chance or mechanical causality. If we allow ourselves to wonder at the fact that our minds are marvelously attuned to, and supported by, the nature of the world, we cannot but recognize the work of a supreme orderer who provides the conditions for human thinking.[18]

We discover, however, that it is not only human thinking but also moral effort that is supported by the order of nature. If nature determined within narrow limits what man could do, there would be little room for developing morally. On the other hand, if there were little predictable regularity in the course of events, men could not learn from their past experience. The balance between freedom and order appears to be nicely calculated for moral development. Hence we may suppose that the purposive intelligence that is responsible for this balance is concerned for moral growth. This is the third link in the argument and is designed to add not so much to our confidence that a cosmic intelligence exists as to our conviction that it is good.[19] It is to the confirmation and clarification of this principle that the next links are added.

In the fourth link we turn our attention to the fact that human effort leads to the achievement of stable values that are supported and sustained by nature. Moral effort leads to moral character, which is the basis on which other values can be developed. Nature and human effort in interaction produce these values.[20]

---

lation of Tennant, to whom he refers with special approval. ("Biblical, Liberal, Catholic," *loc. cit.*, p. 1304.)

16 Peter Anthony Bertocci, *Introduction to the Philosophy of Religion*, Chs. V to VIII.

17 *Ibid.*, pp. 332–339.

18 *Ibid.*, pp. 339–344.

19 *Ibid.*, pp. 347–350.

20 *Ibid.*, pp. 350–357.

We are now prepared to ask directly what the aim of the cosmic mind may be. The preceding links suggest that he has willed a world that is good for man. But this raises many questions in view of the widespread evil in the world. Indeed, if we understood man's good in terms of the quantitative surplus of pleasure over pain, we could hardly call our world good at all. But this is a superficial view. We have seen that our world does support our efforts to achieve values, and we may confidently assert that, in the estimation even of pleasures, qualitative rather than quantitative considerations are decisive. In these terms, we have seen that the world does support man's efforts. It encourages him to share in the process of creation. What man achieves through his cocreativity is transmitted through civilized institutions. Moral principles are those norms by obedience to which human values can be realized and preserved. The moral order in which man lives is such that creative love on man's part contributes to the furtherance of values. All this enables us to affirm, as the fifth link, that the world is good for us and that its creator, judging from his creation, creatively seeks our happiness.[21]

The adjustment of the world to our experience and need is not limited to the moral sphere. In the sixth link we note that aesthetic experience is a further remarkable gift of the world to man. That man should enjoy beauty certainly appears to be the intention of the creator.[22]

Finally, in the seventh link we turn to religious experience itself. For some this experience is quite sufficient reason to believe in God, but Bertocci, like DeWolf and Mascall, refuses to regard it as in any way a substitute for the hard task of philosophic thought. Only when we have seen that it is entirely reasonable to believe in a creative, purposive intelligence that wills and seeks man's good can we confidently see, in the claims to direct experience of that intelligence, confirmation of our argument.[23]

In addition and in contrast to the kinds of arguments employed by DeWolf and Bertocci, another line of reasoning has been developed by Boston Personalists, especially by Edgar S. Brightman. Brightman's argument may be characterized as ontological in distinction from both the metaphysical arguments of the Thomists and the cosmological arguments we have just been considering. This difference requires brief explanation, especially in view of the fact that Brightman is altogether opposed to what is usually called "the ontological argument."

Thomism requires for the acceptance of its arguments only the acknowledgment that there are finite things. Whether these things are mental or material does not matter. Once this one acknowledgment is granted,

[21] *Ibid.*, pp. 357–372. [22] *Ibid.*, pp. 374–381. [23] *Ibid.*, pp. 382–384.

Thomism claims to present demonstrative proof of God's existence as infinite being.

DeWolf and Bertocci generally argue from the nature of the world as our present scientific knowledge reveals it to us. They insist that the most intelligible explanation of the present condition of the world, in the light of what we know of the processes by which it developed, is that it has been formed by a purposive, loving intelligence. Like the Thomists they leave open the ontological question of the relation of matter and mind except to the extent that they assume that mind is not merely epiphenomenal.

Brightman, however, raises the ontological question centrally and builds his case for a personal God upon his solution. He calls our attention to the fact that all of our thinking begins with our conscious experience as such. This is the unavoidable datum self or shining present.[24] We do not need to posit a mental substance underlying the datum self and thereby expose ourselves to the objection of Hume against Berkeley.[25] But we can quite empirically point to continuities within experience that are not subject to the charge of unknowability. In other terms, what we are given is not a general impersonal flow of qualities but quite concretely our own personal existence including all the qualities, sensory and nonsensory, that comprise our experience.[26]

Experience within the shining present points to that which is beyond it as essential to its self-understanding. This beyond which illuminates what is given Brightman calls the illuminating absent.[27] By definition this is never open to direct inspection, hence it cannot be known in the same way as the shining present. However, the task of the reason that functions in the shining present is to develop an inclusive view that is both empirically accurate and adequate with respect to the shining present and coherent in its interpretation of the illuminating absent as it illuminates that present.[28]

In developing a conception of the illuminating absent we are confronted with two basic alternatives, which we may label realism and idealism. Realism argues that much, at least, of the illuminating absent is ontologically unlike the shining present, whereas idealism affirms that one

24 Edgar S. Brightman, *Person and Reality: An Introduction to Metaphysics*, p. 36, n. 3. The terms "mind," "consciousness," and even "person" are also used as virtual synonyms.

25 *Ibid.*, p. 267. This does not mean that the term "substance" is rejected, but it is applied to the experienced unity which is the person, not to an underlying unperceived unity. (*Ibid.*, p. 199.)

26 The rejection of a narrow view reducing the shining present to sensory qualities is crucial to the argument. (*Ibid.*, pp. 39–40.)

27 *Ibid.*, pp. 31 ff.

28 *Ibid.*, pp. 37–38, 247.

ontological category is all-sufficient. The realist cannot supplement his negative assertion that the illuminating absent is nonmental by any positive account of what the nonmental can be, but in itself this is not adequate grounds to reject his thesis.[29] Furthermore, the realist has the disadvantage of providing a less economical scheme of concepts,[30] but this, too, leaves open the question of philosophical superiority. The decisive issue is the issue of which system leaves less sheer mystery in its final explanation.[31]

To answer this question we must first consider Brightman's own ontological scheme and then determine whether the introduction of nonmental entities will reduce or increase the mystery. Brightman sees the illuminating absent as composed in two clearly distinguished ways. First, it includes other shining presents or selves. Of these, our most confident examples are other persons like ourselves, but we also recognize the existence of subhuman selves in the animal world. Even an amoeba is a shining present. However, the bodies of animals, plants, and the inorganic world cannot be understood in these terms. Instead, they can be understood as the content of a cosmic mind that acts on our minds and thereby constitutes nature.[32]

The realist either omits the cosmic mind from his scheme and treats nature as an autonomous reality of nonmental but unknown character or retains God and adds this nonmental reality. In either case, he introduces a major complexity into the ontology and adds to the mystery about relations. From any point of view it is difficult to understand how entities are effectively related to each other, but some clue can be found to the relations among minds. To introduce nonmental entities that are intimately related to minds is to introduce new problems that are insoluble and only serve to increase the mystery.[33]

The counterargument of realism is that scientific thought demands it and that the Personalist's idea of nature is incredible.[34] Brightman devotes extensive attention to showing not only that Personalism is fully compatible with scientific thought but also that the basic categories of such thought — time, space, motion, cause, and substance — are better understood in terms of personalistic idealism.[35] Furthermore, the Personalist's understanding of nature is no more strange to common sense than is the understanding of modern science.[36] Therefore, Personalism can be shown to account for everything that realism explains, to employ fewer concepts, and to leave less mystery unsolved.

[29] *Ibid.*, p. 358.
[30] *Ibid.*, p. 356.
[31] *Ibid.*, p. 351.
[32] *Ibid.*, p. 248.
[33] *Ibid.*, pp. 363–364.
[34] *Ibid.*, pp. 360–362.
[35] *Ibid.*, Part II.
[36] *Ibid.*, p. 361.

A further argument is required to show that the cosmic self, mind, or shining present is a personal God. One can readily show that the functions ascribed to this mind could not be carried out by a subpersonal entity; hence the cosmic self must be personal or superpersonal. Further, one can show that this Cosmic Person is worthy of worship.

All the arguments of the Boston Personalists converge on the one affirmation that God exists and is a Person. Further, in varying ways they point to the fact that he is personally concerned with his creatures. In view of this emphasis, Personalism faces acutely the question of why there is so much evil in the world.

At this point there appears a major debate between DeWolf, on the one hand, and Bertocci and Brightman on the other. All agree that much of the evil in the world results from man's misuse of the freedom that God gave him.[37] Much other evil can be seen as needed if man is to be stimulated to inventiveness and to the achievement of high moral character.[38] The causal order needed for the achievement of values also inevitably produces suffering.[39] But there seems to be a residue of evil that is neither beneficial to man's moral growth nor caused by his sin.[40]

Brightman and Bertocci argue that the amount of this evil is so great that we must acknowledge that God cannot be both altogether good and all-powerful. Since the whole movement of the evolutionary process has been toward a world that sustains human values, we cannot question God's goodness toward us. Hence we must understand the slow and sometimes thwarted course of progress as an expression of God's struggle against something that resists his will. After considering several possible interpretations, both agree that there must be within God himself a resistant given that blocks his immediate realization of all that he wills.[41]

DeWolf, on the other hand, opposes any hypostatization of that which limits God's will. He acknowledges that in some sense God's power is not absolutely unlimited. As Brightman and Bertocci agree, God is limited by his delegation of power to his creatures and by his own rational nature. Furthermore, however great his power may be, it is simply what it is and not more. God's power is limited in this sense but not in the sense that something other than it imposes a limit.[42]

This difference, although philosophically and theologically interesting,

[37] Bertocci, *op. cit.*, pp. 360–362; DeWolf, *A Theology of the Living Church*, p. 139.
[38] Bertocci, *op. cit.*, pp. 395–398; DeWolf, *A Theology of the Living Church*, pp. 140–141.
[39] Bertocci, *op. cit.*, p. 402; DeWolf, *A Theology of the Living Church*, pp. 139–140.
[40] Bertocci, *op. cit.*, p. 402; DeWolf, *A Theology of the Living Church*, pp. 141–143.
[41] Bertocci, *op. cit.*, Ch. 17.
[42] DeWolf, *A Theology of the Living Church*, p. 141.

is not central to our concern with theological method. Hence, we leave it without further comment. What is important is the vast area of agreement among the Personalists, all of whom hold that reason by itself is capable of providing an adequate conviction of the existence of a personal God who is concerned about the world he has created.

Such a confident claim for the power of reason may appear to reduce divine revelation to a minor role. But DeWolf does not see the relation of reason and revelation in these terms. He rejects the view that what is learned through revelation is not learned through reason and that when reason suffices revelation plays no role. In opposition to this view, he argues that all knowledge in every field is based upon the conjoint working of reason and revelation.[43]

There is no such thing as reason discovering truth apart from data that are presented to it. Likewise, the sheer presentation of stimuli does not itself create knowledge. Reason must operate upon that which is received by the mind from its environment.

Thus far all except extreme rationalists would follow the argument. But when DeWolf speaks of revelation he does not mean simply the world's self-disclosing to man in his experience. He means quite seriously that this experience can be understood only as the product of God's activity. Certainly, physical conditions are directly responsible for the particular character of our experience. But once we have understood that the whole order of the world and the adaptation of the mind to its environment is God's creative work, we can no longer distinguish the natural from the divine. God's activity is a decisive ingredient in every acquisition of knowledge. But his activity alone does not simply produce knowledge in us. We exercise our own voluntary co-operation with him in the use of the reason that he has given us. Hence, again, we can understand our knowledge only as the product of co-operation between the divine and human agents, of revelation and reason.

It is important to grasp clearly this meaning of the term "revelation." In many natural theologies the term "revelation" has a much wider reference than distinctively Christian revelation. But usually natural revelation is distinguished from other aspects of natural experience by virtue of its direct relevance to knowledge of God. In this case, experience is not called revelation because God is active in its production but because it leads the mind to think about him. Therefore, while all experience may be thought of as having some slight revelatory potentiality, attention is concentrated on quite limited aspects of it. DeWolf, by contrast, defines

[43] *Ibid.*, pp. 63–64, 33–36.

revelation entirely in terms of the agency of God in producing the experience.[44] Since this agency is absolutely universal, there is no basis for distinguishing that part of experience which is especially relevant to his natural theology from that which is the basis for historical research or technological improvements. Revelation is that part of all experience which is not the result of man's free activity.

Thus far we have operated entirely within the limits of natural theology or philosophy of religion. But DeWolf is concerned to function specifically as a Christian theologian. If we are to make the transition from natural theology to Christian theology, we must introduce a conception of special revelation to supplement general revelation.

DeWolf points out that in addition to the rational thinking about God that is possible on the basis of general experience, men do have particular experiences that are peculiarly illuminating to them. Sometimes, for example, a word or gesture of an acquaintance rather suddenly illuminates the motivation of his behavior in a new and decisive way. History shows that this kind of event has been crucial for the development of religious movements and institutions. An event in which an individual or a community has found significant new insight into the nature of God is what DeWolf calls " special revelation." [45]

Once again we must pay close attention to what DeWolf means. Special revelation has often been understood as an act of God in history of a different order from other historical events. It has meant, therefore, a supernatural occurrence to be distinguished from natural occurrences by the directness of God's intervention. DeWolf does not think in these terms. He has established once and for all that every event involves the activity of God. He does not believe that this activity functions more directly in some events than in others.[46] An event is not objectively a special revelation by virtue of God's special act in it. Rather, any event is a special revelation when in fact it functions as such for some individual or group.

This means that the concept of special revelation can be developed within a strictly historical context. In recognizing that a great diversity of events has functioned as specially revelatory, we are asking for no new act of credulity. Once we have established that God exists, and once we have accepted the fact that human religion is related to him, we must acknowledge that the diversity of religions reflects in part the diversity of experiences which have been decisive for the particular ways in which God is understood in the several traditions.

We must also note that there is a positive valuation of special revelation

[44] *Ibid.*, p. 33. [45] *Ibid.*, pp. 65–67. [46] *Ibid.*, pp. 65, 66.

when religion is understood in this way. Although particular beliefs are not guaranteed by the revelatory experiences that lie behind them, we do see these experiences as genuinely revelatory. Special revelation occurs only when God's presence is actually felt and when through the experience something about his nature and will is grasped.[47] Special revelation does provide a basis for *knowledge* about God.

Here we find a crucial doctrine that allows for a transition from natural theology to Christian theology. As long as we see the diversity of experience of God as so much data from which we must generalize about the nature of religions, we must remain at the level of philosophy of religion. If, however, we see that some events give new insight into the nature of God, then the exposition of the truth about God that is given in such special revelations becomes a partly independent discipline. DeWolf understands Christian theology as such a discipline. It does not simply describe what Christians have experienced and believed. Rather it formulates critically the truth that has been learned through Christian experience.[48] Since what it formulates is the truth, its affirmations are not merely confessions relevant to Christians; they are assertions that are claimed to be true for all men.

At the same time, however, it is clear that the problem of relativism does not disappear. Adherents of other faiths have equal right and duty to formulate the truths that their experiences have given them. Presumably these truths are binding also for Christians. This fact raises problems to which DeWolf is only beginning to give extended attention.[49]

DeWolf guards against overenthusiastic dogmatic claims by the adherents of each tradition by insisting that theology must be a critical discipline. This means not only that clarity and coherence are required within it but also that the theologian must not make affirmations that are in conflict with what is known about God on the grounds of general revelation. Every theology should presuppose the truth of the basic understanding of God, man, and the world that natural theology has attained.[50]

The Christian theologian must always keep in mind the knowledge about God and man that is given by natural theology and then ask with respect to each topic what further light is thrown upon it by the special experience of the Christian community. This experience is not limited to

[47] *Ibid.*, p. 67.
[48] *Ibid.*, p. 18.
[49] See DeWolf, "The Interpretation of Christianity and the Non-Christian Religions," *The Theology of the Christian Mission,* Gerald H. Anderson, ed., pp. 199–212; and *Acknowledgments of Non-Christian Contributions to Christian Faith,* the Boston University Lecture for 1960–1961.
[50] DeWolf, *A Theology of the Living Church,* p. 46.

a few extraordinary events but has been articulated into a tradition embodied in the Bible. Hence it is especially the Bible to which the theologian turns in his quest for a richer understanding of religious reality.

We need hardly note at this point that the authority that the Bible enjoys in this view is not that of an infallible oracle.[51] DeWolf does not hesitate to distinguish more and less inspired passages[52] and to subject all to critical reason. Both what is known of God from natural theology and the message of the high moments of the Biblical revelation itself can be used as criteria.[53] The Bible is understood as a source of insight and illumination, not as a final norm by which every affirmation is to be tested. We are to accept it as authoritative in religious matters because we recognize its unique spiritual wisdom, not because we claim an objective supernatural guarantee for its accuracy.

Given these methodological principles, it is not surprising to find that much of what DeWolf as a Christian theologian tells us about God closely resembles what Bertocci as a philosopher tells us about God. The accent on God's righteousness and love may be heightened, and DeWolf resists Bertocci's emphasis on God's finitude. Throughout his discussion, DeWolf supports his own position from the Bible and in the process he deals with questions of Biblical interpretation. But what is impressive is that his reading of the Bible extensively supports and reinforces the understanding of God that is also derivable from philosophy.

Much the same can be said for DeWolf's theological doctrine of man. His discussion of man's dependence, limits, moral responsibility, freedom, and survival of death parallels closely the position developed by Bertocci on philosophical grounds. Once again Christian experience is understood as reinforcing natural theology rather than as adding wholly new beliefs to it.

The situation here is not unlike that in Thomism. Both have great confidence in the power of reason to show the truth of many doctrines that have often been regarded as dependent upon special revelation. This confidence is, however, less qualified among the Boston Personalists than among modern Thomists like Mascall. Mascall recognizes that the kind of reasoning on which Thomistic natural theology depends became possible only through the historical impact of special revelation. This is because the particular vision of entities in the world as finite existents cannot be regarded as universally prevalent in all human cultures. We saw that the systematic implications of this fact for the relation of natural and revealed theology were not fully faced in Mascall's own work.

The Boston Personalists do not see a similar need for moderating their

[51] *Ibid.*, Ch. 8. [52] *Ibid.*, pp. 76–77, 82–83. [53] *Ibid.*, pp. 84–85.

claim to the objective rationality of their position. This is because they base their primary arguments upon the understanding of the world that has been produced by the advance of scientific knowledge. Presumably they recognize that their formulations could not have been employed apart from the historic fact of scientific achievement, but given the virtual universality of the acceptance of science, this limitation does not relativize the results in any important sense. One may ask whether future scientific advances may not render present conclusions out of date, and Personalists would not rule out this possibility. But since the Personalists only claim that we should now act in terms of what it is now reasonable to believe, this is no objection to their system.

The contrast with Mascall may be stated in a further way. Mascall recognizes that many people do not actually perceive the world in such a way as to have within their consciousness the starting point of the argument for the existence of God. However, he insists that the argument itself is demonstrative.[54] For one who has the starting point, God's existence is objectively certain whatever fluctuation there may be in his subjective certitude. For the Boston Personalists the data for reasoning about God are accessible to anyone who will take the trouble to read the appropriate scientific treatises. No special state of mind is required other than the openness and sensitivity that are necessary for any learning experience.[55]

Thus the starting point is, for practical purposes, universal. The arguments, however, can show only the superior reasonableness of one interpretation with respect to others. They can lead to a judgment of objective probability. The reasonable man will adapt himself to this situation by treating such objective probability as if it justified subjective certitude, although he will remain open to new evidence.

In principle the approach of the Thomists means that special revelation may supplement natural knowledge of God but cannot change it. That which is objectively certain is beyond alteration. For Boston Personalism, on the other hand, the data of special revelation might affect the scale of probabilities on some point. In practice, however, it is Thomism in which the specifically Christian affirmations introduce the greater tensions with the philosophical doctrines. This is because the philosophical arguments employed lead to affirmations about God that seem to conflict with the personalistic thought of the Bible. The basic harmony in Boston Personal-

[54] Mascall, *Existence and Analogy,* p. xi.

[55] The data of Christian theology are not, of course, accessible apart from the moral and spiritual disciplines of the Christian life, but I do not understand DeWolf to say that this applies to the data of natural theology. *A Theology of the Living Church,* p. 20. See also the fuller discussion of the point below, pp. 77–83.

ism is due to the fact that it regards the philosophical evidence as pointing precisely to an understanding of God as Person. Hence in Boston Personalism the convergence and harmony of philosophy and theology are almost complete.

Thomism regards its argument for the existence of God as leading to a conception of God's transcendence that enables us to accept all manner of occurrences in strictly supernatural and suprarational terms. Boston Personalism, on the other hand, basing its understanding of God upon rational probabilities, has no place for this kind of supernaturalism. Hence, in its theological expression, as well as in its philosophy, it limits itself to the rationally plausible. This might seem to be a very restrictive principle indeed, but in fact it does not prove to be so.

DeWolf shows that the occurrence of miracles,[56] the existence and activity of angels,[57] and judgment after death[58] are all intelligible ideas and reasonable beliefs coherent with all else that we know about God, man, and the world. Whether or not we have sufficient evidence to accept any particular belief of this sort remains a separate question, but at this point the special experience of the Christian community adds considerable weight of probability to otherwise plausible beliefs. Biblical accounts must be critically examined, but this does not imply that we should approach them with an incredulous spirit.

The crucial test of the harmony of theology with philosophy is found in Christology. This doctrine cannot be developed simply in terms of natural theology. Furthermore, many of the historic Christian affirmations about Jesus Christ would break the bounds of possibility imposed by personalistic natural theology. We turn now to a brief summary of DeWolf's understanding of Jesus.

Jesus must be seen first of all to be a man among men.[59] He grew and developed normally, had human intellectual limitations, and experienced temptation and suffering.[60] He was uniquely endowed for his unique vocation, but nothing about his native equipment forced him to perform any distinctive mission.[61] DeWolf makes it clear that, ontologically and by nature, therefore, Jesus was a man and not God.[62] At this point DeWolf stands unequivocally in the liberal tradition and, he believes, in the Synoptic tradition against some of the creeds. Furthermore, he rejects the relia-

[56] DeWolf, *A Theology of the Living Church,* pp. 126–127.
[57] *Ibid.,* pp. 128–129.
[58] *Ibid.,* pp. 285–286.
[59] *Ibid.,* pp. 225–226, 234.
[60] *Ibid.,* pp. 227–229.
[61] *Ibid.,* pp. 248, 254.
[62] *Ibid.,* pp. 243–244.

bility of the stories of the virgin birth both on historical grounds and because they misrepresent Jesus' status as human.[63]

If Jesus was a man in the full, unqualified sense, he was free to fulfill or not to fulfill God's will for his life. What makes Jesus unique is that the mission God asked of him was one spiritually decisive for all time. While everyone is called to take a special individual place in God's Kingdom, Jesus was called to reveal to men the Kingdom itself. Because this mission was so distinctive, it required special historical preparation and need never be repeated.[64] Whether other men were called to fulfill this mission and failed to do so, we do not know.[65] We do know that Jesus was called and that he voluntarily accepted God's will for his life. This total devotion to God's will also marks Jesus off from other men.[66]

Because Jesus wholly subordinated his will to God's will, he came to share God's purposes. Thereby he became revelation to us in two ways. As man he shows us what man can become as he yields himself wholly to God. As one who shared God's purposes he shows us what those purposes are and how they impinge upon daily life. Therefore, he may justly be called the Word of God.[67]

The revelation that we find in Jesus, and especially in his voluntary death on the cross, does not merely enlighten us as to the true character of God and the human situation. It also moves us to that repentance of sin and acceptance of God's forgiving love which bring us to reconciliation with God.[68] Hence, through revelation we experience also reconciliation as an objective change in our relationship to God.[69]

Another Christian doctrine that DeWolf does not derive from natural theology is that of the Trinity. For many theologians the doctrine of the Trinity is necessitated by their Christology, in which they declare Jesus to be the incarnation of a divine pre-existent being who is equal with God. Since only God can be equal with God, this being must be God. Yet he must not be identical with the Father to whom Jesus prayed. For these and other reasons a second person is introduced into the one Godhead. Similar considerations lead to regarding the Holy Spirit as the third person.

This motive for trinitarian formulation is mentioned only to show that it does not operate for DeWolf. Thereby he is saved from a doctrine that would be severely in tension with the rational view that God is one supreme Person. To say that God is three persons, as orthodoxy has done, is clearly incompatible with the assertion that he is one person. Since at least

[63] *Ibid.*, pp. 231–232.
[64] *Ibid.*, pp. 248–249.
[65] *Ibid.*, p. 253.
[66] *Ibid.*, pp. 248–251.
[67] *Ibid.*, pp. 251–253.
[68] *Ibid.*, p. 267.
[69] *Ibid.*, pp. 268–269.

some forms of traditional trinitarianism are impossible for a Personalist, and since the usual reason for adopting the trinitarian position does not operate in DeWolf's theology, one might expect a direct acceptance of unitarianism.

However, DeWolf believes that the Biblical basis for formulating trinitarian doctrine is preserved in his thought, and that a trinitarian doctrine can be formulated that is harmonious with his Personalism. He accepts what he understands to be the New Testament view that God the Father is the ground of all that is, that Jesus Christ is the incarnate Word, and that the Holy Spirit is continually present to us in guidance and comfort.[70] He insists also that the God we know in these three ways is himself unqualifiedly one.

Furthermore, he argues, we would misunderstand the historic creeds if we supposed that when they spoke of three persons they meant persons in our sense, or specifically in the sense in which Personalism speaks of God as the supreme Person. Although some contemporaries have moved in this direction, the creeds are better understood when we remember that the Latin word originally referred to masks worn by actors. Therefore, we are faithful both to the Bible and to the deeper sense of the creeds when we assert that one personal God is given in three modes of revelation. DeWolf does not object seriously if his view is labeled as a form of Modalism, whether or not this is taken as an accusation of formal heresy.[71]

◈ ◈

The foregoing is sufficient to illustrate the remarkably consistent procedure followed by DeWolf. The fundamental understanding of God and his relation to the world provided by natural theology is never challenged or substantively altered by the statement of Christian theology. On the contrary, it is given further support in terms of distinctively Christian experience. This experience requires that special attention be given to understanding the events that have been decisive for it and the way in which those events exercise their influence. Hence discussions of the authority of the Bible and of Christology and the church are added to what can be learned directly from natural theology. These additions are made in terms of what it is reasonable to believe on the grounds of natural theology and what the experience of Christians gives sufficient evidence for believing.

[70] *Ibid.,* p. 274. For fuller discussion of the Trinity, see *The Case for Theology in Liberal Perspective,* Ch. V. DeWolf has recently called attention to the increased role of this doctrine in his thought, especially as expressed in the structure of *The Enduring Message of the Bible.* (" Biblical, Liberal, Catholic," *loc. cit.,* p. 1305.)

[71] DeWolf, *A Theology of the Living Church,* pp. 276–279.

There is no leap as in Mascall into a realm of supernatural affirmations in some tension with the natural theology. There is, however, a further specification and enrichment of what is left undetermined in natural theology.

The existence of a personal creator-God is the most central assumption of DeWolf's theology, and this belief is established primarily in natural theology.[72] Hence we may devote our primary attention to the evaluation of the ways in which philosophy functioning as natural theology supports this belief. If any of the arguments advanced demonstrate that belief in a personal, creator-God is the most reasonable of positions, then the theological position developed on this basis will have great strength. If the arguments fail in their purpose, then the theological method that assumes their adequacy must be reconceived.

The obvious objection against relying heavily upon the arguments advanced by Personalists for the existence and nature of God is that most contemporary philosophers do not accept them. If we are to base our lives upon a calculation of rational probabilities, we might suppose that we would place great weight upon whatever consensus there may be among leading thinkers. In some ages this would give considerable support to Christian faith, but in our own time this is hardly the situation. Hence we must be persuaded of the reasonableness of believing in God in spite of the fact that the grounds for such belief are not widely accepted.

The Personalists are far from unaware of this problem. They do not offer us, therefore, a general philosophical consensus but, rather, specific rational grounds for belief. They share constructively in the philosophical discussion of the facts that confront us, and they ask us to accept their conclusions on the strength of their arguments.

However, to find a clue to the problem that lies behind these arguments we must ask why they have no greater acceptance among contemporary philosophers who should be in position to judge their philosophic worth. Mascall, we noted, held that the lack of acceptance of his arguments results from failure to contemplate the world in the right way. But the Personalists do not explicitly ask for any comparable mind-set or practice in contemplation as the basis for accepting, for example, the wider teleological argument. Hence, the failure to accept their conclusions would seem to be due to ignoring or misunderstanding the question, to a negative prejudice, or to lack of persuasiveness of the argument.

This does not mean that Personalists suppose that reason can operate in

72 Without rejecting this view, DeWolf has recently stressed that it is in its specifically Christian form that theism is most defensible rationally. ("Biblical, Liberal, Catholic," *loc. cit.*, p. 1305. See also a passage added in the 1960 revision of *A Theology of the Living Church*, pp. 59–60.)

abstraction from the ongoing life processes or even from basic faith commitments.[73] But they do not seem to regard the faith commitments required as distinctively Christian or as historically conditioned in any decisive way. DeWolf, for example, notes that the rationalist must have faith that there is kinship between reason and reality. He must commit himself to basic moral principles, such as honesty, necessary for the successful pursuit of knowledge. He must believe in the inherent value of some goals and achievements.[74]

Although there is no indication that DeWolf supposes that this faith, required for the functioning of reason, is historically dependent on Christian revelation, he does not exclude this interpretation. In his definition of natural theology he states that it is *logically* independent of Biblical revelation and faith.[75] This definition is open to the interpretation that the data for natural theology factually depend on Christian faith but that we have no basis for asserting that this dependence is logically necessary. If this is what DeWolf means, we should call his natural theology a Christian philosophy or Christian natural theology [76] to make clear its actual derivation from Christian faith, and we should not expect it to be rationally acceptable to persons with quite different backgrounds. If what DeWolf calls natural theology can be regarded in this way, most of the objections raised below are irrelevant.

However, this interpretation of DeWolf raises more questions than it solves. First, it seems to conflict with his statements that man can and does formulate natural theologies that are correct as far as they go — presumably independently of distinctively Christian revelation; [77] that natural theology can provide a common platform with non-Christians; [78] and that the arguments of natural theology can rationally persuade non-Christians of theism.[79] Second, this interpretation would demand a recognition of a theological circle and its complex methodological consequences that is not found in DeWolf's writings. For these reasons, I am interpreting DeWolf as affirming that belief in a personal creator-God is neither factually nor systematically dependent upon Christian revelation, that on the contrary it is presupposed by Christian thought on the basis of independent rational considerations.

I wish to argue, however, that in fact the validity of these rational con-

[73] DeWolf, *A Theology of the Living Church,* revised edition, pp. 44–45.
[74] L. Harold DeWolf, *The Religious Revolt Against Reason,* pp. 176–178.
[75] DeWolf, *The Case for Theology in Liberal Perspective,* p. 19.
[76] For clarification of these terms, see n. 83 in Chapter 2.
[77] DeWolf, *The Case for Theology in Liberal Perspective,* p. 30.
[78] *Ibid.,* p. 33.
[79] *Ibid.,* p. 34.

siderations does depend on a distinctive apprehension of the world in much the same way as in the case of Thomism. If one accepts fundamentally the need for the kind of explanation of the data that Personalists undertake to give, their explanations have considerable persuasive power. If, however, one does not see the data as requiring explanation in this sense, then the whole argument, however cogent it may be in itself, appears simply empty.[80]

The point may be seen most readily by considering the distinction of description and explanation that is crucial to DeWolf's second argument explicitly and to his other arguments and that of Bertocci implicitly. Is there a real difference between description and explanation, and, if so, what is it?

A certain kind of common-sense point of view (which I share with the Personalists) holds that there is a difference. A description simply asserts *how* a thing is, and an explanation tells *why* it is as it is. In scientific inquiry, however, it has become increasingly clear that an explanation is only a more inclusive description. An isolated phenomenon is held to be explained when the formula that describes it can be shown to be derived from a formula that describes a wider range of phenomena. Hence scientists, and those philosophers who seek to escape the endless confusions of philosophy by staying close to the proven methods of science, hold that the distinction between description and explanation is only one of degree. A complete description of the phenomenon would also be its complete explanation if the description showed the mathematical relations of all the formal patterns described.

If this scientific point of view is adopted, most of the above arguments are entirely undercut. A complete description of causal law constitutes the only explanation for which it is meaningful to ask. A complete description of evolutionary development leaves no room for some other kind of theory that DeWolf and Bertocci see as explanatory. The ideas of eternal truths and objective moral principles are also seen as illusory. If the truths of which we speak are mathematical or formal truths, they are understood as tautological. They come into existence with the definitions that entail them. If the truths in question are empirical truths, they are functions of human experience and have no eternal suprahuman status.

If we argue against the scientifically oriented philosopher that there is, nevertheless, an immediate perception of an ultimate difference between explanation and description, we must recognize clearly what we are doing. The idea of explanation with which we are now dealing is derived from

80 Bertocci is aware of this situation, but the need for explanation is so clear to him that he does not take it very seriously. Cf. *op. cit.,* pp. 280–281.

our experience of our own purposes affecting our acts. When I write these words, a complete *description* of my act would subsume this interaction of forces under general laws of such interaction. But I feel that the *explanation* of my writing these words lies in my desire to clarify and communicate my thoughts. The category of explanation may then be applied to other persons and to higher animals. How much farther it may be applied is a question of great importance. It is clear that we can decide how far to apply it only by determining the pertinent resemblances of the object in question to ourselves.

Now we must ask to what degree the cosmos as a whole resembles us with respect to its entertainment of purposes and capacity to put them into effect. That is, is the cosmos personal? But how shall we decide such questions? If we believe that the distinctive category of explanation can be applied to cosmic activity, we must suppose that the cosmos is personal, for there is no such thing as a nonpersonal explanation that is other than generalized description. But we are then assuming what we are supposedly inquiring about. Either the cosmos is personal and we do right to seek an explanation of the world, or the cosmos is not personal and we can only describe phenomena. This much we can show, but it is difficult to see how any arguments of the sort used by DeWolf and Bertocci can demonstrate the superior rationality of one position over the other.

The merit of Bertocci's work is that it helps to destroy an intermediate conception of explanation that often confuses the real issue. Many have thought they had given an explanation in distinction from a description of an event when they fixed its place in a deterministic order. Objective causality has been supposed to work on the model of a machine. As long as the mechanical conceptuality could be used, the emptiness of this kind of explanation was not recognized except by a few philosophers. Hume showed that in the objective view we cannot in principle attribute necessity to the relation between two events however frequently they succeed one another in a regular way. But an important psychological need to understand was fulfilled by subsuming events under a mechanical model.

Still others, when the mechanical model collapsed in the life sciences, employed a language of forces or emergence. Bertocci does well to show us that such terms in no sense suggest explanations of anything.[81] Clearly, if we are to explain rather than describe we must do so in terms of purposes, and if we are to explain cosmic phenomena we must do so in terms of cosmic purpose. The halfway houses between positivism and theism can be successfully demolished from either side. But the result depends

[81] *Ibid.*, pp. 34 ff.

upon whether, with the abandonment of such intermediate types of "explanation," the demand for an explanation in distinction from a description remains at all. If it does, then the case for theism requires only the demonstration that the purposes of the persons within the cosmos cannot account for the existence, order, or change of the cosmos as a whole. To such an end effective arguments can be formulated. But for those who give up the demand for explanation, any argument will be irrelevant.

Much the same difficulty is more commonly raised in terms of meaningfulness. With some diversity among themselves, the dominant schools of recent philosophy have tried to relate meaning closely to verification. The meaning of a statement consists in some way in its observable implications. If I assert that a given object is square, one may measure the sides and angles and thus test my assertion. The meaning of the assertion consists in its testable implications. If I assert that there is rational life on planets circling distant stars, it is possible to conceive of certain observations that could support my statement even if we are not now in a position to make such observations, and indeed even if man can never in fact make the required observations. But when I assert that the theological order of the universe is the product of a supreme intelligence, there seems to be nothing implied thereby of a testable sort.[82] Hence many philosophers declare such statements to be meaningless.

We may, of course, reasonably complain that a statement is meaningful whether or not it can be verified, that truth and falsity consist in the correspondence of an idea to a reality whether or not we can prove this correspondence, and that the claim that a supreme intelligence exists either corresponds or fails to correspond to an enduring reality. But once again, we can only confront one philosophical orientation — one now prevalent — with another that happens now to lack wide acceptance in the philosophic community.[83] Hence we do not escape the difficulty that our argu-

[82] Note, however, the interesting argument of Hick that on the hypothesis of survival of death, evidence might be attained for or against the truth of the affirmation of God's existence. On this basis Hick argues that the affirmation is meaningful whether or not it is true. (*Faith and Knowledge: A Modern Introduction to the Problem of Religious Knowledge,* Ch. 7.) The whole discussion is very fluid at present, and I do not want to imply any clear consensus against the meaningfulness of affirmations about God. The point is only that in the present situation the meaningfulness of such language cannot be simply assumed.

[83] I do not wish to press the question of the relative strength of the two philosophical orientations. Although I believe that my judgment of the dominance of the orientation alien to Boston Personalism is correct, all that is necessary to my argument is to point out the seriousness of the dispute. It should go without saying that current popularity of a position is no index to its "truth." The only reason for introducing this point is to stress that the theologian who today appeals to philosophy for support cannot appeal to any philosophical consensus but must

ments persuade us only if we already share in a particular perspective.

The Personalists appeal to the criterion of empirical or comprehensive coherence to justify their philosophical position.[84] I have already indicated my own view that when we once grant the need for explanation in distinction from description theism wins out over the pseudo solutions of materialism and creative evolution. But this criterion is useless for establishing the right of the demand for explanation in the first place. In so far as the understanding of comprehensive coherence includes the idea of explanation, it begs the question that in our day is most acute.

The criterion of empirical or comprehensive coherence does have value when we turn from the basic justification of introducing the question of God to the further question as to his nature. For example, Personalists have faced the question of how God's goodness can be affirmed in the light of the evil in the world with candor and originality. In doing this they have been guided by the need to bring their assertions about God into coherent relationship with the data of honest observation of the world. They have made important contributions in demonstrating again in the twentieth century the reasonableness of Christian theism.

Systematically, however, Personalism assumes as rationally given a set of beliefs that are in fact radically disputable. The issues at stake cannot be settled by appeal to probability, for no clear meaning can be assigned to this idea that is neutral to the disputants. Hence, one's acceptance of Personalism cannot be finally on the grounds that Personalists themselves have offered, but rather on the grounds of a much more basic decision. Until one has seriously explored how that decision is to be made, one is not in a position to settle questions about the relation of faith to reason or about the relation of Christian theology to natural theology.

This objection to Personalism might not be serious if professional philosophers alone found its philosophic assumptions dubious. Actually, however, Personalism's assumptions run deeply counter to the increasingly prevalent mood of our day. Personalism has great confidence in the reliability of a kind of common-sense speculation about the cosmos as a whole, whereas sophisticated moderns generally find such confidence naïve and out of date. Even when sympathetic to such inquiry they find the results too suspect and humanly unreal to serve as a basis for ultimate decisions of life and death. Hence, it is not philosophers only, but spiritually sensitive moderns generally, who feel an ultimate frustration and

---

defend the philosophy to which he appeals against vigorous philosophical attack. I am in my criticisms questioning the adequacy of the Personalists' defense.

84 Bertocci, *op. cit.*, pp. 55–59; DeWolf, *A Theology of the Living Church*, pp. 28–29.

emptiness before Personalism's staggering claims about reason's ability to know God.

Although this discussion is relevant to most of the arguments of DeWolf and Bertocci it is not equally relevant to that summarized above from Brightman. The objection to DeWolf and Bertocci has been that they presuppose a basic way of apprehending reality and understanding the function of reason that is radically at issue in our day. Hence we should direct our attention to how that issue can be settled, and it seems at least likely that we will be driven to acknowledge the role of some kind of faith at that point. Such acknowledgment would throw an entirely different light upon the character of natural theology and on the relation of faith to reason.

Brightman's argument deals directly with the most fundamental of philosophic questions, and although in his case, too, the need to explain rather than simply describe plays a decisive role, it is by no means so simply assumed.[85] This is to say that Brightman raises directly the question of the nature of being as such, and his argument for the existence of God follows from his answer to this question. Critics may object that the raising of this question is just as alien to the modern temper as are the less technical speculations of the other Personalists, but against this objection we may note an increasing recognition that the long effort to avoid the ontological questions shows signs of collapsing. Analysis shows that those who have claimed to avoid this question have in fact operated with ontological assumptions. Even those who restrict themselves to the study of language cannot avoid some judgment as to the relation between language and things.

Brightman's argument in essence is very simple. Our present experience points beyond itself for its own intelligibility and existence.[86] This beyond includes other shining presents that explain a part of our own shining present. That which cannot be explained in these terms must be explained either as the work of a cosmic shining present, or as something wholly different in nature from shining presents, or as some combination of the two. Of the three alternatives, the second and third are more complicated, less clear, and leave us with greater mystery than the first. Hence it is reasonable to believe in a cosmic shining present. Further analysis of its functions shows it to have the properties of a personal God.

If we are to criticize Brightman seriously we must ask whether the comparison of personalistic idealism and realism in fact shows the superiority of the former to the degree claimed. Or can we suggest a kind of realism,

[85] Brightman, *op. cit.,* Ch. 9 and p. 149, n. 18, pp. 205, 229, 310.
[86] *Ibid.,* p. 269.

or compromise between idealism and realism which is equal or superior by Brightman's own criteria?

I believe that if realism is understood as materialism, Brightman's objections are well taken. However, Brightman usually identifies realism with any doctrine of a reality that is not conscious. The datum self or shining present is equated by Brightman with *conscious* awareness or experience. Might we not posit *un*conscious subjectivity as real without introducing the weaknesses of materialism?

Before attempting to sketch such a position, we need to look closely at the difficulties into which Brightman's principles lead him. First, he must draw a very sharp line between entities that are selves or shining presents and those that are not, and he must do so on the basis of his conjecture as to the presence or absence of consciousness. He judges that an amoeba is conscious whereas a cell in an organized body is not.[87] Whether he is correct in this conjecture is not the point. What we must note is that wherever he draws the line he must separate that which exists in itself as an object both for the human and the divine mind and that which exists *only* as the content of God's thought. Thus empirical differences which seem to be matters of degree must be taken as clues to the most fundamental of all ontological distinctions.

A second difficulty appears in understanding the unconscious in man. Brightman has two choices. Either it is really unconscious, in which case it belongs exhaustively to the divine environment of man, or it is really conscious, only inaccessible to the normal personal self.[88] Each alternative has strange consequences, which we can consider in the reverse order.

If the unconscious is in fact a consciousness, it is also a datum self or shining present. There are, then, two or more selves associated with each human body, both of them conscious. All of them presumably have considerable influence on the behavior of the body, including its speech. Do I then identify my friend with one among the several conscious selves in the body? By what means do I distinguish him from the others? By the element of rationality? But are we to think of conscious selves devoid of all rationality? Surely what we usually mean by personality or character must be the conjoint product of all these conscious selves; yet it is this which excites our esteem and love.

Am I to understand my own relation with the other selves inhabiting my own body in the same way as my relations with persons inhabiting other bodies? If the relation is radically different, do we not surrender the

[87] *Ibid.*, p. 201.
[88] This is Brightman's favored view. *Ibid.*, pp. 179, 209, 273.

economy that was one of the advantages over realism by introducing now a third radically distinct way in which relations between selves occur?[89] These questions and objections are not systematically decisive, but they do indicate that Brightman's ontology raises difficulties that increase the mystery he seeks to reduce.

If we follow the alternative of treating the unconscious as truly not conscious, we draw a still sharper line between consciousness and the unconscious.[90] Consciousness is actually extant as an entity in the world created by God and given real autonomy. Unconsciousness is the direct working of God for consciousness, with no being of any sort in itself. Here again, very slight empirical differences might become the basis for positing an absolute ontological difference.

Consider for example, a dull discomfort in one's leg. At one moment one may attend to it and bring it into full consciousness. Then he shifts attention to something else and for some time " forgets " about it. At other times he is very dimly aware of it at the edges of his consciousness without attending to it. At all times it qualifies his mood to some extent, adding, perhaps, to his irritability. What seems to occur often is a very gradual fading from consciousness correlative with the degree of intensity of concentration on other subjects. Sometimes one realizes suddenly that for some moments the discomfort has greatly increased. It seems rather arbitrary to identify the exact point at which the discomfort passes from what may without qualification be called consciousness into total unconsciousness. Yet, in Brightman's view either this line must be drawn and must be held to have decisive ontological significance, or else the discomfort must be held to pass over to another self inhabiting the same body.

Consider also the phenomenon of subliminal sensation, which has direct consequences for motivation. Must we say that the words flashed upon the screen are simply not experienced at all? They seem to be experienced unconsciously. But in Brightman's view this event must be understood as existing only in God or else as occurring in a self other than the one motivated to act by the stimulus.

Still another difficulty occurs in connection with sleep. Brightman recognizes dreams as a mode of consciousness, but while the sleeper is not

[89] The first two are relations between created selves and between such selves and nature understood as God's immediate " physical " activity. (*Ibid.*, p. 275.) There is also a still different relation between the present of the person and his past. In the philosophy of Whitehead and Hartshorne all of these can be reduced to one.

[90] In this view the subconscious would be classed with the body as part of the environment of the person, which Brightman holds is simply and literally God in action in co-operation with the human self. (*Ibid.*, p. 272, n. 28.)

dreaming he is not a self at all.[91] Indeed his existence is only as an unconscious entity, hence as no entity at all except in the divinely constituted natural environment of waking selves. The discontinuity introduced by sleep into personal existence is, therefore, of ontological significance. In each dream and in each awakening an ontological transformation or re-creation occurs. Once again, however gradually one may rouse, some exact point in the continuum must be identified as that at which an absolute ontological change occurs.

It is this feature of Brightman's position which I must confess personally strains my credulity. This does not make it philosophically untenable, but it does suggest that we should consider alternatives in which the ontological judgments are less artificially related to experience.[92] If in experience we seem to find a continuum of being rather than two radically different ontological orders, and a continuum of experience in which consciousness shades off into unconsciousness, then an ontology that expresses this continuum would seem more coherent with experience than one which introduces radical dualities.

For this reason, we should consider the idea that experience or subjectivity is a broader category than consciousness. Psychologists find it useful to think in these terms, and we have seen that in personal experience it is difficult to draw a sharp line around consciousness. Brightman has already radicalized the idea of consciousness when he extends it to the "subconscious," dreams, and amoebae, but his limitation of experience to consciousness forces him somewhere to draw a line of utmost ontological import. If we argue that already in his application, consciousness has lost clear, distinctive meaning, and that it would be better to agree that certainly there is experience in the "subconscious," in dreams, and in amoebae, although different from what we usually mean by conscious experience, then we can be free to extend the one category of experience still farther. Essentially we mean only that all these entities are something for themselves as well as functions in and for the experience of others. Then cells and molecules and electrons as well as mosquitos and amoebae can be acknowledged to have experience.

Brightman refers to the position suggested here as panpsychism and asserts that its acceptance would have little effect upon his conclusions.[93]

[91] *Ibid.*, p. 179. Presumably one or more of the other conscious selves might be awake or dreaming during this time, but we are here considering one of these selves as the sleeper.

[92] Bertocci, however, in Brightman's name does regard incredibility as a relevant philosophical consideration. (*Ibid.*, p. 361.)

[93] *Ibid.*, p. 202. If he means only that the status of a cell in a multicellular organism is not systematically important, this is readily granted. The issue is whether a line

I prefer to call it pansubjectivism to avoid special connotations of the psyche, but whatever the position is called, its adoption does affect Brightman's argument. This argument moves from the fact of elements of experience that cannot be caused by other human and subhuman minds to the probability of a cosmic mind. The position suggested here allows for the attribution of all experiences to the causal efficacy of human and subhuman subjects. This does not mean that no argument for the existence of God can be developed from this position, but it does mean that this argument must take a different form from the one we have been considering.[94]

It has been necessary to devote some time to this discussion in order to meet Brightman on his own grounds. We could have simply noted that in his case as in that of DeWolf and Bertocci certain fundamental assumptions underlying the whole argument point to prior commitments. But this would have been unfair in view of Brightman's extensive consideration of the categories and his explicit arguments against positivistic thought.[95] Positivism, he holds, would be justified only if the mind's natural quest for a more inclusive understanding broke down.[96] Even then it would itself have presuppositions that pointed beyond its own doctrines. Hence, at least the effort at a wider philosophic viewpoint seems to be justified. Once this quest is allowed, no criteria seem fairer than those of empirical coherence, and the arguments on these grounds against materialistic realism appear strong.

I have tried to suggest, however, that another view is more empirical and more coherent. Specifically, what I have called pansubjectivism is more economical in that it understands all of our experience epistemologically as having one rather than two or three types of causes, and it is more coherent with experience in that it accepts gradations as such and is not forced to impose ontological dualities where experience suggests a continuum. The chief objection that may be expected from Brightman's point of view is that we cannot imagine an experience that is not conscious. But we cannot imagine an amoeba's kind of consciousness either, or God's, except in the sense that we can imaginatively project a con-

---

is to be drawn anywhere between that which has some reality in itself and that which *is* only as the direct activity of God.

94 The dependence of my counterproposals on Whitehead and Hartshorne is gladly acknowledged. For both these men, the developed position *does* require the affirmation of God's existence.

95 I believe, nevertheless, that in Brightman's thought as in *everyone's* thought there is a circularity of starting point and conclusion that could be pointed out on careful analysis.

96 *Ibid.*, p. 310.

tinuum of which we can grasp a small range of much greater distances in either direction. Once this kind of imagination is allowed, pansubjectivity is also allowed.

If pansubjectivity is as reasonable an interpretation of our total experience as Brightman's Personalism, then the inadequacy of this support for theology is shown. Natural theology must show the superior reasonableness of belief in the personal creator-God of Christian faith. I have argued that the particular way in which Brightman argues for this belief can be countered by a theory that does at least equal justice to the data and that disallows Brightman's argument for the existence of God. Even those readers who find Brightman's cosmology more plausible than my counterproposals should be forced to acknowledge that the possibility of such counterproposals indicates the highly subjective, if not arbitrary, character of adopting Brightman's conclusion as *the* conclusion of objective, neutral reason.

The foregoing criticisms of the Personalists' arguments for the existence of God are not intended as refutations. In my opinion all their arguments have some weight, although I would wish to reformulate most of them. I have tried to show two limitations of these arguments. First, those personalists who attempt to operate without commitment to a particular ontology make basic assumptions that they cannot justify adequately in their own terms. Second, Brightman's argument, based upon the development of an ontology, fails to exclude counterproposals that undermine his conclusions. The possibility of a more rigorous ontology's eventuating in belief in a personal God is not excluded by these criticisms, but I wish to suggest that the ideal of a purely objective rational conclusion supportive of personalistic faith is unlikely of realization.

We have given rather extended attention to the arguments for the existence of God advanced by the Personalists because we will not be able to understand the predominant theological view of the status of these arguments until we have seriously explored their limitations. None of the theologians to be treated from this point on in this book acknowledge reliance upon arguments for the existence of God.

Only Wieman can be regarded as avowedly accepting natural theology, and in his case we will see that the whole effort is to turn from speculative to purely descriptive categories. As long as one is secure in his conviction that reason provides an adequate basis for faith in a personal God, this situation must appear strange and to Christian theologians, by and large, eccentric. If, however, we recognize not only intellectually but also personally or existentially that reason supports faith only when it begins with a self-understanding or vision of reality that is not shared by the intellectual leadership of our time, then we can understand the fear of acknowledging dependence upon natural theology that characterizes modern theology as a whole.

The opponents of natural theology often introduce a second objection. They argue that the idea of God that emerges from philosophic speculation is alien to the living God of the Bible.[97] My critique of Mascall in the preceding chapter follows this line of thought in part. However, I believe that it is largely irrelevant to the criticism of Personalism. One may argue that Personalism tends to minimize the gulf that is felt between man and God in the Bible and to impose human criteria of judgment upon him, but such argument presupposes disputable interpretations of the Bible and also fails to recognize the very strong affirmations of God's otherness that can be found in such writers as DeWolf.[98] It is true that Personalists have tended to a higher estimate of the moral capacity of man than some other theologians, but they have certainly not minimized the reality of sin and evil, and the question of who is more faithful to the Bible here is an open one.[99] Furthermore, the basic issue is not whether one agrees in detail with Personalist theology but whether the fundamental approach *necessarily* leads to such conclusions as may be thought to be un-Biblical. Here, at least, the question remains undecided, and the evidence would seem to favor the Personalists.

The Personalists may also be attacked because within the context of their method they cannot affirm without severe qualifications the deity of Jesus. I believe that this inability is ingredient in the approach. The affirmation of Jesus' deity cannot be based upon the criterion of comprehensive coherence. It also depends upon a metaphysical context alien to Personalism. But that the affirmation of the ontological deity of Jesus is an essential or desirable part of Christian theology remains, again, an open question. A plausible case can be made for its absence from most of the New Testament.

The point of the above comments is twofold. On the one hand, the philosophic commitments of Personalism in its natural theology do restrict the range of assertions that can be made in its Christian theology. On the other hand, it is by no means self-evident that Personalism is prevented from affirming with considerable adequacy the faith of the New Testament. Criticism on this point must be based upon study of the New Testament that goes beyond any present clear consensus.

97 For DeWolf's defense against this charge, see *The Case for Theology in Liberal Perspective,* pp. 22–30. Cf. also *The Religious Revolt Against Reason,* Ch. 3.

98 DeWolf, *A Theology of the Living Church,* pp. 96–103.

99 For DeWolf's impressive discussion, see *ibid.,* pp. 130–143, 179–200.

We may summarize our conclusions as follows. The Personalists have achieved a remarkable synthesis of philosophy and theology that satisfies their own criterion of comprehensive empirical coherence. In this way they have shown the reasonableness of the Christian faith and the absence of any necessity of absurdity and paradox in its formulation. We have not tried to judge whether their understanding of Christian faith is adequately Biblical or existentially acceptable.

On the other hand, the whole circle of Personalist thought fails to make contact with increasingly prevalent kinds of reason in our day. The criticism of Personalism here is not that this gulf exists or that those on the other side of the gulf are philosophically wiser or more reasonable. The criticism is only that the theological method that is advocated largely ignores this gulf. Unless it is possible to argue for the Personalist conception of the function of reason on grounds that seriously challenge the phenomenalistic and positivistic philosophies of our day, we must abandon the effort to establish belief in a personal God on the basis of a reason that is independent of Christian revelation.

4: Henry Nelson Wieman

IN THOMISM AND BOSTON PERSONALISM WE FIND VIGOROUS EXPRESSION OF two quite different types of natural theology. In one respect, however, they resemble each other. Both affirm the existence of God on the basis of inference from data that are more immediately given than God. We have seen that the data are conditioned and that the justification of any inference whatever has been called in question. This does not mean that the arguments are not well taken, but it does reveal that their conclusions cannot be taken as the unequivocal dictates of objective reason. If faith depends upon prior acceptance of these conclusions, then it rests upon the shaky foundation of doubtful speculation.

Some of the theologians whom we will consider in subsequent chapters reject every effort to rest faith upon any general human experience or thought. They are convinced that faith can be faith only if it is the work of God as his immediate act and gift. If human agency is allowed at all, they believe, not only must we rely on the broken reed of rational argument but faith's own nature is misunderstood. Hence modern Protestant theology has seen efforts unmatched in previous history to exhibit faith in its total autonomy and separateness from the rest of man's beliefs and convictions.

In principle, if faith is wholly God's act in and for us, then all criteria for its justification are surrendered. Faith occurs as and where it occurs, and no discussion of it is possible except where it has in fact occurred.[1] Before proceeding to a discussion of those positions which accept and glory in this situation, we will consider one supreme effort that has been made to avoid alike the speculative character of the natural theologies

[1] See Wieman's critique, *The Source of Human Good,* pp. 32–37; *Intellectual Foundation of Faith,* pp. 110, 133.

considered earlier and the apparent arbitrariness of the positivistic positions treated in the later chapters.

The alternative to speculation on the one hand and the " leap " of faith on the other must be some kind of empirical description. Such description has played some role in all theologies, and in some cases has played a very large role. But in most Christian theology it has been assumed that what can be described is only the effect of God's activity, and is hence only a source of data from which inferences to God's existence and nature can be drawn. If we are to avoid such inferences, and the doubtful speculations they always entail, then we must assert that God is given directly in experience and hence subject to direct description and verification.

This kind of claim can be made in several ways. First, there is mystical experience, with its claim to immediate participation in the divine life or immediate encounter with the divine person. Its difficulty is that the witness of mystics is diverse and is always conditioned by the theological heritage they bring to their experience. That there is mystical experience is clear, but to believe in God on the basis of its occurrence is to accept another doubtful inference. For the mystic himself, something more may be said; but for those who are limited to normal experiences, an empirical theology cannot be built upon hypernormal experiences.[2]

Second, psychologists such as Jung claim to have discovered through clinical observation what they call the God-archetype as a structure in man's unconscious psyche.[3] For all practical purposes they then identify the God-archetype with God. On this basis, an empirical theology appears possible in which the situation of man universally in relation to God can be described. However, a twofold objection must be raised. First, one must question whether in fact considerable speculative inference is not involved in the identification of the God-archetype and the " description " of its functions. Second, it can hardly be demonstrated that none of what has been historically understood as religious faith has been directed toward an extrapsychic reality instead of toward this intrapsychic one. As long as this possibility is open, most Christians will prefer to understand by " God " something quite different from the God-archetype.

If an empirical theology is to be taken seriously, it must describe a nonsubjective reality that is directly accessible to normal experience. But so long as men think in terms of substances, such a venture is impossible. Every empirically accessible substance must be a spatiotemporal entity, which it would be idolatrous to regard as God. Systematic development

[2] For Wieman's interpretation of mystical experience, see *The Source of Human Good,* pp. 186–187; *Man's Ultimate Commitment,* p. 142.

[3] Carl Gustav Jung, *Psychology and Religion.*

of thoroughgoing empirical theology required first the abandonment of these categories of thinking. In this sense it was the radical philosophy of Hume that prepared the way for empirical theology.

Empirical theology receives its most adequate expression in the work of Henry Nelson Wieman. Wieman's theology can be understood only when we have first entered into the philosophicospiritual situation of modern man, in which the stable world of substantial entities has been abandoned. The sticks and stones, tables and books, vegetables and human bodies, which were once regarded as the individuals out of which the world is composed, are now seen as strands that in various conjunctions with one another and with strands of perceiving and feeling constitute events.[4] Events are the conjunctions of such strands, or rather the events are the actualities through analysis of which we isolate these strands. A human person is itself one of these strands and not, as the Boston Personalists suppose, the inclusive event.[5]

These events, which constitute the ultimate reality, are qualitative in nature. That is, they are complex qualities that may be analyzed into simpler qualities in particular relations. Among these qualities no priority can be given either to sensory or emotional elements. They occur in conjunction, and this conjunction is the given reality itself.[6]

This vision is so important for the understanding of Wieman's empirical theology that some further exposition and illustration are demanded. What still seems to us more "common sense" is an understanding of reality as composed of separate entities in interaction. In this view my mind constitutes one such entity, and my body, my typewriter, and the paper on which I am writing constitute other such entities, along with the chair on which I sit and the table that supports the machine. These entities seem to be the primary realities and my act of typing seems to be secondary. But the history of modern philosophy has shown that this view assumes an idea of substances underlying the observed qualities of things that cannot stand under analysis. The typewriter *is* a togetherness of qualities and potentialities. But these qualities do not exist simply in themselves. They occur only in conjunction with the sensitive organism and mind of man. By the same token this organism does not exist in itself.[7] It always occurs as an interaction with its environment. What is primary, what is the source for all other knowledge, what is prior to all speculative inference, is the event of my typing, which includes all the qualities of color and

[4] Henry Nelson Wieman, *The Directive in History,* pp. 7–8.
[5] *Ibid.,* pp. 19, 21.
[6] *Ibid.,* p. 14.
[7] *Ibid.,* p. 19.

sound and touch as well as of emotion, memory, and expectation that constitute it.

When we shift the focus of reality from substances to events we also move from static to dynamic categories. A substance could be thought of as enduring unchanged through time. The typewriter could be understood as a self-identical substance on successive days. But every event is absolutely unique.[8] The event of my typing today is numerically and qualitatively different from the event of my typing yesterday. Furthermore, within an event, however broadly or narrowly conceived, there is a qualitative flow rather than an unchanging being. The qualities are the concrete, objective realities that constitute events and hence processes.[9] Therefore, process is the all-inclusive term for reality. We may speak of the one total cosmic process, or we may speak of the myriad of processes that make it up. The point is that the most concrete division of the whole, whether into few or many parts, always yields qualities, events, or processes. These processes can be analyzed also into those relatively stable structures which we call strands, but this analysis requires abstraction from the qualitative concreteness of the processes or events.

The replacement of the dualism of substantial matter and ideal experience by the monism of event means that we are no longer confronted by the problem of explaining spirit in terms of matter or matter in terms of spirit. The physical and the spiritual occur at opposite poles of a single continuum of events. They are known in the same basic way, if they are known at all.[10] There may be differences between firsthand knowledge and secondhand knowledge — acquaintance with and knowledge about — but all knowledge is fundamentally of one piece. It cannot be divided into types according to its subject matter.

For this reason, the methods of knowing that are successful in one area of investigation can be applied to others. Of course, instruments, experimental techniques, and specific procedures vary according to whether one studies atoms, the stars, or the behavior of children. But in all cases there is required careful observation guided by hypotheses formed out of previous experience and subject to modification in the light of new experience. What must be rejected is the dogmatic spirit that holds some ideas or practices to be beyond criticism, beyond testing in the ongoing process.[11]

[8] *The Source of Human Good,* p. 303.

[9] *The Directive in History,* p. 14; *Man's Ultimate Commitment,* pp. 82–83.

[10] *The Source of Human Good,* pp. 181–184, 211–212.

[11] *Ibid.,* pp. 210–211; Henry Nelson Wieman, *The Wrestle of Religion with Truth,* pp. 63–64.

This fundamental fact about how knowledge grows has the utmost significance for man's religious quest. Just because religion is of supreme importance to man, he seeks to protect its teachings from questioning. But as the body of reliable knowledge grows, those beliefs that are kept unaffected by this knowledge appear increasingly dubious and even incredible. Hence, more and more, dogmatically affirmed religious doctrines are losing their hold on the modern mind. Since many identify religion with the dogmatic spirit, they turn their backs upon religion itself to their own untold loss.[12]

This situation can be remedied only as the realities of religion are located within the all-embracing process and are subjected to the most careful scrutiny. Then the verified results of such study can play their rightful role in providing guidance in the most important areas of life.[13]

The central concept of religious thought is God. By "God," men have often understood a substantial being outside experience. But such a concept is at best exceedingly doubtful — at worst, meaningless. Men cannot really put their trust in that about whose reality honesty compels them to be skeptical. "God" must be redefined if he is to be sincerely worshiped in our age. But redefinition cannot mean that we arbitrarily call something else "God," something quite different from what religious faith has always meant by "God." On the contrary, we must push behind the now outgrown concepts of God to that which is more deeply meant by "God." The substantial being outside experience was not worshiped as God because it was substantial or because it was outside experience. It was worshiped because it was acknowledged as the author of all that is good and as that one to which man should give his devotion wholly.[14]

The property of being altogether worthy of devotion follows from the property of being wholly good in the sense of being responsible for all good things. Hence, the essential character of God is his creativeness of good. Wieman's most famous book is entitled *The Source of Human Good*. Our task now is to develop a concept of the source of our good that will enable us to guide our devotion intelligently.[15]

At one stroke we thus solve the problem of the existence of God. If God is understood as a nonempirical entity speculatively conceived, his existence is always suspect. But speculative conceptions have changed repeatedly in Christian history without basically affecting faith itself, for

[12] *The Wrestle of Religion with Truth,* pp. 43–45.
[13] *The Source of Human Good,* pp. 34, 53; *Intellectual Foundation of Faith,* p. 57.
[14] *The Source of Human Good,* pp. 263–268; *Intellectual Foundation of Faith,* pp. 55–56.
[15] *The Source of Human Good,* pp. 16–17, 293; *Intellectual Foundation of Faith,* p. 80.

faith has been dependent on a functional understanding of God as he to whom man owes all that is most precious, rather than on a particular conception of what philosophical attributes are his.[16] Once we have recognized this clearly, we can identify God in terms of his function as an experientially given actuality. We can and should then proceed to conceptual formulation.

This preliminary statement of Wieman's approach is, however, subject to serious misinterpretation. Granted that there is human good and that there must, therefore, be sources of that good, do we not falsify man's religious experience if we call all such sources " God "? Does not this mean that my parents, my teachers, and even the crops in the field become " God "? These questions pave the way for a much more precise formulation of Wieman's teaching.

We do not mean by " God " the proximate causes of specific goods. Anything and everything can serve in such a capacity. We are concerned in religion with a much deeper question and must delimit our inquiry in two additional ways. First, what interests us is human good itself, that is, that which is inherently worth-while in human existence. Secondly, we are concerned with that self-identical process which is at work wherever this human good appears, not with this or that entity that plays an incidental role. Therefore, our need is, first, to identify the ultimate good and, second, to describe the process by which the good is brought into being.

Wieman identifies the good with qualitative meaning.[17] To understand what he means we must return to the distinction between events as qualities and as conjunctions of strands. We must recall that it is the qualities which are concrete and the strands which are abstracted from the series of events. Meaning is a factor in relation both to the qualities and to the strands. In both cases meaning is a connection between qualities now appearing and other qualities remembered or anticipated.[18] But this connection may function in two quite different ways.

The meaning may consist in a relation between certain qualities now given and memory or anticipation of functions and their sequences. For example, one may identify certain qualities as a stick, referring thereby the presently given quality to past operations or to the anticipation of the consequence of future functions. The focus is upon the accurate identification of one strand in the event in terms of how it functions in other events. Attention is thereby directed away from the felt immediacy of the qual-

[16] *Intellectual Foundation of Faith,* p. 177; *Man's Ultimate Commitment,* p. 12.
[17] *The Source of Human Good,* p. 17; *The Directive in History,* p. 18.
[18] *The Directive in History,* p. 16.

ities that are involved. In this case the present experience is treated as an instrumental value.[19]

On the other hand, the meaning may focus upon the qualities themselves. Memory of the past and anticipation of the future may enrich and heighten the present enjoyment of quality.[20] There is no known limit to the enrichment of quality that associations of this sort can introduce.[21] They transform the sheer qualitative event into qualitative meaning. This qualitative meaning, and it alone, constitutes intrinsic value. To increase qualitative meaning is, therefore, necessarily to increase the good.[22]

This identification of good with qualitative meaning is of central importance for Wieman's thought. Since God is understood as the creative source of good, the definition of good determines where we look for God and hence the whole direction and form of religious faith.[23] Therefore, we must consider briefly how Wieman defends his doctrine of the good.

First, we see that Wieman's definition serves to identify good with concrete actuality. An event is good to the degree that it has complexity, unity, and intensity.[24] He is consciously opposing any doctrine that the good should be identified with certain qualities as opposed to others — to pleasure, for example, as opposed to pain.[25] An element of pain may be indispensable to intensity and richness of experience, whereas pleasure may be quite compatible with dull mediocrity. The difference between Socrates and the pig is not that Socrates is more contented but that Socrates has incomparably greater richness of experience, including far more pain, than the pig is capable of experiencing. The thrust of life is toward this richness, not toward the insipidity of porcine contentment.[26]

Second, we must remember that an intrinsic good may also function instrumentally as an evil. That is, the entertainment of a qualitative meaning may lead to action that will destroy other men. But the qualitative meaning does not thereby become evil or even neutral.[27] Even in the extreme case of the sadist, the qualitative meaning in his experience is intrinsically good whatever the destruction of qualitative meaning for others may be. This makes it clear that we must distinguish the question

[19] *Ibid.*, p. 17.
[20] *Ibid.*, p. 16.
[21] *The Source of Human Good*, p. 307.
[22] *The Directive in History*, pp. 62–67.
[23] Note, however, that he believes his call for devotion to the creative event follows also from other theories of value. See below, pp. 106–113.
[24] *The Source of Human Good*, p. 134.
[25] *Ibid.*, pp. 13–15.
[26] *Ibid.*, pp. 93–97; *The Directive in History*, pp. 32–34, 47–48.
[27] *The Directive in History*, pp. 62–63.

of intrinsic good from the question of moral good.[28]

We cannot say that the pursuit of intrinsic good as such is always morally good. This is blatantly true in the example of the sadist we have just noted. But it is also apparent when we take the intrinsic good of a whole community into account. Again this is most apparent when the good of one community conflicts with that of another, but Wieman insists that this is not the only basis of the inadequacy of this kind of moral norm. Even if we seek the greatest good of the greatest number, we will still not be fulfilling the moral law.[29]

Wieman takes this antiutilitarian approach because he is convinced that in fact the greater good is not served by the effort to harmonize maximum individual achievements of good. There are two reasons that need to be noted. First, the attempt to harmonize the good of each with the good of all tends to lead to a decline of the intensities promoted by conflict.[30] Second, and more important, the identification of the greater good with any imagined state of affairs is limited by the inadequacy of our present imagination. The really creative forces will break through our fancied utopias, and our commitment to these ideals will hamper rather than promote these forces.[31]

This means that the greatest good is promoted, not when we project ideal situations and seek the means to achieve them, but when we discover that process which produces good and increases the conditions that facilitate its action.[32] In other words, the moral law is that we should serve God. Any other principle will express our culturally conditioned values and will lead to mutually frustrating conflicts with other ideals. Only if we abandon commitment to ideals in favor of commitment to the source of good will fruitful universal co-operation be possible. This means, of course, that we must not attempt to identify the service of God with obedience to any historically determined commands or laws.[33]

We see now that the question about the nature of God is not of limited "religious" interest but is decisive for the adequate direction of all man's striving. To accentuate this fact, and to gain a hearing among those who are not conventionally religious, Wieman sometimes writes about the

[28] *Ibid.*, pp. 34–35.

[29] *Ibid.*, pp. 36, 48; *The Source of Human Good*, p. 224; *Man's Ultimate Commitment*, pp. 122–124. However, in his latest book Wieman does define morality in utilitarian terms, thereby distinguishing it from faith. *Intellectual Foundation of Faith*, pp. 18–20.

[30] *The Directive in History*, pp. 46–47.

[31] *Ibid.*, pp. 48–50; *The Source of Human Good*, pp. 23–26, 46.

[32] *The Directive in History*, pp. 71–72; *The Source of Human Good*, pp. 224–225.

[33] *The Directive in History*, pp. 50–52.

creative process without speaking of it in theological terms. Yet he is sure that the service of this process requires worship and the kind of devotion that has characterized historic religion.[34] Furthermore, he is convinced that the supernaturalist categories of religion have in fact functioned to guide devotion in the right direction even when they have also confused and hindered it.[35] Hence it is right and proper to speak of the creative event or process as God, however different the conceptuality suitable for modern man may be from that of earlier centuries.

We are ready now to ask the crucial question: What is the process that produces human good? That is, how does the growth of qualitative meaning occur? This is an empirical question that can be answered only through careful observation. This observation is in principle open to all who will discipline themselves to look with sufficient care. Our first answers may be quite inadequate, and no answers will ever exhaust the reality. But in answering the question we appeal neither to inferences to an unobservable reality nor to a leap of faith. We ask only for attention, care, and openness. Our conclusions should be equally acceptable to all men of good will whatever their traditional faiths may be, just as the findings of science are open equally to all.

In recent writing Wieman has identified five aspects of those events in which qualitative meaning grows. The first is an expansion of the range of the individual's capacity to know, control, and appreciate. The second is increase in the appreciative understanding of oneself and others as individuals. The idea of appreciation in both of these aspects includes the discrimination of positive and negative values. The third aspect of the creative event is a progressive integration of all that the person is acquiring. The fourth is increase in the capacity to meet suffering, failure, and death creatively. The fifth is the increase of freedom.[36]

This total event is one that Wieman often calls "creative interchange." By this he means any situation in which individuals encounter other persons or possibilities with openness and sensitivity. Even when the other persons are morally evil, the encounter with the qualitative meanings that they embody can be an occasion of growth. Hence the one great enemy of the creative event is rigidity, commitment to limited values, closedness to new experiences and possibilities.[37]

Wieman believes that every child's development offers us an example

[34] *Ibid.*, p. 130; *Intellectual Foundation of Faith*, p. 21.

[35] *The Source of Human Good*, pp. 264–265.

[36] *Intellectual Foundation of Faith*, pp. 61–62, 125–126. Wieman's best-known analysis of the creative event into four sub-events is found in *The Source of Human Good*, pp. 58–65.

[37] *The Directive in History*, pp. 66–67.

of creative interchange in which qualitative meaning increases. Hence the process that is God is fully accessible to our study. But man's problem is that with the attainment of adulthood he generally becomes closed to the further operation of creative interchange except in very limited ways.[38] Our urgent need is to learn how to keep ourselves open throughout life to ever continued growth. To say this is to say that our problem is to achieve genuine surrender to the working of God in our lives.

We have thus far shown that when we understand God as that process which is creative of human good we can identify God empirically and begin the important task of empirical description. However, before proceeding to a consideration of what this means for Christian theology, we must face an important objection. Many may protest that what they mean by God is not only that which is the source of their good but also one who stands over against them in grace and judgment. God is not only creator and redeemer but also lord and judge. If the process that Wieman identifies as God does not function in this way, if it is after all only a part of nature subject to man's control and manipulation, then to call it "God" is blasphemous.

For Wieman, too, this objection is entirely valid. But now the question is a purely empirical one. Is that process by which human growth occurs one that men can manipulate and control or one to which they can only submit themselves in faith? To Wieman it seems overwhelmingly clear that we are not the authors of our own good. Can I really pretend that I have produced in myself such spiritual growth as has occurred? Or can I suppose that I am able to produce it in my children? Can any psychiatrist claim to produce growth in his patients? Or can any minister suppose that he produces it in his congregation? To ask such questions is to answer them. A farmer cannot make crops grow. He can only help in faith to provide conditions in which growth occurs. At the very best we cannot claim to do more than this with respect to our spiritual development. The author of our good acts freely among us as our lord rather than as our servant.[39]

Careful investigation serves only to heighten this realization that we are dependent for our good upon a process that we cannot control. It is not only that this process cannot be forced by us; it is also that we cannot even foresee its ends. We can understand good states of affairs only in terms of our present spiritual discernment.[40] Hence, what is beyond that

[38] *Ibid.*, pp. 67–68.
[39] *Man's Ultimate Commitment,* pp. 25, 73, 76.
[40] *The Source of Human Good,* pp. 75–76, 224–225.

discernment we humanly fear and distrust. But to avoid that which we cannot imagine or understand is to limit drastically the amount and kind of good that may be attained. Over and over again maturity brings us to stages of life that are deeply rewarding but that could not entice us until we had tasted of their worth.

On the other hand, this cannot mean a blind effort after change for its own sake. Modes of life that we do not understand may in fact be destructive rather than good. We cannot be guided either by our present understanding or by the ideal of novelty for its own sake. We can, however, discern the process that has been at work in the creation of every past good, and we can trust that process to lead to still greater future good.[41]

This means that if greater good is to be created in us and through us we must so relate ourselves to the creative process — God — that we will be continuously remade by it. This relation must be one of trust and devotion in the fullest degree. So long as we cling to the particular attainments that are already ours, whether they are the products of our own efforts or of the past working of God, we block the new working of God. Hence, we cut short our own growth. True growth occurs only in a continuous surrender of all that we have and are.[42]

Thus far in our exposition of Wieman's thought we have operated on a purely empirical basis, without special reference to any historical tradition. Hence, we have been dealing with what may be called philosophy of religion rather than with theology. However, two unusual things about this philosophy of religion must be noted. First, Wieman is not developing a theoretical system of thought for its own sake but is so describing experience as to challenge men to commit their total selves to God. In the second place, Wieman's empirical conclusions have remarkable affinities with the religion of the New Testament.[43]

Wieman recognizes that the religion that is a vital option for us in the Western world is Christianity.[44] This does not prejudge the question as to whether Christian claims have unique relevance for all men, but it does indicate that for us in the West the task is to recapture the vital reality of our own religious heritage. To do so is to reinterpret that heritage in

[41] *Ibid.*, p. 81.
[42] *Ibid.*, pp. 276–279.
[43] *Ibid.*, pp. 263–265; *Intellectual Foundation of Faith,* pp. 34–35.
[44] *The Source of Human Good,* pp. 39, 263. In recent years Wieman has de-emphasized this primary role of Christianity. In his as yet unpublished reply to this chapter, "In Defense of My Faith," Wieman stresses that our need is for a faith that can guide our culture and that Christianity does not have that power.

terms of the kind of empirical knowledge of God that is now available to us.

Our religious heritage centers in the events surrounding the life, ministry, and resurrection of Jesus Christ. In those events the creative event became present in history in a new way. Jesus' interchange with his disciples so transformed them that they became capable of having such interchange with one another.[45] With the death of Jesus this interchange seemed to cease, only to rise to new heights in the resurrection experience. Whereas during Jesus' life it had been restricted in scope to its Jewish context, with his death and resurrection it broke through this cultural limitation and became universal in its scope.[46] Hence, this event is the most decisive of all history.[47] The victory of the creative event over all other processes in history is far from evident in all of life, but in principle that victory has been won.[48] We can be transformed today by the power of that victory.

The impact of the Christ-event upon us today is not through some magical force overleaping the centuries. On the contrary, it is quite specifically through the church. Whereas the creative event has occurred often and to varying degrees throughout history, the Christ-event became decisive by virtue of producing a community in which creative interchange has been permanently continued.[49] In this community, men are called to devotion to the source of good rather than to particular created goods. They are placed under obligations so demanding that their pride in their own virtue is destroyed and they are opened to mutual forgiveness. A bond is established between them more binding than congeniality or kinship. The witness of this community has opened men to a transformation that could never come from human effort directed by human ideals. Thus the symbols, the myths, the worship of the Christian church have sustained through the centuries those conditions in which the creative event could continue to transform men and bring them to new heights of qualitative meaning.[50]

In the preceding paragraph I have followed Wieman's frequent practice of avoiding theological terminology. Wieman is convinced that he has

[45] *Ibid.*, pp. 39–40.

[46] *Ibid.*, pp. 41, 43–44, 278.

[47] *Ibid.*, pp. 233, 274. In the same book Wieman speaks of the atomic bomb as having cut history in two more decisively than the star over Bethlehem. But he does so only to emphasize the urgency of service to creative good which we know theologically as the living Christ. (*Ibid.*, p. 37.)

[48] *Ibid.*, pp. 271–272.

[49] *Ibid.*, pp. 42–43, 269–270.

[50] *Ibid.*, pp. 263–265.

as much right as any to the use of the term "God,"[51] but he is also convinced that readers are often misled by the term. Popular religion thinks of God as a person who transcends space and time. Many theologians who use personalistic language acknowledge that this language is wholly inadequate to speak of God, but by continuing its use they confuse the common people. Wieman wishes to be as explicit as possible about the difference between his concept of God and the concept of popular Christianity because he believes that faith cannot regain vitality until men regain confidence in the sober truth of Christianity's objective foundation.[52]

Once we have cleared away the danger of being misunderstood, we must and should use the ritual and symbolism of historic faith. It is God who is incarnate in the Christ-event. Our salvation is given only by him. Our task is only to yield ourselves wholly to his will and to work to be born again into his Kingdom. Life in this Kingdom is the life of ever-renewed commitment, sacrifice, and devotion, sustained by the community of faith in its regular worship. All this Wieman can say in soberest truth and in full loyalty to the searching demands of empirical verification.

Furthermore, although Wieman does not acknowledge a realm of being that transcends space and time, he does insist upon God's transcendence. His whole theology is a rejection of a humanism in which God is identified with any function or possession of man.[53] Man cannot predict or control the working of God. Indeed, the effort to impose his own norms and his own ideals upon the course of events, however noble or worthy these may seem, is the one absolute evil.[54] God is man's sovereign Lord, and every effort of man to usurp that Lordship to himself is doomed to hinder the working of the good. But the redemptive work of God is never stopped by man's rebelliousness. Even in his rebellion man experiences the forgiveness of God as always ready to redeem him when he turns in true repentance.[55]

To use other theological language, we may say that for Wieman salvation is by grace through faith. All works-righteousness is excluded. Yet man is not freed from responsibility. He cannot save himself; he cannot even foresee what his salvation will mean. But he can give up his confidence in the created goods that so easily absorb him. He can contribute to creating the conditions in which God's work is most effective. He can

[51] *Intellectual Foundation of Faith,* pp. 104–105.
[52] *The Source of Human Good,* pp. 265–266.
[53] Cf. Edward Farley, *The Transcendence of God: A Study in Contemporary Philosophical Theology,* Ch. VI, esp. pp. 186–191.
[54] *The Source of Human Good,* pp. 90, 273.
[55] *Ibid.,* pp. 278–279.

submit himself to being remade by God, even though that means dying to his old self and rising in Christ. Even these acts are not his in the sense that they are independent of the prior working of God. His capacity to yield himself to God is already the work of God in him.[56] Furthermore, no matter how effectively he has been transformed by God he never arrives at a stage that he can regard as one to be permanently possessed. The Christian life is an ever-renewed dying to the good that God has worked in us in order that God's greater good may be born.

One traditional problem of Christian theology Wieman solves with a clarity and radicalism that are rare in Christian history. This is the problem of evil. This problem is that of reconciling God's omnipotence with the presence of evil in the world. Those who think of God as a cosmic or supercosmic being, even when they acknowledge some limit to his power, are nevertheless driven to deny in some way the ultimacy of the apparent evil in the world. Wieman rejects all such claims. It is far from clear that good is certain to triumph in our world or that its ontological status is more ultimate than that of evil. On empirical grounds such sweeping judgments cannot be made. Furthermore, they are not religiously and morally helpful. They contribute to the idea of faith as believing that which is in itself improbable or at best radically uncertain. It is far better to face with unbiased honesty the realities as they can be seen and tested.[57]

Wieman's affirmations about God, therefore, must not be understood as precluding other assertions about the processes that make for evil. What is supremely important for us is to know that there is a power not ourselves that dependably produces human good. We need further to know how to relate ourselves to that process in order that we may contribute to its effectiveness in ourselves and others. But we have no evidence at all that this is the *only* process in the universe or the most powerful. These processes and their results are a problem in the sense that they pose many practical difficulties for us, but their occurrence is no occasion for raising questions about the goodness of God. God's power is inexhaustible, but we have no reason to suppose that no other powers exist. We may believe that whatever evil befalls us God will not cease working, but that working is no guarantee that evils of the most devastating sort will not befall us.[58]

We are now in a position to ask how Wieman directs us to think as Christian theologians in distinction from philosophers of religion or natu-

[56] *Man's Ultimate Commitment,* p. 20.

[57] *The Source of Human Good,* pp. 87–93; *Intellectual Foundation of Faith,* pp. 118–120.

[58] *The Source of Human Good,* pp. 81–82; *Intellectual Foundation of Faith,* p. 79.

ral theologians. He himself, it must be acknowledged, is rather indifferent to this methodological question. Wieman believes that religion must recover its concern for truth, and that this truth must be sought by rigorous empirical inquiry. He is passionately dedicated to the proclamation of the gospel that this inquiry discloses. He knows that he has himself found God within the Christian tradition and that this is the situation of Western man.[59] He also affirms of the Christ-event a real decisiveness for all of history.[60] Yet he does not deeply care whether the gospel he proclaims be called Christian or not.[61] In this sense he does not concern himself with the particular methodological problems of Christian theology. In so far as Christian theology is committed to any dogma that it is not willing to subject to empirical tests, Wieman repudiates it. He is quite ready to take the onus of heresy if that is required by loyalty to the empirical evidence and that gospel which this evidence yields.

However, all that Wieman says is fully compatible with a confessional or perspectival Christian theology. Granted that the knowledge of God's existence and working is not systematically dependent on any particular historical event, Wieman himself sees its factual dependence upon the community that arose from the resurrection of Jesus as the Christ. We must confess, then, that it is in this community originating from this event that both understanding and salvation have come to us. Our task is not to attack other confessions and perspectives; it is to witness to the grace that is given us. With this vision the confessing Christian theologian is in a position to consider the doctrines that come to him through his tradition and to treat them both appreciatively and critically as efforts to witness to that one reality of salvation in Christ which he shares with the fathers in the faith.[62]

Wieman's own attitude toward this kind of use of his position is ambivalent. He recognizes the necessity of rooting faith in tradition, ritual, and institutions. Hence he must approve the systematic effort to do this. But at the same time he fears the tendency to relapse into a misleading terminology and to avoid the hard issues of demythologizing. He wishes to stress that the empirical approach to the study of God is available to all

59 *The Source of Human Good,* p. 263.

60 *Ibid.,* p. 274.

61 One senses a definite shift here between *The Source of Human Good,* 1946, and his most recent writings, in which he is increasingly concerned to transcend the diversities among faiths. Cf. *Intellectual Foundation of Faith,* pp. 5, 27–28, 34, 166–167, 179.

62 Daniel Day Williams has developed a perspectival position based largely on Wieman's general orientation. See *God's Grace and Man's Hope,* pp. 50–51. Although based on a different ontology, H. Richard Niebuhr's confessional theology is also methodologically compatible with Wieman's position. See below, Chapter 11.

men everywhere and that its results are to be affirmed not only confessionally but also with all the objectivity that attaches to the conclusions of any empirical investigation.[63] It is of supreme importance today, as cultures and religious traditions interact and conflict, that devotion be directed to that which can be known independently of any culture or tradition. Thus the desire to substitute a universal philosophy of religion or life for all the particular theologies clashes in Wieman with the recognition of man's need for the richness of traditional symbol and myth. But this clash is more pragmatic than theoretical. In principle there is no conflict except in emphasis, and the extensive harmony between Wieman's empirical findings and the Christian understanding of man's relation to God renders the use of Wieman's philosophy of religion an open possibility for the theologian — a possibility that has been explored to some degree by Wieman himself.

◈ ◈

The analyses of Mascall and DeWolf both led to the conclusion that the Christian theologies of these men rested upon speculative inferences from historically conditioned data. Our interest in Wieman has centered in the possibility that by the rigorous use of empirical method we might base Christian theology on fundamental convictions that are beyond speculative disagreement. Hence, further examination of his position must be directed by the question as to whether he has in fact achieved this end.

I propose to focus my criticisms at two points. First, can Wieman identify the good, and the process that produces good, without committing himself to one among several defensible value theories? Second, is the identification of the creative event with God legitimate? Does this identification depend upon any prior speculative commitments?

In the preceding presentation of Wieman's theology, we saw that he identified good with qualitative meaning. We saw that this identification had much to commend it and that Wieman was able to develop an impressive position based upon this understanding. At the same time, we have to recognize that there are other ways of understanding what value is. If Wieman's whole theology rests upon the acceptance of this value theory, he is hardly freer of dependence upon philosophical speculation than are Mascall and DeWolf.

Wieman is fully aware of this fact, and he deals with it quite explicitly. He lists six theories of value, which he regards as exhaustive of the possibilities for practical purposes, and he argues that the process he has identified as the source of human good increases value as understood by any of

[63] *Intellectual Foundation of Faith*, pp. 179–180.

these theories.[64] For example, if the good is understood as satisfaction of human desire, we find that it is the creative event that leads to the greatest of such satisfactions.[65]

This does not mean that Wieman regards the existing value theories as adequate. On the contrary, he thinks all six are inadequate as a guide to conduct because they leave the impression that men should work directly for the increase of value as they define value or else they make no serious effort to guide action at all. The major point of Wieman's view is that when men work directly to increase value as they see it they in fact fail to achieve their goal.[66] Value is increased only when men commit themselves to that process which increases it and abandon the effort to manipulate events toward idealized ends. If this one point is established by empirical investigation, then the ethical and theological consequences follow without regard to the philosophical position adopted about value.

Thus far, Wieman's defense appears adequate. He confronts an apparently more difficult problem when we contrast to this whole way of approaching ethical questions the deontological approach. This approach takes " right " as a primitive term and denies that one can derive what one ought to do from an inspection of what is good in itself. For example, some philosophers argue that one ought to keep promises regardless of the anticipated consequences.

Once again, Wieman is not oblivious to this philosophic doctrine. He agrees with the deontologists that moral principles cannot be derived from foreseen consequences.[67] But he believes that this ethical school offers no adequate alternative. He rejects the appeal to intuition, presumably on empirical grounds.[68] Apparently he feels that his own theory does full justice to the real basis for the deontological opposition to the primacy of foreseen consequences, and hence he does not give further consideration to the philosophical rejection of the position.

At this point, therefore, we must recognize a philosophic commitment on Wieman's part that is not acceptable to all contemporary philosophers. If we follow the deontologists in the view that breaking promises is inher-

[64] *The Source of Human Good,* pp. 297–298.

[65] In Wieman's later work, *Man's Ultimate Commitment,* the greatest good is understood as the most complete satisfaction of the whole person (p. 98). This would seem to require considerable revision of my exposition based on *The Source of Human Good* and *The Directive in History,* but he asserts that what is most satisfying to man's whole being is the richest content of felt quality (p. 97). I assume this is virtually the same as qualitative meaning. In *The Source of Human Good,* Wieman also asserts that qualitative meaning satisfies human want (p. 19).

[66] *The Source of Human Good,* p. 46.

[67] *Ibid.,* p. 222.

[68] *Ibid.,* p. 223.

ently wrong regardless of foreseen consequences and also regardless of the demands of the creative event, then we will not be able to identify the moral demand with the service of Wieman's God. Life might confront us with real dilemmas in which we must choose between doing our duty and serving God. To say the least, serious complications would be introduced into Wieman's position.

The solution of this problem most favorable to Wieman would be as follows. Even the most thoroughgoing deontologists recognize that there is a plurality of moral obligations that may conflict with one another and that, therefore, the concrete demand upon the individual can only be that he take full account of each of the principles involved. Furthermore, among these principles the increase of human good plays a major role.[69] Further analysis is likely to show that the amount of weight given to promise-keeping when it conflicts with increasing the foreseen good is proportionate to the extent that promise-keeping is an important contributor to the sustaining of those relations of mutual trust which are essential to the working of the creative process. If so, the remaining theoretical divergence between a deontologist and Wieman would have little or no practical or theological significance.

There remains a third contemporary view of moral and valuational discourse that is less adequately confronted by Wieman. This is the view that this whole realm of discourse lacks cognitive significance. For example, it may be held that the assertion that a certain state of affairs is good is an expression of emotion or an effort to influence behavior rather than a communication about that state of affairs. If so, then all the theories of value and deontological ethics are alike empty, and Wieman is reduced to saying that a certain describable process leads to ends about which he or others emote in a certain way or that he exhorts others to view favorably or unfavorably.

Wieman's response to this line of thought is that it is purely verbal. One may, of course, always raise verbal objections against anything, but the reality of valuation continues.[70] Men do respond positively and negatively to situations and possibilities, and at its simplest level we mean by "good" just that to which this positive response is directed.[71] Wieman agrees that the content of this good varies immensely and that there may be legitimate disagreements in the effort to identify the universal characteristics of this good. We have seen this already in his recognition of alternative value theories. His own view is that what is common to all

[69] *Ibid.*, p. 222.
[70] *Intellectual Foundation of Faith*, p. 113.
[71] *The Directive in History*, pp. 31–32.

men's good is qualitative meaning, but if he is in error here he asks only to be corrected.

Once again, I believe that Wieman's response is largely adequate. Even extreme noncognitivists do not deny that men make discriminatory responses. They only deny that in the English language the word " good " is not equivalent to the words " positively responded to by someone." They argue that the word " good " suggests a rightness in this positive response. For example, they think that we cannot call the sadist's satisfaction in the pain of others " good." Wieman, however, affirms unabashedly that this is good, although it is a limited good, and decidedly not a moral good.[72] Whether or not his usage conforms to that usage common in English is not a matter of critical importance. Given his intelligible usage, Wieman's discourse about the good and the source of good appears fully cognitive.

The real crux of the problem comes at the point at which the deontological and the noncognitivist positions sometimes meet. We might call this the existential point, although neither position is likely to use this term. Granted that a certain process can be described that increases good, understood in any of several ways, why serve that process? Why concern oneself to promote the good in this way?

We arrive here at the central test of every ethical system, not of Wieman's only. It is because of the difficulty of answering such questions as these that the noncognitivists deny that the good can be treated cognitively. They believe that as the term " good " is used in English (and equivalent words in other languages) it implies its own demand for actualization. But as soon as some other terms are substituted for it, this implication becomes questionable. Hence, these other terms are not real equivalents, and the word " good " must be understood as emotive, hortatory, or imperative rather than as cognitive.

The same difficulty is responsible for the turn to deontological ethics. However the good is understood, if it is to make a claim upon us, we require an additional principle, namely, that we *ought* to actualize or increase it. But if we recognize the necessity of this principle of obligation here, we have no reason to deny that there may be other such principles. Indeed, introspection reveals that such other principles do in fact exist.

The third possibility is that the good is implicitly understood as what all men want. In this case, once men are shown that a certain process will increase the good, they will serve that process because they want to do so. No new moral principle is required because clarification of the already ex-

[72] *Ibid.*, pp. 34–35.

isting goal is sufficient. Failure to serve the good is due to ignorance.

Wieman's position must be the third of these. He requires acceptance of the view that there is such a thing as objective, intrinsic value, even though he does not require acceptance of his particular characterization of that value. He requires also acceptance of the view that the awareness of this value has decisive existential import for the human individual. But his philosophic position does not allow for the kinds of intuitions to which the deontologists appeal.[73]

We must consider, therefore, the difficulties that have been widely noted in any ethic of consequences, that is, in any value theory that does not introduce special principles of obligation. First, the good must be identified with that which men in fact are most concerned to achieve. But men's desires are extremely diverse; so the good must be stated very abstractly and, even so, great difficulty is found in any formulation. Wieman's formulation in terms of qualitative meaning faces the difficulty that many men seem to themselves and to observers to prefer security to increase of qualitative meaning. Wieman must distinguish between what men really want and what they seem to want.[74] This procedure is in line with that of the Greek philosophers and much Christian ethics, but Wieman advances the argument through his reference to modern psychological knowledge.

What men really want is the greatest possible satisfaction of their total being.[75] But society compels the repression of many of their needs; so these cannot function consciously.[76] This means that we cannot solve our problem as the classical thinkers supposed, for we are not capable of recognizing consciously that state of affairs in which we would experience maximum satisfaction. We must, instead, identify that process in which greater satisfactions are progressively achieved and submit to its working in us and with us. This process is that in which qualitative meaning increases. Hence, as men are released from the psychological mechanisms that prevent them from recognizing their own real wants and needs, and are enlightened as to how to achieve their real ends, they will be motivated to submit to the creative event.[77]

If the increase of qualitative meaning always occurred for the individual who submitted himself to the process, I would regard Wieman's solution to the problem of motivation as adequate. However, he is quite aware

[73] *Man's Ultimate Commitment,* pp. 122–123.

[74] *Ibid.,* pp. 108–109, 200–201. Wieman is clear that men may not "like" the good. (*The Directive in History,* p. 32.)

[75] *Man's Ultimate Commitment,* p. 98.

[76] *Ibid.,* pp. 101–102.

[77] *Ibid.,* p. 134.

that this is not the case. Submission to the creative process may lead to death.[78] Presumably it may also lead to straightened circumstances in which one will be denied further opportunities for creative interchange, for example, protracted solitary confinement under conditions destructive of human dignity and personality. Can we say that all men really desire the results of the creative process in spite of these possible outcomes?

Wieman may well reply that there is no other hope for man and that he must take his chances,[79] and this may very well be sound advice. However, differences of temperament and disposition will surely come into play at this point. Some desire a rich and zestful life at all costs and are willing to forego all security for its sake. But to say that this is true of all men is to make an assertion for which there is little empirical evidence.

Another possible reply is that, whatever happens to us individually, the service of the creative event leads to a larger good for the wider community.[80] Here, too, there might be occasional circumstances in which factually this would not be correct, but let us assume that a life devoted to the creative event would on the whole lead to a far greater increase of good than any other kind of life. Could we then say that this kind of life leads to that end which all men ultimately desire? This would mean that man's deepest desire, when freed from all repression and confusion, is for the increase of good as such rather than for the increase of his own participation in the good. Once again, such an affirmation seems to have but little support in the empirical evidence.

Since Wieman does not wish to make affirmations about human psychology that are not warranted by the evidence, his imperatives must be formulated hypothetically. *If* one desires that greater qualitative meaning be attained, *then* he must surrender himself to the creative process. Or *if* one desires that greater total satisfaction of human desires be achieved, *then* he must serve the creative process. But whether men do have this desire remains a purely empirical question, and nothing can be said to the effect that they *ought* to have it. Wieman may remain confident that the

78 *Intellectual Foundation of Faith,* p. 89.

79 See, for example, his strong statement that the individual cannot find satisfaction except as he commits himself to creative good, in *Man's Ultimate Commitment,* p. 107. In "In Defense of My Faith" Wieman states that security can be attained only by commitment to divine creativity, but there does seem in fact to be a kind of quest for security that operates against such commitment.

80 *The Source of Human Good,* p. 293. Here Wieman is explicit that faith in the creative event will at least in some major crises involve the subordination of the private to the public good. He believes that the satisfaction received from this commitment will be sufficient recompense for this sacrifice. *Intellectual Foundation of Faith,* p. 89.

number of " men of good will " is large and that the practical need is for directing their efforts rather than proving that they should seek the good, but the situation that emerges may be more dangerous than Wieman realizes.

In part, at least, men of good will are motivated by the idea that there is an intrinsic good that demands their support. They do not think of themselves as simply attempting to further their own desires, which happen to be for the general good. To the extent that one is really persuaded that his *preference* for the good is the *only* reason for seeking it, his willingness to sacrifice in its service is likely to diminish.

In our day it is not idle speculation to point out this weakening of commitment to the good, which comes from the loss of the sense of its inherent rightfulness and absolute claim. The problem of meaninglessness is widely recognized as the spiritual problem of our time, and this problem grows precisely out of the loss of self-evidence of goods and goals. Men of good will in large numbers have suffered disillusionment. New generations arise nurtured on radical relativism, for whom the passion to produce the good is hardly comprehensible.[81] There is great value in giving clearer direction to those who do seek to increase good. But in our day an ethic that does not face the problem of motivating new generations toward the good, however conceived, has only limited relevance.

From one point of view it may seem unfair to single out Wieman for this criticism. He has done more than most theologians and moralists to come to terms with these problems. But the systematic approach of Wieman to theology requires of him a degree of success here that is not required of others. Traditional theology may appeal to love or gratitude toward God as the motivation for moral behavior. It may hold that to know God is to love him, and that hence religious experience can provide the needed motivation. But Wieman cannot escape his problem in this way.

For Wieman, we devote ourselves to the service of God because God produces the good. Our devotion to God is a function of our concern for the good. Knowledge of God cannot provide the motivation for that concern. If the good lacks power to claim us, God also lacks that power. He may continue to work among us, but the human submission to his working, apart from which his working is thwarted and impeded, will be lacking. Everything depends upon the power of the good to evoke our devotion to itself and to that process by which it is created. As long as that power exists, Wieman's analysis of how we can most effectively respond will be

[81] *Intellectual Foundation of Faith*, pp. 207–208.

relevant. But the more ultimate question of how this devotion can be effectively evoked and sustained remains unanswered.[82]

The conclusion of this discussion of Wieman's theory of value is that his theory has a remarkably wide range of relevance but fails to achieve the universality he seems to claim for it. The acceptance of his position does not depend upon defending one theory of value against all others, but it does depend upon a genuine commitment to the good, which transcends the theory.[83] The presence or absence of this commitment is presumably conditioned by the effective religious and cultural tradition, as well as by the particular life history, of each individual. Hence, Wieman's theology, like the theologies of Mascall and DeWolf, depends upon a conditioned historical situation for its acceptance.

Having developed this criticism rather fully, it is now necessary to show that it is far from decisive for an evaluation of Wieman. Although he sometimes writes as though only confusion and obstructing psychological mechanisms prevent the universal service of the creative event, at other times he shows clear recognition of the difficult problem of motivation. He is convinced that unless men can be persuaded to serve the creative event, mankind is doomed, but he is by no means certain that men care enough about the salvation of mankind to undergo the kind of transformation that is required.[84] He sees a large amount of convergence between private and public good in this service, but he does not pretend that this convergence is complete.[85] He does not inform us that men will spontaneously serve the creative good when they see it for what it is. Rather, he appeals to men to do so for their own sake and for the sake of mankind. He understands that men are unlikely to serve the creative good until they despair of satisfaction in created goods, and he knows that even then other responses are likely.[86] He knows that such service can be developed and sustained only as it is cultivated by private and public worship.[87]

Even those who see the source of motivation to the good in our experience of God do not suppose that information about God produces devotion of itself. So Wieman also need not show that information about the nature of the good and the process by which it is created spontaneously

[82] Although this paragraph must be understood as my criticism and not a summary of Wieman's statements, Wieman does recognize that the function of knowledge of God is at least primarily to direct an existing devotion and not to engender it. (*The Source of Human Good*, p. 48.)

[83] *Intellectual Foundation of Faith*, pp. 113–114.

[84] *Man's Ultimate Commitment*, p. 59.

[85] *The Source of Human Good*, p. 293.

[86] *Ibid.*, p. 278; *Man's Ultimate Commitment*, p. 58.

[87] *Intellectual Foundation of Faith*, p. 91; *The Directive in History*, p. 130.

evokes our commitment. In both cases commitment can be encouraged and guided, but its occurrence is an event beyond human manipulation. Wieman's argument is that when such commitment is evoked toward a transcendent deity no direction is given to human life.[88] He believes, and with much right, that he can provide the needed guidance to all those who are committed to the good. He believes further that men can accept his direction without first accepting any particular cultural or religious tradition.

The more serious question that we must pose is whether the creative event can function for us as God. Granted that it is the source of human good, can it be for us also the object of ultimate commitment?

The obvious objection to Wieman's position here is that the creative process can be only instrumental to good. Good itself is a property of experience or states of affairs. We may commit ourselves to the achievement of such situations on the basis of the great good we perceive that they will contain. But that which produces them we regard as means to be used and cast aside when they are no longer needed. If the creative good is understood as a process creating good, then our attitude toward it is properly instrumental.[89] We cannot identify any such instrument with God.

This objection, however, largely misses the point. The error lies in the fact that it assumes that persons, situations, and processes are ontologically distinct. It treats the first two as achieved realities and the latter as a series of somehow less real events connecting them. Wieman's view, in contrast, is that processes are the ultimate and only concrete reality. Persons and situations, if they are contrasted with the concrete processes, must be abstracted from them. The real value must inhere in the concrete process, not in that which is abstractly isolated from it.

As Wieman sees the relation of the creative process and the goods that it produces, he does not think of means and ends. The process is the ongoing reality in which stable structures emerge. But these structures are not intrinsically better than the process. The process itself is the becoming of higher values and contains, therefore, the value of these values. The created good is intrinsically less good than the creative good.[90]

This becomes clear when we see how Wieman actually describes the source of human good. The term " source " suggests a means to an end

88 *The Source of Human Good,* pp. 32–34.

89 Wieman recognizes the kinship of creative good with instrumental good, but the latter term refers properly only to created goods employed for foreseen ends. (*The Source of Human Good,* p. 57.)

90 *Man's Ultimate Commitment,* p. 107.

that is other than itself. But Wieman's actual analysis is quite different. He examines the events of the becoming of greater good to identify structures common to all of them. The occurrence of these structures he sees as sub-events within the inclusive event. The conjunction of these sub-events constitutes the common structure of all creative events. Thus, that by which the creative event is characterized is a complex structure that as such is abstracted from the event and lacks the intrinsic value that can occur only in the concrete event itself. But the relation of this structure to the event is not of means to ends but of structure to totality.[91] This totality, which is precisely the occurring of the greater good, is God. Hence, devotion to God is devotion to that event which is the becoming of the greater good and which has, therefore, the full intrinsic value of that good.[92]

We may go farther and say that Wieman has clearly identified that event which is intrinsically best. If any event is God, surely it is this supremely valuable one. But can any event as such be the object of our devotion? Is not devotion directed to persons who by their character or personality evoke our love and commitment?

Once again the objection betrays a refusal to accept Wieman's basic ontology. Devotion must be directed to that which is most real, not to abstractions. In Wieman's philosophy persons are strands within events and are isolable only by abstraction from the events.[93] These events are themselves the entities fundamentally constitutive of reality. There can be no higher object of devotion than that event in which good is always brought into being.

But this defense betrays in its turn the dependence of Wieman's whole position upon his ontology. *If* we take persons as ontologically real and regard the interactions among persons as ontologically abstract, *then* Wieman's theology must be profoundly shaken. It is true that he can still argue that we can serve the good of persons only when we produce the conditions in which the creative interchange he has described can be freely operative. But in this case, it becomes clear that this event is instrumental to the good of the persons. The values that occur have their onto-

[91] *The Source of Human Good,* p. 299.

[92] *Man's Ultimate Commitment,* p. 107.

[93] This is very clear in *The Directive in History,* e.g., pp. 19, 21; but in *Man's Ultimate Commitment* the individual is often spoken of as a concretely real entity. The shift in the focus of the good from qualitative meaning to human satisfaction reflects this change. I take it, however, that the change is terminological and for purposes of communication, and not an acceptance of a personalistic metaphysics. This interpretation is supported by the statement in his latest book, *Intellectual Foundation of Faith,* that the process of creativity is ontologically prior to persons (p. 63).

logical locus not in the event but in the persons among whom the event occurs. We may serve the event in the sense of encouraging its occurrence, but we do so because we are committed to the persons who are benefited by the event. We may even retain Wieman's insight that we serve persons better when we contribute to this process of creative interchange without attempting to control its outcome than when we attempt to control the course of events toward foreseen ends, but the process remains something to make use of rather than that which claims for itself our final sacrificial commitment.

This does not mean that Personalism is right and Wieman wrong. It means only that Wieman's creative event cannot seriously be regarded as God unless we agree that what he understands by events constitutes that which is ultimately real. *If* Wieman's ontology is correct, *then* it may well follow that Wieman's theology is also correct. But on what basis are we to decide as to the correctness of his ontology?

Wieman would have us accept his ontology on empirical grounds. It is based upon the recognition that nothing is real that is not of the order of experienced reality. It takes the immediacy of experience as its starting point and refuses to draw inferences to an unknown realm. But cannot almost the same thing be said about Brightman? He too takes the sheer givenness of immediate experience as his starting point and refuses to posit any other kind of ontological reality except such "shining presents."[94] It is true that he posits a plurality of shining presents rather than just his own, but Wieman also posits events other than that one in which at any given time he participates. How can one position be taken as superior to the other?

Brightman appeals to empirical coherence, which allows him to introduce explanations of his experience in addition to description. Wieman rejects explanation in this sense in favor of description.[95] Brightman would find Wieman's description confused at the point of Wieman's neglect of the discontinuity between the privacy of one experiencer and that of another. Wieman would find Brightman driven to speculations increasingly remote from the givens of experience. Once again, how can we decide between them? By what neutral criteria shall we judge alternative ontologies?

My point is that however we decide ultimately to answer such questions, we shall be forced to enter extensively into philosophical discussion of highly debated questions. If our acceptance of Wieman's theology de-

[94] See the discussion of Brightman in the preceding chapter.

[95] Causes are the systems of events in which an event occurs. Hence, explanation is complete description. (*The Directive in History,* pp. 25–26.)

pends upon our agreement with him on these speculative ontological questions, then Wieman's position does not have the freedom we have sought from speculation.

Wieman is aware of the plurality of metaphysics, as he is aware of the variety of value theories, and he does not wish to base his religious position upon any commitment to one or another. He recognizes that it would be idle to attempt to refute all the philosophies that refer to a reality transcending all possible experience. He argues only for their irrelevance to the practical affairs of man, with which he is concerned.[96]

Furthermore, Wieman does not rule out the possibility of ontologies that take mind or matter as the central terms. Against them he urges only that they must not take one term or another in such a way as to give that term exclusive ultimacy. Also, he expresses his opinion that greater pragmatic value is found in an ontology of events.[97]

Wieman's position here seems so moderate and reasonable as to disarm the critic. However, I must restate my criticism. Wieman intends that his fundamental religious position be independent of prior commitment to any metaphysics or ontology. To a considerable degree he succeeds. That is, he shows what men must do if human satisfactions are to increase. He shows this in such a way that persons with very diverse ontologies can agree with him on the grounds of empirical evidence.

In another respect he fails. He believes that since the process of creative interchange is that in which the human good grows, therefore — independently of ontological views — it is available as an object of personal devotion. I am arguing that devotion can be given only to what is perceived as ontologically concrete, and that there are ontological positions in terms of which a process of interaction must appear as an abstraction.

One might object that as long as one is persuaded that the good is achieved by creative interchange and is willing to further this achievement, it would make little difference what attitude one adopted toward the interchange as such. But I do not think this is true. Wieman is deeply convinced that religious devotion is needed, and he is seeking to point us to that which is supremely worthy of that devotion. It has seemed to be a fact that Personalists have been unable to understand how devotion can be given to an interaction, and I am trying to demonstrate systematically the cause of their difficulty.[98] My argument is that this central feature of

96 *The Source of Human Good,* pp. 72, 208–209. The avoidance of ontological debate is especially noticeable in *Intellectual Foundation of Faith.*

97 *The Source of Human Good,* pp. 209, 301.

98 I have taken Personalism as my one example of a position opposing Wieman's ontology. Actually, a variety of ontologies exist and operate in a similar way as obstacles to accepting Wieman's religious position.

Wieman's position does depend for its acceptance on the prior acceptance of his ontology of events.

In the end we find that the methodological situation of Wieman is not very different from those of Mascall and the Personalists. If, with Mascall, we see the world composed of entities that do not contain within themselves the basis of their own existence, then we must agree with him that there is a ground or power of being that does contain the principle of being and that is therefore radically other than all these finite entities. If, with Brightman, we see the self as the only entity that is given to us and seek an explanation of its contents, then we will find the most reasonable explanation to be in terms of the activity of other selves, and in one way or another we are almost certain to be forced to posit a supreme self as the explanation of much that is otherwise incomprehensible. If, with Wieman, we see the given as the qualitative flow of events and reject the demand for explanation in distinction from description of this process, then we must accept his identification of the supremely valuable process as that which is supremely worthy of our devotion.[99]

In each case a basic ontological judgment, expressing a distinctive sensibility, mode of vision, or primitive datum, is the ground of the natural theology. The very plurality of such grounds and the apparent incompatibility of the theologies that are built upon them tends to destroy confidence in the claim of any one of them to escape the relativities of private opinion or historical conditionedness. If natural theology, however ably pursued, leaves us with this fundamental relativity, many theologians are convinced it must be rejected. Its claim has been to ground the specificities of Christian faith in a rational context accessible also to the unbeliever. But we are forced to acknowledge that this claim is exaggerated. The rational context turns out to be hardly less relative to personal decision or prior conditioning than the distinctive act of Christian faith. Hence, we turn in the following chapters to a consideration of theologians who call for the radical autonomy of theology as witness to a divine act for whose occurrence no rational evidence is relevant.

Before leaving this discussion of natural theology, however, we may

[99] In "In Defense of My Faith," Wieman has shown that creative interchange is essential to the formation of any ontology or perspective and hence prior and superior to all. He seems to hold that for this reason the relativity of his position is transcended. However, the Personalist holds that the working on us of the personal God is prior and superior to all, and the Thomist calls attention to the fact that existence itself as God's act has this priority or supremacy. I do not believe that the relativity of each position can be escaped in this way. The defense against the charge of relativity in each case presupposes the particular position that is defended.

note that important elements in the positive affirmations of the three positions studied are compatible with one another. Within a more inclusive context the Thomist vision of God as the principle of being and the Personalist vision of God as supreme Person may be reconciled. Wieman's sensitive account of how good grows in human history may well contribute decisively to any understanding of how this personal principle of being acts among us. Indeed, I believe the context for such partial reconciliation is available in the work of Whitehead and Hartshorne. Thereby a partial transcendence of the relativity of natural theologies may be attained.

Part II
THEOLOGICAL POSITIVISM

5: The Nineteenth-Century Background

IN PART I WE HAVE CONSIDERED A VARIETY OF THEOLOGICAL POSITIONS THAT allow autonomy to man's rational activity and that develop the statement of the content of faith in relation to the independent results of that activity. In each case we have seen that the philosophy employed profoundly affected the content as well as the form of the affirmation of faith. Furthermore, the implication of the whole program is that Christian faith depends for its intelligibility and acceptance upon the prior acceptance of a particular philosophy. In our day, when no one philosophy has general acceptance among philosophers, and when all ontology and metaphysics are widely suspect, the precariousness of this procedure is apparent.

The employment of natural theology or a philosophical prolegomenon to theology is a common characteristic of much Roman Catholic theology and of liberal Protestant thought of the English-speaking world. It is criticized from a variety of points of view, which may be grouped under the headings of Augustinianism, existentialism, and theological positivism. Of these points of view, the first, although often viewed favorably, has little articulation today except to the degree that it appears in conjunction with one of the other two. We will consider it briefly in the concluding chapter. Existentialism, to which we will give extended consideration in Part III, is widely influential but has an ambiguous relation to natural theology. The most unequivocal rejection of the use of philosophy by theology is in theological positivism, the subject matter of this part.

The term " theological positivism " is used here to refer to a movement whose chief contemporary representatives may also be classified as Neo-Reformation theologians. The movement reaffirms the hostility of the Reformers to the Scholastic confidence in philosophical reason, and it employs this hostility more systematically as a methodological principle than was possible or necessary for the Reformers themselves. It is, therefore, both a recovery of Reformation thought and a response to the particular theological-methodological situation into which Christian thought has come as a result of modern relativism and the accompanying skepticism with respect to the capacity of reason to attain ultimate truth.

The origins of positivistic theology may be traced back to the New Testament itself. Although it may be doubted that the New Testament writers made any systematic attempt to avoid dependence on philosophy, none of them felt any need to justify their affirmations by appeal to philosophy or to express their faith systematically in categories provided by philosophy. In so far as there were presuppositions for their affirmations not given in the Christian revelation itself, they were thought of as given in earlier revelation or in common sense.

The issue of theological method arose only with the need to present the message to the cultured Greek world and to defend it against criticisms. This need had already driven Judaism to make extensive use of philosophy in its self-understanding, and to a considerable degree the Christian synthesis with classical philosophy followed lines already laid down by such Jews as Philo.[1] Protests were heard against the accommodations involved even in the earliest period, but on the whole the program of synthesizing the Greek and the Biblical won out in the development of the Roman Catholic Church. In the Middle Ages, with the progressive accessibility of the major works of Aristotle, this synthesis comprised a systematic union of Aristotle's philosophy and Biblical revelation that continues to the present to dominate most Roman Catholic thinking.

The Reformation protest against what it regarded as the corruption of the pure faith in the empirical church of its day took many forms. Central was its attack upon a form of piety that too easily sought to obtain status before God by good works. This was vehemently rejected in the name of Paul's doctrine of justification by faith. But this doctrine was understood to have much wider significance. Not only the purchase of indulgences but also the whole ecclesiastical system was repudiated in so far as it was based upon a claim to some kind of control over the movement of God's grace.

For our present purposes, however, the issue of central concern was one that appeared to be decisive for the Reformation only with the passage of time. Luther's attack upon indulgences was based upon an appeal to the Bible against the current practices of the church. The church opposed

[1] This is a major thesis of Wolfson. See *The Philosophy of the Church Fathers*, pp. v–viii and *passim*.

Luther on the grounds that the church as such, and not the individual Christian, is the authoritative interpreter of the Bible.[2] If this view is accepted, then the individual Christian can appeal to no other authority against the authorized teaching and practice of the church. Since the church had developed its doctrinal justification for its practices through the Scholastic theology of the immediately preceding centuries, Luther's appeal to the Bible was necessarily a rejection of the prior authority of human reason as philosophically employed by the Scholastics.[3]

There was another, more direct basis for Luther's hostility to the natural theology of the Scholastics. The popular piety of Luther's day was typified by the Brethren of the Common Life, who taught a simple, direct obedience to Christ as he appeared in Scripture, and who set aside the elaborate intellectual and institutional machinery of the church as entirely secondary to intense personal faith. This spirit deeply appealed to Luther. He was influenced also by the mystical piety of the *German Theology,* which he highly praised despite its divergence from his later theological position.[4] Throughout his life he preferred the simplicity of personal faith to the intellectual subtleties of philosophical theology.

Furthermore, Luther lived in a day when humanism was very much in the air. Although in many respects Luther lacked all sympathy for this movement, he nevertheless shared directly or indirectly in its concern to recover a direct confrontation with classical sources.[5] This meant a rejection of the approach to those sources through the eyes of the Middle Ages. Such a direct recovery of the Scriptures opened Luther's eyes to the gulf between primitive Christianity and the practices of his own day. The humanistic assumption of the superiority of the classical source in comparison with later interpretation and elaboration caused him to accept with little question the normativeness of the plain teaching of Scripture. Like the humanists, Luther had little sensitivity to the problem of inevitable distortion in all interpretation, his own included.

Finally, Luther's own theological training was under the influence of the school in which the tensions between reason and revelation were most fully recognized.[6] The Occamists could not agree with Thomas that the fruits of reason could lead to the very threshold of Christian revelation,

[2] Rupert E. Davies, *The Problem of Authority in the Continental Reformers: A Study in Luther, Zwingli, and Calvin,* p. 22.

[3] *Ibid.,* p. 18. Cf. also Pelikan's point that Luther's attack on Aquinas followed primarily from Thomas' theological doctrines. *From Luther to Kierkegaard: A Study in the History of Theology,* p. 4.

[4] Etienne Gilson, *Reason and Revelation in the Middle Ages,* pp. 91–94.

[5] Pelikan, *op. cit.,* p. 9.

[6] *Ibid.,* pp. 5–6.

because they understood reason much more nominalistically than did Thomas. They stressed the supremacy of the will both in God and in man and thus depreciated the capacity of reason to grasp the ultimate nature of things.

All these influences combined to cause Luther to regard the Scriptures and the theological pretensions of philosophy as incompatible opposites. He assumed without question, in harmony with the universal belief of his day, that the Scriptures are the Word of God. Since he contrasted Scripture with philosophy, as well as with the whole tradition of the church as it had developed by means of philosophy, both tradition and philosophy could be understood only as the words of man.[7] Hence, the humanist's preference for the classical expression as over against the later distortions became for Luther the radical preference for God's truth against human distortions.

The systematic implication of this view of the relation of the Bible to philosophy is clear. Responsible theology is not essentially different from Biblical exegesis. It can have no second norm beside the revealed Word of God. Since that revelation is self-authenticating and self-interpreting, it needs no second norm.

Luther's own work was complicated, however, by his remarkable sensitivity to the historical character of revelation and to the humanness and variety of the Scriptural witness. The Word of God is not simply identical with writings bound between the covers of the Bible;[8] it is rather the command of God and the gracious gift of salvation through faith which come to us through the Bible and are authoritatively witnessed to in the Bible.[9] There is no attempt on Luther's part to achieve a perfect agreement of everything that is said in the Bible after the manner of some later harmonizers. On the contrary, he finds in Christ the center in terms of which the Biblical writings in their real variety are to be understood and judged.

The antithesis of Scripture as the Word of God and philosophy as the words of man led also to strong antipathy to philosophical doctrines of God. Luther rejected these doctrines on two counts. First, since God has revealed himself to us, any effort on our part to come to him in some other way expresses an absurd and stubborn pride. We need no knowledge

[7] Davies, *op. cit.*, p. 18.

[8] *Ibid.*, p. 31. Note, however, the criticism of Davies in Johnson, *Authority in Protestant Theology*, pp. 36–39. Johnson shows that Luther does not exclude James or other writings in the Bible from being "Word of God."

[9] Pelikan, *op. cit.*, pp. 17–18. Johnson shows that the law is just as much Word of God as is Gospel, *op. cit.*, p. 36.

of God that God has not himself granted us in Jesus Christ. The philosophical effort to discover God is both unnecessary and sinful.[10]

Second, the ideas that are attained by philosophical speculation are nothing but products of the human mind. They do not and cannot have reference to the living God. Hence, any reverence directed to God as philosophically understood is idolatrous.

Luther's rejection of philosophy as a channel for gaining knowledge of God continued throughout his life, but his attitude toward the Bible altered somewhat. In the face of what he perceived as dangerous misinterpretations of Scripture in the religious excitement generated by the Reformation, Luther was forced to recognize the need for authoritative interpretations. These were formulated as occasion arose in confessional statements, and when necessary, secular authority was required to suppress false teaching. The appeal to the Bible against both Roman Catholics and Spiritualists tended to weaken the differentiation of the words of the Bible and the Word of God. Finally, even while Luther was still alive, the need for subtle distinctions in protecting the Lutheran view from misinterpretation led to the renewed use of Aristotelian philosophy.[11] Protestant orthodoxy came to differ from Roman Catholic Scholasticism chiefly in its rigid Biblicism and in its defense of specific confessional statements.

The two major works that gave systematic expression to the Scriptural positivism of the early Reformation were the 1521 edition of the *Loci Communes* of Melanchthon[12] and the *Institutes* of Calvin. In his early work under the influence of Luther, Melanchthon listed such major topics as free will, sin, law, and grace, and defended the Reformation position in terms of the teachings of the Bible on each subject. Thereby he achieved a systematic presentation of the Christian faith with a minimum of human interpretation. Successive editions of the *Loci Communes* reflect an increasing use of interpretation and even of philosophical tools.[13]

Calvin's *Institutes* go beyond Melanchthon's early work in imposing an order upon the material but continue to reflect the Reformation principle of appealing only to Scripture. Calvin retains the distinction between the words of Scripture and the Word of God, but for him this does not imply the freedom to criticize or reject parts of the Scripture.[14] It means, rather, that the words become the Word of God only as the Holy Spirit makes them such for us individually. Hence, there is less explicit use of a norm

[10] Davies, *op. cit.*, pp. 18–19.
[11] See the discussion in Chapter 1.
[12] An English translation is found in *The Loci of Philip Melanchthon*, pp. 63–267.
[13] Pelikan, *op. cit.*, p. 33.
[14] Davies, *op. cit.*, pp. 109–114.

within the Scripture and a greater concern to organize systematically the whole corpus of Biblical teaching. The rejection, as idolatrous, of human efforts to know God outside of Scripture continues, although man's failure to recognize God in nature is at the same time understood as culpable.[15]

Much of Calvinism, like Lutheranism, became scholastic both in its proliferation of subtle distinctions and in its use of Aristotelian philosophy as an aid for this purpose. In both alike, protests arose in the name of individual piety against the intellectualization of the faith. However, the orthodox synthesis of reason and faith remained dominant until shaken from without by radical attacks upon the kind of reason with which faith had made its alliance.

The role of Hume in systematically undermining the rational arguments in favor of Christian doctrines was noted in Chapter 1. The relevance here is that by shattering the complacent acceptance of rational support, Hume reopened for theologians the possibility that faith must work out its form and content in independence of all speculative reason. The history of nineteenth-century German theology is largely the story of this attempt.

However, the nineteenth-century efforts differed profoundly from those of the Reformation, especially in their treatment of the doctrine of God. Luther and Calvin unhesitatingly affirmed the initiative and activity of God in terms differing little from those of the Biblical writers. Their rejection of the role of philosophy with respect to the doctrine of God was based on their full security in the evident reality of God. They did not need philosophic support.

In the nineteenth century, by contrast, the existence of God was problematical, and theologians hesitated to affirm God's ontological reality as such on the basis of revelation. This seemed to be making on the grounds of faith an affirmation that belonged properly to the sphere of philosophy. Once theology trespassed upon the territory of philosophy, it seemed that theology must stake its case upon the philosophic acceptability of its assertions. But this would leave theology endlessly dependent upon a discipline that was increasingly unsympathetic.

The effort of the nineteenth century was to distinguish the spheres of philosophy and theology in such a way that the former could not cast doubt upon the affirmations of the latter. At the same time the idea of a supernatural revelation that guaranteed the truth of statements about man or God was abandoned. This left little choice but to conceive theology in confessional terms as an account of the faith of the church. That the church existed as a community of believers was an empirical fact that no

[15] I have tried to express the subtle but important difference between Calvinism and Lutheranism in *Varieties of Protestantism,* Ch. II.

philosopher could deny. Hence, an account of the faith of the church was an unexceptionable field of investigation.

The question at issue, however, is the status of the result of such an investigation. If faith is simply a description of the opinions held by a certain group of people, it seems to provide only sociological and psychological information. If, on the other hand, it affirms the content of the group's beliefs as true, faith would seem to require some other justification than the mere fact of belief.

This problem can be solved in so far as what is described is not the objective content of what is believed but the experiential faith of the believer. If a man has actually experienced redemption, then the account of his experience has normative as well as descriptive interest. However, his experience as such could not be warrant for accepting his interpretation of the experience as a work of God.

For this reason, theology in the nineteenth century tended to become anthropocentric. In Christian experience it had a datum that could not be denied by philosophy. This experience appeared in the eyes of Christians as supremely precious. Hence, its description and affirmation could be a means of showing the unique power and value of Christian faith. Men could be attracted to the faith by its own inherent efficacy without being first forced to accept speculative opinions in the sphere of metaphysics. Natural theology is replaced by a positive account of faith itself.

Twentieth-century theological positivism developed as both a continuation of and a reaction against this kind of nineteenth-century theology. It continued its rejection of natural theology, but it radically opposed the tendency to anthropocentric thinking. Since this nonphilosophical German theology provides the immediate background for Brunner and Barth, a brief exposition of the theological methods of the two most famous exponents is in order. These are Schleiermacher and Ritschl.

Schleiermacher divides the totality of human life or consciousness into three great areas. These are the area of knowing, the area of doing, and the area of feeling. The first two constitute the active side of life, whereas feeling is the passive side. The former are ways of securing mastery over the world, whereas feeling is the purely receptive and therefore self-surrendering side of life. Feeling is the sheer immediacy of conscious existence conceived as prior to all inference and action, and as distinguished from all representation. It is not simply an accompaniment of other elements in consciousness, for at times it dominates the whole of experience.[16]

One of the fundamental theses of Schleiermacher is that religion, or piety, belongs to the area of feeling and participates in the freedom and

[16] Friedrich Schleiermacher, *The Christian Faith,* iii. 2, 3.

priority that this area enjoys in its relation to knowing and doing.[17] Piety is related to this area of feeling as a part to the whole. To differentiate it from other feelings, Schleiermacher adopts the criterion of absolute dependence. In most of man's feeling there is some element of dependence, at least in so far as he is modified by what is given in his consciousness, but for the most part man experiences his relations as those of mutual dependence. No matter how trivial his influence upon the other object may be, as in his relations with the stars, the fact of such an influence sharply distinguishes the feelings associated with his relations with human society and nature from the feelings of piety. It is only in so far as man feels related to that which he can in no way affect, and which is at the same time the very source of his existence, that his feelings are pious.[18] In this feeling man may identify himself with the whole of finite existence, and thus he may realize the dependence of this whole upon the infinite.[19]

This feeling of absolute dependence in itself is undifferentiated, that is, it is the same in all men and at all times. It is never altogether absent from consciousness, but the vividness of its presence differs greatly, and the extent to which it is present is the degree of piety of a particular person or experience. On the other hand, piety never comprises the whole of the self-consciousness, for it is always accompanied by other feelings. The universal coexistence with the feeling of absolute dependence of these other feelings, derived from the relationship with nature and society, affords the basis for the differentiation of religious feelings, both within individuals and between persons and religions.[20]

Placing religion in the area of feeling does not mean that it is irrelevant to doing and knowing. Piety can be expressed in either, but it remains essentially feeling throughout.[21] It is expressed in relation to doing as religious ethics and in relation to knowing as doctrine or dogmatics. Of these expressions, the expression of piety in knowing is more relevant to the present concern.

Doctrines are accounts of religious affections set forth in speech. They include every proposition that can enter into preaching, and they can be classified as poetic, rhetorical, and descriptively didactic.[22] Dogmatic propositions fall within the third type and are those in which the highest degree of definiteness is sought.[23] These propositions are formulated both in the service of the church and in the interests of science.[24] The purposes that lead to their formulation lead also to their collation in dogmatic systems.[25] Dogmatics, therefore, is the most fully systematic statement of the

[17] *Ibid.*, iii. 4.
[18] *Ibid.*, iv.
[19] *Ibid.*, xxxvi.
[20] *Ibid.*, v.
[21] *Ibid.*, iii. 5.
[22] *Ibid.*, xv.
[23] *Ibid.*, xvi.
[24] *Ibid.*, xvii.
[25] *Ibid.*, xviii.

beliefs of any religious community.[26]

It is clear, therefore, that systematic theology, or dogmatics, is positivistic in the sense that it directly presents the faith of the religious community. It does not include a prior appeal to the evidence of universal reason as is the case where natural theology is employed. However, it is also clear that there are, or should be, as many systematic theologies as there are religious communities. Since their beliefs vary and even conflict with one another, the systematic statement of these beliefs would seem to lack any reasonable claim to truth. That is, theology has the criterion of precision and coherence with respect to what a given community in fact believes,[27] but it provides no basis for reconciling or judging among conflicting beliefs in terms of the reality of that toward which the beliefs are directed. In other words, theology becomes that branch of sociology which deals with the religious beliefs of the communities studied and abandons all normative claims.

Schleiermacher, however, did not intend to reduce theology to this radically relativistic function. He sought to avoid this result in two ways. First, he understood the theologian to be one who shared the beliefs of his community. Hence, his objective description of the beliefs of his community is in intention a statement of the truth. He may clarify and even correct beliefs by referring them more carefully to the actual movement of religious feelings to which they give expression, but as he shares in those religious feelings he can acknowledge no further norm.

At the same time Schleiermacher recognized that the fact of relativity of experience and accompanying beliefs posed a problem that could not be ignored. Unless one sees the relation of the religious experience of his own community to that of others in a way that somehow vindicates one's own, his commitment to the beliefs of his community must be weakened. Schleiermacher dealt with this problem in his " Introduction " partly explicitly and partly implicitly by displaying Christianity as the highest religion.

Schleiermacher argues that the movement from animism and polytheism to monotheism is unequivocally a movement from lower to higher.[28] Hence, Christianity as a monotheism stands as the highest level of religion. However, along with Christianity at this level he recognizes also the Jewish and Mohammedan religions. Even here, he claims that both Judaism and Islam have lingering affinities with lower forms of religion, so that Christianity can be objectively affirmed as the highest form of religion.[29]

The problem becomes much subtler when Schleiermacher distinguishes

[26] *Ibid.*, xix. [27] *Ibid.*, xxviii. 1, 2. [28] *Ibid.*, vii, viii. [29] *Ibid.*, viii. 4.

the communions within Christendom. Chiefly, his problem is to differentiate Protestant theology from that of Roman Catholicism. Here he makes no explicit claim that Protestant piety is higher than Roman Catholic; yet he so presents the difference that at least to the Protestant reader the preference for Protestantism is strengthened. In Roman Catholicism, he says, the believer's relation to Christ depends on the mediation of the church, whereas in Protestantism the church expresses and embodies the common life that emerges where individuals have received redemption in their direct relation with Christ.[30]

The purpose of these comments on Schleiermacher's method is to show the role of what he calls " borrowings " from philosophy of religion and apologetics. Since theology as such simply presents systematically the faith of a community, its persuasive power depends upon the conviction that the faith of the community is the highest and purest faith. Thus in the nineteenth century much of the energy that had previously been devoted to showing that Christian beliefs are true was transferred to the task of showing that Christianity is the highest or final religion. The escape from natural theology to positive theology was only partial.

Furthermore, presupposed by this whole approach is the view that religion as such is a desirable phenomenon. If religion is simply a texture of illusion or an obstacle to personal and social development, the fact that Christianity is better than other forms would hardly be sufficient commendation. Actually, Schleiermacher's greatest contribution may have been in his defense of religion as such rather than in his vindication of Christianity and his account of systematic Protestant theology.

The positive valuation of religion depends on two things. First, one must believe that religion is not based fundamentally on illusion. The function of natural theology had been to show that reason indicated the existence of that God about whose specific dealings with the world Christianity made such impressive assertions. Schleiermacher reacted against this kind of dependence of theology upon the conclusions of philosophy and showed that religion is not primarily a matter of beliefs of this sort. Yet he could not escape altogether the problem of the reality of God.

His solution of this problem was based partly on the claim that religious experience itself, that is, the feeling of absolute dependence, warrants belief in that on which man is absolutely dependent,[31] and partly on a minimization of statements about God and his dealings with the world. Primarily, he speaks of man's religious experience, not about its object. What

[30] *Ibid.*, xxiv.

[31] Cf. Richard B. Brandt, *The Philosophy of Schleiermacher: The Development of His Theory of Scientific and Religious Knowledge*, pp. 110–130.

he does say about the object has caused many who formerly thought themselves unable to accept the Christian teaching about God now able to believe without difficulty. Schleiermacher requires little more than that the universe as a whole be understood as a living and infinite unity on which each of its parts must be seen as absolutely dependent.[32] Specifically, Schleiermacher finds fully acceptable the philosophy of Spinoza. Systematically, we cannot say that Schleiermacher escapes all dependence on an implicit natural theology by this approach, but we can see how he was able to turn attention away from the problems of natural theology.

Much more important in Schleiermacher is the second and positive basis for the high evaluation of religion. He could assume that the critics of religion agreed with him that the fullest development of the highest capacities of man constitutes his greatest good. He had only to show, therefore, that religion is a human capacity capable of development, and that this capacity represents the very highest expression of man's human potentials, the development of which is essential to satisfactory development of other aspects of personality as well.[33] Since religion is man's relationship to the highest and most inclusive of all things, Schleiermacher's task was not a difficult one once he had shown that religion is a spontaneous response rather than a set of outwardly imposed ideas and behavioral norms.

Even on the basis of this brief comment on Schleiermacher's theological method it is possible to see that his influence could lead both to the development of a positive confessional theology and also to the scientific study of religion in its unity and historical diversity. The greatest nineteenth-century exponent of the former development is Albrecht Ritschl.

Schleiermacher began with the quality of subjectivity definitive of all religion and distinguished Christianity as a species within this larger genus. Hence, although the theologian as such confesses the faith of his community, he needs also the apologete to justify him in his commitment to this one among many forms of religion. Ritschl, by contrast, begins with Christian faith as such and focuses directly upon its object. The theologian does not describe primarily the movement of subjective experience within the believer but rather the object toward which the faith is directed and from which it is received.

To this extent Ritschl represents a return from anthropocentric liberalism to the objectivism of orthodoxy. However, no simple return was possible. Even more clearly than Schleiermacher or the Reformers, Ritschl

[32] Schleiermacher, *The Christian Faith,* xxxiv. 2.
[33] Friedrich Schleiermacher, *On Religion: Speeches to Its Cultured Despisers,* pp. 21, 39.

saw the necessity of dissociating theology from cosmological and metaphysical inquiry.[34] Hence, theology's object could not be God understood as a metaphysical first principle or a supreme cosmological entity. Theology's object could only be God as revealed in history, which means, Jesus Christ. Furthermore, when treating Jesus Christ, the theologian cannot deal with the mysteries of natures and persons in their ontological interrelations.[35] His object is Jesus as historically given, his acts and sayings, his personality and character. Finally, what is of concern is not the sheer factuality of this or that event or character trait, but Jesus' meaning for the believer as revealing God to him. Thus, despite the stress on the object, we find that our attention is directed to the practical (or what today we would call the existential) meaning of the object for the subject. The escape from the anthropocentric circle is far from complete.

Nevertheless, Ritschl directed research away from the study of religion in general and Christian experience in particular toward the historical Jesus. Christian theology consists in confessing his supreme and ultimate significance, and it does so on the basis of what objective inquiry guided by faith shows to be the actuality of the historic person.[36] In this way, faith and science are united, and the question of the relation of Christianity to other religions is largely avoided.

Ritschl's position has systematic difficulties in its doctrine of God. Although successful in turning attention away from the nature of God in himself to God as revealed in Jesus Christ, Ritschl does not mean that God is simply identical with the historical individual. Jesus has the value of God for the believer, but when Jesus reveals God, he reveals a reality that is not only his own person. Hence, the question of the basis of believing that such a reality exists is not escaped.

Much more decisive for the decline of Ritschlianism, however, was the difficulty with respect to the marriage of faith and objective historical research, which Ritschl supported. Such research seemed to lead to the conclusion that our historical knowledge of Jesus warrants few if any assertions about his life, character, and personality. If faith depends upon reliable knowledge about such matters, its situation is indeed precarious. Ritschl's effort to escape relativism by positivistic historical research must be declared a failure.

Schleiermacher's effort to deal with the problem of relativism by showing Christianity to be the highest religion met its nemesis in the work of Ernst Troeltsch, who brought out clearly the implications of Schleier-

[34] Albert Temple Swing, *The Theology of Albrecht Ritschl,* pp. 27–59.
[35] *Ibid.,* pp. 96, 100.
[36] Albrecht Ritschl, *Instruction in the Christian Religion,* in Swing, *op. cit.,* p. 200.

macher's anthropocentric starting point.[37] He saw that once Christianity is understood as a historical phenomenon it must be seen as one such phenomenon among others. It can be judged superior only by its own standards. Hence, there is no objective claim that can fairly be made either as to its truth or value that transcends the community that is formed by it. Only within and for this community can we proclaim the value of Christian religion as the most acceptable expression of man's spirituality. In Troeltsch, theological positivism appeared to have worked itself out to inescapable conclusions that contradicted its own principles of faithfulness to the church's experience.

It was in the context of a situation to which Troeltsch gave extreme and frightening expression that younger continental theologians rediscovered another nineteenth-century thinker who had prophetically grasped the deeper significance of his epoch and had offered a radical corrective. This man was Sören Kierkegaard, little noticed in his own day outside his native Denmark, but destined to exercise incalculable influence over the twentieth century. Both the theological positivism discussed in Part II and the theological existentialism discussed in Part III can be understood only against the background of his work.

Kierkegaard accepted the orthodox teaching of the Lutheran church of his day as an essentially adequate statement of the content of Christian doctrine. He did not think of himself as a theologian charged with the task of reconstructing his doctrine or measuring it against the norm of the New Testament. His problem was rather that of how the individual human being can come to terms with this already defined Christian teaching.[38]

He was quite sure that he could not come to terms with it by demonstrating its truth. The great speculative philosophy of Hegel intrigued him, especially as it undertook to expound the truth of Christianity as a necessary part of a system whose content is determined by pure rationality. But Kierkegaard held that such an approach erred in at least three ways. First, it attributed to pure, impersonal rationality a power of construction which in fact it does not have.[39] Second, it was unable to account for the concrete individual in his passionate concern, even though only such an individual could have created the system. Third, it profoundly misunderstood the nature of Christian faith.

Christian faith is not to be identified with the rational conviction that

[37] Hermann Diem, *Dogmatics,* pp. 4–9.

[38] Hermann Diem, *Kierkegaard's Dialectic of Existence,* pp. 81 ff., 189–190; and *Dogmatics,* pp. 20–21.

[39] In this respect, Kierkegaard anticipated much of the criticism by logical empiricism.

certain affirmations are true. Equally objectionable is any view which suggests that faith consists in treating as true a belief which is in fact only probable to a certain degree. Both of these interpretations imply that faith could exist only on the sufferance of speculative philosophy, whereas in fact it has always been entirely independent of speculation. So vehement was Kierkegaard's hostility to the interpretation of faith as involving rational belief that he taught that any objective evidence for the truth of Christian doctrine would be harmful, depriving faith of its proper province.

What, then, is faith if it is unrelated, or even negatively related, to objective evidence? It belongs to the sphere of inwardness or subjectivity. The question is not the objective one of the defense or criticism of a set of ideas in terms of their intelligibility or probability. It is the subjective one of how the existing individual responds to the encounter with these teachings. This response must be either an offended rejection or a voluntary acceptance. Faith is the decision of the subject to believe, and it is grounded only in the subjective existence of the individual.[40]

The revolutionary implications of this analysis with respect to the intellectual and scholarly work of Christian thinkers can hardly be exaggerated. Through most of Christian history, thinkers have been attempting to justify the content of Christian belief to themselves and others as worthy of belief. They have recognized, of course, that intellectual assent is not sufficient to salvation, but they have taken it as an important part of faith and specifically as that part to which the thinker should naturally address himself.

There have been repeated protests against the quality of Christian self-understanding engendered by this intellectualism. The Reformation itself, we have seen, may be understood as such a protest. Pascal represents another great protest, which remained within the Roman Catholic Church. Kierkegaard was himself deeply influenced by the protest of Johann Georg Hamann.[41] Hence, Kierkegaard stands in a long tradition of defenders of the faith who have seen the dangers in the effort to justify rationally the content of Christian teaching.

Kierkegaard, however, went farther than any of his predecessors in spelling out the basis and the significance of the protest. He turned his attention to the inner life of the individual and explored this with a subtlety and depth that have never been excelled. Furthermore, he focused

[40] J. Heywood Thomas, *Subjectivity and Paradox,* Ch. III.

[41] Walter Lowrie, *Kierkegaard,* pp. 164–167. A volume on Hamann, including selections from his writings, has recently appeared in English: Ronald Gregor Smith, *J. G. Hamann, 1730–1789.*

attention upon the radical difference between the inner life of subjectivity and the outer world of objectivity in such a way as to show that the categories used to investigate the latter are irrelevant to the investigation of the former. The objects with which science and speculative philosophy are concerned are properly treated by objective thinking, but far more important to man as man is the world of subjectivity, which is altogether misunderstood when it is objectified.

The radical character of Kierkegaard's emphasis on subjectivity appears in his strange assertion that subjectivity is truth.[42] This doctrine he developed against those who seek to achieve truth by surrendering their individuality to the impersonal universal reason. That this procedure may lead to a grasp of objective truths such as those embodied in mathematics, Kierkegaard never questioned. But the grasp of such truths is compatible with madness.[43] Sanity demands that the truths that are grasped be those which are relevant to the actual situation of the existing individual, and this means, his subjectivity.

Furthermore, the truth of the existing individual is not an appropriate selection from the previously defined sphere of objective truth. Objective truth deals only with objects and universals, whereas the decisive truth is concerned with subjects and individuals. There is no rational transition from the former to the latter. Subjective truth is *sui generis,* incapable of the kind of verification that characterizes objective truth but infinitely more important to man as man. The grasp of this truth is correlative with the intensity and passion of subjectivity, not with the amount of detached deliberation that precedes its acceptance.

Kierkegaard analyzed the alternative ways of life open to man to show how the decisions involved in choosing one or another are not based upon any objective calculus of truth or probability. Reason can show only its own limits by raising without answering the question of existence itself. By showing its own limits it points to the absolute otherness of that which lies beyond those limits with respect to what lies within them.[44] By that very fact, it makes clear that with respect to what lies beyond there can be no evidence whatsoever. Every argument that God exists presupposes its conclusions and is rationally useless. The only way of moving from subjective acceptance of the truths of reason to belief in God is by a leap, a decision of the whole person centering in the will.

It must be made clear that the leap of faith has nothing in common with the acceptance as probable or true of the opinion that what is beyond is of

[42] Sören Kierkegaard, *Concluding Unscientific Postscript,* pp. 169 ff.
[43] *Ibid.,* pp. 173–174.
[44] Thomas, *op. cit.,* pp. 108–109.

a certain sort. Whether God exists is a matter of absolute concern to the individual. The leap of faith is a decision for a way of existing, not for the entertainment of an opinion. That which is believed in is not God if it is not a matter of infinite personal concern. The leap is the decision to believe, that is, to live in subjective certitude. Neither before nor after the leap does this involve any evidence for the truth or falsity of the opinions involved or any objective certainty about them.[45] This complete disproportion between subjective certitude and objective uncertainty is the heart of the paradox of which Kierkegaard often speaks.

But Christian faith involves a still more striking paradox. It asserts that God became man, that the man Jesus is God. This doctrine is absolutely absurd to rational man. It affirms that that which is wholly unlike became that which is like without ceasing to be what is wholly unlike. This claim is the offense of Christianity and can never be made rationally acceptable. Therefore, it confronts the individual with an absolute either/or. Either he must believe this claim, or he must reject it.[46]

Objectively, of course, one may remain in doubt or vacillate between two opinions. Degrees of conviction are possible. But subjectively one finds himself confronted by a question of infinite concern. If the Christian claim is true, then one's eternal welfare hinges upon the decision. There is only belief or unbelief, and the decision belongs to each individual in his utter solitariness.

For this decision no historical evidence is of help. So far as objective knowledge is concerned, the historian is always limited to approximating knowledge that is necessarily wholly disproportionate to the absoluteness of decision. But in any case the deity of Jesus is in no sense accessible to historical investigation. Even the contemporaries of Jesus could only believe or disbelieve; they could not see his deity or base their conviction on cumulative evidence.

The decision of faith is a radically individual one, and it is a decision for a life of suffering. The disproportion between subjective commitment and objective evidence is paralleled by the disproportion between Christian existence and the life of comfort and culture. Just as Kierkegaard attacked all theological accommodation to what seems plausible, he also attacked all personal accommodation to what is socially acceptable and compatible with worldly success. Hence Kierkegaard, who accepted and defended the inherited teaching of the church, bitterly attacked its hypocrisy and complacency. For him, Christianity is a radically individualistic faith.

Although Kierkegaard intended to deal only with the question of the

[45] *Ibid.*, Ch. IV. [46] *Ibid.*, Ch. V.

subjective appropriation of Christian teaching and not with the objective content of that teaching, which he accepted as such, in practice the distinction repeatedly breaks down. His analyses of human existence are rich in transforming significance for the doctrines of faith, sin, repentance, justification, and sanctification. Furthermore, in relation to these analyses of subjectivity he also develops distinctive doctrines about God and Jesus Christ. In its formulation of all these doctrines, modern theology has been deeply influenced by him. However, those who have been led by this influence to identify the subjective analysis of believing as the grounds for developing Christian doctrine as such have in fact profoundly betrayed Kierkegaard's basic intention.[47]

In conclusion we may note, first, how Kierkegaard became the source of philosophical existentialism and, second, the implication of his thought for theology in the twentieth century. Kierkegaard gave a profound stimulus to philosophical existentialism by forcing attention upon the otherness of subjectivity from objectivity and by demonstrating the possibility of treating subjectivity with clarity and rigor without employing the categories of objectivity. He contributed many specific analyses, such as his famous discussion of anxiety, that have been influential among philosophical existentialists. He called attention to the necessity of decision and of the element of the absurd, in the face of which man decides.

The theological position that Kierkegaard supports is a thoroughly orthodox and dogmatic one. The implications of his thought move radically counter to any accommodation of theology to culture or philosophy or any effort to redetermine the content of the faith. He assumed a harmony of the orthodox teaching of his day with the New Testament, and he did not foresee how New Testament scholarship would undermine this apparent unity. Hence, one cannot say just how he would have dealt with some of the specific theological problems of the twentieth century.[48]

In addition to the specifically existential influence that has implications for theology as well as for philosophy, Kierkegaard contributed three principles that have played a prominent role in determining the methodology of much twentieth-century theology. First, he stressed that God is radically beyond the grasp of reason and can be known only in faith, hence that the Christian affirmation of God has nothing in common with any philosophical affirmation whatsoever. Second, he stressed that Chris-

[47] Diem, *Dogmatics,* pp. 21–23.

[48] Diem points out that the dissolution of dogmatics by historicism cannot be dealt with in Kierkegaard's terms. (*Dogmatics,* p. 32.) Thomas' argument that Kierkegaard's understanding of the absolute paradox of the God-man is not disturbed by modern Biblical studies is not entirely persuasive. (*Op. cit.,* p. 114.)

tian faith is based upon the absolute paradox that God became man in Jesus, and that the concern of the thinker can be only to point to this affirmation and to show how its affects the human situation — never to explain or justify it. Third, he dissociated faith from the communal and sacramental life of the empirical church and affirmed it as a relation between the individual and God.

Throughout the nineteenth century there were not lacking conservative Protestants who kept alive the Scholastic, pietistic, and to some degree the Reformation, approach to theology. In recent decades there has been a marked revival of sensitive Reformation thinking in both Europe and America. It eschews the violent obscurantism and indiscriminate hostility to modern ideas that partly justified the earlier caricature of fundamentalism. It turns the focus of its attention away from the issues that are specifically in dispute with modernists to the central affirmations of historic orthodoxy, thereby escaping the danger of becoming cultic.[49] Its leaders have contributed critiques of liberalism and other forms of modern theology that have been recognized as responsible and damaging.[50] But it remains profoundly loyal not only in general but in detail to the doctrines of the Reformation and especially of Calvin and his early followers. Some of its leaders make considerable use of philosophic reasoning, but others deserve not less than Barth and Brunner the name of theological positivists. Among these perhaps the most impressive is G. C. Berkouwer.

Berkouwer represents the finest flowering of a Calvinist tradition that has developed primarily in terms of its own inner dynamics rather than as a response to the changing intellectual environment. He is, however, surprisingly open to the new winds that are blowing in other theological circles and has written one of the most perceptive accounts of the theology of Karl Barth.[51] He takes to task his conservative brethren when they simply dismiss the theology of Barth because of its differences from the system of thought that they have identified as orthodox.[52] For Berkouwer the only final criterion is loyalty to the Word of God, and in so far as Barth is open to that Word, his thoughts are to be considered seriously and appreciatively.

Berkouwer is even more sensitive than Barth to the dangers of using

[49] Cf. Edward John Carnell, *The Case for Orthodox Theology,* Ch. VIII.

[50] J. Gresham Machen, *Christianity and Liberalism;* Edward John Carnell, *The Theology of Reinhold Niebuhr;* Cornelius Van Til, *The New Modernism: An Appraisal of the Theology of Barth and Brunner;* Gerrit Cornelis Berkouwer, *The Triumph of Grace in the Theology of Karl Barth;* Carl F. H. Henry, *Fifty Years of Protestant Theology.*

[51] Berkouwer, *The Triumph of Grace in the Theology of Karl Barth.*

[52] See criticism of Van Til, *ibid.*, pp. 384–393.

philosophical categories in theological exposition.[53] Nevertheless, he does not simply dismiss those who do make use of such categories.[54] Each man is to be judged in terms of the degree to which the Word of God controls and directs his thought, whatever the terminology may be. For his own part, he remains remarkably close to the language of the Bible and the Reformation confessions, although he also defends ideas couched in the more speculative language of the ecumenical creeds and of much orthodox theology.[55]

To a considerable extent the conservative Calvinist tradition from which Berkouwer comes, although avoiding philosophical entanglements, worked out the rationally consistent implications of key doctrines that it found in the Bible. For example, some of its spokesmen so interpreted the doctrine of divine election as to set beside it, as on the same level, the doctrine of reprobation.[56] Thus God's rejection of the many is treated as a divine act in just the same sense as his election of the few. Berkouwer recognizes a certain rational neatness in such a scheme, but he deplores the theological tendency to affirm such rational coherences in the face of the silence and even the opposition of Scripture.[57] The Bible, Berkouwer argues, attributes only the divine election to God as its cause. On the other hand, this does not mean that Berkouwer questions that many are lost or that the divine sovereignty is less clearly manifest in condemnation than in election. He rejects also any effort to make the divine condemnation conditional upon God's prevision of man's lack of faith.[58] To accept any of these alternatives to the doctrine of double election would be just as unfaithful to Scripture as is that doctrine itself. The theologian's task is to faithfully affirm what is affirmed in Scripture, and not to attempt to reconcile apparently conflicting emphases in a rational scheme.[59]

Although Berkouwer feels free to criticize Calvin and the Calvinist confessions at those points where they have gone beyond the teaching of Scripture, they function for him as guides and norms by which to check his own reading of the Bible. Hence, on each doctrine that he investigates, he devotes much of his attention to the teaching of the church in

[53] *Ibid.*, p. 16, n. 21, pp. 20, 21.
[54] *Ibid.*, pp. 21, 389.
[55] E.g., the cautious defense of the idea of the impersonal humanity of Jesus Christ. (Berkouwer, *The Person of Christ*, pp. 305–326.)
[56] Berkouwer criticizes Van Til for taking this position. (*The Triumph of Grace in the Theology of Karl Barth*, pp. 391–392.) He also criticizes some assertions of Calvin and the Canons of Dort that are subject to misinterpretation in this direction (*Divine Election*, pp. 173, 181, 188, 190.)
[57] Berkouwer, *Divine Election*, p. 173.
[58] *Ibid.*, pp. 197–201, 203.
[59] *Ibid.*, pp. 181, 207–209.

which he stands. Since this teaching includes the acceptance and reaffirmation of the ecumenical creeds of the early church, these also function as guides to the interpretation of Scripture.[60] However, for Berkouwer, these creeds are accepted ultimately because they accurately reflect the meaning and intention of Scripture, not because they have been accepted by the church.[61] As a faithful reader of God's Word, Berkouwer stands in dialogue with others who acknowledge this same Word, convinced that in the main it has been faithfully reflected in those creeds and confessions by which his church lives.

In order that we may grasp the relationship of this conservative Biblicism to the positions with which Part II is primarily concerned, we should note first its relation to the theology of the Reformers. Conservative Biblicism differs from Reformation theology in several respects.

First, and by necessity, it differs precisely in its attempt to be loyal to the Reformers' teaching. The spirit of Luther is highly individualistic and even revolutionary in that he relied upon a quite fresh grappling with the Bible. He did not concern himself much with how others had understood it, but counted upon its power to offer its meaning directly to him. Although Calvin was partly guided by Luther and other early Reformation figures, his spirit remained much the same as theirs. He confronted the Bible freshly, seizing the meaning that it gave him as the Word of God.

For later generations impressed by the work of the Reformers a choice is necessary. On the one hand, one can simply attempt again the fresh confrontation with the Word of God, allowing it to lead wherever it may. But the history of Protestantism, even in the time of the Reformation itself, shows that this leads to endless multiplication of sectarian interpretations. One can therefore avoid this consequence by learning to read the Scriptures basically through the eyes of the Reformers. This does not exalt the work of Luther and Calvin into a new canon, but it does give to them an authority with respect to the interpretation of the one canon which is not wholly unlike that claimed by the more moderate advocates of the Roman Catholic Church for its tradition.[62] The argument, then, becomes that as to which tradition is in fact more loyal in its interpretation to what it intends to interpret.

On the whole we may say that whereas Barth takes the risk of the first

[60] Berkouwer, *The Person of Christ*, p. 75.

[61] *Ibid.*, pp. 159, 161 ff. Here Berkouwer defends the creedal affirmation of the deity of Jesus from Scripture.

[62] Cf. George H. Tavard, *Holy Writ or Holy Church: The Crisis of the Protestant Reformation*, pp. 244–247.

alternative to a very considerable degree, Berkouwer tends strongly to the second. It is for this reason that we may call his Biblicism conservative in a sense that does not apply to Barth.

A second divergence from the Reformers — or at least from an element perceived in the Reformers by the adherents of Neo-Reformation theology — is manifest. The Reformers taught, according to this view, a nonidentity of the written words and the Word of God.[63] For the Neo-Reformation theology, this provides an opening for accepting many of the conclusions of the critical scholarship of the past two centuries and for supporting in principle the continuation of critical study of the Bible.[64] Berkouwer, on the contrary, takes as his starting point for theological work the identity of the canonical Scriptures and the Word of God.[65]

Berkouwer does not suppose that any rational proof can be given for the identity of the Bible and the Word of God. Only the Holy Spirit can convince us of the truth.[66] However, this faith can be supported without defensiveness against the attack of critics within and without the church. Also, the need of the world for the clear affirmation of the unqualified authority of the Bible can be shown.

The problem confronted by theological positivism in the twentieth century may be gathered from what has now been said. It must continue and complete the task of establishing the total independence of its starting point from philosophy and contemporary culture. It must witness to the faith in such a way as to overcome all tendency to relativism. It must recapture the radically theocentric character of Christian faith.

All this can be done fairly easily by those who, like Berkouwer, first establish the inerrancy of Scripture. But for the major spokesmen of theological positivism in our day this possibility is ruled out. Both the historical research of the nineteenth century and the nature of faith itself make the return to an objective Biblical authority of this sort impossible for them.

The special problem for them centers around the doctrine of God. In the first century and also in the sixteenth the reality of the revealed God was simply not in question, but today it is everywhere doubted. Some philosophers still provide rational arguments on varying grounds in favor of belief in deity, but the use of reason in this way is repudiated by theological positivists. Nineteenth-century theology made belief in God a function of human experience, but the anthropocentrism that this implied is

63 I have suggested above that this had a somewhat different meaning for Luther than it had for Calvin.

64 For example, the vigorous assertions of Brunner, *The Theology of Crisis,* pp. 19–20; and *The Word and the World,* pp. 92–104.

65 Gerrit Cornelis Berkouwer, *Modern Uncertainty and Christian Faith,* pp. 12–16.

66 *Ibid.,* p. 14.

emphatically rejected. Conservative Biblicists can affirm God's reality on the basis of the inerrancy of Scripture, but no such argument is available for the major positivists.

In the two following chapters we will examine and evaluate the solutions of Brunner and Barth to the methodological problem posed by this situation. Since Barth initiated the movement and profoundly influenced Brunner's development, it would seem that one should treat him first. However, the thought of Brunner is more readily comprehensible to American readers and provides a useful foil against which to set that of Barth. Furthermore, the Barth of the *Church Dogmatics* appeared in full self-consciousness only after the influence of the early Barth had led Brunner to formulate a quite different systematic position. Hence Brunner is treated first.

6: Emil Brunner

WHEN NEO-ORTHODOXY, NEO-REFORMATION THEOLOGY, THE NEW BIBLICAL theology, or theological positivism is spoken of in America, the first name that comes to mind is that of Karl Barth. Yet when one undertakes to state the position in question, it is more likely to sound like that of Emil Brunner.

Brunner associated himself so closely with Barth's theology that he was long taken as its spokesman in this country. In 1934, disagreements between them came to focus in public debate,[1] but Brunner has ever since then continued to stress their agreements rather than their differences. Only gradually has the full meaning of these differences become clearly apparent.

In approaching Brunner's theological position, we are fortunate that it is available to us in a recently finished systematic form, complete with methodological prolegomenon.[2] Brunner's work runs to some 1,200 pages, but in comparison with Barth's monumental and still unfinished opus, it is a model of clarity, brevity, and simplicity. Basically, Brunner's *Dogmatics* is only a clarification and reorganization of the ideas that he has been expressing for several decades. Hence, it can be used here quite safely as the basis for expounding his general position.

Brunner has formulated his theology as a third way, rejecting both

[1] The essays in question are Brunner's "Nature and Grace" and Barth's "No!" published in *Natural Theology,* Baillie, ed.

[2] Of the three volumes of Brunner's *Dogmatics,* the first two, which are most directly relevant to methodological questions, are in English. They constitute Brunner's doctrines of God and of creation and redemption. The third volume, published in Switzerland in 1960, contains his treatment of the Holy Spirit and eschatology. The methodological section of the *Dogmatics* is supplemented in a valuable way by *Revelation and Reason: The Christian Doctrine of Faith and Knowledge*. Other books by Brunner have been used only incidentally.

liberalism and orthodoxy, both subjectivism and objectivism.[3] Liberalism, he declares, has become man-centered and has sought to subject the mystery of God to human reason. As a result, it has become an expression of human religiosity rather than of Christian faith, and its spokesmen have substituted the science of religion for Christian theology.

On the other hand, Protestant orthodoxy has treated the human words of the Bible idolatrously. It has failed to distinguish God's Word from the all too human ideas about science, history, and cosmology that abound in the Bible. Hence, it has been forced to defend all manner of indefensible beliefs or to allegorize statements that are plainly intended to bear a literal meaning. In its exaltation of the book it has obscured the Christ.[4]

Brunner's alternative is that we should recognize that in the Bible we have God's Word in a very human medium. He likes to quote Luther's statement that the Bible is the crib in which Christ is laid.[5] Jesus Christ is God's self-disclosure to man. The Bible expresses man's hope for, and witness to, that disclosure. Our need is to encounter God in Christ, not to believe that certain propositions recorded in the Bible are precisely accurate.

These ideas, so exciting thirty years ago, have lost much of their interest today just because of their success in refashioning the thought of the church. Almost all the theologians treated in this book could agree in general with what has been said, but this does not preclude the widest variety of interpretations among them. Hence, we must ask much more precisely what Brunner means and how he understands the implications of his teaching.

The rest of this chapter is devoted to explaining and criticizing Brunner's distinctive formulation of the third way beyond liberalism and orthodoxy. Brunner holds that the great error of liberalism (and some forms of orthodoxy) has been its effort to begin thinking outside the sphere of faith. In contrast, Brunner wishes to develop a theology that begins with faith and is wholly the servant of faith.[6] For this reason, we will first attempt to understand what Brunner means by faith and how he understands it to arise. Second, since theology is a cognitive activity arising from faith and bound to faith,[7] we must see how Brunner understands faith as articulating itself reflectively. Third, since theology as a reflective enter-

[3] Emil Brunner, *The Theology of Crisis,* p. 22. This third way is the theme of the entire book. See also Brunner, *The Divine-Human Encounter,* Ch. 1.

[4] *The Theology of Crisis,* pp. 19–20; *The Word and the World,* pp. 92–104; *Dogmatics* I, p. 34.

[5] *The Theology of Crisis,* p. 19; *The Word and the World,* p. 94.

[6] *Dogmatics* I, pp. 3, 8–81.

[7] *Ibid.,* pp. 28–29, 38–40, 62; *Revelation and Reason,* p. 40.

prise claims to speak truth,[8] we must learn how Brunner justifies this claim and what this means for the method by which theology is developed. We can then turn to a brief consideration of some major doctrines that are affirmed by Brunner to see how they articulate the implications of his method. Finally, we will critically analyze Brunner's position to determine whether the doctrines he affirms are actually warranted by the method he proposes.

Brunner understands faith as the human response to God's revelation of himself in Jesus Christ.[9] This revelation is a definitely supernatural act.[10] To regard Jesus as revealing God because of his ideal human obedience does not, in Brunner's opinion, safeguard the distinctive teaching of Christian faith. In the person of Jesus, God as Person meets man.[11] This is the central affirmation of Christianity, and everything hinges upon it.

But on what grounds is this to be believed? The authority of Scripture cannot be appealed to, for this depends upon its witness to revelation, not on independent evidence of its inerrancy.[12] Obviously, philosophy cannot help us, since no philosophy could demonstrate such a supernatural event. Hence, it seems we must appeal in some way to personal experience. But the appeal to personal experience has usually been understood either subjectively or objectively. When it is understood subjectively, as is primarily the case with Schleiermacher and Bultmann, theology can deal only with Christian experience as such and surrenders its authentic focus on God and his acts. If it is understood objectively, as by orthodoxy and Barth, man's responsibility before God is endangered.[13]

These consequences can be avoided if we revive the authentic Biblical understanding of the personal relationship between God and man. God meets or encounters man in Jesus Christ. This is neither an occurrence objective to man, nor an event within man's private subjectivity. It is a relationship between two persons that involves the personal centers of both.[14]

In answer, then, to the question as to how we can know that God has supernaturally revealed himself in Jesus Christ, the unequivocal reply must be that we have encountered him there.[15] If we have not done so, we cannot affirm the truth of Christian faith. There can be no rational

[8] *Dogmatics* I, pp. 14, 43, 50, 60, 61, 63, 80, 84; *Revelation and Reason,* pp. 3, 362.
[9] *Dogmatics* I, pp. 61, 309; *Revelation and Reason,* pp. 32–37.
[10] *Dogmatics* II, pp. 328, 330–332, 340, 356; *Revelation and Reason,* pp. 40, 99–100.
[11] *Dogmatics* I, p. 61; *Revelation and Reason,* p. 409.
[12] *Dogmatics* II, p. 343; also I, p. 110; *Revelation and Reason,* pp. 169 ff.
[13] Cf. *Dogmatics* III, pp. 245–252, for treatment of Barth and Bultmann in these terms.
[14] *Dogmatics* I, p. 61; *Revelation and Reason,* pp. 33, 134.
[15] *Dogmatics* II, pp. 241, 255.

proof to the unbeliever that Christian claims are true. By the same token, there is no need of rational defense of the truth for the believer. In this sense the starting point for Christian theology is frankly a-rational.

But this does not mean that Christian faith is *ir*rational. It is clearly not rationalistic in the sense of deducing its content from universal principles of reason, but few thinkers today believe that any truth about life or the world can be learned in that way. Faith is entirely open to the use of reason in explicating its implications.[16] Hence, faith differs from the intention of philosophy and the natural sciences in its use of reason only in that the datum on which it rests in its entirety is not acknowledged as such by all men.[17]

The essential difference between Brunner (and indeed most of the theologians to follow) and those treated in Part I lies precisely at this point. The latter may acknowledge a special experience that gives rise to the specific doctrines of faith, but they do so within a context that makes the occurrence of such special experiences intelligible on objectively established grounds. Brunner, by contrast, rests the entire case for Christian belief upon the occurrence of the encounter with God in Jesus Christ. Christian thinking begins only with and after this encounter.

We must further understand that the encounter is not subject to human control. A man cannot take certain steps and thereby place himself in the presence of God. It is God who encounters man, not man who encounters God. It is essential that man throughout recognize the priority of the act of God. Brunner unequivocally rejects any view that gives to man's independent deeds a place in the scheme of salvation.[18]

But this does not mean that man is a merely passive object upon which God acts.[19] When God encounters man, man is placed in the position of responding. He can accept or reject the grace proffered in Jesus Christ.[20] Brunner unequivocally rejects any doctrine of predestination that denies to man the final responsibility for how he reacts to God's offer. God's act is always primary and unconditioned by human merit. But God's act places man in a position of freedom and responsibility. His freedom is entirely conditioned by God's prior act in encountering him, but his response is his own.

When man responds affirmatively to God's offer of grace in Jesus Christ, he enters into the life of faith. This does not mean that he has infallible

16 *Dogmatics* I, pp. 62, 79; *Revelation and Reason*, pp. 16, 213; Emil Brunner, *Man in Revolt: A Christian Anthropology*, p. 61.
17 *Revelation and Reason*, p. 363.
18 *Dogmatics* I, p. 310.
19 *Ibid.*, pp. 311, 315; *Revelation and Reason*, p. 48.
20 *Dogmatics* I, p. 338; III, p. 27; *Man in Revolt*, p. 537.

information heretofore denied him. But it does mean that he apprehends reality in a new way.[21] First and foremost, for the first time he knows the living God. In the second place, he knows himself and his fellow Christians in a way that is quite impossible apart from faith. In the third place, he understands nature and natural man much more fully than the natural man can understand himself.

There is, then, a cognitive element in the encounter, but this is not of the sort that is usually meant by knowledge.[22] It can be regarded neither as the objective knowledge appropriate to the inanimate world nor as the subjective understanding appropriate to apprehending other persons,[23] nor as the self-understanding on which the understanding of other subjects depends.[24] In all these forms of knowledge, man is the agent and source of knowing.[25] Our autonomous self-understanding leads us to the limits of our being, where we know ourselves called to authentic existence and guilty for our failure to respond to that call. But none of the modes of cognition that we usually call knowledge enable us to discover the source of the call or to respond to it.[26]

It is here at the boundary of our existence that we encounter the revelation of God in Jesus Christ as the answer to the question posed by our existential situation. Thereby we know the source of the call in God the creator and recognize our guilt as sin. At the same time we know our sin as forgiven in the cross and resurrection of Jesus Christ.[27] This knowledge is a subjective understanding of ourselves, but only of ourselves as receiving our true being from the personal impartation of God. It is a knowledge *of* ourselves but not *from* ourselves, hence, a unique form of knowledge. We know ourselves in faith as known and loved by God.[28]

[21] *Dogmatics* I, pp. 176, 308–309; II, pp. 154, 257; *Revelation and Reason,* pp. 49, 62, 425; *Man in Revolt,* pp. 65–66, 81.

[22] *Dogmatics* III, p. 294.

[23] *Ibid.,* III, pp. 285–288, 292.

[24] *Ibid.,* III, pp. 288–289.

[25] *Ibid.,* III, p. 295.

[26] *Ibid.,* III, p. 292.

[27] *Ibid.,* III, pp. 292–293.

[28] *Ibid.,* III, pp. 294–295. The discussion of faith and knowledge on which these two paragraphs are based is Brunner's most recent effort to formulate his position on this point. Taken by itself, it could be understood to imply that theology can deal only with existence in faith as received from God and not with God directly. Since, however, his *Dogmatics* deals extensively with God, I assume that Brunner does not intend this understanding. The encounter, for him, gives knowledge of the God who encounters as well as of the self who is encountered. Otherwise, the criticisms he directs against Bultmann in this same volume would apply equally to his own position. (*Dogmatics* III, pp. 247–249, 254). An anticipated new edition of Brunner's *Wahrheit als Begegnung* (*The Divine-Human Encounter*) may clarify the obscurities that remain.

The central expression of the new understanding of faith is in prayer. Prayer continues the encounter relationship with God and expresses without describing the new apprehension of self and world. Thus prayer is the spontaneous language of faith.[29] However, prayer is by no means the only language appropriate to the man of faith.

The new understanding of God, self, and world that is given in the encounter can and must also be considered reflectively. Brunner shows that three motives have been at work in the church from early times, requiring such reflection.[30] First, there is the need to defend the faith against misinterpretations and distortions. Second, there is the need to instruct candidates for membership in the church. Third, there is the need to give guidance in the understanding of the Bible and to summarize its teaching.

These three functions are concerned with aiding Christians in the understanding of their faith. They presuppose the faith with which they deal. In so far as they replace the I-Thou relation with God by a reflective attitude toward that relation and what it signifies, they are even dangerous to faith.[31] But this reflection is a necessary danger, and it can be prevented from damaging faith by being constantly referred back to its center and goal in the encounter itself.

The reflective process is responsible not only to that upon which it reflects but also to the norms of reason that govern all reflection. It must live in the tension between these two authorities.[32] If it pays too little attention to rational criteria, it will constitute poor reflection and be unable to give direction and clarification to Christian thought. If it pays too little attention to its source and goal in the encounter with God in Jesus Christ, it will be led into barren speculations which weaken rather than strengthen the faith that Christian reflection should serve.

The final outcome of reflection upon faith in the service of the church is dogmatics. Dogmatics aims at clarity and systematic comprehensiveness.[33] But it aims at this in the service of the church, bound to faith itself as its decisive norm.

There are other theological tasks within the church that do not culminate in dogmatics. Dogmatics has as its function the clarification of the teaching of the church for believers. But Christian thinking must also be related to unbelievers. Hence, the church must also practice eristics on the one hand, and missionary theology on the other.[34]

Eristics may also be called apologetics, but this is unfortunate if it suggests defensiveness in relation to criticism.[35] The function of eristics is

29 *Dogmatics* I, p. 38.
30 *Ibid.*, I, pp. 9–13, 93–96.
31 *Ibid.*, I, pp. 41, 83.
32 *Ibid.*, I, pp. 84, 85.
33 *Ibid.*, I, p. 79.
34 *Ibid.*, I, pp. 3, 98–103.
35 *Ibid.*, I, p. 98.

not to defend Christian faith but rather to attack the ideologies that oppose it. An important part of this attack may consist in distinguishing the faith itself from the teaching and the practice of the empirical church, both of which may be justifiably subject to criticism. But eristics makes no effort to prove the truth of Christian claims themselves. Attacks by Christian theologians such as Barth upon this whole enterprise are justified in so far as there was for a long time a tendency to regard the discussion with unbelief as a kind of prolegomenon to dogmatics itself. This is wholly inappropriate, since dogmatics is a believing thinking which in itself takes no account of unbelieving thinking. But from the perspective given in faith as articulated in dogmatics, the Christian thinker must undertake to unmask the errors of hostile beliefs. Pascal and Kierkegaard are the great examples of eristic theologians.[36]

Missionary theology is also addressed to the unbeliever from the viewpoint of faith. Its task is to make contact with the unbeliever where he actually stands with his questions and objections. Whereas eristics in its negative function attacks the errors of non-Christian views, missionary theology as the positive form of eristics attempts to remove the obstacles that interfere with the understanding and acceptance of the gospel.[37] It concerns itself with the condition of man apart from Christ, so that by illuminating that condition for the unbeliever, he may be brought to a sense of his need for Christ and to a willingness to acknowledge that need.

Having indicated something of the range of forms taken by believing reflection, we must turn to the question as to the norms by which every claim to Christian truth is to be judged. We have already seen that while rational criteria of consistency and comprehensiveness are recognized, the distinctive norm is loyalty to faith itself. But how is this loyalty to faith determined?

Systematically, the whole of Brunner's theological work rests upon his answer to questions of this sort. He is clear and emphatic that theological judgments claim to be true[38] and that this claim is warranted only by their loyalty to faith. At the same time he is equally clear and emphatic that faith is not in itself an assent to propositions.[39] Hence, the crucial question is that of the transition from faith to true theological propositions. To examine Brunner's answer to this question we must consider again his central category of the encounter as the locus in which revela-

[36] *Ibid.*, I, pp. 99–100, 103.
[37] *Ibid.*, I, p. 103.
[38] See references to n. 8.
[39] *Dogmatics* I, pp. 28, 53; III, pp. 199, 205, 218–220; ***Revelation and Reason***, pp. 9, 11.

tion occurs, faith arises, and theological knowledge becomes possible.[40]

The knowledge that arises in me when another person discloses himself to me is entirely independent of my ability to articulate what I know of that person. But some articulation is possible and even natural. The spontaneous form of that articulation will be in expressions of affection, compassion, gratitude, or loyalty. We have seen that the spontaneous response to the encounter with God is prayer. But that is not the only form that articulation can or should take. I can and should tell others about this meeting, the person whom I have met, and that which I have learned about myself and my world through this meeting.

The language that is appropriate for speaking *about* the person who has disclosed himself to me is the I-It language of reflective discourse. To this degree it will fall short of expressing the true personalness of the one who has been met. Nevertheless, it can point to that personalness with greater or lesser success. The account of the new knowledge that I have gained in this meeting can also be more or less distorted, but the intention will be to speak truth.

Here lies the key to Brunner's whole theological position. In Jesus Christ we meet God as Person, that is, God discloses himself to us as Person. If we respond in faith, we acknowledge him as Person and speak to him. In this encounter we gain knowledge of ourselves and of God, not of that sort which science seeks but the kind of knowledge we have of persons through personal relations. We can and should tell others what we have learned. To do so we will have to give up the I-Thou language of the encounter, and we will have to recognize that what we say will be more or less distorted, but the intention will be to speak truth.

Truth about a person, whether human or divine, cannot be tested in the same way as truth about things in the public world. Others may not have met that person. Even if they have met him, there may be differences in the way in which he discloses himself to them. But this does not mean that the affirmations made on the basis of that person's self-disclosure are not true affirmations about that which exists in itself quite independently of the varying opinions of men.

This analogy of theological truth about God with truth about human persons is absolutely essential to Brunner's thought.[41] Yet there are obviously special problems with which he knows that he must deal. God

[40] *The Divine-Human Encounter*, Ch. 2.

[41] This analogy is essential in spite of Brunner's emphasis on the different origins and character of our knowledge of God and of other human persons. (*Dogmatics* III, pp. 293–296.) If the uniqueness stressed in these pages is pressed too far, Brunner's whole position would have to be reconstructed.

does not simply meet us as other persons meet us, not only in the sense that our organs of vision and hearing do not come into play in the same way, but also in the sense that the encounter with God is always mediated.[42] The witness of Christian faith is that we meet God in Jesus Christ and not elsewhere.

Our meeting with Jesus Christ likewise is mediated and not direct, like our meeting with persons living with us on the earth. It is analogous, rather, to our becoming aware of persons through mutual friends or the writings of strangers. Such persons can become very important to us. They can even have a meaning for us that they do not have for those who tell us about them. But the encounter with them as persons is dependent upon the testimony of others and is fundamentally determined by the way in which these others have themselves encountered them. We must assume some fundamental trustworthiness of these witnesses if we are to suppose that they can mediate an encounter with a real person.

In our relations with Jesus Christ we are thus bound to the witness of early Christians preserved for us in the New Testament. It would seem, then, that we must first believe that the writers of the New Testament books were essentially honest and reliable witnesses before we can trust the encounter with Jesus Christ that they mediate. Roman Catholicism and Fundamentalist Protestantism have alike made much of this problem and have made the infallibility of church and Scripture respectively into the rational warrant for believing the testimony to Jesus.

Brunner refuses to follow this path. He must, therefore, affirm that the encounter with Jesus Christ is self-authenticating. Granting that it is mediated by the witness of others, Brunner teaches that we finally trust their witness because through it we have come to an encounter that is analogous with their own and that gives itself to us as real.[43]

We may perhaps conjecture that there are analogies to this experience in other mediated encounters. I may, for example, approach the dialogues of Plato and of Xenophon without any prior knowledge of Socrates or any particular interest in him. I may also have no prior convictions as to whether Plato and Xenophon are presenting a real man or a fiction. Yet, while I am reading these testimonies to Socrates, Socrates may become for me so real and vital a figure that I no longer have any doubt of his historical actuality. I may be far more challenged by him than by Plato or Xenophon, through whom I have come to know him. I may even begin to judge Plato and Xenophon in terms of what I now feel to be the in-

[42] *Revelation and Reason,* p. 148.

[43] *Dogmatics* II, pp. 241, 255. At one place Brunner specifically argues that it is revelation's disclosure of us to ourselves that authenticates it (pp. 257–259).

justices that they do to their master in their portrayals. Thus, paradoxically, they have mediated to me an encounter with a man in terms of which I then judge the adequacy of their testimony. We must now ask whether this is the fashion in which Brunner conceives of our encounter with Jesus Christ.

To some degree, at least, this analogy appears to hold. Brunner does believe that the witness of the apostles mediates an encounter with the person of Jesus that is not simply an encounter with their witness to him. He does believe that this encounter is the norm by which we judge even their witness. But this position seems to be in line with that of the now notorious nineteenth-century thinkers who sought the historical person of Jesus behind the records and criticized the records from that vantage point. Brunner is not oblivious to the dangers of this program. His justification of his own position in the face of his approval of the rejection of the nineteenth-century quest of the historical Jesus clarifies for us what he understands by the person of Jesus and our own encounter with him.

First, Brunner approves Schweitzer's exposure of the unhistorical character of the nineteenth-century quest.[44] The biographers of Jesus assumed that he was a man who fulfilled their own ideals of humanity but no more. Hence, they attempted to portray him as an understandable and admirable human being. Since the apostolic witness presents him as the Messiah who preaches the imminent consummation of God's Kingdom, they were forced to invent an almost wholly different person. Hence, in their effort to reconstruct the historical reality they used illicit imagination and projected their own ideals.

Schweitzer himself drew the conclusion, not that nothing can be known of Jesus, but that what can be known of him is precisely the messianism and apocalypticism that the nineteenth-century biographers had tried to discard. Brunner generally accepts this judgment of Schweitzer, although he regards it as extreme. He does not understand Jesus' teaching to be wholly determined by his expectation of God's future acts. Jesus' awareness of the present work of God also plays an essential role.[45] But he agrees that Jesus confronts us as a person who claims to be something more than a virtuous man, and that any attempt to find behind this person who proclaims himself, another, who is merely human, is doomed to failure.

From the form critical school, however, and culminating in the work of Bultmann, there has arisen a more radical objection to any attempt to en-

[44] *Ibid.*, II, pp. 260–263.

[45] *Ibid.*, II, pp. 262–263.

counter the person of Jesus.[46] The Gospels are understood as consisting entirely of materials made use of in the preaching and worship of the early church. This church was not interested in the person of Jesus but rather in the mighty act of God. Hence, the materials with which they provide us are unsuited to any reconstruction of the historical figure.

Brunner does not reject the form critical study of the Gospels; but he does believe that its legitimate implications have been seriously exaggerated. In the first place, the skepticism that has arisen with regard to the accuracy of our information about Jesus is only partly due to the fact that this information is given in the form that it assumed in the church's preaching. It is also due to assumptions on the part of such critics as Bultmann that the actual facts could not have been as they are reported, assumptions rooted in an already outdated understanding of the modern scientific world view.[47] In the second place, Brunner shows that even the most skeptical accounts leave us with a historical figure, and with a figure who does witness to his own person as decisive.[48] In the third place, the witness of the church to Jesus is a witness to the historical figure and hence, does mediate an encounter with him. The Christ of faith *is* the Jesus of history. The encounter with Jesus *is* the recognition of him as the Christ.[49]

In view of all this, the hypercritical doctrine that we know too little of Jesus as person to encounter him as such must be rejected. The analogy of this encounter with other mediated encounters with historical figures can be retained. However, Brunner distinguishes the encounter with Jesus from other such encounters in two important ways. First, the one we meet in the apostolic witness to Jesus Christ is one who confronts us with divine authority.[50] Second, the acknowledgment of that authority, which is of the essence of the meeting, is given to us in the present act of God in the form of the Holy Spirit.[51] Ours is not, therefore, an intuitive act of reconstructing a personality from fragmentary witnesses. Ours is a confrontation with divine reality to which we receive immediate divine testimony. Hence, the relativity of personal opinions is radically transcended.

46 *Ibid.*, II, pp. 242–243, 263–270; III, pp. 246–250, 388–391.
47 *Ibid.*, II, pp. 190–191, 269–270; III, p. 248.
48 *Ibid.*, I, p. 211; II, pp. 242–243, 247, 249, 328.
49 *Ibid.*, II, pp. 240–241, 244, 327; III, pp. 209–211, 216–218.
50 *Ibid.*, II, pp. 325–326.
51 *Ibid.*, I, pp. 29 ff.; III, p. 29; *Revelation and Reason*, pp. 169 ff.; *Man in Revolt*, p. 67. Brunner understands that the work of the Holy Spirit is not strictly limited to this testimony, but he does not discuss his other work extensively. See *Dogmatics* I, p. 31; III, pp. 29–30.

Although in this way the authority of the present witness of the Holy Spirit is decisive, theology does not appeal to that authority. The Holy Spirit makes possible the response of faith to Jesus Christ as he is mediated to us in the witness of the early Christian community. He does not give us additional information about Jesus or about ourselves. He is the presupposition of theology but not the norm of theology.

The norm of theology is determined by its task. Its task is to tell the truth about God as he has revealed himself in Jesus Christ. Since faith is the acknowledgment of this revelation, it is the starting point and goal of theology, but it is not as such the primary subject of theology. Theology deals with God and his self-manifestation first, and only secondarily with the human response to that act. Theology is the accurate account of what God reveals to man in his self-disclosure in Jesus Christ.

This does not mean that the theologian simply reflects upon God's revelation as he has personally experienced it and ignores the testimony of others. On the contrary, he can serve the church only when he takes seriously the whole story of how it has witnessed and formulated its understanding of revelation.[52] The theologian must take the confessions of his own communion with special seriousness. Finally, he must acknowledge the privileged position of the apostles and the importance of the fact that his own encounter with Jesus Christ is mediated through theirs.[53]

This last fact is the basis for the correct Christian doctrine of the authority of Scripture. This authority lies primarily in the apostolic witness to Jesus Christ. This witness is absolutely necessary to our faith, because apart from it we could not have heard the gospel at all. Its particular form has relative authority as well, because despite its mediation through the human thought and experience of the apostles, it must be recognized that they shared in the revelatory events themselves in a way that later generations have not. This means that we must pay profound attention to the way in which the apostolic witness is formulated and test our own teaching against it. It does not mean that all the opinions of the apostles are beyond criticism. They share in the world view of their time, and their testimonies are not in perfect harmony with one another.[54]

It is time to summarize the distinctive third way of Brunner, by which he avoids the Scylla of liberalism and the Charybdis of orthodoxy. On the one hand, the subject of theology is God in his supernatural self-disclosure to man in Jesus Christ, testified to us by the apostles and guaranteed by the present witness of the Holy Spirit. On the other hand, every proposi-

[52] *Dogmatics* I, pp. 19–20, 50–59.
[53] *Ibid.,* I, pp. 45–47, 80–81; *Revelation and Reason,* p. 124.
[54] *Dogmatics* I, p. 46.

tional formulation of the truth that is disclosed, even that through which we come to the meeting with God in Christ, is subject to human error and must be tested against the revelation itself. That these two views can be held together depends upon the concept of encounter with God as communicating a preverbal understanding that is nevertheless susceptible of rational articulation.

We are now ready to see how Brunner applies these principles in the formulation of some aspects of his doctrine of God. What does God disclose to us of himself in his revelation in Jesus Christ?

First of all, God discloses himself to man as Person.[55] This fact can hardly be overemphasized in our understanding of Brunner. It is the central point in terms of which all other doctrines about God are formulated. Non-Christian doctrines of God may declare him holy, omnipotent, omniscient, omnipresent, and glorious; but all these terms mean something entirely different because they are applied to a universal principle, a metaphysical entity, an immanent process, or a primal cause.[56] Unbelieving reason, furthermore, constantly attacks this Christian Personalism as anthropomorphic and irrational. All too often, theologians have compromised with these criticisms and have tried to identify the Christian God with the God of some philosophy. But in Jesus Christ, God discloses himself to us as a Living Person. Any theological doctrine that is unfaithful to this primary Christian fact is to that degree unchristian.

Brunner's stanch adherence to Personalism in spite of what he takes to be philosophical unanimity against it does not involve him in irrationalism. On the contrary, he does not see any legitimate philosophical argument against the Christian view.[57] The philosopher's rejection shows only the inadequacy of reason that is not in the service of faith. This inadequacy is based on pride and self-defense.[58] Since reason is competent to derive only principles, essences, and causes to account for what is empirically given, it wishes to restrict the area of belief to these abstractions. It is unwilling to acknowledge finitude before the Living God.

But if we begin with faith in the Living God, we may talk quite intelligibly about his relations with the world. We may even relate our discussion to the various conclusions of philosophical investigation. Especially, we may show from the perspective of Christian Personalism the errors in both deism and pantheism which have so often seemed, mistakenly, to constitute the decisive alternatives for thinking about God. Faith under-

[55] *Ibid.*, I, pp. 61, 121–124, 139–141; *Revelation and Reason,* pp. 43–44.
[56] *Dogmatics* I, pp. 143–147.
[57] *Ibid.*, I, pp. 139–141.
[58] *Ibid.*, I, pp. 126, 156; *Revelation and Reason,* pp. 66, 73.

stands that the Absolute Person, God, wholly transcends the world, but that he also constantly gives himself to and in the world. From this perspective we may criticize many of the greatest theologians of the church, including the Reformers.

For example, both Zwingli and Calvin, among others, were deceived by the proper idea of God's absolute Lordship and power into formulating doctrines of God's causal efficacy for all that occurs in the world.[59] Since man must be purely receptive in his relation to God's personal self-disclosure, they argued that faith must be simply the effect of God's causal action. Thereby they left the revealed context of understanding the relation of God and man in terms of personal encounter and unknowingly introduced alien categories. The results were disastrous. If God is the cause of faith in this deterministic sense, human responsibility ceases. The way is open to the doctrine of double predestination, with all its horrible implications for the understanding of God, which are so contrary to the Biblical witness to his love.[60]

If in contrast we understand God's disclosure of himself as personal, then we understand that our response must also be personal. In personal relations the category of cause as it is employed in the objective sphere is simply inapplicable. There is an initiative and a response to which the concepts of determinacy and indeterminacy are alike inappropriate. When God encounters us as Person, we in our total being are freed for faith, but we are not compelled. God desires, but does not force, our acceptance of himself.[61]

The second major truth about God that is given in his self-disclosure is his agape-love.[62] His manifesting of himself to us in the encounter is an act of pure love, which we have done nothing to merit. Jesus embodies this pure love of God in his relations to men, culminating in the cross. It is precisely as love that God reveals himself to us in Christ.

But we cannot deduce from God's infinite love that all men will receive the benefits of that love.[63] To do so is again to misunderstand the personal

[59] *Dogmatics* I, pp. 315–317, 345; II, pp. 154, 172–175; *Man in Revolt,* p. 541.

[60] *Dogmatics* III, p. 465.

[61] Although I believe this way of stating matters is faithful to the spirit of most of Brunner's writings, it should be said that in his latest statement Brunner sounds much more like Bultmann. From personal relations the emphasis shifts to the existential situation. The question of the fate of unbelievers is rejected except as it is the question of my response to God's judgment upon me. (*Ibid.,* III, pp. 472–474.) I have ignored this in the text because it would raise far more difficulties than it would solve, and if taken as the clue to his position as a whole, it would require reconstruction of his whole system.

[62] *Dogmatics* I, pp. 183–199.

[63] *Ibid.,* I, pp. 348–353; III, p. 468.

relation of God to man. It is to think again of God's love as a cause operating upon man as an effect. Once we accept that image we must choose between the terrible decree of double predestination on the one hand and universal salvation on the other. In the light of the love of God, we would have to choose the latter. But the premise is wrong.

God offers himself for all men in Jesus Christ. In this we know his love for all men. But he offers himself to men in such a way as to make them personally responsible. This responsibility must be taken with utmost seriousness, so that the possibility of man's rejecting God's gift must not be ruled out. God's love is not contradictory to his wrath when we understand his wrath as his rejection of man's rejection of him.[64]

In the third place, God meets us in his revelation as our Lord.[65] This means, first of all, that we apprehend him as one who actually exercises sovereignty over us. It means also that we meet him as one who claims our willing, grateful obedience to his will.[66] Once again, it is only as we hold fast to the understanding of God as Person that this duality can be understood and maintained.

The understanding of God as creator arises from this meeting with God in Jesus Christ as Lord.[67] Even in the history of Israel, God was acknowledged as Lord first, then as creator of heaven and earth. The Christian belief that God is creator does not follow from the acceptance as authoritative of the first chapters of Genesis. Whatever wisdom these contain, they must be recognized as mythical in form and content. We know God as creator of all that is because we know him in Jesus Christ as sovereign Lord.

In the order of knowledge, therefore, we know God as our personal redeemer in Jesus Christ before we know him as the creator of heaven and earth. In the order of being, however, we must recognize that he was creator of heaven and earth before he manifested himself in Jesus Christ.[68] This means also that he stands in the relation of creator even to those who do not acknowledge his revelation in Jesus Christ. For this reason, the Christian understands a great deal about the unbeliever that the unbeliever cannot understand about himself.[69]

The believer understands, for example, that God is visible in his creation and that the failure of the unbeliever to recognize him there is due to a rebellious refusal rather than to an objective impossibility.[70] The believer sees in the unbeliever's understanding of himself and his world a per-

64 *Ibid.*, I, p. 337.
65 *Ibid.*, I, pp. 137–150.
66 *Ibid.*, I, p. 147.
67 *Ibid.*, I, p. 148; II, pp. 8–9, 52–53.
68 *Ibid.*, II, p. 9.
69 *Ibid.*, II, pp. 46–47.
70 *Ibid.*, I, pp. 132–136.

verted misunderstanding of the revelation that God makes of himself in his whole creation.[71] The Christian may then describe what is objectively visible even apart from Christ, although he must always recognize that he himself sees it only because of the encounter with God in Jesus Christ.

At one time Brunner spoke of this knowledge as a Christian natural theology.[72] It is a natural theology in that it shows the knowledge of God that is available in abstraction from Christ. It is a Christian natural theology in that it can be formulated only by one whose eyes have been opened by Christ.

So vehement was the objection to the positive use of the expression "natural theology," especially by Barth, that Brunner retracted the term and apologized for the confusion he had caused by introducing it.[73] He did not, however, withdraw the idea that the term expressed. It should, he agreed, be called simply "the Christian doctrine of creation." However, it continues to have a function as a point of contact with unbelievers.

This function is the responsibility of eristics and of missionary theology. These disciplines deal with the same data as are available to non-Christians, but show the inadequacies in the non-Christian interpretation of the data.[74] They do this from the perspective of Christian revelation, but they present their truth in terms of its intrinsic adequacy to the shared data.

Barth opposed the idea of the point of contact just as vehemently as the idea of natural theology. Even here, Brunner recognized that there was truth in Barth's position. A point of contact sounds like some positive element in the belief of non-Christians on the basis of which they may be led rationally to accept Christian faith. But this is not what Brunner means.

Brunner's point of contact lies first in the common data of all men, man's total being in his environment. It does not lie in the interpretations that unbelievers place upon this data. All their interpretations are perverted by their unbelief. Hence, there can be no point of contact in the sense of common beliefs shared by faith and unbelief. The search for this kind of point of contact is erroneous and, as Barth has seen, has led to results that dilute and endanger the substance of the faith.

But man's real situation, however falsely he interprets it, does have

[71] *Ibid.*, II, p. 23; *Revelation and Reason*, pp. 66, 73; *Man in Revolt*, p. 530.

[72] Brunner, "Nature and Grace," Chs. IV and V, *Natural Theology*, Baillie, ed., pp. 35–60.

[73] *Dogmatics* I, p. 132; *Man in Revolt*, pp. 527.

[74] *Dogmatics* I, p. 103; II, pp. 70–72; *Revelation and Reason*, pp. 425–426. Brunner has recently avoided the use of the expression "point of contact," but it still expresses his meaning.

some bearing upon his thinking and believing. Although he cannot acknowledge if for what it is, he does have some capacity to recognize the truth of the Christian interpretation when it is proclaimed to him. Man is guilty for his refusal to see himself as he really is before God. This guilt, and man's capacity for recognizing the truth of the Christian gospel when it is proclaimed to him, constitute the point of contact. It is through this point of contact that man can be led to recognize the desperateness of his plight and to be willing to accept God's grace.

If we deny a point of contact in this sense, we make mockery of man's responsible humanity. Then God's act in revealing himself is no longer an encounter between the divine Person and the human person, but an act worked upon a purely passive entity that might equally well be a dog or a stone. Man's capacity to respond to revelation is given only with revelation, but man's capacity to hear, to acknowledge, and to reject truth is part of his nature as man.[75] This much man brings with him to his encounter with God in Jesus Christ.

The affirmation that faith has an understanding of man and his world, even in abstraction from Christ, that is lacking in the unbeliever opens up vast fields for Christian reflection. The believer's interpretation of the findings of historiography, science, and common sense must take full account of the data and of the logical requirements placed upon all thinking.[76] No interpretation of data can be put forward as Christian on the authority of Biblical statements as such or on the authority of the empirical church. Interpretations can be put forward only as they bring the light of God's self-disclosure to bear upon the particulars of God's creation.

The relevance of revelation to the interpretation of data is on a graded scale.[77] At one extreme, in mathematics and the more technical aspects of the natural sciences, the relevance is very slight indeed. At the other extreme, where man is trying to understand his own existence, the relevance is very great. Hence, it is as we approach the center of man's personal being that the conflict of Christian belief with unbelieving distortions becomes most critical. In order to carry out this discussion with the unbelieving world, the Christian must be fully conversant with the status of the sciences in each field. He must know what their legitimate autonomous provinces are, so as not to intrude his own judgments illegitimately. He must not ally himself too closely with particular scientific views just because they seem more congenial with his own vision. But at the same time he must be willing to enter the discussion both as one who honestly in-

[75] *Revelation and Reason,* p. 65; *Dogmatics* I, pp. 338–339.
[76] *Dogmatics* II, pp. 46–47, 87, 151.
[77] *Ibid.,* II, p. 27; *Revelation and Reason,* pp. 383, 429.

quires and as one who has decisive light to throw upon the ultimate interpretation.

Even when Brunner is discussing the breakdown of the Newtonian world view or the importance of depth psychology, we must recognize that his thought is Christocentric. So long as he operates as theologian at all, whether his work is dogmatic or eristic, it all depends upon and serves God's revelation of himself in Jesus Christ.[78] Hence, the act of God with which the theologian must be especially concerned is that act of revelation itself.

This does not mean that theology must begin with a doctrine of Christ. Brunner actually turns to this topic only in the latter section of Vol. II of his *Dogmatics*. In Jesus Christ it is God who reveals himself. Hence, we may speak of the God who is revealed as he is revealed without explicitly dealing with the channel of revelation. We may even talk about God's self-revelation in creation before we settle the questions of Christology. But Jesus Christ remains the basis of our faith, in relationship to whom all else is judged.

Brunner distinguishes the work and the person of Jesus and treats them in that order. This is proper because it is from Jesus' work that the early Christians moved on to the questions about his person.[79] It was because of what he did for them that they proceeded to define who he was. If we reverse this order, we are likely to obscure through a deductive process the vitality of the personal encounter through which faith arises.

The work of Jesus may be distinguished in the traditional way according to his prophetic, priestly, and kingly offices. The prophetic office consists in the proclamation of the Kingdom of God, with its demand of radical obedience in love and its offer of the forgiveness of God.[80] The priestly office is the ministry to sinners, which culminates in his reconciling death upon the cross.[81] The royal office consists in his actual victory over the powers of evil in his inauguration of the Kingdom itself.[82] The three offices may be summed up as revelation, atonement, and kingship, and these in turn may be understood as three mutually related aspects of one work, in which each includes the others.[83]

This can best be understood when we realize that in each of these three offices Jesus points to his own person.[84] He differs from the prophets in that they proclaim the Word given them by God, whereas he offers himself as the Word of revelation in his own person. His work of reconciliation is consummated only in his self-offering on the cross. His kingship

[78] *Dogmatics* II, pp. 239–240.
[79] *Ibid.,* II, pp. 271–273, 322.
[80] *Ibid.,* II, pp. 275–281.
[81] *Ibid.,* II, pp. 281–297.
[82] *Ibid.,* II, pp. 298–305.
[83] *Ibid.,* II, p. 305.
[84] *Ibid.,* II, p. 274.

is embodied in his own personal claim for obedience and love. Thus in every direction Jesus' work is his person.

The ultimate identity of Jesus' work and his person returns us to the central characteristic of Brunner's theology. That which God has done for the world is to reveal himself personally. We may distinguish aspects of this one work of self-manifestation, but we cannot think of some other work of God for us that is not this one, all-decisive self-disclosure. We cannot, for example, discuss God's work in regeneration and sanctification as something other than his work in revealing himself. Revelation is the all-inclusive category for God's saving work; this work always takes place in the self-disclosure of personal encounter; and this encounter never occurs except through the person of Jesus Christ.[85]

This means that the doctrine of Jesus' person is not less important to us than it was to the early church. Since Jesus points us constantly to himself we cannot finally, but only provisionally, distinguish his work from his person. Furthermore, we must recognize that by his work he points to himself in such a way that we cannot simply regard him as man. The authority by which he fulfilled his work in his person must be divine authority. In some sense God must be present in Jesus.[86]

Brunner recognizes that the Bible does not explicitly settle for us the many questions that arise as to the mode of God's presence in Jesus. The whole apostolic witness does make clear, however, that in Jesus the man we encounter God. It is precisely to this encounter with God in Jesus that the Holy Spirit testifies in the immediacy of present experience. Hence, for Christians there can be no question that Jesus is in some sense God; there can only be questions as to how he is God.

Brunner considers systematically and historically the options that have been tried and concludes with the church that no statement is satisfactory that does not affirm both Jesus' full manhood and his full deity.[87] He does not claim that this affirmation can be made fully intelligible. He simply affirms that making this affirmation is the only way of remaining loyal to the revelatory encounter itself. Such loyalty is ultimately more important than clarity and consistency, although these latter are not to be despised.[88]

Brunner leaves us thus with a mystery. However, we should not understand this as an expression of a love of paradox and mystery on his part. He leaves us with a mystery because he has not been able to achieve greater clarity, not because an inherent value attaches to mystery. He is glad to go as far as he can to make sense of this mystery. The task of reflection is to prevent misconceptions of the faith and to answer as many

[85] *Ibid.*, II, pp. 305–306.
[86] *Ibid.*, II, p. 343.
[87] *Ibid.*, II, p. 359.
[88] *Ibid.*, II, pp. 349–350.

honest questions as it can. It is also the task of reflection to acknowledge its own limits as it encounters them.

◈ ◈

We have surveyed only a fraction of the topics treated by Brunner. However, we may hope that these samples illustrate his method fairly and give sufficient indication of the kind of theological position in which it is articulated. It is time now to raise critical questions.

It is *not* the intention of any criticisms in this volume to debate such questions as whether the supernatural events referred to by a theologian in fact took place. In this case, therefore, we do not ask whether in fact Jesus was both God and man or whether the Holy Spirit does assure us that in him we meet God. On the other hand, we do not ask whether Brunner is right or wrong in denying the absolute authority of the written word in Scripture and creed. Our questions are solely those of internal criticism. Granting Brunner's central convictions, do his conclusions follow? Are there other consequences that he has not so clearly drawn that cast a different light upon the situation?

We will consider first the question as to how Brunner relates reason and revelation and, specifically, philosophy and theology. He has written extensively on this topic, but important ambiguities remain.

Brunner allows to reason unaided by revelation in Jesus Christ the capacity to work out formal relations in logic and mathematics, to assemble empirical data, and to construct and verify scientific hypotheses. However, such reason goes astray when it attempts to interpret its findings to the degree that these impinge upon matters of specifically human concern. He denies to such reason any competence whatsoever with respect to the knowledge of God.[89]

Brunner teaches that reason liberated by revelation can interpret findings of the sciences more critically and more realistically.[90] Hence, he affirms that there is such a thing as Christian philosophy, which is better as philosophy than non-Christian philosophy and constitutes a proper exercise of Christian thinking. This Christian philosophy seems to be almost identical with the Christian doctrine of creation, which is a branch of theology.

The question is whether Christian philosophy is also competent to deal with the doctrine of God. On this point Brunner can be quoted both ways. On the one hand, he asserts repeatedly and vehemently that all knowledge of God is given in the revelation encounter with Jesus Christ. He explicitly

[89] *Revelation and Reason*, p. 383. [90] *Ibid.*, p. 393.

rejects the principle of *credo ut intelligam* on the grounds of the fundamental contradiction between revelation and reason.[91] He protests warmly against any alliance of theology with philosophy.[92]

On the other hand, he teaches that there is a real analogy of being in creation that can be perceived by the eyes of faith.[93] He recognizes the cosmological and teleological arguments for the existence of God, which are part of Christian philosophy, as rational forms of the Christian doctrine of God.[94] These teachings seem to imply that the Christian knows God not only in Christ but also in creation. Therefore, reason informed by faith *is* a source of knowledge about God.

I do not believe that these two emphases of Brunner are mutually compatible. If reason, even when informed by faith, cannot proceed from creation to God, then Brunner should not defend the analogy of being or treat philosophical arguments for God as a legitimate part of Christian philosophy. He would have to take the position that even to Christian eyes creation allows no inference whatsoever with regard to the creator. If he does allow that Christian reason can perceive evidence of the creator in his creation, he must acknowledge that this does provide a second basis for thinking about God alongside his revelation in Christ. He can consistently insist that this possibility exists only on the basis of the revelation in Christ, but he cannot reasonably deny it altogether.

There is a second closely related but distinguishable question on which Brunner's statements are equally confusing. Distinct from the question of *how* we arrive at an idea of God is the question of the form of the idea itself. Can the Christian idea of God be philosophically formulated? Brunner seems to say that it cannot, but his arguments are far from clear.

Personalistic theism, Brunner recognizes, is that philosophy which most closely approximates the Christian understanding of God. However, he denies that the idea of a personal God which it espouses is the personal God himself.[95] On this basis he reiterates his objection to identifying the revealed God with the God of any philosophy at all, even the most Christian philosophy.

This argument, however, is far from decisive. There is, of course, no identity of any idea of God with God himself. But this is true of the reflective theological ideas of God as well as philosophical ones. Theology also shifts from the language of I-Thou to that of I-It. Hence, this non-

[91] *Ibid.*, p. 17.
[92] *Dogmatics* I, pp. 135–136, 154–155.
[93] *Ibid.*, I, p. 176; II, pp. 42–45; *Revelation and Reason*, p. 80.
[94] *Revelation and Reason*, pp. 343, 347–348.
[95] *Dogmatics* I, pp. 122, 155.

identity is no special objection to a philosophical idea. The question must be rather that of the relation of the philosophical idea to the theological idea.

Presumably, these two ideas will not coincide. One is articulated in relation to considerations of a general character, and the other arises in a particular encounter. But nonidentity is no objection to integration unless there are inescapable incompatibilities between the two ideas. Certainly in other spheres of experience, such as our knowledge of other persons, both general considerations and the individual encounter come into play. They may at times be in some tension with each other, but they cannot be held radically apart.[96] The issue is really the factual one as to the possibility of articulating philosophically a conception of God with which our encounter-knowledge is compatible.

Sometimes Brunner seems to argue that in the case of God there can in principle never be any compatibility between our encounter-knowledge and any other thinking about him. All human thinking, including that based upon our experience of other persons, and including the idea of transcendence itself, falls within the circle of immanence.[97] Only God's self-disclosure breaks through that circle. Hence, all human thinking is irrelevant to God.

We are not here questioning this account of the situation in so far as human thinking is understood as thinking unenlightened by revelation. However, Brunner does not regard the Christian theological doctrine of God as interdicted by this limitation of the competence of reason. Hence, he is not excluding all thinking that is informed by faith from relevance to God. The line seems to be drawn between Christian theology and Christian philosophy. But on what basis is it drawn?

Christian theology in its reflection on God as revealed in Jesus Christ does not limit itself to the language of prayer or Scripture. On the contrary, it makes considerable use of philosophical language, at least in Brunner's own formulations.[98] How, then, can the relevance of philosophi-

[96] Sometimes Brunner speaks as if there were a chasm between all personalistic thinking and all rational thinking, which must deal with abstractions only. If we then understood philosophy as committed to rational thinking, we could see its necessary irrelevance to considerations of both the human person and the divine Person. However, Brunner acknowledges that reason may talk about persons at both levels. See *Revelation and Reason,* p. 365. He concludes from his survey of the scientific study of man that subjective understanding plays an increasing role there. See *Dogmatics* III, pp. 287–289. Hence, I have ignored this line of argument in the body of the text.

[97] *Revelation and Reason,* pp. 365–367; *Dogmatics* III, p. 295.

[98] *Revelation and Reason,* p. 375; *Man in Revolt,* p. 243.

cally formulated ideas about God be denied in principle when theology lacks any clearly distinct categories?

Brunner actually does not argue the issue primarily along these lines. Instead, he criticizes from the perspective of Christian revelation those ideas of God at which philosophy, including Christian philosophy, has arrived. He finds all philosophical ideas of God resistant to the Biblical understanding of a God who acts selectively in history. He mentions panentheism as a philosophy which, like Christian theology, avoids the errors of pantheism and deism, but dismisses it as an expression of the Christian view because it is not sufficiently dynamic.[99] Perhaps he is correct in these and similar judgments, but he has not shown anything intrinsic to the nature of philosophy that would prevent a Christian philosophy from allowing for God's selective activity or from formulating a more dynamic version of panentheism.

Brunner's total position could be made much clearer and more consistent if he abandoned his strictures on philosophy as such and limited himself to distinguishing sharply between all thinking that is informed by faith and all thinking that is not informed by faith. He could then recognize without the present ambiguity that Christian theology and Christian philosophy are distinguished by their focus on the particular and on the universal, but that no sharp line can be drawn between them. The Christian philosopher cannot as a philosopher speak of the unique act of God in Jesus Christ, just as he can say nothing of particular events in any area, but he can and should so structure his ideas as to allow for such unique acts and particular events. The theologian cannot as a theologian enter upon detailed discussions of the interpretation of the modern scientific world view and its relevance for theological assertions, but he can and should show the need for such discussions and their significance for his own work. The task of showing the interrelations of all the areas of thought is the philosopher's task.[100]

The greater part of Brunner's statements can be understood in these terms. If he should give up those other statements in which he tries to circumscribe the competence of Christian philosophy more narrowly, the content of his doctrines would be affected very little. However, his influence, which has hitherto tended to weigh against rigorous philosophical study on the part of theologians, would instead work for such study. By retaining the unequivocal affirmation of the priority of faith over reason, while giving free rein to the work of reason guided by faith, Brunner's

[99] *Dogmatics* I, p. 175. [100] *Revelation and Reason,* p. 395.

position would become that of what I have called Augustinianism in the preceding chapter. But the actual shift involved would be quite minor.

If we are to raise really basic questions about Brunner's position, we must direct our attention to his understanding of revelation in encounter as the basis for all theological reflection. The decisive principle of Brunner's whole theology is that we encounter God in Jesus Christ in such a way as to gain knowledge about God, the world, and ourselves. If the encounter does not eventuate in new knowledge, it is clear that, in Brunner's view, theology could not take place. If the encounter with God occurred apart from Jesus' essential mediation, it is clear that the theology that would result would not be Christian in Brunner's sense. If the encounter with Jesus were simply an encounter with a historical figure, however great a religious genius or prophet, it would give us new knowledge of Jesus, but it could not give us, in Brunner's terms, new knowledge of God.

Let us begin by granting to Brunner his basic contention that an encounter with a person has cognitive consequences that can be reflectively articulated. At least in direct personal encounters such knowledge is gained. In mediated encounters this is much less clear, for the new knowledge seems to be learned through the mediating reports rather than from the one mediated. Yet there does seem to be a sense in which the person witnessed to can come alive for us and encounter us as something more than the sum of the propositions about that person which we have read and heard. Hence, let us grant that something may also be learned in such an encounter.

However, we must ask of Brunner, what person is encountered through the mediation of the apostolic witness. Is it God or Jesus? Of course, Brunner must regard this as a misleading question in so far as it implies that Jesus is not God. Yet he too recognizes some distinction between God and Jesus. God's personhood antedated the coming of Jesus and cannot be simply identified with Jesus as person.[101]

If, then, we insist upon our question as to which person is encountered, initially the answer must be that it is Jesus.[102] It is Jesus who is mediated to us through the apostolic witness, and apart from him Brunner insists that there is no personal encounter with God. What Brunner affirms is that when we encounter Jesus aright we also and at the same time encounter God.

Now this can be understood in two ways. First, we might suppose that the encounter with the person Jesus "triggers" another encounter, namely, one with God. We might say that Jesus directs our attention to

[101] *Dogmatics* I, pp. 229–231; II, p. 360. [102] *Ibid.*, I, pp. 35, 37, 124; II, p. 322.

God, or that he is transparent to God, or that we can come to share his own vision of God. But Brunner emphatically rejects these views. Jesus does not point us to God; he in his own person reveals God. When Jesus says "I," it is God who says "I."[103] We must take Brunner's affirmations here seriously.

Brunner asserts the second alternative, namely, that the encounter with Jesus *is* the encounter with the Person, God. That this is a mystery he certainly acknowledges; so it would be foolish to press for full clarification. But we must note again the ambiguity that arises by virtue of the acknowledged fact that there is no simple identity of Jesus and God. Jesus prays to his Father, and Brunner does not suppose he is simply praying to himself. God is really present in the person Jesus, but not in such a way as to be simply identical with him.

This point is too self-evident to require emphasis. The church has never identified God with Jesus in such a way as to raise questions about the continuance of God's functions of sustaining the creation independently of Jesus. Even God the Son, when conceived as the Logos, continues to fulfill his eternal functions in some autonomy of the events in Palestine.

However, it is necessary to stress this simple and obvious fact in order to point to the acute and crucial difficulty in Brunner's whole theological system. He claims that knowledge is given with revelation and that that knowledge is about him who reveals himself. By this he means and must mean God as he eternally is. Furthermore, absolutely central to all that Brunner affirms about God on the basis of revelation is that God is Person. What are the grounds of this affirmation?

If we followed the first alternative indicated above, there would be no difficulty here. Jesus certainly understood God as Person; so if we were looking with him toward his Father, we, too, would see God as Person. But Brunner has rejected this view. If, on the other hand, we could simply identify Jesus and God, then it would be clear that God is Person because it is a person that we encounter when we encounter Jesus. But Brunner certainly does not mean this. He wants to say that when we encounter the person Jesus we thereby encounter, also as Person, God, who is not simply identical with Jesus. But he gives us no basis for his view that it is *as Person* that God is present in the person Jesus.

I am not here objecting to the mystery of the two natures of Jesus. The problem here is with persons — and persons in the full modern sense that is Brunner's intention. It is hardly intelligible to say that there are in this sense two persons in Jesus who are simultaneously encountered. We may

[103] *Ibid.*, I, pp. 227–228.

say with orthodoxy that in encountering the person of Jesus we encounter also his nature as deity, but then we have no basis for affirming God as Person. We may believe that God is Person, but we must do so on other grounds, such as the authority of Jesus' teaching, direct personal experience, or rational probability.

Brunner can, of course, save his doctrine of God by appealing to the teaching of Jesus or to the Old Testament prophets. The point here is only that he cannot in fact derive his doctrine of God as Person in the manner in which he claims to derive it, namely, from God's self-revelation in personal encounter. This could be done only by affirming a direct encounter by men with God as Person. But Brunner regards any talk of experiencing God apart from Christ as unchristian.[104]

The same must be said a fortiori of Brunner's discussion of creation. This is undoubtedly a Biblical doctrine playing a role in both the Old and the New Testaments. But we cannot really derive this doctrine from the personal encounter with God in Jesus Christ. The person Jesus does not disclose himself to us as the Creator of heaven and earth. It is true that he refers us to the Father in terms of this sort, but Brunner's method ostensibly is not that of systematizing the teachings of Jesus. Jesus may be said to encounter us as one who claims Lordship over us, but the Lordship that he claims does not directly imply anything about creation. Brunner appeals explicitly to the prologue of John and to certain sayings of Paul, but surely one who is as emphatic as he in rejecting the authority of Scriptural teachings as such does not mean to say that we accept the doctrine of creation because of the presence of these passages in the New Testament.

The plain fact seems to be that both the Personhood of God and the doctrine of God's creation of heaven and earth were accepted by the authors of the New Testament with little question because they were already accepted in Judaism.[105] The disciples of Jesus did not first come to believe these things in their encounter with him. They brought these ideas to that encounter. Their beliefs were probably reinforced by Jesus' belief, and we may suppose that Jesus' personal experience of God gave to his teaching on these matters an authority partly independent of his inherited tradition. But even today Jews continue to believe in the personal Creator quite apart from any encounter with Jesus Christ. Indeed, it is

[104] *Ibid.*, III, pp. 20–21, 31–32.

[105] Brunner, of course, is fully aware that Judaism knew God as Person. (*Revelation and Reason,* pp. 89, 92.) But he says that God was not personally present before Jesus. (*Ibid.*, p. 93.) This seems to reinforce the view that his personal presence was not the historical basis for believing him to be Person.

somewhat ironical that Brunner's own formulations are deeply indebted to a Jewish philosopher, Martin Buber.

If Brunner will agree that factually the doctrines of God as Person and as Creator antedated Jesus in the Jewish community, he may still wish to argue that for us the encounter with God in Jesus is the only ground for affirming them. If so, I can only conclude that the grounds are confusing and shaky. Furthermore, they are not the grounds on which these doctrines have historically been affirmed by the church.

In actual fact, does it not seem more likely that Christians bring to the interpretation of the encounter with Jesus some understanding of God? This understanding may not at all depend upon secular philosophy or culture. It may be formed in the Judaeo-Christian community through the whole corpus of the Biblical writing; or it may be dependent specifically upon the teaching of Jesus or Paul. Once given this preconception, we may certainly understand how the awareness of the presence of God in Jesus is the awareness of the presence of the personal creator-God. From this point on, we might follow Brunner's presentation with little alteration.

But this would mean that Brunner must acknowledge that there is a decisive preconception with which the encounter is entered. This preconception may owe nothing to philosophy. It may be wholly dependent on the previous encounters of others with God. But if we trace these encounters to their source, we must in all honesty go beyond Jesus to the Jewish prophets. The authority for the view of God as personal creator seems to lie in the total experience of Israel with its Lord rather than in the specific encounters of Christians with God in Christ.

If so, we must raise questions about Brunner's radical Christocentricity. Israel's experience must also include a revelation that is presupposed by that in Jesus Christ. Some of our knowledge of God seems to arise through that earlier revelation. If that revelation can be assigned no independent authority for us, then we must see this aspect of our knowledge of God in all its conditioned relativity. But we are dishonest if we attempt to found it upon the one encounter with God in Jesus Christ. The whole history of Christian theology makes it clear that those who come to Christ with other preconceptions about God are able to understand their encounter with him apart from any implication that God is Person in the modern sense.

Like many of those who seek the moderation of the middle way, Brunner is forced to incorporate a profound tension within his own system. He wishes both to make the single encounter with God in Jesus Christ all-determinative for Christian thought and to keep within that thought the full richness of traditional theology which has fed on the more extensive sources of reason and Scriptural authority. Hence, he is driven to attribute to this one relationship of encounter cognitive consequences that it factually has not had. If he accepts other norms besides this, then he must return to some identification of revealed propositional truth, admit some other encounter with God than that which occurs in Jesus Christ, or allow authority to the conclusions of philosophical speculation. If he takes seriously his limitation of the source and norm of Christian thought to God's self-disclosure in the encounter with Jesus Christ, then he must restrict the corpus of theology to a discussion of Jesus as Person and of what happens to man when faith is awakened in him by the encounter. If he follows the former course, he must accept the typical consequences as they are expressed in orthodox and liberal theologies. If he follows the latter course, he must limit theology almost entirely to an account of the life of Christian faith.

Karl Barth early sensed the precariousness of Brunner's position and dissociated himself from it as sharply as possible. In the next chapter we will consider whether Barth has succeeded in maintaining the radical Christocentricity of theology on the one hand while avoiding its restriction to anthropology on the other.

7: Karl Barth

BARTH'S THEOLOGICAL IMPORTANCE FOR OUR GENERATION IS SO GREAT, AND the sheer volume of his writings is so vast, that I am more conscious here than anywhere else in this volume of the presumptuousness of my undertaking. Furthermore, Barth needs to be understood in terms of the development of his thought more than most of the men treated. Through it all lies a profound consistency, and he himself sees his latest work as the fulfillment of intentions already expressed in 1919.[1] Nevertheless, with regard to questions crucial to this study, Barth would have to be presented quite differently in his different periods.[2]

Barth notes that it was in the middle part of the second decade of our century that he reacted sharply against his liberal teachers.[3] This revolt found vigorous expression in the two editions of *The Epistle to the Romans* of 1919 and 1922.[4] It was especially in the second of these editions that the existentialism of Kierkegaard became a decisive factor in his thought.

T. F. Torrance sees the first of these editions as still within the categories of the liberalism against which Barth was revolting.[5] From this point of view we might identify a critical liberalism as a first stage of Barth's public career and consider the second edition as the inauguration of a second stage of clear rejection of liberalism under the influence of Kierkegaard. For this period, extending through the twenties, the Kierke-

[1] Gerrit Cornelis Berkouwer, *The Triumph of Grace in the Theology of Karl Barth,* pp. 37, 43.

[2] For an account of Barth's three periods see T. F. Torrance, "Karl Barth," *Ten Makers of Modern Protestant Thought,* George Hunt, ed. Esp. pp. 59–63.

[3] Karl Barth, *The Humanity of God,* p. 40.

[4] Of these, only the latter is available in English translation.

[5] Torrance, *op. cit.,* p. 59.

gaardian principle of the infinite qualitative difference between the divine and the human was determinative.[6]

Whether or not we accentuate the divergence of the second edition of Barth's *Romans* from the first, we can say that it was the second edition which inaugurated a new era in continental theology. Brunner, Bultmann, and Tillich give expression to this new era and specifically to the influence of Kierkegaard, which is its most distinctive mark. For Barth himself, however, the last major expression of this period is found in the first volume of what was to have been his *Christian Dogmatics*.[7]

The third period begins roughly with the publication of Barth's book on Anselm in 1930. It is clarified in his repudiation of Brunner's theology and along with it that of Kierkegaard as well.[8] It receives its monumental expression in the still unfinished *Church Dogmatics,* which begins with a thorough rewriting of the first volume of the *Christian Dogmatics.*

In an exposition of Barth, one must, therefore, choose between the pre-existentialist, the existentialist, and the post-existentialist stages of Barth's theological development. The first is of importance chiefly because of the light it throws on the background of the others. But the second and third have enormous systematic and historical importance. The Kierkegaardian stage has been carried through in its distinctive implications by Brunner and Bultmann in quite divergent ways. Hence, although a systematic analysis of Barth's own writings in the years from 1922 to 1929 would be of great intrinsic interest, the remainder of this chapter will deal entirely with the Barth of the third period, who has repudiated every alliance with philosophy, even the most negative.

Even within this third and most productive period of Barth's development, his writings are full of surprises.[9] Indeed, so great has been the shift of emphasis and the significance of new ideas that in 1951 Brunner began to write of the " new Barth."[10] Of all men Barth is most emphatic in his refusal to be his own disciple. Therefore, a statement that may be carefully documented from one book may appear very misleading in the light of Barth's later explanations. Only the man who has read and pondered all has the right to pronounce upon Barth's doctrines, and I am not that man! Hence the special diffidence that I cannot forbear expressing as I approach this chapter.

[6] Karl Barth, *The Epistle to the Romans,* p. 10.

[7] This has not been translated.

[8] In John Baillie, ed., *Natural Theology,* pp. 114 ff. See also Barth, *Church Dogmatics* I. 1, p. ix.

[9] Berkouwer, *op. cit.,* pp. 13–14.

[10] *Ibid.,* p. 15.

Yet I am convinced that underlying the endless richness and unexpected variety of Barth's doctrinal formulations there is a basic coherence of method.[11] Indeed, it is precisely this one method which explains the manifoldness of expression. Perhaps it will be possible to state this method fairly and to indicate in broad outlines some of the remarkable ways in which it bears fruit, without attempting to fix in simple propositions the fluid forms of the dynamic thinker. At any rate, it is to that task that I direct my efforts.

We have seen that in the theology of Brunner the central and decisive concept is that of the divine-human encounter. Man as responsible person meets God as Person in the person of Jesus. The Biblical witness makes possible this encounter and is authenticated by it. The encounter has a transforming effect upon man and upon his capacity to see truly that which he had previously distorted.

We may begin our examination of Barth by pointing out the negative fact that he does not share Brunner's understanding of revelation. Barth is interested in the presence of God as Person to man or even the unity of God and man, but not in an encounter between the divine Person and the human person.[12] Man as responsible person is not a partner in this event of presence or union. The Scriptures are not to be understood as mediating a personal encounter with Jesus or as being authenticated by such an encounter. Barth is indifferent to any general enlightenment that may or may not follow the event.[13]

This should make clear in advance of further exposition that in Barth we confront a theological method that is not to be understood primarily as more one-sided, more extreme, or more consistent than that of Brunner but simply as different. It should make clear also that the difference of the theologies as a whole is rooted in the differences of their views of revelation, which is for both the all-determinative ground of theology. We turn, therefore, to a discussion of what Barth understands by revelation, focusing, however, not on his own elaborate exposition of the diversity and unity of its forms, but on that characteristic of his view which seems decisive for the difference between Barth's whole elaboration and that of all the other theologians treated in this volume.

Revelation *is* God's Word or personal presence. As such it is identical with reconciliation. It is also identical with Jesus Christ. But we have seen

[11] Barth himself stresses the unity of the *Church Dogmatics* IV. 2, p. xi.

[12] Barth does not deny that in some sense God "meets" man. See *Church Dogmatics* II. 1, p. 9. But Barth does not understand this as Brunner does after the analogy at the encounter between two human persons. The agency of the meeting is entirely on God's side. See also, *ibid.*, I. 1, pp. 234–235.

[13] Barth, *Church Dogmatics* I. 1, pp. 272–277.

already that God's presence is not to be understood as something available for human encounter. Much less is it available for human appropriation. It is sheer event that simply transpires according to God's sovereign freedom.[14] There is no characteristic of man that can be understood as a capacity for God's presence in his Word. This possibility belongs entirely with God.[15] God's presence is real presence in Jesus, in church, in sacrament, in Scripture, in preaching, in the elect. But in every case, it is a presence whose occurrence is wholly God's decision and which cannot be identified with any changes in the form or content of the earthly vessel. It is a presence to which the earthly vessel has no claim and which occurs or does not occur quite independently of all psychological or physical factors associated with the vessel. Hence it is a presence that can be believed or acknowledged only as and when it in fact happens.[16]

The fundamental significance of this understanding of the mode of God's presence can be brought out by examples. Let us consider God's presence in proclamation that includes both preaching and sacrament. First we must note that it really happens, that is, God really speaks from time to time in human proclamation.[17] This absolutely mysterious fact is the basis of the church's ministry. But man can make no predictions whatsoever about this presence. He cannot suppose that it can be brought to pass by his earnestness, his rhetorical power, the vividness of his presentation of Jesus, his success in portraying man's guilt, or his theologically correct preaching. God's presence occurs in the proclamation according to his own free determination, which remains to man wholly mysterious. When it occurs man can acknowledge that it occurs, but that is all. He thereby acknowledges that man's fallible words of proclamation have in fact in this instance by God's grace become God's Word, hence, revelation and reconciliation, hence, the presence of Jesus Christ himself. He does not for this reason suppose that the human words that were uttered are thereby sanctioned or sanctified. They remain as fallible as ever.

This illustration of the mode of God's presence can be applied with little modification to Scripture. God's presence in Scripture is always *event,* wholly uncontrollable and unpredictable from man's side. Hence, the Roman Catholic understanding of the church's authoritative definition of doctrine through its interpretation of Scripture and tradition must be vehemently rejected as denying God's free sovereignty.[18] In a similar way Protestant orthodoxy by its identification of the Bible with the Word

[14] *Ibid.,* I. 1, pp. 19, 24, 30, 177.
[15] *Ibid.,* I. 1, p. 224.
[16] *Ibid.,* I. 1, pp. 234 ff., 280, 282.
[17] *Ibid.,* I. 1, pp. 57, 79.
[18] *Ibid.,* I. 1, p. 43.

of God attempted to divinize a human and worldly entity and to bind God's freedom.[19] Church and Bible become God's Word when and as God freely chooses, but they do not thereby attain some permanent divine quality.[20] They remain in themselves wholly fallible, wholly human and worldly.

At the same time it must be understood that Barth's view is an even more vehement rejection of what he calls Modernism or Neo-Protestantism. By this he means the whole tendency of Protestantism since the Enlightenment to see a broader base for its thinking than the objective Word of God and to find such a base in an understanding of man. From the standpoint of Neo-Protestantism as Barth sees it, Christian religion is one modification of general human possibilities and can be understood only in terms of these possibilities. This view does not merely falsely identify God's Word with human forms of its expression; it implicitly denies the whole idea of God's Word as the free event of God's presence. It understands God's presence as a universal characteristic of man and even of nature that may then be judged by some empirical or psychological criterion as greater or lesser.[21] If we are to defend God's freedom from bondage to the church and Scripture in which he has promised us his presence, much more must we defend it from the view that it is a universal property of man or nature. Hence, Barth's rejection of Roman Catholic ecclesiasticism and Protestant orthodox Biblicism must not be understood as having anything in common with the Neo-Protestant rejection. The latter attacks these positions because they threaten the autonomy of human thought and action. Barth attacks them solely because they fail to acknowledge the absolute freedom of the sovereign God.[22]

What we see in the above examples is Barth's strong determination to distinguish absolutely the Word of God as the miraculous supernatural event of God's presence from the worldly human entity in which it occurs. It is, of course, precisely this entity which becomes the Word of God, but its becoming the Word of God has no effect upon its status as purely human and worldly. The event of its becoming the Word of God must be understood *sui generis* and simply acknowledged as such.[23] Both God and the worldly object are fully and unqualifiedly present together without any lessening of the deity of God or of the worldliness of the worldly ob-

[19] *Karl Barth, Against the Stream: Shorter Post-War Writings, 1945–52,* p. 217.
[20] *Church Dogmatics* I. 1, p. 127.
[21] *Ibid.,* I. 1, p. 40.
[22] *Ibid.,* I. 2, pp. 661 ff.
[23] *Ibid.,* I. 1, pp. 178 ff.

ject, which remains altogether worldly before, during, and after the event of God's presence.

What has been said of church, sacrament, Scripture, and proclamation must be said with renewed emphasis of the believer. The believer is one for whom the event of God's presence, the hearing of the Word, has occurred and does occur from time to time.[24] He cannot understand this as an encounter with God to which he brought his own responsible humanity. He cannot discuss the prior emotional or intellectual development that enabled him to accept God's gift. He can only acknowledge that he heard God's Word, that this event occurred and occurs.

By the same token he cannot discuss himself, the believer, as the product of this event in terms of new cognition or psychological characteristics or powers.[25] This event has made him *invisibly* a new man and *may* have experiential consequences.[26] But he cannot hold up some new development in his own life as belonging to or as a product of God's work. He can only understand himself before, during, and after the event of God's presence, the event of hearing God's Word, as thoroughly and unqualifiedly human, hence, as wholly other than the event that he acknowledges.[27]

Even when we turn to Jesus Christ as he who lived in Palestine in A.D. 1–30 we find a not altogether different situation. Here again Barth sees the human Jesus as truly human. As such he is a witness to the presence of God.[28] He is not exalted into a suprahuman, semidivine being by that presence.[29] He is very man of man. But he is also very God of very God. God's presence in his case is different in kind from God's presence to believers.

The believer acknowledges God's presence to him but remains simply and only human. Jesus as human testifies to God's presence in him and is both purely human and wholly God. The analogy of God's presence in Jesus with God's presence in church, Scripture, proclamation, and believer holds at the point of the preservation of the absolute worldliness of the worldly and the absolute deity of the divine in their conjunction. But in all these cases we can only say that by God's good pleasure the worldly object *becomes* the event of God's Word. It is true that in the case of Jesus Christ we may say, in a somewhat similar way, that Jesus Christ is God's Word. But we do not mean that this is an event in the sense that from time to time he becomes God's Word for us as is the case with Scripture and proclamation. He becomes God's Word for us in Scripture and proc-

24 *Ibid.,* I. 1, p. 216.
25 *Ibid.,* I. 1, pp. 276–277.
26 *Ibid.,* I. 1, pp. 239, 254.
27 *Ibid.,* I. 1, pp. 280, 282.
28 *Ibid.,* I. 2, p. 855.
29 *Ibid.,* I. 1, p. 470; I. 2, p. 162.

lamation because he first antecedently in himself is God's Word. To make this clear we must also say that God's Word is Jesus Christ.[30]

There is, of course, no position outside of the acknowledgment of God's Word from which such acknowledgment of its content can be explained. Theology always presupposes in general and in detail the actuality of the Word, which is its only object.[31] Even within the sphere of faith God remains precisely a mystery in his self-revelation. Hence, although many misconceptions can be cleared away, and although the relations among God's revelation in Jesus Christ, in Scripture, and in proclamation can be explained, God's presence as such can only be acknowledged. The function of rational inquiry is to make the mystery visible as such.[32]

The foregoing should suffice to indicate the very distinctive conception of the God-man relation that characterizes Barth's whole view. In terms of it we can see that a theological method very different from that of Brunner is demanded. Brunner seeks a humanly intelligible encounter with the person Jesus Christ in order that thereby we may encounter God. The Scriptures are the indispensable means of this encounter, but it is our encounter as such that authenticates the witnesses and even allows us to pass judgments upon them. Therefore, although the theologian should exhibit his extensive agreement with the earliest and hence privileged witnesses, he is bound only to Jesus Christ himself and the understanding that comes to him in the encounter. Thus Brunner develops a Christocentrism rather close to that of some forms of Ritschlian liberalism.

In *this* sense, Barth is *not* Christocentric. There is for Barth no encounter with the Jesus Christ of A.D. 1–30 mediated by Scripture that then makes possible critical evaluation of Scripture. On the contrary, in accordance with God's absolute freedom he makes himself present for us now in the testimony to Jesus Christ in Scripture and proclamation. This event of God's presence which is God's Word is that to which all life and thought within the church is directed in openness, obedience, and acknowledgment. Hence, theology also is directed finally only toward the Word of God.[33]

Barth distinguishes dogmas from the dogma. The former are humanly formulated propositions. The latter is the reality that they attempt more or less successfully to assert. In itself, the dogma remains beyond human formulation as the norm for every formulation.[34] Dogmatics as a human enterprise can deal only with this never-finished process of approximating dogma. Again, therefore, in dogmatics we have the strong emphasis on the

[30] *Ibid.*, I. 1, pp. 131–132, 476; I. 2, p. 162.
[31] *Ibid.*, I. 1, pp. 30–33, 285; I. 2, pp. 7, 775.
[32] *Ibid.*, I. 1, p. 423.
[33] *Ibid.*, I. 1, pp. 284 ff.; I. 2, p. 883.
[34] *Ibid.*, I. 1, p. 307.

unqualified humanness of every human creation, however devout and intelligent its author may be.

However, the Word of God is not only an ineffable norm toward which believing thinking strives. It is also the Jesus Christ of A.D. 1–30 to whom the Scriptures witness and who is proclaimed in the church's preaching. It is that Jesus Christ who makes himself present in that proclamation and who is its norm. The function of dogmatics is to criticize the human proclamation of the church in terms of its faithfulness to its norm and content, Jesus Christ. Concretely, this can only mean measuring the proclamation of the church by the testimony to Jesus Christ in the Scripture. We do *not* suppose that this testimony is anything more than a human testimony to God's Word, that is, to Jesus Christ. But equally we do not suppose that we have some other basis for witnessing to Jesus Christ than the Scriptural witness. Hence, the task of dogmatics is to test the proclamation of the present church by the Scriptures.[35]

Furthermore, we must understand that when we appeal to Scripture we appeal to Scripture as a whole. The canonization of the Scriptures was a human and therefore fallible act of the human and fallible church, but it was not an arbitrary act. Those books were canonized which in fact became for the church from time to time according to God's good pleasure the Word of God. If the church finds itself drawn to revise the canon, it is always free to do so. But this revision must be an act of the whole church in obedience to God's Word, not of individual theologians in accordance with their personal preferences.[36]

Still further, Barth forbids us to interpret the whole Biblical witness in terms of one principle, however central this may truly be. For example, we should not take the atonement, although it is indeed central for faith, as the key in terms of which all other teachings of the Bible, such as those on creation and eschatology, are to be understood. We are not to do this precisely because the Scriptures do not do this, and we have no higher court of appeal available to us. There is a unity of all the teachings of Scripture in the Word of God himself, but as such this unity is not accessible to us.[37] It is the eschatological truth that judges and condemns to error all our partial truths. Thus it reminds us of the entirely human character of our dogmatic efforts, but these efforts themselves can be obedient only as they reflect the independent treatment in the Bible of the great themes of God, creation, reconciliation, and redemption.

This conscientious loyalty of Barth to the whole of the Bible as total and normative witness to God's Word must be stressed because it is this as

[35] *Ibid.*, I. 2, pp. 812–813. [36] *Ibid.*, I. 2, pp. 473–479. [37] *Ibid.*, I. 2, p. 877.

much as anything else which distinguishes Barth's position in general and in detail from that of every other figure given major attention in this book. Brunner, we have seen, appeals to Jesus himself as the norm by which the Scriptures are to be judged. Many contemporaries appeal to the kerygma, the message of the primitive church found in the Scripture, as the norm. Still others seek the distinctive characteristics of the prophetic-Christian tradition or the peculiar motif of primitive Christianity and treat these as the decisive principles that must guide all Christian thinking. Barth, however, insists that the theologian is in no position to make such selective abstractions from the total Biblical witness. Only the Word of God to whom the Bible witnesses is the Lord of the Bible, and we are loyal to that Lord only as we listen for the Word throughout the Bible.

This means that Barth rejects "systematic" theology.[38] System implies the development of the whole from a center or key principle regarded as capable of illuminating all else and of placing it in proper perspective. The systematic theologian may derive his key from the Scripture, but once this is securely in his possession he is free to display its implications independently of the Scripture. Barth says we have no such key. Every doctrine must be developed in terms of a new questioning of the whole of Scripture — never by deduction from the conclusions of other aspects of our investigation.[39]

Here lies the explanation of Barth's peculiar unpredictability. He cannot predict his own conclusions. A systematic theologian can be counted on to develop each new doctrine in consistency with his central commitment. But Barth insists on simply interrogating the Scriptures again. The reader of the "Prolegomena" is unprepared for Barth's doctrine of election because Barth himself did not have in mind, when he wrote the "Prolegomena," precisely the doctrine that he developed in Volume II.[40] Likewise, Barth's doctrine on baptism could hardly have been predicted on the basis of the positions taken by him on other topics.[41] In each case a fresh study of Scripture, and not the logic of his earlier statements, is determinative for his conclusions. This is what Barth means by repudiating all Barthianism. He asks faithfulness to Scripture and not faithfulness to any interpretation of Scripture that he may have put forward.

Thus far in this exposition of Barth we have discussed only two points: first, his conception of how God is present, and second, his loyalty to Scripture. It is the thesis of this whole presentation of Barth that these two principles jointly explain his actual procedure and conclusions, whereas either one by itself fails to do so. That is, if we simply began with

[38] *Ibid.*, I. 2, p. 861.
[39] *Ibid.*, IV. 2, p. xi.
[40] *Ibid.*, II. 2, p. x.
[41] Berkouwer, *op. cit.*, p. 13.

Scripture as such and as a whole, we might well find it saying some things to us quite different from that which Barth hears. We might, for example, read it as history of the mighty acts of God in the fashion of *Heilsgeschichte* or in terms of a succession of covenants. We might understand human decision as qualifying the effectiveness of God's gift of grace to each individual. We might understand God's presence in the Christian era in his Holy Spirit as a felt presence that was perceived directly in communion and indirectly in the new psychological qualities of love, joy, and peace that he produced. We might understand that sin and guilt are the actuality of the human situation apart from Christ and that this can be seen separately and independently in Adam and natural man. But Barth does not find these things in the Bible, and to this extent we may say it is predictable what he will find. He always understands the Bible as witnessing to the Word of God as that which freely makes itself present in the witness and which *is* Jesus Christ.

Barth, of course, believes that his understanding of the Word of God as God's revelation and presence to man is itself the understanding of the Bible. Hence, he appeals to one principle and not two. But it must be said that at some points Biblical scholars find his exegesis strained. It cannot be supposed that Barth simply approaches each text afresh without any conception of the kind of message that is to be sought in it. On the contrary, he approaches each text seeking its witness to the one Word of God, Jesus Christ, and inevitably his conception of the way in which the Word of God is revealed affects the way in which he understands the text's witness.[42] In a sense, therefore, Barth does have a system of the sort he disavows, in that a single central principle derived from Scripture guides the interpretation of all Scripture.

At the same time, however, it must equally be said that in fact Barth does not proceed by tracing out the most reasonable implications of his understanding of the Word of God. He is open as few theologians have ever been to new light from Scripture. He is never satisfied to maintain any view unless he can first convince himself, if not others, that this is indeed the meaning of Scripture. Hence, it is the two principles, which he would reduce to one, in terms of which the vast corpus of his writing is to be understood. On specific doctrines he feels free to change his views and sometimes does so in startling ways.[43] But all these changes occur

[42] *Church Dogmatics* I. 1, p. 131.

[43] E.g., his reversal on doctrine of continual creation from affirmation to rejection. See Weber, *Karl Barth's Church Dogmatics: An Introductory Report on Volumes I:1 to III:4,* p. 166.

within, and on the basis of, these two fundamental principles of his thought.

Dogmatics is the testing of the church's proclamation by the Scriptures, which are understood as testifying in their entirety to the one revelation in Jesus Christ. It accepts no other object or norm besides this. Hence, it cannot hold itself responsible to the contemporary world view or to any philosophy.[44] In this sense, Barth's rejection of all human thinking not bound to revelation is total. But this does not mean that either proclamation or dogmatics is bound to the language of Scripture. This is a purely human language that is in no way sanctified by its use in the primitive witness. Our proclamation and our dogmatics must be in our language, and this means in a language that has been influenced by philosophy.[45]

Furthermore, dogmatic propositions must be rational through and through.[46] Barth is not troubled by the fact that such rationality is affected by purely human intellectual traditions, for he never pretends in any respect to escape the situation of an altogether worldly humanity. In dogmatics we use the best concepts available to express the meaning we find in the Word of God. But we do not thereby commit ourselves to the philosophical context in which these terms receive their meaning. We commit ourselves only to the Word of God. When philosophical categories show signs of hindering the free expression of that Word, they must be abandoned. Thus Barth himself purged his *Church Dogmatics* of the vocabulary of existentialism when it became clear to him that this led to misunderstanding on the part of others and unclarity on his own part. The dogmatician's attitude toward philosophy is not one of hostility or fear, but one of perfect freedom.[47]

Dogmatics is bound only to the Word of God, and it must in intention be a dogmatics of the church as such. Nevertheless, the dogmatician must also recognize that he speaks within and for a particular branch of the

[44] *Church Dogmatics* I. 1, pp. 287 ff.

[45] *Ibid.*, I. 1, pp. 86, 91–92, 184; I. 2, p. 778.

[46] *Ibid.*, I. 1, p. 340.

[47] *Ibid.*, I. 1, pp. 93–94, 142, 321; I. 2, pp. 774–775, 819. Barth develops his highly positive view of philosophy and its relation to theology most fully in "Philosophie und Theologie," his contribution to *Philosophie und christliche Existenz, Festschrift* for Heinrich Barth, Gerhard Huber, ed., published in 1960. Here he stresses that both are responsible to the one and same truth, that each must deal with the problems treated by the other, and that they differ only in the priority they give to these questions. This difference of priority, he sees, creates many inevitable differences in treatment and formulation, but he calls for a free conversation in which each can learn from the other without any attempt on either side to triumph over the other. See especially pp. 93–95.

church.[48] In Barth's case this is the Reformed Church, which sees in the Calvinist tradition the most adequate human approximation to the Word of God. Therefore, Barth treats with special respect the theological positions of the thinkers in this tradition and especially of Calvin.[49] He remains essentially loyal to this tradition even when he criticizes its formulation. In this way he distinguishes his understanding of the faith from that of Lutherans and Anglicans as well as, much more drastically, from Roman Catholics and Neo-Protestants.[50]

However, the Reformed theologian never argues from the Reformed confessions as authorities but employs them only as guides.[51] The confessions are affirmed ultimately only so long as one can affirm them as useful and adequate guides to the Scripture testimony. The latter alone is authoritative, and in it lies the principle of unity of all evangelical confessions.

A distinctive feature of Barth's theology in contrast with both orthodoxy and liberalism is the determinative role that he assigns the doctrine of the Trinity. This doctrine is actually expounded in the "Prolegomena" to the *Dogmatics*! Historically it has been usual to treat the doctrine of God first, and then in terms of what is said about God as such to discuss the Trinity. But Barth regards such an approach as un-Biblical. It presupposes that we know something of God in some nontrinitarian way prior to our knowledge of his threefoldness. But precisely such knowledge is what is excluded by our understanding of Jesus Christ as God in his revelation.[52]

To understand Barth's position here we must remind ourselves of his fundamental understanding of how God is related to man. For God to approach man is for him to be present to man in revelation and reconciliation. Apart from this approach there is no relation of man to God, and in this approach God is unqualifiedly God. At the same time God in his presence to man reveals that which also *is* apart from that presence. That is, we cannot identify God wholly with a series of events that touch man in his history and thereby reconcile man and God. What is given in those events is God, but it is God only in one of his modes of being, which we call his Son. God reveals himself to man only in his existence as Son, but this very fact points also to his existence as the Father who sends the Son.[53]

With respect to the relation of Father and Son we must say two things. First, the Son is not the Father and the Father is not the Son. Second, God who reveals himself in the Son is also the God who is the Father. The

48 *Ibid.*, I. 2, p. 831.
49 *Ibid.*, I. 2, pp. 824–827.
50 *Ibid.*, I. 2, pp. 829–832.
51 *Ibid.*, I. 2, pp. 836–838.
52 *Ibid.*, I. 1, pp. 345–346.
53 *Ibid.*, I. 1, pp. 343–344, 372.

point is that although on the one hand we must never dissolve God's being in himself into his being for us, we must also not attribute to God the Father any will or purpose or nature that is not revealed in Jesus Christ.[54]

It would not be wrong, I think, to suppose that when Barth insists that we must begin with God the Trinity, he has in mind primarily the duality and unity of Son and Father. He begins with the Trinity because it is only so that he can begin with revelation. Any other starting point would begin with some idea held to be revealed but not with revelation as such. To begin with revelation as such is to begin with the Son, who can only be understood as revelation when he is understood as the Son of the Father.

However, Barth is fully aware that the doctrine of the church is a doctrine of trinity and not of binity, and he shows no disposition to minimize the importance of the third person. The Spirit is the Spirit of Father and Son,[55] the mode of God's presence which works faith in the Son in the believer's heart. The Spirit, therefore, has no content or object other than the Son but is precisely the means by which God's revelation and reconciliation in Jesus Christ becomes actualized anew in each believer.[56] Thereby the Spirit points to the eschatological consummation in redemption, which, as the new coming of the Son, is the content of Christian hope.[57]

Barth is critical of the use of the term " person " to refer to these three modes of existence of God.[58] The term was appropriate in the early church because the concept of person at that time did not have its present-day meaning. In one sense of person we must say that God is *one* Person who exists in three modes. At the same time he vehemently rejects historic Modalism as failing to do justice to the real threeness-in-one and oneness-in-three of the three modes of existence of the one Person, God.[59]

God and his three modes of being provide the basic outline of the entire dogmatics. Volume II deals with " the doctrine of God "; Volume III, with the doctrine of creation, which Barth understands as God the Father; Volume IV is entitled " the doctrine of reconciliation," which Barth understands as God as Son; and Volume V will deal with " the doctrine of redemption," which Barth associates with God as Holy Spirit. Thus we see how the entire dogmatics deals in one sense only with God, only with the Trinity, while at the same time dealing continuously with man, his world, and his future. For Barth, God and man cannot be treated as two topics of theological inquiry, for both are known only in the one God-man,

[54] *Ibid.,* I. 1, pp. 436–437.
[55] *Ibid.,* I. 1, pp. 546–547.
[56] *Ibid.,* I. 1, p. 517.
[57] *Ibid.,* I. 1, pp. 528–531.
[58] *Ibid.,* I. 1, p. 412.
[59] *Ibid.,* I. 1, pp. 438–439.

Jesus Christ. Ultimately, the one topic of all that is said is the way in which God makes himself present to and for man in his one Word, Jesus Christ.

It is time now to turn from this discussion of method and principles to illustrations of their application to crucial doctrines. For this purpose the two problems of election and creation are selected. It is highly significant for Barth's treatment of both these doctrines that he places election first and in the context of the doctrine of God as such.[60] In one respect Barth's doctrine of election is predictable from his basic understanding of the way in which God makes himself present in his Word. Since this presence is purely an event subject *only* to God's freedom, there can be no question of human merit or response before, during, or after the event as conditioning its occurrence or effect. Hence, Barth consistently affirms that the human decision with respect to faith and obedience always follows upon and depends on the divine decision and in no way conditions it.[61]

The scattered references to this situation in Volume I of the *Church Dogmatics* suggest that Barth assumed in common with the Calvinist tradition generally that there is also a human decision of unfaith and disobedience that similarly follows upon and depends on a divine decision. Although it appears that even here Barth did not want to place these two decisions on the same level,[62] still they both appear as human decisions reflecting prior divine decisions. Since this position is fully consistent both with Barth's fundamental understanding of the divine freedom and sovereignty and with the traditional Calvinist reading of the Bible, there seemed no reason to expect a change.

Nevertheless, he does depart from the Calvinist view in his extended treatment of the doctrine of election, and he does so in a highly original and interesting manner. It is here that what Berkouwer has called the "triumph of grace" in Barth's theology becomes clearly apparent, and although it may be seen as foreshadowed in his earlier work, Barth himself expresses surprise at his own development.[63]

Barth was driven to modifications of his traditional Calvinist view of election partly by his close study of the Bible and partly by his basic principle that Jesus Christ is the revealed God. If Jesus Christ is our *only* ground for knowledge of God, then we cannot know of God anything that we do not see in Jesus Christ.[64] This seems quite simple and evident, but Barth shows that the whole Christian tradition has failed to remain strictly faithful to this principle. Even Calvin, for example, separates the

[60] *Ibid.,* II. 2, pp. 3–506. Creation is the subject of Vol. III.
[61] *Ibid.,* I. 1, pp. 65, 184, 235, 237–238.
[62] *Ibid.,* I. 1, p. 171.
[63] *Ibid.,* II. 2, p. x.
[64] *Ibid.,* II. 2, pp. 25, 103–104, 115, 422.

electing God from Jesus Christ in such a way that he can attribute to him an eternal decree of nonelection, which is not revealed in Jesus Christ.[65] It is this which creates the tension between the revealed love of God and the horror of the decree of damnation of the nonelect.

Brunner avoided the implication of God's arbitrary damning of most men by insisting that God offers himself to all men in the encounter, but that men can fail to respond. Essentially he thereby repeats the Arminian and Wesleyan responses to the rigidities of orthodox Calvinism,[66] although he strives hard to differentiate his position from theirs through his categories of encounter and response. Barth, however, will have nothing to do with any view that regards a human response as conditioning the efficacy of God's act. If we use such language at all, we must understand that the human response is included within the act of God, that it is a predicate of God and not of man. Barth's problem is, therefore, on the one hand, to retain the Calvinist view of the sole effective agency of God in his absolutely free sovereignty while, on the other hand, rejecting any idea of God's will and purpose that is other than that revealed in Jesus Christ.

What God reveals in Jesus Christ is his gracious election of man. The man who is elected is the man Jesus Christ. What is revealed about election is not some information about his past activities and future plans but rather this particular election of Jesus Christ. Hence we know nothing of any other election of God. We do know, however, that in electing the man Jesus Christ, God did not elect simply one man from among others but rather elected man as such, for the human Jesus Christ is not to be understood as an individualized person except as he becomes so through his election.[67] By uniting himself with man in Jesus Christ, God united himself decisively with man as such. Hence man is elected to unity with God in Jesus Christ.[68]

For this reason the Christian is never to take unbelief seriously.[69] We can and should set no limits to the efficacy of God's grace. Every individual is always to be approached as one who is already elect in Jesus Christ.[70] The difference among men would seem to be only the degree to which they acknowledge the one, all-decisive fact of their election.

The apparent implication of this line of thought is that despite all ap-

[65] *Ibid.*, II. 2, p. 111.
[66] Cf. Berkouwer, *op. cit.*, p. 264.
[67] *Church Dogmatics* I. 2, p. 163.
[68] *Ibid.*, II. 2, pp. 94, 116–117, 120–121, 351.
[69] *Ibid.*, II. 2, pp. 296, 416; *Against the Stream*, p. 216.
[70] *Church Dogmatics* II. 2, p. 415.

pearances all men are elect, and Barth has been accused of this doctrine.[71] His sharp distinction of God's presence in his Word from any human response to that presence seems to open the way to some such position.[72] But Barth finds himself forbidden by the Bible from accepting such conclusions.

In the first place, he stresses that any human doctrine of universal salvation makes salvation a predicate of man, something that happens to him by virtue of his being a man.[73] But the Bible treats election as a free act of the sovereign God. We can neither affirm that election is limited in its scope nor that it is unlimited.[74] We can only proclaim that it has occurred in Jesus Christ.

In the second place, alongside this rather moderate qualification of the doctrine of universal election, we find Barth identifying election closely with faith in Jesus Christ and membership in the church.[75] Again Barth is bound here much more by the explicit teaching of the Bible than by the logic of his own position. The Bible as he reads it knows no other election than that in Jesus Christ and knows this as occurring only with its acknowledgment by faith and by sharing in the fellowship of believers.

This means that alongside the apparent universalism of the effective election of man in Jesus Christ, Barth sets a strict exclusiveness that identifies the body of the elect with Israel and the Christian church. He affirms quite clearly that there is a crossing over of individual men into a state of election in a sense that does not seem compatible with the view that their election precedes their crossing over.[76] In other words, although he attributes sole effective agency to God, he takes very seriously man's acknowledgment of God's grace as the mark of election and even as the occasion of its occurrence for the individual.

We are left here with an acute problem for understanding. In Jesus Christ, God has elected man, yet among empirical men most seem to be in a state of rejection. We cannot attribute this state of rejection to successful resistance of God's grace. But we are also forbidden to attribute it to a decision of God to reject them. The only alternative appears to be that of denying real actuality to rejected men! And it is just this course that Barth adopts.[77]

[71] Cf. Berkouwer's discussion of this whole tendency in Barth's thought, *op. cit.,* pp. 262 ff.
[72] *Church Dogmatics* II. 2, p. 340.
[73] *Ibid.,* II. 2, p. 295.
[74] *Ibid.,* II. 2, pp. 417–418, 422.
[75] *Ibid.,* II. 2, pp. 345, 410 ff., 422–423.
[76] *Ibid.,* II. 2, p. 417.
[77] *Ibid.,* II. 2, pp. 450–454, 539.

So extraordinary is Barth's position at this point, and so significant for the development of the later parts of the *Dogmatics,* that we must pause briefly to consider what is meant. All other theologians have started with the assumption of the equal reality of all men. Salvation and damnation distinguished between two equally real conditions that befall them. Theological questions centered around the respective roles of God and man in determining which condition would occur.

Barth, however, sees man only in Jesus Christ. This means, for example, that only Jesus Christ is a person and that we achieve participation in personhood only in him. Even in Jesus Christ, personhood is a predicate of deity rather than of humanity, hence also in us it is not a state of being of which we have possession.[78] Apart from believing participation in Jesus Christ there are no persons at all. Indeed, outside the humanity of Jesus Christ there is no humanity at all! [79]

When Barth first develops this point, one might conjecture that we are dealing with a terminological question. One might suppose that he simply chooses to define personhood in this way. But as we proceed we see that with increasing seriousness Barth affirms that reality as a whole is a predicate of God and of God only, that it appears to us only in Jesus Christ, and that we share in it only in him. Furthermore, Jesus Christ is nothing other than God's presence to the world in grace. Hence only this grace is real. Evil, rejection, sin, cannot be set alongside grace as opposing realities.

Since we are forbidden to affirm that all empirical individuals are, despite appearances, elect, we are forced to affirm that despite appearances those who are not elect are not independently real! Again one might suppose that our need is for terminological clarification. Obviously, Barth does not mean that the rejected are imaginary entities or that they would not meet empirical tests of existing. Hence, he is using " real " in a very special sense. Yet it would be an illusion to suppose that a few terminological distinctions would enable us to incorporate Barth's doctrine within our accustomed modes of thought. It can be grasped, if at all, only by imaginatively sharing in his own vision of the sole agency of God and the unlimited graciousness of that agency. From this point of view we must see by faith, and in spite of all appearances, that what resists God's grace is *really* nothing — is already negated, wholly negative. Hence those men who attempt to stand in that rejection have in fact nothing to stand upon and no being or power to oppose to God's grace.

Barth does, it is true, allot a certain limited and negative reality to the

[78] *Ibid.,* II. 1, pp. 284–286. [79] *Ibid.,* II. 2, p. 541.

rejected, but this he insists is derived from the elect. One exists as rejected by virtue of being known as such by the elect.[80] He represents man in his need for election and in that negative condition which is the only alternative to faith.[81] As such he too exists by the will of God as the shadow of his gracious election.

We should now be prepared to understand Barth's doctrine of creation. It had seemed to observers that at this point Barth could have little to say, and Barth himself confessed to uncertainty as he approached this problem.[82] We shall begin by noting the reasons for skepticism as to Barth's ability to handle this topic.

If we affirm that nature and natural man are the creation of God, it seems that they must in some way bear the imprint of his will and purpose. The order of nature and natural society must reflect God's intentions. The structures of being of created entities must have some positive relation to the being of the Creator. As the psalmist says, "the heavens are telling the glory of God; and the firmament proclaims his handiwork."

But if all this is true, then there must be some objective possibility of knowing God through his creation. One may, of course, argue that sinful man refuses to see what is objectively there to be seen, and on this basis one may deny that non-Christians know anything truly about God from nature. Their philosophy and religion may be held to reflect only a distortion of the truth that objectively confronts them. But then one must acknowledge that the Christian through the forgiveness of sins is enabled to see the glory and purpose of God directly in his handiwork. To deny this seems to deny that nature objectively is God's creation, hence to deny the Biblical doctrine of creation as such.

This position of denying to nature any significant relation to God has been adopted in some of the theological trends influenced by Kantian and post-Kantian developments. It has even been supported by the hostile attitude of some New Testament passages toward this world and its rulers. Hence a consistent position may be developed that excludes nature from consideration and treats of God's act only in election and redemption.

However, Barth has precluded adopting either the view that nature potentially offers us direct testimony to God's being and nature, or the view that God's creation of nature can be dismissed by Christian theology. He rejects the first in his radical protest against any natural theology, even a Christian natural theology. He rejects the second by virtue of his refusal to select certain Scriptural teachings to the exclusion of others. Clearly, God's creation of the world is taught in the Bible.[83] Hence the apparent

[80] *Ibid.*, II. 2, p. 451.
[81] *Ibid.*, II. 2, pp. 455–458.
[82] *Ibid.*, III. 1, p. ix.
[83] *Ibid.*, III. 1, p. 23.

dilemma found by Barth in developing his own Christian doctrine of creation.

We have already noted that in the order of presentation Barth develops his doctrine of election prior to his doctrine of creation. This is because election and that alone can be identified as God's final, decisive, and all-inclusive purpose for man. This is known in Jesus Christ, to whom all Scripture testifies. This means that also the story of creation cannot be read independently of the one purpose of God known in Jesus Christ. Creation has no purpose other than election. Hence it embodies no structure or actuality that points to some other truth about God than the one truth of his election of man in Jesus Christ.[84]

Now we arrive at Barth's remarkable and novel solution of his problem. God does manifest himself in his creation. The Bible tells us this and the Christian, therefore, knows it. But what God manifests in his creation is nothing other than Jesus Christ![85] Therefore, apart from Jesus Christ there is *no* knowledge of God in creation, neither correct nor distorted. Hence, also, the Christian whose eyes are opened to God's manifestation in creation sees nothing there other than the reality he sees in Jesus Christ.[86] The doctrine of God's creation of the world implies nothing whatsoever about the possibility of finding in the world any clue to the nature of God except that knowledge of God which is given once for all in Jesus Christ.

From this position we can throw new light upon Barth's startling doctrine of the lack of independent reality on the part of rejected man. Since Adam has been understood by other theologians as man as created by God, Adam's reality and nature have been seen as the embodiment of what man is by nature apart from a new and special act of grace in Jesus Christ. This has made man's fallen nature a topic of special theological inquiry. The understanding of its limitations and need has provided the context for understanding the work of Jesus Christ. Thus Christology has depended upon anthropology.

But Barth sees that this presupposes that creation had some other purpose and outcome than election or that God's purpose in creation was not effective. Only in this case could Adam, hence natural man as such, be understood as having reality in himself. But just this view is what Barth has rejected in his doctrine of creation.

The purpose and meaning, and hence the actuality of creation, is election and nothing else. In so far as man is not elect, he lacks the purpose, meaning, and actuality of creation. He lacks, therefore, created nature as

84 *Ibid.*, III. 1, pp. 18–19. 85 *Ibid.*, III. 1, pp. 31–33. 86 *Ibid.*, III. 1, pp. 23–25.

such and can be understood only as a shadowy anticipation of his own reality. Elect man, and hence man as the creature that he really is, is seen only in Jesus Christ.[87]

This means that the usual order of theological inquiry is sharply reversed. Barth does not speak of Adam and Christ but of Christ and Adam! We cannot learn of the need for Christ or the nature of his work by first considering man's condition apart from him.[88] We can consider man's condition apart from Christ only in the light of that which he overcame and negated. The doctrine of creation and created man, like the doctrine of election and elected man, has no other object than Jesus Christ.[89]

Although Barth can in this way subsume all doctrines about man under the one doctrine of Jesus Christ, he must face the fact of evil. He must face it, not primarily because of its empirical factuality, but because of its importance in the Bible. If creation can be understood as having its meaning in Jesus Christ, Jesus Christ must nevertheless be understood as victor over evil. Hence evil must have some status for Barth.

The problem is, of course, that Barth must give some account of the source or origin of evil. It cannot be attributed directly to God's creative act, since that has no other end than election. On the other hand, it cannot be attributed to misuse of freedom on the part of man, since Barth assigns to man no freedom to overrule or even effectively to resist God's purposes. It would seem, then, that evil must be somehow antecedent to creation as an eternal enemy of God. But this would imply a dualism that Barth knows to be wholly un-Biblical.

Barth faces here a traditional theological dilemma. How can the reality of evil be reconciled with the omnipotence of God? If we rule out the possibilities of placing the blame on man and of affirming an ultimate dualism or some limitation upon God's power or goodness, we seem to be left with the single possibility of declaring evil to be unreal.

Indeed, it is in this direction that we are to seek Barth's answer. Barth equates evil with nothingness,[90] and he absolutely denies to it any autonomous existence or reality. Yet it is precisely this nothingness which, as the enemy of God, is overcome in Jesus Christ! Clearly, nothingness is a very

87 Karl Barth, *Christ and Adam: Man and Humanity in Romans 5,* pp. 29, 30, 36, 46, 47, 58, 59.

88 *Ibid.,* pp. 33–35.

89 It is characteristic of Barth that he is not satisfied with this view on the basis of its harmony with his general position. He affirms it explicitly on the basis of exegesis of Paul. *Christ and Adam* is an exegesis of Romans, ch. 5.

90 The German term "*das Nichtige*" has no adequate English translation. Since the translators of the *Church Dogmatics* have decided to use "nothingness" as the translation, confusion will be minimized if we conform. See their footnote on this problem in *Church Dogmatics* III. 3, p. 289.

active and powerful nothingness—and not, as nothingness, simply negligible.

This strange concept of a powerfully active and dangerous nothingness is essential to Barth's total position. Nothingness, so far as it is, cannot be understood either as an eternal reality or as a created entity. Yet it has such importance that it is overcome by God only in Jesus Christ.

This last statement is the key to the understanding of nothingness. It *is* that which is overcome by God in Jesus Christ. It *is* that possibility which is rejected by God in creation. It is that which *is* by virtue of God's eternal rejection. Thus its being is both negative and dependent upon God, but nevertheless, as that to which God says No, still real and potent.[91]

Perhaps we may risk a schematic summary of Barth's total vision of reality that will help the reader to make some sense of the foregoing expositions. From this scheme we may omit completely any reference to plants and animals and heavenly bodies and the like—the nonhuman creation—since this is of little importance.

Any such scheme must begin with God as Trinity, creator, reconciler, and redeemer of man—equally God in his hiddenness and in his revealedness. At the opposite pole we must set nothingness. Nothingness is real and exists, but its reality and existence are *sui generis*.[92] That is, nothingness does not share in the kind of reality that God has or imparts to his creation. Nothingness has its reality only as that which is rejected by God, therefore, as that which is negated and overcome.

Between God and nothingness we must place man, the creature. But in man, too, we find a parallel duality of the elect and the rejected.[93] The elect are those who have become as creatures what the creature really is. That is, God has presented himself to the elect in such a way that they acknowledge his Lordship and their creaturehood. Their existence and reality consist in the Word that God has spoken to them. Thus they neither have nor claim any autonomous existence, but just in this acceptance of existence from God they fulfill their true being as creatures.

The rejected also have their peculiar reality and existence. They remain creatures even in their denial of their creaturehood. By their rejection of God's grace they submit wholly to nothingness and are thereby plunged into nothingness. But their nothingness is not sheer nonexistence, and it is not to be equated with the reality of nothingness itself. Like nothing-

[91] *Church Dogmatics* III. 3, pp. 351–353; Berkouwer, *op. cit.*, pp. 56–60.

[92] *Church Dogmatics* III. 3, p. 352.

[93] The same kind of duality characterizes angels and demons, although in the case of the demons their lack of existence and their identity with nothingness are virtually complete. See Weber, *op. cit.*, pp. 200–204.

ness, which exists by virtue of God's rejection of it, and which can be understood only in God's overcoming of it, the rejected man exists only in and for the elect. His reality can be seen only in the creaturehood manifested in the elect and denied in him. Even the denial is visible only in and for the elect.

Even this highly negative account of the status of the rejected, however, does not really explain how Barth can deny to natural or rejected man a special place in Christian thinking. Barth must do so if he is to maintain clearly his distinction from Brunner. Brunner agrees that natural man cannot understand himself, that, therefore, there can be no doctrine of natural man as creature except from the point of view of faith. However, Brunner holds that when a man's eyes are opened by faith, he can see the condition of natural man as fallen creature. At that point a Christian doctrine of fallen man becomes possible and even mandatory. On the basis of what has just been said there seems no reason for Barth to deny this possibility.

But Barth does deny to the discussion of natural man any proper province in Christian theology. Neither nothingness nor rejected man becomes an independent topic for theology. The kind of reality they have is such that they can be seen *only* as that which grace has negated. Hence the theologian knows *only* the grace and its negating, and the negated only as the negated.

This means that there is nothing to be said about rejected man except that in Jesus Christ man's rejection is overthrown. Even the rejection, or perhaps we should say precisely the rejection, which might otherwise constitute an object for theological investigation, is now impotent, even unreal. It is not to be taken seriously; therefore, it is not to be talked about as if it were an effective human act on the part of the rejected. Barth even speaks repeatedly of the ontological impossibility of sin, although this never implies that sin lacks reality and danger for man.

◈ ◈

Barth has written so extensively and has developed novel solutions to so many problems that in one sense criticism is easy. It is hardly doubtful that there are inconsistencies, confusions, ambiguities, and simply meaningless sentences scattered throughout the thousands of pages of his *Dogmatics*. There are few readers who are not sometimes frustrated by Barth's failure to give direct, clear-cut answers to what seem to be direct, clear-cut questions.

Furthermore, we may take it for granted that in Barth's extensive work in exegesis he must come frequently into conflict with more specialized students of the Bible. Presumably, Barth is often wrong even on matters that can be more or less settled by scholarship. Certainly his interpretations of many passages differ markedly from those which are generally taken as standard.

But all of these criticisms, however effectively they might be made, would be irrelevant to our central concern in this volume. Our concern here is to determine whether Barth has provided us with an intelligible and self-consistent theological method. Can dogmatics accept as its total function the testing of the church's language by Scripture in the way that he has proposed?

In order to answer this question, we must remind ourselves what the Biblical norm is for Barth. First, it is quite clear that he never regards the Biblical norm as binding him to Biblical language. Further, it is evident that his understanding of the Old Testament is, and must be, very different from the Jewish understanding. Finally, despite Barth's objection to system and his recurrence to Scripture for new guidance on new doctrines, it can hardly be denied that he is often guided in his understanding of Scripture by the systematic demands of his own position.

In summary, this means that there are key principles of Scriptural interpretation that are decisive for the outcome of Barth's thought. According to his own view, these principles must be derived from, and justified by, Scripture itself. Otherwise they would constitute foreign importations that we might trace to a cultural or philosophical preunderstanding. Barth knows, of course, that the theologian cannot be free in detail from such preunderstanding. But it is essential to his whole approach that its basic procedures and principles *not* depend on commitments that are not authenticated by Scripture.

The major presupposition that must be pointed out, then, is the assumption of the unity of Scripture. Of course, this does not mean for Barth what it has meant to some fundamentalists. He is not concerned to harmonize in detail different accounts of the same incident in Israelite history or Jesus' life. It does mean, however, first, that the Scripture understands itself as a united witness to God's acts, and second, that we can now see that throughout Scripture that to which testimony is given is in fact one, namely, God's reconciling self-revelation which is Jesus Christ.[94] Still more specifically, Barth's whole position rests on the accuracy of his understanding of the way in which God is present to, and in the world as, an exposition of the understanding of that presence characteristic of Scripture as a whole and in each of its parts.

[94] Barth, *Church Dogmatics* III. 1, p. 24.

One cannot question that Barth has made an impressive case for his view, and it would be out of place here to affirm or deny its accuracy. It must be noted, however, that most Biblical scholars are impressed by the deep diversities of understanding that characterize the Biblical writers even on such central questions as are decisive for Barth.[95] Barth knows that he diverges at crucial points from the entire church tradition, including the Reformers, and that he differs from virtually all contemporaries except those who take their cue specifically from him. What Barth sees as the decisive understanding of the mode of God's revelation and the unity of the whole of canonical Scripture is, in its exact form, his own new discovery!

This does not necessarily mean that Barth is wrong in his understanding of Scripture. The favorable and quite plausible explanation would be that throughout Christian history theologians have failed to guard themselves sufficiently against the importation of extraneous patterns of thinking into their interpretation of the revelation attested by Scripture. Certainly no one has ever been more self-consciously careful at this point than has Barth. We must be alerted by Barth's novelty, however, to careful criticism of the steps by which he moves from the embracing of the Scriptural norm to his specific teachings.

In the earlier exposition of Barth's method I have suggested that most important of all for his whole development is the understanding of the mode of God's presence as occurring to and in man but not in such a way as to become a part of his empirical being. In subtle but important ways this conception differentiates Barth's understanding of Scripture and theology from that of every other theologian treated in this book. Hence, a careful critical inquiry into the Biblical character of this view would be crucial to an appraisal of Barth.

Such an appraisal is beyond the scope of this volume, but an outline of Barth's argument and its consequences will allow for some tentative judgment. The argument is as follows. God's presence to man is always and as such revelation. All Scripture is testimony to revelation. Revelation is Jesus Christ. Therefore, Jesus Christ is the sole topic of Scripture. That this is so is the decisive principle of interpretation of all of Scripture. If the Christocentric principle of interpretation of all of Scripture follows, as I think it does, from the understanding of how God makes himself present to man, then the Scriptural character of Barth's view of God's mode of revelation may be tested at a second point. That is, we may investigate whether the exegesis that results from the Christocentric principle does

[95] Cf. Hermann Diem, *Dogmatics,* pp. 62–63, 98.

justice to the Scriptural texts themselves. Can we reasonably interpret Genesis on the one hand and Paul on the other, for example, as presenting natural man as real, visible, and theologically relevant only in the election of humanity in Jesus Christ?

We can, of course, say that most Biblical scholars read these accounts differently from Barth, but this is not decisive. Every interpretation of Scripture depends upon some hermeneutical principle. Barth believes that the scholars who find other meanings do so by bringing alien preconceptions to the Scripture instead of finding their principle in Scripture itself. The principle provided in Scripture is the revelation to which it witnesses. Hence, a historical interpretation of Biblical theology in terms of a history of ideas, or an existentialist interpretation in terms of the kind of human existence that results from God's act, is alien to Scripture's own meaning.

The question is whether there may also be a Biblical exegesis grounded like Barth's in the principle that Scripture witnesses to revelation that holds that the Scriptures are *also* interested in expressing a new understanding of the world gained through revelation. We have seen that in order to deny such a province to theology Barth has increasingly developed a doctrine of the purely negative reality of all that is not God's grace. One cannot read Barth's extensive treatment of this theme without feeling that it has an importance in his theology out of all proportion to the direct support it receives in Scripture. It requires utmost vigilance and subtlety for Barth to interpret passage after passage of Scripture in the light of this monism of grace.

One wonders whether it is Scripture itself that drives Barth over and over again to what often appears as strange and strained exegesis on the one hand and to highly novel speculation about nothingness on the other.[96] Is it not rather more probable that the Biblical writers saw no incompatibility between testifying to God's revelation and speaking of the real condition of real fallen men — a condition that persisted in spite of revelation and because of their rejection of it? Is it not probable also that some Old Testament writers took a keen interest in the world that God provided as the scene of election in such a way as to see in it a partly independent witness to God's graciousness? Is not Barth's careful rejection of these possibilities based more upon his judgment as to where their development leads than upon his faithfulness to Scripture as such?

My point here is that in the formulation of the principle that guides Barth's exegesis of Scripture there is operating alongside Barth's openness to Scripture as such his hostility to some of the consequences of other in-

[96] Cf. Berkouwer, *op. cit.*, p. 246.

terpretations of Scripture — consequences that lead to the inclusion, among the significant data of the theologian, of objects other than Scripture. Loyalty to Scripture is qualified by the predetermination that such loyalty must make itself exclusive. Hence it is predetermined that aspects of Scriptural teaching that seem to point beyond Scripture do not really do so. The issue is, then, whether Scripture that is understood as testimony to revelation demands that exclusive status which Barth accords it, or whether this exclusive status is ascribed it on considerations that are alien to Scripture itself. It is my belief that the latter is the case.

It is almost certain that this is the case biographically. Barth recognizes that in his earlier writings he did not carefully and consistently rule out statements about natural fallen man as an object in himself. Indeed, he was heavily indebted to Kierkegaard's analysis of how man subjectively came to the point of decision for or against faith. He did not immediately perceive this interest as contrary to Scripture. He did, however, become aware of the implications and consequences of allowing this interest free development, and he startled his early admirers by radically rejecting and repudiating it, giving as his reason precisely the results that follow from taking this interest seriously.[97]

The real question, however, is not biographical but systematic. Does Scripture teach the monism of grace and the exclusiveness of its own witness to revelation consistently? If not, Barth must employ selectivity and norms based on something else than the united witness of Scripture. These principles may still be found within Scripture, but their selection must point to some preunderstanding on the part of the man approaching Scripture. Then the question of the justification of this preunderstanding raises the whole range of issues that Barth's method is designed to circumvent.

This criticism is by no means intended to suggest that Barth is more bound by a preunderstanding than other theologians. On the contrary, what is truly remarkable about Barth is the extent to which he is able to let the Bible speak in terms of its own understanding of itself. But the criticism is made because Barth alone among all the men treated in this volume professes as the method of theology this pure, nonselective obedience to Scripture's witness to revelation. If the method he proposes is humanly possible, we must acknowledge it at the very least as a stable, coherent, and intrinsically acceptable way to theologize. Indeed, it would be difficult to justify any other method as equally Christian. Every other theology would then appear as some kind of mixture of pure Christian thinking with some concern or presupposition brought in from without.

97 Baillie, *op. cit.*, pp. 114 ff.

If the criticism is valid, on the other hand, we must say that the ideal for theology held up before us by Barth is a false ideal. We must say either that we can find unity in the Bible only by bringing presuppositions to it or that faithfulness to the whole of Scripture requires us to engage also in discussion of and in the world. Probably we shall be forced to say both.

If the criticism is not valid, then Barth confronts us with a profound either-or. Either we must enter with him into a vision of the unlimited sovereignty of God's grace that reduces all else to negativity, finding this vision as the uniform message of Bible and church, or we are forced simply to confess that this vision is not real for us and that we must stand outside the circle of faith defined by it. Few men in our age or any age have come so near succeeding in confronting us with a final choice for or against faith. If Barth has failed, as I believe he has, his has been one of the most brilliant failures of all times.

In conclusion, we may summarize the possibilities as follows. If despite all objections, Barth shows the possibility of a theology of revelation that receives its principles from revelation and applies them in turn only to revelation, then all criticism ceases. We must stand either within or without the closed circle of revelation. There is no path by which we may move into this circle from the wider world of thought and no path by which we may move from that circle back to the wider world. Furthermore, if Barth is right, then every other appeal to revelation is null and void. Our only real choice is between the closed circle of revelation and total ignorance of God that does not even know its ignorance.

If, on the contrary, Barth is able to justify his view that Scripture speaks *only* of revelation in Jesus Christ only by bringing to Scripture certain assumptions that are not derived from it, then we must require a responsible theologian to concern himself with this preunderstanding. This might point us back to the natural theologies treated in Part I or forward to those theologies treated in Part III. In any case, it establishes *some* context that is shared by faith and unfaith and within which revelation is apprehended or interpreted.

If, finally, we can allow the Bible to provide its own principles of interpretation but find that these lead to an inclusion in theology of topics other than God's self-revelation in Jesus Christ, then we must concern ourselves, on the basis of revelation, with the questions that agitate the wider world of thought. This is the alternative suggested in the preceding chapter on Brunner. If carried through, it would lead to a synthesis of all knowledge through a philosophy selected, corrected, informed, and guided by the Christian faith. This is what we have called a Christian philosophy including or supporting a Christian natural theology.

Part III
THEOLOGICAL EXISTENTIALISM

8: What Is Existentialism?

IN THE FIRST PART OF THIS VOLUME, WE HAVE CONSIDERED A VARIETY OF CONtemporary theologies that build upon, or within the context of, specific philosophical positions. All these philosophies stand in that tradition which accepts as its task either the analysis of the structure of being as such (metaphysics and ontology) or the formulation of a world view that incorporates the best theories currently available (cosmology).[1]

Because of our specifically theological interest we have neglected any investigation of those other ontologies and cosmologies whose formulations are antithetical to religious interests. These consist in various forms of materialism, naturalism, and phenomenalism, all of which appear to religious eyes to be reductionistic to some degree.

However, speculative philosophy, whether favorable or unfavorable to the claims of faith, no longer dominates the intellectual scene. It has come to seem pretentious and blind to the limitations of knowledge. Its practitioners have been on the defensive, in part from the time of Hume and Kant, more acutely in the twentieth century with the collapse of cosmological thinking in physics.

In Part II, we considered theological positions that are developed in strict intentional independence of the claims of speculative thought. They have recalled the church to its witness to the one revelation of God in Jesus Christ. They have insisted that this God is known only in his revelation and, hence, has nothing in common with the ideas about deity constructed by speculative thought.

Careful criticism of Brunner and Barth, however, has suggested that

[1] Some of the generalizations of these first paragraphs do not apply to Wieman.

the program may not be a possible one. On the one hand, we cannot escape presuppositions that arise in a wider experience than our apprehension of Jesus Christ. On the other hand, our revealed knowledge of God seems to be relevant to a wider sphere of reality. If either of these points is correct, we cannot rid ourselves as theologians of involvement in philosophy as completely as some had hoped.

A third possibility seems to be to seek help from a philosophy that shares in the rejection of that kind of speculation characteristic of natural theology. In the twentieth-century collapse of idealism and naturalism, two major types of philosophy have arisen. These may be called, in very general terms, existentialism and analysis.

Both movements are now having great influence on Protestant theology. During the past forty years existentialism has undoubtedly affected theology more deeply, especially in Germany; hence, our primary attention will be devoted to it. Since analysis necessarily requires a given body of propositions to analyze, it cannot provide a *basis* for theology. Thus far it has been employed chiefly as clarificatory of the status and meaning of orthodox doctrines and of the kind of theology that was treated in Part II.[2]

In Part III we turn our attention to that contemporary theology which is rooted in existentialism, but before discussing theological existentialism it seems necessary to attempt an interpretation of existentialism in general as a major orientation in modern thought.

The term is widely used and frequently defined, but to most people it remains as confusing as ever. There can be little hope that this attempt at clarification will be more successful than others, but the effort must be made. To this end this chapter presents existentialism in two ways: first, historically, and then, as an ideal type. The historical presentation consists of a comment upon the decisive contribution of Nietzsche and of brief accounts of major aspects of the thought of four twentieth-century philosophers: Husserl, Sartre, Heidegger, and Buber. This list could be greatly extended, but these four accounts will be sufficient to indicate the range and variety of points of view loosely grouped under the heading of existentialism. Those themes which have emerged out of this wealth of creative thought and which tend to group themselves together as distinctively existentialist will then be presented in an effort to describe the ideal type that the term " existentialist " suggests.

[2] Cf. Willem Frederik Zuurdeeg, *An Analytic Philosophy of Religion;* John Hick, *Faith and Knowledge: A Modern Introduction to the Problem of Religious Knowledge;* Antony Flew and Alasdair Macintyre, eds., *New Essays in Philosophical Theology.*

By common consent the two greatest existentialist thinkers of the nineteenth century are Sören Kierkegaard and Friedrich Nietzsche. Since a summary of Kierkegaard's position and its implications for theology was offered above in Chapter 5, it will not be repeated. We must also bear in mind his immense importance for the thinkers treated in Part III.

Kierkegaard affirmed the absolute otherness of God from man and from all that man's objectifying reason can conceive. Nietzsche proclaimed that God is dead. These two views have in common the rejection of all popular, comfortable religion. Both recognize that the rational arguments by which faith has so often been supported are useless. Both understand that man's ordinary moral values are wholly irrelevant to the experience of ultimate reality. Both perceive that the lives of churchmen and outsiders alike in fact deny the reality of God. But whereas for Kierkegaard this situation posed the challenge to recover authentic faith, for Nietzsche it required that men should face honestly and fearlessly the consequences of their atheism.

The vast majority of those who had abandoned belief in God went on living as though this made little difference. The ethics of humility and sacrifice, the special concern for the poor and the weak, and the ideal of equal rights for all men simply because they are men were supposed to be humanistic principles independent of belief in God. The moral law or the inherent value of human personality replaced God as the objective determinant of the meaning of individual existence.

The death of God proclaimed by Nietzsche should be understood much more comprehensively than as a denial of the existence of the God affirmed by the Christian church. Such denial might be made in the interests of classical philosophy, Indian mysticism, or even modern humanitarianism. What Nietzsche perceived to have ended for Western man was every understanding of the world in terms of supersensuous reality.[3] The finite world of particulars must henceforth be understood as the only source of meaning, the only sphere for thought and existence. This for Nietzsche is the essential meaning of nihilism.[4]

On the basis of this nihilism Nietzsche with prophetic genius exposed all the illusions of his humanistic contemporaries. If God is dead, then there is no objective demand upon man whatsoever. He becomes his own God, and he must lay down for himself the end of his own existence. Man is what he makes himself and can find the meaning of existence only in this act of self-creation.

[3] Martin Heidegger, "Nietzsche's Wort, 'Gott ist tot,'" *Holzwege,* p. 203.
[4] *Ibid.,* p. 205.

The acceptance of the death of God and the development of these consequences have characterized the dominant trends of twentieth-century existentialism. Hence, in many respects philosophical existentialism is more Nietzschean than Kierkegaardian, more nihilistic than Christian. Theological existentialism, by contrast, however much it may respect the brilliance of Nietzsche's insight, must retain against him elements of Kierkegaard's position. In the efforts of theological existentialists to come to terms with contemporary philosophical existentialism we will see the tensions introduced by the Nietzschean element in the latter.

Nevertheless, even theologians may recognize and employ the profound meaning of Nietzsche's dictum. Martin Buber writes of the eclipse of God, and many recognize that we live in a post-Christian age. The whole understanding of theology in such a situation is radically altered.

Kierkegaard's existentialism became profoundly influential in Protestant theology with the publication of Karl Barth's *Epistle to the Romans,* especially the second edition in 1922. The whole tone and tenor of theological debate since then has been set against that background. Twentieth-century philosophical existentialism made a similar impact upon the philosophical community through the appearance in 1927 of Martin Heidegger's *Sein und Zeit.* Although Heidegger was aware of, and interested in, Barth's work, the modern emergence of philosophical existentialism should be understood as relatively independent of the theological revival. At the same time, it posed a profound challenge to the existentialist theologians by presenting existentialism in a new and much more systematic fashion.

Mounier draws an interesting diagram of the historic development of existentialism in the form of a tree.[5] He shows Kierkegaard as the trunk of this tree. But across the top of the trunk, just before it branches, he writes the word "phenomenology." The founder of phenomenology was Edmund Husserl, who, ironically, was far from being an existentialist himself. He taught that philosophy must set aside the question of existence and concentrate entirely upon the realm of essences, of meanings, or of ideas. Philosophy must become an exact science of ideas.

But in order to turn philosophy into an "eidetic science" Husserl was forced to develop systematically a method of inquiry that had until then been employed without critical, methodological self-consciousness. This method he called "phenomenology," and it is the phenomenological method that has subsequently been employed in the work of the major existentialists. Both Sartre and Heidegger studied under Husserl and both developed their own philosophic programs in relation to their teacher.

[5] Emmanuel Mounier, *Existentialist Philosophies,* p. 3.

Heidegger's *Sein und Zeit* is dedicated to Husserl and appeared first in Husserl's phenomenological yearbook. Although the later Heidegger can be called an existentialist only in a very loose sense, his whole development can be understood as determined by his commitment to phenomenology.[6] Sartre's major work, *Being and Nothingness,* is subtitled " An Essay on Phenomenological Ontology," and in other works as well he writes explicitly as a phenomenologist. Hence, a brief exposition of Husserl's phenomenology is essential.

Husserl was convinced that philosophy could attain scientific precision only if it limited itself to description, and for him, as well as for his pupils, the phenomenological method is understood as purely descriptive. But phenomenological description differs from ordinary empirical description in several ways.[7]

In the first place, ordinary empirical description is affected by an interpretive framework based on earlier experience. What we see in an entity is affected by what we suppose ourselves to know about it. Thus we may " see " the sun in terms of our knowledge that it is ninety-three million miles away and that the earth revolves around it. For many purposes the conditionedness of our " seeing " by our past experiences is unexceptionable, but it is disastrous for philosophy. This is because the function of philosophy is to clarify the fundamental assumptions underlying our knowledge, and it cannot, therefore, afford to be influenced by the conclusions of such knowledge. Phenomenology is that description which sets aside, or in Husserl's words " brackets," all extraneous information or theory and sees the object just as it presents itself apart from all interpretation.[8]

In the second place, ordinary empirical description understands itself as describing existent entities. But the *existence* of entities is already a theoretical interpretation that introduces the whole gamut of metaphysical speculation. Husserl, therefore, insists that we must bracket the existence of that which we describe. This does not mean that we describe it simply as a subjective impression. On the contrary, we do not experience it as such, and to describe it in this way would itself be a function of a speculative theory. We describe each entity precisely in terms of that objectivity with which it gives itself to us.

In the third place, ordinary empirical description takes its objects to be particulars as such and proceeds to generalizations about them. Phenome-

[6] Heinrich Ott, *Denken und Sein,* pp. 45–52.

[7] For Husserl's criticism of empiricism and naturalism, see *Ideas: General Introduction to Pure Phenomenology,* I, pp. 82–88.

[8] Edmund Husserl, *Cartesian Meditations,* Meditation 1.

nology, on the other hand, takes its object to be forms, meanings, or ideas. It is not concerned with the contingent fact that event A caused event B to occur. But it may describe what is meant or intended by event, cause, or occurrence. To achieve such a description it must use examples, but what it seeks in the particular is that idea whose meaning it seeks to expose. Only by expounding the meaning of such primitive ideas can philosophy fulfill its function of clarifying the foundations of all knowledge.

In the fourth place, ordinary empirical description ignores the process of consciousness by which the object being described is experienced. Phenomenology, by contrast, understands each object as the " intentional " object of consciousness and, hence, must describe also the process of intending that constitutes the object as such. Every experience has content. In this sense there is no consciousness that is not the intention of some object. But the object is also such, only as the object of that intention. Hence, its objectivity is a function of the intending process.[9]

Husserl affirms that consciousness " constitutes " its objects. This does not mean that we can choose to constitute or not to constitute a stone when we attend to it. Its intended objectivity precludes this freedom on our part. But it does mean that everything we perceive in the object is a correlate of our way of perceiving. It is the *how* of experience that structures the world and in terms of which everything in that world must be understood as a correlate. This *how* is certainly supra-voluntary, but at the same time, it is a property or function of consciousness. More precisely it is this *how* of experiencing which in its most universal aspects comprises pure consciousness, the absolute subject of all experience. It is the analysis of this pure consciousness which constitutes the whole world of objects as its correlative sphere that is the supreme function of transcendental or pure phenomenology.[10] It seems clear that for Husserl this transcendental subject and this alone ultimately exists.

That this position is an idealism is recognized by Husserl.[11] He calls it a transcendental phenomenological idealism and differentiates it from all other kinds of idealism. It leaves us with a view of the status of physical things that we can sustain only as long as we remain in the transcendental standpoint. They are the autonomously real objective correlates of pure consciousness. It is as such that we perceive, think, mean, or intend them,

[9] For Husserl's clarification of the relation of the *how* and the *what* of experience, see the discussion of *noesis* and *noēma* in *Ideas* I, Sec. III, Chs. III and IV.

[10] *Ideas* I, pp. 17–18, 253–254, 285.

[11] *Ibid.*, pp. 18–19.

but it is only as intended that they have this autonomous objectivity. Hence, they are secondary in ontological status, dependent upon conscious intention, yet, as intended, objective to the intending consciousness.[12]

The position into which we come may seem not only idealistic but also solipsistic. It may seem that it is not only consciousness which constitutes the world but specifically my consciousness which constitutes my world. Husserl, however, was certain that this is not the case, or at least that it is true only in a very limited sense. Indeed, Husserl was sure that the objectivity which we intend is an objectivity to a plurality of consciousnesses, that apart from a community of perceivers our meaning is emptied of essential ingredients. Hence, he devoted extensive attention to our knowledge of other minds.[13]

We must remember that for Husserl the question is never whether we know that there are other persons than ourselves. We ask only what we mean by such a thought. We can answer this question only by examining *how* we come to think of such persons. The process is mediated by our awareness of animated bodies other than, but like, our own. This leads us to posit that they are accompanied by a psyche like our own and, finally, that this functions like our own on the basis of an absolute, pure, and constituting consciousness.

It is important to note that the objectivity of the other consciousness differs from that of all other objects. It is given mediately, but it is given as radically independent of the process of my constituting it. It can have this independence because it is of the same order of being as my own consciousness. That consciousness and I together function as a we, and the intended objectivity of everything else becomes objectivity for this intersubjective community of personal consciousness.

The full understanding of the " I " presupposes the intersubjective communion of persons. It seems to appear at four levels. There is the I-man, the psychophysical being that interacts with its environment. There is the purely psychological I introspectively observable as object. There is the spiritual I, the I that thinks, wills, and purposes. And there is the transcendental Ego, which can never be objectified but which is the unifying subject of the pure consciousness. The I-man and the psychological I are understood as subject to the causal laws of nature, whereas the acts of the spiritual I are *motivated* but not caused. That is, logical laws and past experiences provide the occasion for thinking or acting in a certain way, but they do not force this thought or action. The thought or action occurs

[12] Note how this dependent status is stressed in *Ideas* III, Ch. III.
[13] *Cartesian Meditations,* Meditation V; *Ideas* II, Part II.

only as a function of *spiritual* purposes and ends. The spiritual I is the seat of freedom.[14]

This account of Husserl's thought provides only the barest indication of its complexity, rigor, and scope. It selects from the numerous available topics on the basis of the relevance of Husserl for theology and specifically for modern existentialism. Hence, it has focused on the general goal and method of phenomenology, on the one hand, and what I would call Husserl's ontological position on the other. However, Husserl uses the term " ontology " in quite a different sense. Since both Heidegger and Sartre concern themselves with what they call ontology, it will be necessary in conclusion to indicate Husserl's use of the term.

Husserl distinguishes " regions " of experienced objects.[15] For example, in the external world as objectified we may distinguish three regions: that of material things, that of animated bodies, and that of the psyche. To each of these regions there corresponds a regional ontology.[16] This consists in the clarification of the system of primitive terms and relations, which are intuitively grasped as necessarily inhering in any object given in the region in question. For example, any material object must be spatial. Hence, it must conform to whatever characterizes space as such. Geometry is the a priori discipline that studies spatiality as such. Hence, geometry is one of the regional ontologies relative to material things. Pure sciences of time and motion would be others.[17]

In addition to these regional ontologies there is the formal ontology that investigates the principles common to all regional ontologies and their regions. This is pure, formal logic, including *mathesis universalis*.[18] The establishment of the foundations of the ontologies is the task of phenomenology.

In Husserl's use of ontology, it retains the meaning of the investigation of the structure of being, but Husserl does not apply it to the absolute existence of the transcendental consciousness. Hence, there are ontologies of the dependent realms only. Furthermore, the regional ontologies, that

[14] Alfred Schutz, " Edmund Husserl's Ideas Volume II," *Philosophy and Phenomenological Research,* Vol. 13, 1953, pp. 406–411.

[15] *Ideas* I, pp. 64 ff., 411 ff. There is also an ontology of values, but this is little discussed.

[16] Generally he refers only to regions of the " real " or empirically given. However, he also speaks of the realm of transcendental consciousness as a region. (*Ideas* I, p. 213.)

[17] Alfred Schutz, " Edmund Husserl's Ideas Volume III," *Philosophy and Phenomenological Research,* Vol. 13, 1953, p. 509.

[18] *Ideas* I, p. 67. Husserl also speaks of a formal axiology and praxis as parallel to formal logic. (*Ibid.,* p. 400.) For the distinction between purely formal laws as logical and as ontological, see *ibid.,* p. 409.

is, investigations of what an entity must be to function in that region, leave open the question of the relationship of different modes of being to one another. One might expect the formal ontology to identify what is common to being in any region, hence, what is common to being as being, but instead it treats only what is common to relations in any region. Hence, what are usually regarded as the ontological questions are not included by Husserl in this category but appear, when they appear at all, elsewhere.

Some of Husserl's pupils and admirers were disturbed by the radically idealistic conclusion to which he came and undertook to use the phenomenological method against it. Jean-Paul Sartre wrote a treatise on *The Transcendence of the Ego,* in which he argues in radical opposition to Husserl that the ego itself is also an intentional object constituted by consciousness rather than a transcendental subject presupposed by consciousness.[19] If so, we must reopen the question of the being of the intentional objects of consciousness, which Husserl had hoped that philosophy could avoid.

Sartre answers this question in terms of a fundamental dualism.[20] His analysis of consciousness, to which he had denied a substantial basis in an unexperienceable ego, reveals it as fundamentally negative in character. This negativity is not, of course, nonexistence or lack of efficacy. The point is rather that consciousness lacks all solidity, endurance, or capacity to sustain itself and that its function is always that of negating through questioning, distinguishing, and desiring. As soon as consciousness acquires a content, it becomes a part of the past and thereby is no longer consciousness. Consciousness is such only as it stands in front of the filled, and thereby fixed, past as an opening to be filled.

Over against this remarkable nothingness is being — that which simply is what it is. Being is in itself completely free of all negation, hence, of all differentiation. It is nontemporal and nonspatial, unchanging and completely full. It is only in the negating work of consciousness, therefore, that this being is fashioned into a world.

As a phenomenologist, Sartre undertakes to describe the structures of consciousness as it creates its world and yet always stands before being. He sees the very essence of consciousness in its freedom, which he takes more radically than any other major thinker in the Western tradition.[21] Consciousness is freedom because it is nothingness, that is, because it is

[19] Jean-Paul Sartre, *The Transcendence of the Ego,* pp. 37 ff.
[20] Most systematically developed in Jean-Paul Sartre, *Being and Nothingness: An Essay on Phenomenological Ontology,* "Introduction" and pp. 617–625.
[21] Wilfred Desan, *The Tragic Finale,* pp. 107, 160. Note, however, his qualifying comment on Sartre's recent development, p. xvi.

lack, absence, or nihilation of being. Since determinateness is a function of being, nothingness shares in it.

But freedom as a lack always aims toward being. Its goal is to achieve the concreteness and substantiality of being without losing the freedom of consciousness.[22] But in principle this goal is wholly unattainable. The human project is a failure, an absurdity. God also is to be understood in terms of this impossible combination of being and freedom — the illusion by means of which men avoid facing the absurdity of their own aim.[23]

Although the absurd aim of uniting being and consciousness is common to all men, each man must be understood in terms of his particular fundamental project.[24] Each specific purpose and act has its meaning in the context of this more basic project. The aim of psychoanalysis is to lay bare this deeper meaning of acts. But Freudian psychoanalysis errs in two major respects.[25] In the first place, it assumes that there is a common fundamental project for all men and erroneously interprets the meaning of acts in these terms rather than seeking their actual meaning for the particular individual in question. In the second place, it regards this fundamental project as an unconscious structure outside the scope of freedom and interprets consciousness as a function of this determinate being. Thereby it attributes even the resistance to therapy to the unconscious, ignoring the real responsibility of the free consciousness.

In other words, psychoanalysis operates in terms of an essentialism to which Sartre opposes existentialism. It treats the individual human person as an example of a species and supposes the individual to be but a special case of the interaction of laws that are independent of his choosing. In sharp contrast to this, Sartre calls for an analysis of each individual in terms of his own freely chosen project and demands that " laws " be understood only as generalizations from the real diversity of individual expressions of freedom.

Sartre does not suppose that our fundamental projects are chosen on the basis of rational deliberation or that we are able to articulate them verbally and thereby bring them to reflective consciousness.[26] Consciousness does not mean for him reflective knowledge, and freedom does not mean reflective decision. The consciousness that is nothingness, and therefore also freedom, is the primitive unreflective intending of a world. There are many aspects of this consciousness which are absent in that consciousness

[22] *Being and Nothingness*, pp. 565–566.
[23] *Ibid.*, p. 566. See also Norman N. Greene, *Jean-Paul Sartre: The Existentialist Ethic*, Ch. V.
[24] *Being and Nothingness*, p. 567; Greene, *op. cit.*, Ch. III.
[25] *Being and Nothingness*, pp. 571 ff.
[26] Desan, *op. cit.*, pp. 149–150; Greene, *op. cit.*, pp. 30 ff.

of being conscious which raises consciousness into the realm of availability for discourse. Hence, the affirmation that our fundamental projects are both conscious and freely chosen does not constitute as radical an opposition to Freudian psychoanalysis as it seems.

Nevertheless, the difference is important. Since our fundamental project in terms of which all more immediate aims are to be understood is freely chosen, it may also be freely changed. Conversion is a possibility with which we must always reckon.[27] Furthermore, the individual who recognizes this freedom to be something quite different from what he is must accept radical responsibility for what he is. From this point of view Freudian psychoanalysis appears as the great evasion.

The ideas of conversion and responsibility point again to the implications of Sartre's emphasis that consciousness always stands before being as the lack of being. This means that my consciousness always stands before my past. This peculiar relation necessitates a highly paradoxical account of selfhood. Sartre says that I am not what I am. By this he means that I am not as present consciousness the sum total or net product of what I have been in the past. The present consciousness takes up a relation to that past, but what relation it will take is not determined by the past. To conceal this fact from myself and to pretend to myself that I am only what my past has made me is to adopt a form of bad faith which Sartre calls sincerity. On the other hand, to suppose that one *is* something other than one's past is equally an act of bad faith.[28]

The point is that as freedom, as consciousness, one *is* nothingness. That nothingness is not simply nonbeing but rather a form of being is indicated by the fact that Sartre also calls consciousness being-for-itself. In this characterization it is opposed to being-in-itself, which in opposition to nothingness was called simply being. But being-for-itself is distinguished also in a different way from being-for-others. Sartre notes that we are conscious of the fact that others objectify us, and this consciousness of our being for them profoundly affects our being for ourselves.[29] However, the two never simply merge. Rather, they constitute a duality in terms of which much human experience is to be understood.

Sartre expounds the meaning of human relationships in terms of this duality of being-for-itself and being-for-others. His analyses are extraordinarily subtle and often persuasive. They share with the analyses based on the duality of being and nothingness the characteristic of always pointing

[27] Desan, *op. cit.,* p. 106; Sartre, *Being and Nothingness,* pp. 573; also 496–504.
[28] *Being and Nothingness,* pp. 62–64.
[29] See especially Sartre's discussion of "The Look." (*Being and Nothingness,* Part III, Ch. I, Sec. IV.)

up the futility and absurdity of man's projects. Every relationship aims at an end which in the nature of the case cannot be achieved.[30]

In a brief presentation such as this it is inevitable that the structural elements of Sartre's thought appear to predominate over the detailed phenomenological exposition. It must be understood, however, that in Sartre's intention the structures emerge out of the phenomenological investigation. Indeed, the persuasiveness of his basic dualism depends primarily on the illuminating power of the phenomenological descriptions that involve it.

Sartre employs his skill as a phenomenologist primarily to expose the particularities of the individual consciousness. The universal structures of consciousness as such are recognized and brilliantly articulated, but they are presented more to show how they provide the basis for individual freedom than as decisively important in themselves. In this respect Sartre resembles Kierkegaard.

The philosophical project of Martin Heidegger provides an interesting contrast to that of Sartre. He overlaps extensively in his analysis of the structures of existence, but he does not employ these as a basis for studying the peculiarities of individuals. On the contrary, he regards the ontological analysis of existence as a means of raising the questions of the meaning of being. Whereas Sartre treats the duality of being and nothingness as fruitfully illuminating the diversity of human behavior, Heidegger studies man for the sake of recovering the meaning of being.

Husserl had understood the function of phenomenology as that of developing a series of regional ontologies, but he had not worked out a regional ontology of human existence as such and indeed rarely indicated that he conceived this as a region at all. This may be because the most important part of human existence as he understood it, the transcendental ego, transcends all regions. Heidegger, however, agrees with Sartre in denying that the ego is transcendental. It is a constituted object, not the subject of all constituting. Hence, he holds that it is the phenomenologically accessible existent self which intends and constitutes the world. This means that a regional ontology of human existence (*Dasein*) is possible and that it is the fundamental ontology underlying all others. As such it should prove a uniquely favored basis for recovering the meaning of being.

Although Heidegger made clear in the introduction to *Sein und Zeit* that the analysis of Dasein was to be a means toward reopening the question of being as such,[31] the body of the published work consists entirely

[30] Cf. Desan's summary of the possible relation with the other. *Op. cit.*, pp. 84–91.

[31] Martin Heidegger, *Sein und Zeit,* Subsection 3. Where possible, references are given by subsections rather than by pages in the German edition, since an English translation is expected shortly. A partial, unpublished translation by Robert Tray-

in the analysis of the structures of Dasein, especially in relation to temporality. The impression long current was that Heidegger identified the structures of human existence, when it fulfills its own proper potentialities, with the structures of being that he sought. It was on the basis of this understanding that Heidegger was hailed as an existentialist philosopher and indeed as the greatest of this century.

Heidegger affirms that Dasein is always a being-in-the-world.[32] By this he means that we cannot first identify Dasein as an entity that has its being in itself and then raise the question of its relation to other beings. Dasein is already, as Dasein, a being-in-the-world. The world in which Dasein is, however, is not a finite or infinite spatiotemporal extension conceived as in a scientific cosmology. Rather it is the experienced world as organized in relation to Dasein. Dasein and the world mutually imply each other without ontological priority on either side. "World" is the world of Dasein, and Dasein is *being-in-the-world*.

However, the being-in of Dasein can be analyzed separately from the worldliness of its world. When this is done two characteristics of Dasein stand out with special finality. These Heidegger calls *Befindlichkeit* (feeling) and *Verstehen* (understanding).

Befindlichkeit is that tonality of feeling which is given for every Dasein with its being.[33] It is not chosen or intelligible in terms of some given goal. It is the sheer givenness of Dasein to itself. Heidegger calls this experience of givenness "thrown-ness."[34]

Verstehen is that mode of its being in which Dasein always transcends itself. It is the projection of Dasein into the future in terms of its possibilities for realization. Dasein always understands itself as being-in-the-world in terms of potentially realizable ends. The entities in the world are what they are by virtue of the ends that they can serve, and the world in which Dasein finds itself is the final context of these ends. Thus it is as a project for the realization of certain ends that Dasein constitutes itself as being-in-the-world.[35]

The ends at which Dasein aims may be either possibilities manifested in the entities in its world or possibilities which it finds in its own distinctive being. In the former case, we may describe Dasein as unauthentic, in the latter case, as authentic.[36] These terms are intended by Heidegger as de-

hern, John Wild, Bert Dreyfus, and C. de Deugd has been of great help to me in my work with this book.

32 *Ibid.*, Subsection 12.

33 *Ibid.*, Subsection 29.

34 *Ibid.*, p. 135.

35 *Ibid.*, Subsection 31.

36 *Ibid.*, p. 146.

scriptive rather than normative, but in the total context of the book they do carry normative connotations.

In all our experience of the things in the world we experience ourselves as sharing them with other Daseins. We do not reason to the existence of these Daseins as Husserl had thought. We simply find them already with us in all our relations with things in the world. Hence, one characteristic of our being-in-the-world is our being-with-others in the world. Here again we find the double possibility of authenticity and unauthenticity.

On the one hand, it is possible that the other Daseins can be recognized in the full individuality of their personal being. On the other hand, and much more commonly, Dasein experiences the plurality of the others in their averageness, discounting their individuation. Reflexively, he understands himself as one like others. He then does what *one* does and thinks what *one* thinks. Dasein functions then simply as an impersonal one like others, thereby subordinating his own distinctive possibilities to the averageness of the others.[37]

Heidegger believes that Western philosophy has understood time from the standpoint of physical objects and their changes. From this perspective the present as the presented status of objects is primary. The past is constituted by those presents which once were but no longer are, and the future by those which have not been but will be. Time then appears as an undifferentiated flow of presents.

There is a legitimate place for this physical conception of time, but it should not be conceived as primary.[38] Present, past, and future are primarily modes of the being of Dasein, not of the presented entities, and when they are perceived in these terms, their character is understood quite differently.

Past, present, and future are three dimensions or horizons of existing Dasein. Dasein exists in these three modes or ecstasies, and all other thinking about time has its ground in their co-existence in Dasein. In this context the future is the primary mode of time. This is because Dasein is a project toward the future. The future *is* Dasein in its mode of projectedness, not a present which is not yet. The projection or future of Dasein determines the mode of pastness, or already-thereness, which always accompanies the project. This past is not that which was once present to Dasein and is no longer, but the thrown-ness of Dasein as appropriated by Dasein. The appropriation of the past in terms of the future results in the

[37] *Ibid.*, Subsections 26–27.

[38] Brock, "An Account of 'Being and Time,'" in Heidegger, *Existence and Being*, p. 92.

presentation, that is, present-making of the entities in the world. This is the present in terms of which public and measurable time is to be understood. But in the order of Dasein, which is time in its primary sense, the present is the third, not the first, mode of time.[39]

Heidegger understands the present as that which is presented to Dasein in the form of objects presented to a subject. Therefore, he denies that the present is the self-authenticating starting point for thought. However, it is clear that there is another sense of present in which it is prior to future and past, for it is that by which the future is apprehended as future and the past as past. We may call this " the now," or perhaps simply the existence of Dasein as such, that now which is already in advance of itself. We may then distinguish our use of the past according as we understand it as a succession of presentations or as a succession of actualized existential nows of Dasein.

It is in this sense, first, that Heidegger rejects objective history. The presentations to past Daseins divorced from the Daseins to which they were present are an empty topic for inquiry. The responsible historian confronts the past Daseins as they were in their existence. In dealing with these past realizations of potentialities, the historian finds, he does not create, his material. In this sense there is objectivity in the study of history.

However, Heidegger rejects the ideal of historical objectivity in a second sense as well. The recovery of past Daseins must inevitably be exceedingly selective. To fail to recognize this is not to escape selectivity but only to deceive oneself and to be guided in one's selectivity by random and uncriticized factors. The historian's responsibility is to select in terms of relevance to future realization. He must find realization of potentialities in the past that challenge us today to realization of our potentialities. Hence, responsible historical work is guided by a projection of the future. At the same time the projection can be responsible only if it, in its turn, is formed by an awareness of the past. The past is recovered in terms of a projection into the future based on a prior recovery of the past. This is the circle within which the historian must proceed.[40]

The understanding of time in terms of what is presented is a manifestation of the unauthentic orientation of ourselves to the entities in the world. Unauthenticity appears in Heidegger's analysis as the natural state of man, that toward which man tends except as some special force intervenes.

This tendency to orient ourselves in terms of the presented world is accentuated by the fact that the final and decisive possibility of Dasein is

[39] *Ibid.*, p. 93. [40] *Ibid.*, pp. 102–111.

death. To live authentically is to live in terms of my own proper project, and this is ultimately to live toward death.[41] But the realization of this possibility of nonbeing causes me anguish and drives me to lose myself in the things of the world.

That authentic life is ontologically possible is clear, but it appears ontically or factually as a rather remote possibility. To show the ontic as well as ontological possibility of authentic existence Heidegger turns to analysis of the conditions of its attainment.[42] These conditions he finds in the phenomena of conscience, guilt, and resolve. Conscience is the call of Dasein to itself in terms of its authentic possibilities. This call reveals the guilt of Dasein, that is, its not being what in its innermost possibilities it already is. The responsible acceptance of this guilt and the aim toward realization of authentic possibilities is resolve.[43]

The development of Heidegger's thought after *Sein und Zeit* is of great intrinsic interest. However, it points in many respects away from existentialism and has only recently begun to exercise significant influence on theology.

Heidegger turned away from the analysis of Dasein not because he repudiated what he had done but because he found that the question of the meaning of being must be asked more directly. Being must be understood as the being of whatever is and not as equivalent to human being.[44] Since metaphysics is the traditional name for the investigation of being, Heidegger turned his attention in that direction. In this connection he pointed out that being can become a problem for man and thereby be rescued from forgetfulness only when man encounters nothingness as the possibility of every entity.[45] Heidegger immersed himself in the study of the Greeks, for whom being had thus become a problem and who provided the context for all Western thinking about being.

But Heidegger found that all metaphysical inquiry has identified the question of the being of entities with the question as to what constitutes them as entities.[46] With this it pairs the question of the ground of all contingent entities in a supreme and necessary entity.[47] This means to

[41] Heidegger, *Sein und Zeit,* Subsection 53.
[42] *Ibid.,* Subsection 54.
[43] *Ibid.,* Subsections 56, 58, 60. See also Brock, "An Account of 'Being and Time,'" in Heidegger, *Existence and Being,* pp. 79–85.
[44] Ott asserts that the virtual identification of being with existence in *Sein und Zeit* was the fundamental weakness of the early Heidegger. (*Op. cit.,* pp. 56–57.)
[45] Heidegger, "What is Metaphysics?" *Existence and Being,* pp. 355–380.
[46] Martin Heidegger, *What Is Philosophy?* pp. 58–59; *An Introduction to Metaphysics,* pp. 17–19; "Postscript" to "What Is Metaphysics?" *Existence and Being,* pp. 381–382; *The Question of Being,* p. 33; Ott, *op. cit.,* pp. 92–93.
[47] Martin Heidegger, *Identität und Differenz,* pp. 56–57; Ott, *op. cit.,* p. 94.

Heidegger that the authentic question of being as such has been lost to Western philosophy and hence to the whole of Western civilization. Heidegger sets himself the task of reopening the question of being through a more original questioning, thereby surpassing metaphysics.

When Heidegger speaks of more original questioning, we should understand him in terms of the phenomenological enterprise. The more original question is the one that sheds more of the incrustations of inherited interpretation. It is the one that succeeds in seeing its intentional object more perfectly as it is in its sheer givenness. We ask about the sunrise more originally, for example, when we free our vision of it from all that we have learned about the motions of the earth and the sun, about clouds and atmospheric conditions, even about colors and their aesthetic significance. To achieve this more original view of the sunrise is not the simply intellectual operation of consciously removing from our description those elements which are brought to it from our training. It is really to achieve a freeing of the experience itself from these interpretive intrusions.

In order to ask the question of the entities as such, all great metaphysicians have had to ask the question with great originality. They have had to overcome the common-sense view of the sheer self-evidence of the entities. Heidegger elaborates the necessity of experiencing in anxiety the possibility of the utter nullity of things to show how it becomes possible to ask the more original question. Only this experience makes possible real wonder at the sheer fact of the being of the entities.[48] Along with the poets who have unsystematically but profoundly achieved the more original visions of the world, the philosophers have formed the vision that constitutes the ground of all Western existence.

But Heidegger calls us to the still more original question. Entities are structures of being. All new understandings of the entities are in fact new visions of being itself. But they have not penetrated to the unmediated vision of being. Now, at the end of Western civilization and its metaphysics, we must penetrate to this original awareness of being as being in order to gain a fresh starting point.

There is no way in which Heidegger can directly tell us what being is. He can only try with utmost patience to awaken in us the awareness of being in such a way that we can share with him in its progressive understanding. We can talk about its relationships, however, and can say something negatively, if not positively, about it.

In the first place, it is clear that being itself precedes and is unaffected

[48] In "What Is Metaphysics?" Heidegger presents this as the way in which metaphysics becomes actualized. From a later point of view it may be seen as the way in which metaphysics is surpassed.

by the subject-object dichotomy. Heidegger never intended that we should understand Dasein as the subject of experience and the other entities as the objects. Yet it is only in his later writings that the radical meaning of Dasein as being-in-the-world becomes clear. Perhaps we should say from the perspective of the later works that Dasein is simply Da-sein, the " there " of being. And the being which is there is no more the being of the particular person involved than it is the being of all the things which appear in the Da-sein. Indeed, in some of the later writings the language of Dasein and other entities disappears, presumably because it suggests too much the self-evident being of particular discriminable entities. We have instead only the actualization of being in the appearing of things, for whose appearing the human ingredient is only one indispensable element. This whole appearing of being is now the Da-sein of being, the being-there of being.[49]

In the second place, this makes evident the radical priority of being with respect to all entities, including Dasein, in so far as these terms continue to be usable at all. If we are to understand Dasein now, we must do so from the perspective of being. The reverse order, which characterized the early work of Heidegger, is radically abandoned. Man is removed from the center of the scene.

In the third place, being emerges as itself *geschichtlich*.[50] Our natural interpretation of this term would cause us to say that being is historical, and this need not be false. However, we must be very careful in using this English word. If we call being a historical phenomenon, we seem to make it a function of a human history, but Heidegger means just the reverse. Human history is a function of the way in which being appears. Being is *geschichtlich,* then, not because of its dependence on the human, but because in its appearing it is endlessly becoming something new. Being is not a static reality behind the flow of phenomena. It is the process of appearing in which it appears and is itself. Human history is a function of the way in which being presents itself in man's initial conceptual structuring of the process that is being.

This historicity of being, which is at the same time the foundation of human history and historicity, determines the fatefulness of human existence.[51] Here Heidegger shows that the way in which original questioning is carried on and answered in any age is not simply a function of the skill of persons in practicing the phenomenological method. Being presents it-

[49] See Ott, *op. cit.,* Ch. 8, for a profound exposition and for extensive quotations from some of the relevant works.

[50] *Ibid.,* pp. 105 ff., 215 ff.

[51] *Ibid.,* pp. 126–127.

self to men, or realizes itself in men, in terms of certain structures. These structures change, but they are not changed by voluntary decisions on the part of men. We do not willfully determine the fundamental vision of being in terms of which we do all our living and thinking. This is given for us and has consequences for us. We can choose only to be open to being as it gives itself to us or to conceal from ourselves the being by which we are. If we do the former, we think and live authentically. If we do the latter, we think and live unauthentically.[52]

The fact that it is now possible for Heidegger — and, following him, for us as well — to ask the question of being more originally is itself a fateful situation.[53] It is because Western civilization is factually dead that we are freed of the fundamental objectifying structure of experience which constituted its apprehension of being. Our freedom and responsibility is to share in this openness to being as it now appears to those who have the authenticity to let it be as it is.

In concluding this discussion of Sartre and Heidegger, their respective attitudes with respect to God may be noted. Sartre is an avowed and emphatic atheist. He explains the origin of the idea of God in terms of the absurd project to unite being and freedom, and he shows that the idea of God is precisely the idea of such a union. Furthermore, he understands belief in God as largely antithetical to the full realization of freedom. Atheism is not only demanded by honest inquiry; it is also a liberating doctrine.

Heidegger, by contrast, denies that he is an atheist. This means not that he is a theist, but only that the question of God is not within the purview of his thought. Metaphysics points to God as the supreme being, but in doing so it conceals the question of being as such. Hence, just in this respect metaphysics must be surpassed. Furthermore, Heidegger emphatically insists that being is not God. If God is, he is an entity, not being as such.[54] Whether such an entity exists is an ontic, not an ontological, question. But we must recognize that in our own day his existence is not effective for human life.[55] Both the ontological analysis and the ontic must now dispense with God.

[52] *Ibid.*, pp. 160 ff.

[53] See, however, Heidegger's reservations as to our capacity to ask most originally the question of being. (*Identität und Differenz*, p. 71.)

[54] *Identität und Differenz*, pp. 52–53, 70–71; *What Is Philosophy?* pp. 57–59; Ott, *op. cit.*, p. 139. Heidegger claims that his vision is more open to God, religiously speaking, than is the doctrine of God as necessary ground.

[55] Heidegger asserts that in our day we should be silent about God (*Identität und Differenz*, p. 51); and that we are too late for God (*Aus der Erfahrung des Denkens*, p. 7).

One would not expect any existentialist theologian to follow Sartre's atheism, but it is interesting to note that none of the three men treated in the subsequent chapters makes use of the small opening allowed by Heidegger. None of them takes the affirmation of God as an ontic affirmation in distinction from an ontological one. However, this possibility is not to be ruled out.[56]

There are several other major thinkers whose thought should be included in any historical account of modern existentialism. One thinks especially of Karl Jaspers, Gabriel Marcel, and Nicolas Berdyaev as well as such major literary figures as Fyodor Dostoevsky and Franz Kafka. But no pretense of completeness can or should be made in this introductory chapter, and for the present purposes the few men treated are generally sufficient.

However, in contemporary Protestantism one other philosopher has exercised a profound influence that, though often correlated with that of the existentialist thinkers treated above, remains quite distinctive. I refer to the Jewish philosopher Martin Buber, who has given to the expression "I-Thou" the status of a major category in modern theology. We will conclude this historical presentation of existentialism with a brief indication of the central themes in Buber's thought with reference to their relation to the work of the existentialists treated above.

The basic categories of Buber's thought center around the distinction of the I-Thou relation and the I-It relation.[57] This distinction is not to be identified with that between man's relation to other men and his relation to things. Buber stresses that man may have an I-Thou relation with a tree or a poem and may have an I-It relation with a human being.[58]

The I-Thou relation is any relation in which one is genuinely open to the concrete other as it is — open to letting it present itself on its own terms rather than categorizing it for purposes of utility or personal security.[59] The I-It relation is any relation in which one imposes upon the other his own ends and meanings and in this sense reduces it to a mere object. Whenever one man exploits another he relates himself to that other as an It. On the other hand, the I-Thou relation can be fulfilled in relations with a person in a way in which it can never be fulfilled in relations with things. One may regard anything as a Thou, but only a person can in

[56] Ott, *op. cit.*, p. 146.
[57] Martin Buber, *I and Thou*, pp. 3 ff.
[58] *Ibid.*, pp. 7, 9; Maurice S. Friedman, *Martin Buber: The Life of Dialogue*, pp. 57 ff.
[59] Friedman, *op. cit.*, p. 170.

turn regard oneself as such. Full mutuality, therefore, appears only in the relation between persons.[60]

Although in one sense only the I-It relation objectifies that to which it is related, there is another sense of objectifying which Buber perceives as prerequisite to both the I-Thou and the I-It relations. This Buber calls the primal setting at a distance and regards as that peculiar human achievement which makes possible relationship of any sort.[61] Relationship presupposes a prior separation of that which is related. Only because man can recognize the otherness of what is not himself can he perceive it as what it is in itself and relate himself to it.

This distancing of the other can pass over into its objectification in the sense of the I-It relation. But this is not the spontaneous consequence of distancing. Distancing first of all allows the other to be itself in the I-Thou relation.[62] This is primary also for the child. But as the I develops in the I-Thou relation it is brought into relationship, through the Thou, with a conceptually structured world of things. Necessarily man relates himself to this public world in the mode of the I-It relation. But the habits of using which develop in this relationship threaten to overcome the habits of openness of the I-Thou relationship. Thereby they become the source of evil in all human existence.[63] We cannot avoid this evil by denial or flight, but we must take it up into a higher unity of good.

The I of the I-Thou relation is not the same as the I of the I-It relation.[64] The latter is simply the individual. Man is born as such. But the former is the person that each individual has the potentiality to become.[65] Personhood is a function of relations with persons as persons.

Relationship is finally fulfilled only in the encounter with ultimate reality as the eternal Thou.[66] But that Thou which is God can never be for us an It.[67] Hence, in this age of the dominance of the I-It relation, God is eclipsed.[68] Hence, also, God has nothing to do with the ultimate of philo-

[60] *Ibid.*, pp. 61, 170–171. Even here it is an ideal limit. (Buber, *I and Thou*, pp. 131–134.)

[61] Friedman, *op. cit.*, pp. 82–84, 164–165. Note, however, that in his earlier work Buber tends to identify the I-Thou relation with a lack of distance. (*I and Thou*, pp. 18–24.)

[62] Friedman, *op. cit.*, p. 83.

[63] *Ibid.*, pp. 62–64, 74, 101, 103, 113; Buber, *I and Thou*, p. 46.

[64] Buber, *I and Thou*, pp. 62–65; *Eclipse of God: Studies in the Relation Between Religion and Philosophy*, p. 128.

[65] Friedman, *op. cit.*, pp. 61, 68.

[66] *I and Thou*, p. 75; *Eclipse of God*, pp. 44–45.

[67] *Eclipse of God*, pp. 68, 128.

[68] *Ibid.*, p. 129.

sophic discourse, which is based upon the objectifying thought of the I-It relationship.[69] Furthermore, despite Buber's early and continuing interests in both Western and Eastern mysticism,[70] the relationship with the eternal Thou must not be understood as union or absorption. It is not even a specifically religious relationship that takes man out of his concrete situation in the world.[71] God is encountered as Thou when the world is encountered as Thou.[72]

However, this does not mean that God is only another name for the Thou-quality of the world.[73] God's reality is prior to his realization in the world,[74] and our direction toward him is most fully achieved in prayer.[75] It does mean that faith remains in the lived concreteness of life and seeks to realize God through the mutuality of genuine relationship.

Buber is fully aware of his divergences from the existentialists treated above. He deeply respects Kierkegaard and acknowledges his debt to him,[76] but he opposes Kierkegaard's preoccupation with man's situation as a solitary existent before God. Certainly man's relation to God is supremely important, but that relation must contain man's relation to the world. To be related to God as Thou is to be open to the whole world as also Thou.[77] In our own day of the eclipse of God only total openness to our neighbor as Thou will enable us to address again the Eternal Thou.[78]

Heidegger's parallel preoccupation with the individual has led him in his early writings to identify man's goal as living out of his own proper potentialities. He recognizes that this also affects man's relations to his fellow man, but he sees the quality of these relations as derivative from the quality of individually achieved authentic existence. Buber reverses this order, pointing out that genuine life can be achieved only in the mutuality of real community.[79]

Both Heidegger and Buber speak of "making present,"[80] but the evaluations that they attach to this function are strikingly different. Heidegger

[69] *Ibid.*, pp. 32, 45.
[70] Friedman, *op. cit.*, p. 27.
[71] *Ibid.*, p. 50.
[72] *Ibid.*, p. 93.
[73] Martin Luria Diamond, *Martin Buber, Jewish Existentialist*, p. 40.
[74] Friedman, *op. cit.*, p. 39.
[75] *Ibid.*, p. 136; Buber, *Eclipse of God*, p. 126.
[76] Friedman, *op. cit.*, p. 35. For Buber's discussion of Kierkegaard see *Eclipse of God*, pp. 115–120; "The Question of the Single One," *Between Man and Man*, pp. 40–82. Additional references are given by Friedman, *loc. cit.*
[77] Friedman, *op. cit.*, p. 54.
[78] *Ibid.*, p. 147.
[79] For Buber's discussion of Heidegger, see *Eclipse of God*, pp. 70–78; and "What Is Man?" *Between Man and Man*, pp. 163–181.
[80] Friedman, *op. cit.*, pp. 82, 171.

sees it as the process of objectifying that which is encountered in the world in terms of projected goals. It is necessary for many purposes, such as science and technology, but its predominance in thought has led to unauthenticity. This must be countered by recognizing the priority of relationship to the future and past within Dasein itself over this presenting of objects. Buber, on the other hand, sees the making present as the condition of authenticity. To make present is to render the entity free to be itself and to speak for itself.[81] It is the condition for encounter with things as they are, and especially for the relationship of I to Thou, through which alone the I becomes a person.

This divergence serves to focus the fundamental difference between Heidegger and Buber. The former seeks the goal and resources for fulfillment with the individual Dasein, whereas the latter insists that man can become himself only in relationship. They agree that we must not regard the relationship of subject to objectified thing as primary; but Heidegger replaces this with the primacy of the relation of Dasein to its own future, whereas Buber replaces it with another kind of relation to the other — the I-Thou relation.

Sartre has discussed at much greater length than Heidegger man's relation to other men. But his elaborate analysis has led to the conclusion that in the nature of the case the ideal community is radically unattainable. Buber does not minimize the difficulties involved or deny that failure is frequent. But he rejects Sartre's approach of beginning with the analysis of the autonomous consciousness and only then proceeding to the question of relationship to other consciousnesses. Buber insists that persons become only in relationships, and that we must, therefore, begin with these relationships. The obstacles to full mutuality are ontic and not ontological; hence, they are subject to overcoming by man.[82]

Although we may be inclined to identify existentialism as such with the radical individualism of Kierkegaard, Heidegger, and Sartre, we should recognize that Buber is far from alone in his concern with the encounter or mutual presence of persons. Both Jaspers and Marcel have developed similar emphases quite independently.[83] Many of those Protestant thinkers most influenced by existentialism have appropriated existentialism with the focus on interpersonal relations to which Buber has given classical ex-

[81] There is another theme in Heidegger, developed in his later thought, in which he speaks of letting things be in opposition to imposing our conceptuality and purposes upon them. This brings him somewhat closer to Buber, but Heidegger still lacks any element of mutuality between persons.

[82] Friedman, *op. cit.*, pp. 14–15. For Buber's discussion of Sartre, see *Eclipse of God*, pp. 65–70.

[83] Friedman, *op. cit.*, p. 162, note.

pression. Even Bultmann, who in so many ways remains closer to the Heidegger of *Sein und Zeit* than any other leading theologian, makes use of a concept of encounter that recalls Buber much more than Heidegger.

Since a number of the themes treated in the presentation of each of the men discussed above can be found also in others among them, the overlapping among these existentialists is greater than may appear. Nevertheless, their real differences are also great. If we added discussions of still other existentialists, the diversity would become still more impressive. Rather than thus add to the confusion, we will now turn from the historical account of individual thinkers and conclude this chapter with an attempt to present a "typical" existentialist position which, while not accurately describing the thought of any major thinker, may serve to clarify the kinds of ideas most commonly associated with the term. We will begin with a nontechnical exposition of the technical philosophic starting point of all existentialism — namely, the doctrine that existence precedes essence.

Most philosophers have observed that what is given to man in his experience is a nexus of qualities structured in certain ways. Out of these qualities are made up all the objects of human knowledge, and the formal sciences of logic and mathematics deal with all the possible structural relations. Qualities and their relations are called forms or ideas by Plato, categories by Hegel.

Now the question is whether existence is itself one of the forms or categories along with the others. Hegel taught that it is. Hence, particular existent things, ourselves included, are exhaustively explainable in terms of the categories. Since the categories are the elements of impersonal thought or universal mind, and therefore subject to rational understanding, everything which is or can be is rational through and through.

Another philosophical tradition has held that existence as such is not one characteristic of an entity along with others, but something radically unique and prior to all characterizing. Thomas Aquinas taught this, and the idea is implicit in most substance philosophies. Indeed, it is almost universal in the common sense of the Western world since this common sense has been informed by Christianity. However, it is ignored by much technical philosophy and scientific thought. Indeed, whenever the analytic approach is paramount, it is endangered.

The term "existentialism," however, is meaningful only when it is understood that the existence which precedes essence is first of all *human* existence. Materialism also affirms the priority of existence to essence, but its "existences" are nonhuman in character and indeed exclude the possibility of the existence of the distinctively human. Existentialism arose in a context in which this kind of materialism and even less dogmatic forms of naturalism had been excluded from consideration by Kantian idealism. Specifically it arose as a reaction to Hegel's all-embracing rational idealism. Today it finds as its chief enemy scientism, whether the science which it universalizes regards itself as dealing empirically with *existent* matter or formally with logico-mathematical symbols. It especially opposes any implication that individual human existence is explicable either as a function of something subhuman or as an instance of the universal phenomenon — humanity. We cannot deduce or explain the individual human existent by appeal to anything else whatsoever. It must be taken as an ultimate and all-important fact.

What is meant by beginning with human *existence* is made clearer when we consider the difference between the inner and the outer view of man.

If we view a man from outside through our sense organs, we observe certain structures of qualities. We can perceive also certain changes in position that are functionally related to his environment. We can hear him speak and note the relations of his words to his movements. We can study the insides of his body through X-rays, incisions, or the insertion of instruments through the apertures of his body, and we can discover correlations between the functionings of his nerves and organs, on the one hand, and his outer behavior, on the other. These are the techniques of objective study favored by science. When we view a man in this way it is easy to think of existence as one characteristic among others that are observed — that characteristic which distinguishes this real person from an imaginary one.

Quite opposite to this way of viewing man externally through the sense organs of another man is the way of viewing ourselves in our immediate givenness to ourselves. Here we find fears and hopes, anxieties and purposes, lust and love, not as observable behavior patterns but as moods and motives. Here we find, above all, the sheer irrational fact that we *are*. We cannot then think of this existence as merely one characteristic of our being along with others. It is primary and absolute and the prior basis of the possibility of all others. It is the presupposition of the effort to explain anything at all, whether externally or internally known, and we cannot in turn get outside of existence in order to explain it.

In the sphere of external knowledge we can be relatively detached and objective. But this is true only because external knowledge is not ultimately of radical importance for us as individual existent beings. We can observe the functioning of other human organisms, for example, with minimal involvement, because how they function does not touch our own self-understanding as subjects. But we cannot approach with comparable detachment any investigation of the possibilities for inner existence. We can understand any way of being as a subject only by experiencing that way of being. We can understand what it means to love only by loving, what commitment means by being committed. Hence, the ideal of objectivity, with its accompanying spirit of detachment, precludes any real understanding of human existence. This indictment applies to most traditional philosophy, modern science, and much historiography, even where the object of investigation is man. Only the poet and the religious man have through the ages provided us with guidance in the understanding of man's real existence, and metaphysicians, scientists, and historians have generally contributed only as they were also poets and religious men.

Existential philosophy, therefore, repudiates all imitation of science in its method, and in so far as historians are influenced by its doctrines, they also abandon their earlier ideals. Thought that concerns itself with the objective, and that is therefore relatively detached in spirit, has, of course, practical value as is shown by the achievements of the natural sciences. But for man as man its role is altogether secondary. The subject of supreme concern to man is his own inner being, and this can be understood only as one is personally involved. Existentialists turn, therefore, to reflection upon their own interior life.

The objective approach to the study of men provides no place for freedom. Man's behavior is exhaustively described and its regular patterns are noted. Residual irregularities are simply that and no more. But man in his own immediate self-awareness knows himself to be, at least in some respects, self-determining. He is free to make decisions, and even the decision not to decide is a decision of sorts.

When the decision not to decide predominates in a man's life, then his existence is determined for him by hereditary and, especially, environmental forces. He becomes whatever others are or appear to be. Thus a person who does not exercise his freedom to think critically for himself is formed in his thoughts by whatever opinions are dominant in his environment. In his attitudes he reflects those of his companions. His purposes are whatever purposes are suggested to him. He is the conformist or the other-directed man.

In this abandonment of individuality and merging of himself into the crowd he seeks escape from responsibility and loneliness. But since he remains an existent, individual human being, he can never escape. He can only partially hide his responsibility and his loneliness from himself. The fact of death faces him with his final solitariness and causes him deep anxiety.

This futile flight from individuality is unauthentic existence. It is the curse of mass, industrial, secular society. It is that from which all existentialists call us. Even the unauthentic man has a kind of freedom. That is, he remains free to decide to be free. But so long as he does not exercise his freedom to be free, he is a product of external forces. Hence, he may be said to be only potentially free.

To assert or actualize one's freedom is the central act of freedom by which one enters authentic existence. The authentic man acknowledges his responsibility for what he is and becomes. He recognizes the influence upon him of his past, but by that act of recognition he frees himself of its control. He can decide not to continue to be the self that has been produced by that past. He can decide, that is, to accept another mode of existence, another self-understanding, another ideal aim, than that which the past presses upon him.

The finally decisive limitation to his freedom is his fear of death. As long as he is unwilling to accept death, society and circumstances can place severe limits upon his choice of mode of existence. He can choose only among those ways of being which are tolerated by society. To actualize one's freedom wholly, one must overcome one's bondage to continued life and accept fully the possibility of death.

At this point we must introduce the Nietzschean element in modern existentialism — the awareness of "the death of God." Apart from this, the primacy of the inner life and the realization of responsible freedom would hardly distinguish contemporary existentialism from the Christian life of prayer and service to God. The difference lies in the fact that in modern existentialism for the first time acute self-awareness has come into being in radical dissociation from prayer. That is, the existentialist is not uncovering for himself truth about himself known already to God. He is not examining his motives in the light of an absolute demand placed upon him by one who loves him wholly. On the contrary, he is examining his condition in the light of the absence of any other who knows him, loves him, or places a demand upon him.

The difference in result is incalculable. For Christian piety the inner life is the one point at which man escapes from loneliness into full communion. Christian introspection is carried out in a context of meaning which is in no way brought into question. The problems that emerge center around sin and forgiveness. Truth about the self, not about the meaning of life, is sought in self-analysis. For the thoroughgoing existentialist, the death of God means the absolute aloneness of the existent individual and the absence of any given structure of meaning whatsoever. Hence, the question of sin and forgiveness in the Christian sense cannot even arise. The all-important quest is for meaning, and this quest is foredoomed to failure in so far as meaning is still conceived as something given for the individual. Since God, the objective source of meaning, is dead, the only possible source of meaning is the self. But the meaning determined by the self cannot be rationalized or justified. In the past, men have wondered whether the good exists for God or is only his arbitrary fiat. The existentialist now discovers that, for man without God, the good is man's own arbitrary fiat. Men create, they cannot discover, the principles by which they live.

Christian freedom is freedom to fulfill or not to fulfill the divine purpose for one's life, but the freedom to set the end itself is God's alone. Existentialist freedom is the inescapable necessity of choosing an end without reason or encompassing purpose — simply as an act of freedom. The Christian knows himself responsible for his failure to fulfill God's purpose, but he experiences no responsibility for the purpose as such. The existentialist finds himself, finite being as he is, in the lonely and sovereign role of God, the author of purposes. The anguish that is thus his lot has dimensions wholly unknown to faith.

This makes it clear that for the existentialist the achievement of authentic life is no guarantee of happiness. On the contrary, it is the acceptance without illusion of anguish and loneliness. Every effort to escape from this situation is a flight from human existence as such. Virtue and happiness are alike false goals. Only freedom remains.

Clearly, Christians cannot simply adopt existentialism in its atheistic form. Notwithstanding, they have been deeply influenced by it. In Chapters 9, 10, and 11 we will consider Bultmann, Tillich, and H. Richard and Reinhold Niebuhr as presenting diverse ways in which Christian theology may develop in relation to this movement. The intention in each case is to reject natural theology. Our guiding question will be whether this goal is achieved and whether a viable alternative is provided.

9: Rudolf Bultmann

THE ONE THEOLOGIAN WHO DID MOST TO INTEREST THE THEOLOGICAL WORLD in existentialism was Karl Barth. But as Barth came to realize that his employment of existential categories involved him in an alliance with, or use of, a particular philosophy, he altered his methodology. His great *Church Dogmatics* is a monument to his endeavor to free theology from all dependence upon systematic philosophical thinking.[1]

However, among those who were aroused by Barth's early work, several major thinkers remained loyal to the existentialist emphasis abandoned by their mentor. Two of the most important of these men are Friedrich Gogarten and Rudolf Bultmann. Of these, the former is a systematic theologian and the latter a New Testament scholar. Nevertheless, it has been Bultmann rather than Gogarten who has riveted the attention of the theological world upon the task of interpreting Christian faith in existential terms. In the process of defending his method of New Testament interpretation, Bultmann has dealt with many of the problems of systematic theology.

If Bultmann's thought is to be accurately grasped, one must begin with his understanding of the relation between God and the world.[2] He understands the world as the totality of spatiotemporal phenomena, the whole object of human knowledge. It may be approached both externally, in an objectifying way that is appropriate to the physical sciences, and internally, in the way that is appropriate to the study of man and human history. In either case, we find a closed system of cause and effect — objective causal relations in the former instance, subjective motivations and human deci-

[1] Barth's mature theological method is treated in Chapter 7.

[2] Cf. Schubert M. Ogden, "Introduction," in Rudolf Bultmann, *Existence and Faith: Shorter Writings of Rudolf Bultmann,* Ogden, ed. pp. 14 ff. Ogden takes the infinite qualitative difference between time and eternity as the clue.

sions in the latter. In so far as our knowledge is concerned, any failure to find a cause simply means that we do not yet have adequate tools at our command. We always properly presuppose that the causes of this-worldly phenomena are this-worldly.[3]

This means that God can never be introduced as a factor into the explanation of this-worldly events. He is radically transcendent, and his acts can never be placed alongside other causal influences in the interpretation of what occurs. From this principle there can be no exceptions, whether we are dealing with events recorded in the Scripture or with the religious experiences of mystics. These events are all subject to explanation in terms of this-worldly causes.

This does not mean that God is irrelevant to our existence. It means only that he is hidden to every eye except the eye of faith. Faith sees God's act alike in objective events such as the healing of a child and in the unobservable happenings of personal existence.[4] The eye of faith is precisely the way of seeing all nature and existence in its boundedness by and radical dependence upon that which altogether transcends it, that is, God. Through the eye of faith, events that are otherwise fully explained in terms of this-worldly causes are seen as the acts of God. But there is no transition from this faith-perception to some conclusion that supports or conflicts with this-worldly knowledge. The perception in faith is a "nevertheless" perception.[5] By this we may understand that what in one way is fully understood, and even correctly understood, as explained in physical or historical categories, is "nevertheless" seen by faith as having an entirely different meaning. This different meaning perceived by faith must not be understood as a novel idea or general truth that may be placed alongside other ideas and truths. It is always only a truth for the believer in the moment of his apprehension of it. The event in question is *for him* the act of God, the place where transcendence is revealed. As such it transforms the way in which he understands his own existence. It does not give him new information about any other subject.

[3] The closedness of the world, including the inner life of man, to the nonworldly is stressed repeatedly, especially clearly in Bultmann, *Jesus Christ and Mythology,* pp. 15–16; Bultmann, "Exegesis Without Presuppositions," *Existence and Faith,* pp. 291–292; and Bartsch, ed., *Kerygma und Mythos: ein theologisches Gespräch* II, pp. 181–182.

[4] Bultmann, *Jesus Christ and Mythology,* pp. 62–63.

[5] Ogden calls attention to Bultmann's extensive use of I Cor. 7:29-31, especially the idea of "as though not." Ogden, "Introduction," in Bultmann, *Existence and Faith,* p. 20. This basic orientation is largely inspired by the work of the early Barth, although Barth did not develop its demythologizing implications and has later explicitly rejected them.

This fact, that an event both is and is not the act of God, is the fundamental paradox of Christian theology. From it arises the dialectical character, that is, the " yes " and " no " character, of the Christian witness. It is from this perspective that Bultmann's specific Christological assertions and his famous advocacy of demythologizing must be understood.

In a preliminary way all religion has been seeking the transcendent. The questions implicit in man's universal quest point toward it. But in all religion there is also a development of answers out of the legitimate questions that, while recognizing the transcendence of God, obscures and qualifies it in such a way as to darken the light that the questions seek. There is no actual way in which man can attain through his question to the faith that the question demands.[6]

The Christian message is that God, the wholly transcendent, has acted decisively for man's salvation in the death and resurrection of Jesus Christ. The proclamation of God's act is the *kerygma*.[7] The task of preaching is to provide the occasion in which God makes this kerygma effective.

But the statement that God has acted is the kerygma only when it is preached. As one piece of information laid alongside of others, it is meaningless.[8] It cannot function as a theory or a hypothesis to be tested or as an affirmation of fact that demands intellectual assent. Any such understanding of the statement that God has acted in Jesus Christ translates it into the sphere of this-worldly phenomena. The affirmation that God has acted in Jesus Christ is understood properly only when it is understood as a call to the radical decision of faith, by which we mean total surrender of the self to God. For a man to believe the kerygma is at the same time for God to act in the present in that man's death to his old self and resurrection to the life of freedom in love.

The kerygma is the proclamation of the act of God in Jesus Christ as the possibility of his act in the here and now. Faith is the authentic response to the kerygma in which God's act becomes present. Neither kerygma nor faith is theology.[9]

[6] Rudolf Bultmann, "The Question of Natural Revelation," *Essays: Philosophical and Theological,* pp. 98 ff.

[7] Hans Werner Bartsch, ed., *Kerygma and Myth: A Theological Debate,* p. 13; Rudolf Bultmann, *Theology of the New Testament* II, p. 239.

[8] Cf. Bultmann, "How Does God Speak Through the Bible? " *Existence and Faith,* p. 169.

[9] The relation of kerygma, faith, and theology is explained in the "Epilogue," *Theology of the New Testament* II, pp. 237–241. The distinction as developed there is much the same as that explained in Bultmann, "Kirche und Lehre im Neuen Testament," *Glauben und Verstehen: Gesammelte Aufsätze* I. See translation and discussion of key passages in Diem, *Dogmatics,* pp. 74–76, 79.

Theology is the methodical exposition of the self-understanding that comes into being with faith.[10] As such, it has to do only with human existence and may even be identified with anthropology.[11] But this is misleading if it is not understood in existential terms. Man's existence is bound up with God and the world, and his self-understanding, therefore, includes an understanding of God and the world.[12]

For the kerygma the New Testament is the one authoritative source. It is there alone that we learn of the act of God in Jesus Christ. Every generation must test its preaching by that original expression of the kerygma. In so far as we are Christians at all, we must be bound by its central intention. But this does not mean that any particular proposition found in the Scriptures is identical with the kerygma. Every assertion, however simple, is already an interpretation in human language affected by the faith of the speaker and hence, couched in mythological or theological form.[13] The New Testament scholar can help us to see the multiform way in which God's act was proclaimed, and at the same time to see that it was always, as such, a call for decision.

The theology of the New Testament lacks the finality of the kerygma, by which it is determined. Christian existence was not a monopoly of the first century, and men of every century have shared in the ongoing effort to expound what this existence is.[14] Still, although nowhere is the ideal exposition available to us, Bultmann by profession and the Christian community by tradition have been specially interested in the exposition of self-understanding of the believer that is found in the New Testament.

The problem that we practically confront today, however, is that both the kerygma and the theology of the New Testament are couched in language that is objectionable. It is objectionable, first, because it is simply different from our own and, therefore, hard to understand. But more importantly, it is objectionable because it communicates a misapprehension of the way in which God acts.[15] The kerygmatic affirmation that God acted in Jesus Christ was phrased in a language that places God's actions alongside this-worldly events. In other words, even the New Testament objectifies in a this-worldly plane what belongs to the transcendent or

[10] *Theology of the New Testament* II, pp. 237–239.

[11] *Kerygma and Myth,* p. 107. That Bultmann had in mind the distinction between theology and kerygma when he identified theology with anthropology is uncertain, but it is clear that the compatibility of this equation with statements about God's act in Christ in the same chapter depends on such a distinction.

[12] *Kerygma and Myth,* p. 203; *Theology of the New Testament* II, p. 239.

[13] *Theology of the New Testament* II, p. 240.

[14] *Ibid.,* II, pp. 237–238.

[15] *Kerygma and Myth,* pp. 11–12.

otherworldly. In still other words, the New Testament language has mythologized the kerygma.

The mythology of the New Testament is expressed in both cosmological and eschatological forms. Cosmologically, it confronts us with a three-story universe in which the supraworldly and the subworldly are treated as objectively real worlds alongside our own. Eschatologically, it confronts us with a picture of a new kind of world that will in the imminent chronological future replace this one. Both forms of mythology include affirmations of the activity of otherworldly beings as influencing events in this world alongside this-worldly causes.[16]

This mythology has always been an obstacle to the understanding of the New Testament message. But during much of Christian history it was not felt to be serious because the mythology of the New Testament continued to be effective alongside the kerygma. Today, however, the mythology of the New Testament has been decisively destroyed for the modern consciousness.[17] Hence, special urgency has been added to what has always been an important task of the church — the task of demythologizing so that the proclamation of the act of God may be understood for what it is and not taken as itself a bit of outdated mythology.[18] The New Testament itself initiates the process of demythologizing, and in continuing that process we are profoundly loyal to its intention.[19]

It is quite useless to attempt to extricate from the New Testament those passages in which mythological ideas are not explicitly present and to regard these as the gospel for our day. It is equally useless to go behind the New Testament to the teaching of Jesus, for this is no less mythological

[16] *Jesus Christ and Mythology,* pp. 11–15; and *Kerygma and Myth,* pp. 1–2. There are, of course, other conceptions of myth, and Bultmann is often criticized for not adopting one or another of them. But such arguments are terminological. If one agrees with Bultmann that events really visible only to faith are presented in the New Testament as if they were objectively present, his conclusions follow whether or not such objectification is taken as the defining characteristic of myth.

[17] *Kerygma and Myth,* p. 4. Bultmann steadfastly denies that mythological categories are really effective in our time. If we speak of the demonic, for example, we do not intend to speak of a transcendent power objectively immanent but of a power that grows up from the acts of men. (*Jesus Christ and Mythology,* p. 21.) The existentialist language about unobservable existence is emphatically not mythological in Bultmann's sense. (*Kerygma und Mythos* II, p. 187; Bultmann, "A Chapter in the Problem of Demythologizing," in Harvey K. McArthur, ed., *New Testament Sidelights: Essays in Honor of Alexander Converse Purdy,* p. 4.) Neither is the language of science or modern philosophy generally. (Bartsch, ed., *Kerygma and Myth,* p. 103.)

[18] *Kerygma and Myth,* pp. 10–11, 34, 210.

[19] *Ibid.,* pp. 34–35. Bultmann especially appeals to the Gospel of John as a demythologizing of the New Testament kerygma. (*Jesus Christ and Mythology,* pp. 33–34.) See *Theology of the New Testament* II, Part III.

than are the New Testament writings.[20] Mythological categories of thought pervade the whole of primitive Christianity. What is required is to identify the intention of myth and to reaffirm this intention in non-mythological categories.[21]

All myth expresses man's awareness that the whole of the this-worldly receives its being and its limits from the transcendent.[22] The particular myths express diversity in the manner in which the meaning of the transcendent for human existence is conceived. Hence, the demythologizing of the kerygmatic proclamation is the reformulation of the affirmation that God has acted decisively for man in Jesus Christ apart from the cosmological and eschatological mythical categories in which the New Testament speaks of this act of God.

This understanding of the intention of demythologizing must be stressed because of the continuing misinterpretation that is so prevalent. The demythologizing of the kerygmatic proclamation does not reduce it to a doctrine of human existence. It does not reduce its mystery or question its claim that God has acted in Jesus Christ. It does not make it more reasonable or less scandalous to modern man.[23] It simply distinguishes the kind of claim that it takes to be the central intention of the original kerygma from any claim that a this-worldly event can be *unambiguously* the act of transcendent being. The claim is that *in faith* the Christ-event is apprehended as the decisive act of God. Any claim that any event can be apprehended as an act of God apart from faith must be rejected as mythology. But any understanding of the Christ-event that does not understand it as the decisive act of God is not the understanding of faith.

In relation to New Testament theology, the primary task is understanding the existential intention that is often embodied in mythological patterns of thought. For example, demons and the Spirit of God are viewed as this-worldly entities taking possession of human beings. These ideas must be rejected not only because they are mythological but also because they threaten the integrity and responsibility of the existent individual and thereby stand in opposition to the central intention of the New Testament itself.[24]

If we would understand the theology of Paul, for example, we must demythologize his expressions of his self-understanding. In order to do so, we must come to Paul with some kind of question. Nothing is learned

[20] Bultmann, "Jesus and Paul," *Existence and Faith,* p. 186.
[21] *Kerygma and Myth,* pp. 9–16.
[22] *Ibid.,* pp. 10–11; *Kerygma und Mythos* II, p. 183
[23] *Kerygma and Myth,* pp. 104, 111, 117, 122–123.
[24] *Ibid.,* p. 120; *Kerygma und Mythos* II, p. 182.

from any document unless explicitly or implicitly some question is addressed to it.[25] Since we have already defined theology as the exposition of the self-understanding of the believer, it is clear that we are to query Paul with respect to the nature of existence in faith. But to raise such a question already involves some conceptuality, and to make the question fruitful by elaboration requires a developed conceptuality. By this we mean that we cannot speak at all without using language, and that we cannot use language without an elaborated interconnection of meanings. We may, of course, conceal from ourselves the fact that our questioning presupposes a context of thought and understanding, but thereby we only make more potent the unrecognized presuppositions. Hence, it is much better to recognize that there is no interpretation of any document, certainly not of the theological writings of Paul, without presuppositions.

Futhermore, the meanings of our terms and categories are profoundly influenced by past philosophy, and their systematic clarification is the continuing task of philosophy.[26] Hence, implicitly at least, our questioning is always affected by philosophy. Once again, we are both more honest and more likely to obtain fruitful results if we consciously acknowledge our dependence upon philosophy for the clarification of the categories of our thought.

This emphatically does not mean that the philosophy that we use will predetermine the results of our query.[27] It assists us in the formulation of questions, but only the document that we are examining can give us the answer. It is true, of course, that the answer will receive its form from the question, and that narrow and unsuitable presuppositions will limit our capacity to see what is there for us in the document. But this only emphasizes the importance of care in selection of the conceptuality with which the document is approached. For example, if we suppose that man must be understood as the union of two substances, soul and body, we will ask Paul how he understands the relation of these and what happens to each in salvation. We can then obtain some answers from Paul, but much of what he has to say to us will be unintelligible in these categories. We might instead ask what philosophical anthropology Paul employed himself. To this question, too, we could receive an interesting, if confusing, answer. But if we limited ourselves to this question, we would not be open to Paul's theological affirmations developed within this conceptuality.

[25] See, for example, *Kerygma and Myth,* p. 191; Bultmann, "Is Exegesis Without Presuppositions Possible?" *Existence and Faith,* pp. 292–295.

[26] *Kerygma and Myth,* p. 193.

[27] Bultmann, "Is Exegesis Without Presuppositions Possible?" *Existence and Faith,* pp. 289–290, 295; "The Problem of Hermeneutics," *Essays,* p. 255; *Jesus Christ and Mythology,* p. 49.

We would have only data for constructing a history of early Christian philosophical anthropology, and we would have learned nothing of theological importance for ourselves.

What we need is a philosophical anthropology that is adequate to our present self-understanding and that provides a conceptuality in which Paul's theology can be formulated. Thereby Paul's understanding of Christian existence becomes available to us and can be placed in vital relation to our own understanding.

We are peculiarly fortunate today in having available for our use the phenomenological ontology of human existence developed by Heidegger.[28] As phenomenology, it attains a kind of objectivity that gives it the widest possible use. As an ontology, it limits itself to the sphere of what is universal to human existence as such and leaves out of its purview the variety of ontic forms that human existence can take. Hence, it provides a basis for asking sensitive and important questions without prejudging the value of the answers.

The usefulness of this approach can be seen by its power to bring to Paul's thought greater clarity and coherence than it has in the form in which Paul left it.[29] In other words, it provides a better conceptuality for grasping Paul's understanding of Christian existence than was available to Paul. Hence, through this kind of exegesis Paul's own intention is given a freedom of self-expression that it can achieve in no other way.

Consider, for example, Paul's antithesis of flesh and spirit. By this antithesis, Paul did not intend the distinction of body and soul or of matter and the immaterial. He was concerned about two modes of existence of the total person. But his own terminology introduced confusions, sometimes in his own mind. Heidegger, however, has distinguished for us unauthentic and authentic existence. He has shown us how unauthentic existence is a way of understanding oneself from the world of things and leads to a care for that world that prevents a man from becoming truly himself. He shows us that authentic existence is life lived in terms of the real potentialities of the existent individual. Hence, whether or not we continue to use the language of flesh and spirit, our grasp of Paul's meaning can be informed by Heidegger's analysis.

The question arises as to whether this does not mean that we are identifying Paul's concept with Heidegger's in such a way that we simply bap-

[28] Bultmann asserts that the philosophy that is needed is one that expresses the understanding of existence given with existence. This is just what existential analysis does. (*Kerygma and Myth,* pp. 193–194.)

[29] Macquarrie believes Bultmann meets this test. (*An Existentialist Theology: A Comparison of Heidegger and Bultmann,* pp. 42–46.)

tize the philosophy of Heidegger as Christian theology. The answer is no, and that on several counts.[30]

In the first place, Heidegger does not give us an account of what in fact constitutes authentic existence.[31] Formally, it is any existence in which resolve is effective, that is, any existence in which a man lives in terms of projects that are authentically his own. But such a life may well be one of despair. Indeed, in the view of Christian faith it can be nothing but despair apart from the act of God. The freedom that it supposedly involves is not really freedom from one's own past, which is the freedom man really needs.[32] It lacks the faith and love and hope and joy that characterize Christian existence.[33]

These are, however, ontic or factual, and not ontological, judgments.[34] Heidegger correctly indicates the nature of the possibility inherent in human existence generally, that is, the possibility of living in terms of its own future rather than in terms of the presented realm of things. As a philosopher, he neither should nor could do anything more.

In the second place, even in so far as Heidegger describes authentic existence in a way satisfactory to a Christian, he cannot prescribe how it is to be attained.[35] He would abandon his role as a philosopher if he should appeal to acts of God. At the same time, nothing in his analysis precludes that, ontically speaking, it is only by an act of God that man is enabled to have faith. This is indeed precisely what the Christian affirms.

In the third place, Heidegger assigns " being-toward-death " a decisive place with respect to existence that Christian faith does not accord it. It is the encounter with a " Thou," and not running forward in thought to one's death, that is decisive. At the same time, as an analysis of natural man Heidegger's account remains valid, and it is only because the Christian dies to his old self and rises to new life that death has lost, for him, its sting.[36] But since the new life and the old are not, in Christian ex-

[30] Bultmann makes this point repeatedly, but its most vehement formulation is found in " The Historicity of Man and Faith," *Existence and Faith*, pp. 92–110.

[31] Bultmann often emphasizes that existential philosophy tells us only *that* we should exist, not *how* we should exist. (*Kerygma and Myth*, pp. 29, 193–194; *Jesus Christ and Mythology*, pp. 55–58; and Bultmann, *The Presence of Eternity: History and Eschatology*, pp. 149–151.)

[32] Bultmann, " The Historicity of Man and Faith," *Existence and Faith*, p. 107.

[33] *Ibid.*, p. 110.

[34] *Ibid.*, pp. 94–95.

[35] This is the emphasis in the demythologizing debate. (*Kerygma and Myth*, pp. 26–29, 205. See also *Jesus Christ and Mythology*, pp. 77–78.) In these later writings, Bultmann seems to allow to the accounts of Heidegger and Kamlah more substantive similarity to Christian existence than the foregoing arguments, taken from " The Historicity of Man and Faith," suggest.

[36] " The Historicity of Man and Faith," *Existence and Faith*, pp. 109–110.

perience, separated in any simple chronological sense, even for the Christian Heidegger's analysis of natural man has meaning.

It has been objected that the use of categories derived from the analysis of natural man is unsuited to the exposition of existence in faith. But this would be true only if Christian faith were a new supernatural replacement of human existence.[37] That is, if man became ontologically new — something other than man — then the categories applicable to natural man would not be applicable to him. But Protestants, at least, have never thought in these terms. Man becomes *ontically* new. He enters into a new kind of existence, but he remains a man, indeed the same man he was before. Ontological categories such as those of Heidegger apply to both natural existence and existence in faith precisely because they are ontological.

This relation of theology to philosophy should make it abundantly clear that theology does not look to philosophy to justify its claims. Philosophy makes possible the *clarification* of ontic claims. It cannot judge among them. Whether Christian existence is as theologians describe it, and whether it comes about as they say, are ontic questions. With respect to the truth or falsity of these affirmations, philosophy as such is silent. If an individual who is a philosopher speaks about these matters, he does so as a theologian — not as a philosopher.

Furthermore, one cannot turn to some other source, such as the science of psychology, to find criteria for judging Christian theology. Theological assertions are not about objective facts that can be observed or treated experimentally. But this does not mean that Christian theology is anything unintelligible or mysterious. The same is true of any statement about the factuality of a particular mode of existence or self-understanding. In this respect, Christian theology is absolutely parallel with every other account of a particular mode of existence. Any such account may be obscurely or clearly stated so as to make itself more or less intelligible. So far as this is concerned, the greater clarity — the less mystery — the better.[38]

But the Bible does not simply provide man with one intelligible way of understanding his existence alongside the ways offered by other historical records.[39] In the Bible, man is personally encountered by the Word of God in a unique way. As kerygma, the message of the Bible can become for him the act of God's offering him freedom from himself in a life of love.

Most of the analysis of Bultmann's position in the preceding pages has

[37] *Ibid.*, pp. 94–95.
[38] *Kerygma and Myth*, p. 122; *Jesus Christ and Mythology*, p. 43.
[39] *Kerygma and Myth*, p. 192.

been based upon a sharp distinction between kerygma and theology. However, little explicit use is made of this distinction by Bultmann himself, and few of his commentators or critics have referred to it.[40] Hence, some attempt at justifying the central methodological role assigned it in this analysis is required.

The basic issue is not whether Bultmann's strict definition of theology in one or two essays is consistent with his use of the term elsewhere. Quite probably it is not. The issue is whether there is in Bultmann's actual performance and proposals a duality that can be explained consistently in these terms. Bultmann is repeatedly criticized for what seems to be a basic inconsistency in his thought. On the one hand, he proposes that the New Testament and its kerygma be demythologized in existential terms. On the other hand, he retains affirmations about the indispensability of the once-for-all act of God in Jesus Christ.[41]

Bultmann undoubtedly has said many confusing and conflicting things on these two points that give warrant to much of the criticism of his work. But the thesis of the present interpretation is that he has also provided us with some clues as to how these two elements in his basic intention can be held together in a consistent whole.

Bultmann's more conservative defenders sometimes claim that he sets

[40] Major exceptions are Diem, *Dogmatics,* pp. 71 ff., and Fuchs, *Hermeneutik,* pp. 98–99, quoted in Ott, *Denken und Sein,* p. 172. Fuchs affirms that the distinction between revelation and preaching on the one side and theology on the other is essential to understanding Bultmann.

[41] Ogden stresses the convergence of criticism on this point from the right and the left. "The Debate on 'Demythologizing,'" *The Journal of Bible and Religion,* Vol. 27, 1959, pp. 23–25; *Christ Without Myth,* pp. 95–111. Ogden rightly emphasizes the importance, for understanding Bultmann, of distinguishing the two terms *existential* and *existentiell.* He keeps the distinction in the English text by retaining the two words in this spelling. Others have translated *existential* by "existentialistic" and *existentiell* by "existential." I have tried to make the distinction clear by the context, without introducing technical terms.

The German *existentiell* has the connotations usually associated with "existential" in English, that is, it refers to man's absolutely individual situation as confronted by the demand to choose the direction of his own existence and the specific character of his individual experience as formed by that decision. The proclamation of the kerygma necessarily calls for such *existentiell* decision.

The German *existential* is a technical term used by Heidegger to refer to the phenomenologically articulated categories of existence. Theology, while expressing an *existentiell* concern on the part of the theologian and intending an *existentiell* impact on the hearer, is primarily an account of Christian self-understanding in *existential* terms.

The problem chiefly at issue in the text is how a once-for-all past event can be affirmed without limiting arbitrarily the process of demythologizing. The answer, in terms of this terminology, is that a past event as presently proclaimed may have a unique *existentiell* importance that can be understood in *existential* terms.

limits to the demythologizing proposal[42] and thereby enables himself to make orthodox Christian affirmations that would otherwise be forbidden him. Others have agreed that he in fact fails to carry through the demythologizing program consistently but point out that he denies explicitly that any limits should be set to it.[43] What seems to be missed by both parties to this debate is that the New Testament is to be demythologized completely but that demythologizing can be applied only to what is mythological.

Furthermore, although to demythologize is always to interpret the mythology in terms of its existential meaning, it does not follow that whatever is not existential is thereby mythological. Mythology is not defined as the nonexistential but as the representation of the otherworldly as if it were objectively this-worldly.[44] There may be affirmations in the New Testament that are neither mythological nor existential. Indeed, one would suppose that many odd bits of information about historical fact would have this character, but these are not important.

The question is whether there is any affirmation in the New Testament that is neither mythological nor existential and that is nevertheless important. By affirming that it is important, we mean that it must be *existentially* important; so in this sense it must necessarily be existential. But there may be an affirmation that is not itself an existential statement that yet has existential importance. Information given to a drowning man about the location of a sandbar, for example, might be of such a nature.

Now it seems that, despite certain ambiguities, this is precisely what Bultmann asserts about the New Testament kerygmatic affirmations of the act of God in Jesus Christ. These are not, as such, mythological assertions, although they are regularly associated in the New Testament with mythological ideas.[45] These mythological ideas must be, in accordance with Bultmann's over-all program of demythologizing, exhaustively interpreted in existential terms. But this only brings out with greater force the strangeness or scandalousness of the New Testament affirmation that God acted decisively in Jesus Christ.[46]

The claim that this affirmation is of importance, indeed of supreme importance, is the claim that it is existentially decisive for every man. Hence,

42 John Macquarrie, *The Scope of Demythologizing: Bultmann and His Critics,* pp. 11, 222–223.

43 Ogden makes this point in his criticism of John Macquarrie's *Scope of Demythologizing,* in *Christ Without Myth,* p. 172.

44 *Kerygma and Myth,* p. 10, note; *Kerygma und Mythos* II, p. 183.

45 *Kerygma and Myth,* p. 34. Mythological language is used to bring out the meaning of the past event. (*Ibid.,* p. 37.)

46 See references for n. 23.

its existential meaning must be explained in existential terms. This is an essential part of the intention of the affirmation, apart from which it is not kerygmatic at all. But this does not imply that the intention of the affirmation is exhausted by its existential meaning. On the contrary, the affirmation intends the past act of God just as essentially as it intends its present existential meaning for the hearer.[47]

Those who argue that so far as the kerygma is concerned only existential affirmations can be existentially important will point out immediately the limitation in the analogy of the drowning man and the sandbar. The information there provided consists of objective facts about the objective world, whereas the kerygma gives no such facts at all. The kerygma can be proclaimed only by the believer, for its truth is apprehended only by the eyes of faith. Hence, the affirmation of the kerygma is always already involved with theology as the interpretation of faith, and we have recognized above that theology is exhaustively existential. There may be some theological statements that have little or no kerygmatic import, but there are no kerygmatic statements that do not involve theological interpretation.

Does this mean that there is, after all, no nonexistential element in the intention of the kerygma? This does not follow. It means that the kerygma always intends its existential meaning for the hearer and that it always expresses the self-understanding of the speaker. But there seems to be no inconsistency in affirming that the proclamation of the kerygma always also intends an existentially experienced nonexistential object—the act of God in Jesus Christ. And surely the overwhelming majority of Bultmann's discussions of the kerygma and the Christ-event requires this interpretation.

If the foregoing account of Bultmann is generally accurate, the misunderstanding that underlies many of the usual criticisms of his position should be clear. Conservatives have regarded Bultmann as destroying the supernatural character of Christian faith.[48] But unless this supernatural element is understood necessarily to mean that the otherworldly is *unambiguously* manifest in this-worldly forms, that is, in such a way as to lend itself to scientific and historiographical verification, this criticism is erroneous. Bultmann emphatically retains, and insists, upon the act of God in Jesus Christ as in radical discontinuity with all natural and historical causes. And by this he certainly means that the transcendent, otherworldly, and in this sense supernatural, has appeared in this world—

[47] *Kerygma and Myth,* pp. 22, 27, 110–111, 207–209.

[48] Most of the criticisms of Bultmann in the *Kerygma und Mythos* series are from the conservative side.

only it has so appeared as to remain hidden to all but the eyes of faith. If this is to be attacked from the side of supernaturalist orthodoxy, it must be in terms of a view of miracle as an occurrence observable apart from faith and explicable only in terms of supernatural suspension of natural law. Certainly Bultmann rejects this eighteenth-century conception, and he denies with some warrant that it is central to the intention of the New Testament.

Orthodoxy may also attack Bultmann on the grounds of his denial of final authority to the *theology* of the New Testament. But Bultmann can reply as a New Testament scholar that there is a plurality of New Testament theologies and that all of them are human accounts of how men have come to understand themselves in the life of faith. He himself in no way depreciates their central importance for the Christian community. Quite the contrary, his whole effort is to make them come alive for our generation. When we speak of the *final* authority for Christian faith, we must point to the act of God, and not to the human response to that act.[49] As a witness to the decisive act of God, the Christian has no other appeal than the New Testament.

More serious is the question that must be raised about Bultmann's Christology. What is the relation of Jesus, the existing individual, to the act of God? Bultmann seems to make the faith that God acted in Jesus irrelevant to the understanding of Jesus. Jesus was a Jewish prophet of the imminent eschatological consummation.[50] The Christian faith is grounded in the belief that God acted in him, but it is essentially indifferent to what Jesus did or said or how he understood himself.[51] Therefore, in reconstructing Jesus' message and deeds the historian is perfectly free to ignore the Christian claim that God acted in him. Whether Jesus believed himself to be the Messiah or not is quite irrelevant. Indeed, the truth or falsity of his opinions in general is quite irrelevant to faith. Hence, the objection may be raised that Bultmann separates the Jesus of history so radically from the Christ of faith that the Christian teaching of the incarnation is destroyed.

This criticism has much justification, but at the same time it loses its sting when it is set in the context of Bultmann's own thought. It is because the acts of God are always and necessarily hidden to all eyes but the eyes of faith that the *historical* Jesus is irrelevant to faith. For by the *his-*

49 *Theology of the New Testament* II, p. 240.

50 Cf. Rudolf Bultmann, *Jesus and the Word; Theology of the New Testament* I, Part I, Ch. 1; *Primitive Christianity in Its Contemporary Setting*, pp. 71–77, 86–93; *Jesus Christ and Mythology*, pp. 12–14.

51 *Theology of the New Testament* I, p. 26; *Kerygma and Myth*, p. 117.

torical Jesus we mean precisely that Jesus who is accessible to investigation apart from faith. Faith knows that what is seen apart from faith is always explicable in categories that make no reference to the act of God and that no kind of historical event points more clearly to God than any other. But faith sees that *nevertheless* precisely these events are the act of God for the believer. Hence, *for faith,* the events that for the historian are the historical Jesus are the act of God. Faith connects the act of God to the historical event, not on the basis of historical evidence that such a connection is warranted, but precisely *by faith* in spite of the lack of objective reason of any kind.

This whole debate with orthodoxy points to the fact that the basic issue is that of the fundamental understanding of the relation of God and the world sketched in the beginning of this chapter. If the transcendent is related to the this-worldly as Bultmann says, then the consequences that he derives from this conception seem to follow, and his Christology can hardly be challenged. Since many of Bultmann's orthodox critics have shared this understanding, although they have generally been less clear and consistent, most of their criticisms have missed their mark.

The liberal criticism of Bultmann takes an opposite line, although it converges with the orthodox criticism at some points.[52] The liberal, too, must point out the dependence of Bultmann's theology upon a philosophical preunderstanding of the relation of God and the world, but even if that preunderstanding is accepted, it seems to the liberal that the orthodox elements in Bultmann's theology do not follow.

First of all, is it really the case that the Christian self-understanding is achieved only by an act of God? Bultmann himself frequently stresses that the existent individual is free to choose for himself. When we are confronted by any particular possibility for self-understanding, we are put into decision. That is, in so far as we apprehend self-understanding as really a possibility for us and different from that by which we have lived, we are placed in the position of accepting or rejecting it. Is this not also our situation with respect to the Christian self-understanding? What, then, is added when we call this particular human, existential decision, by which

52 Among liberal critics may be listed Karl Jaspers, Fritz Buri, and Schubert Ogden. The following works may be consulted: Jaspers and Bultmann, *Myth and Christianity: An Inquiry Into the Possibility of Religion Without Myth;* Ogden, *Christ Without Myth;* Ogden, "Bultmann's Project of Demythologizing," *The Journal of Religion,* Vol. 37, 1957, pp. 156–173; Ogden, "The Debate on Demythologizing," *op. cit.,* pp. 17–27; Buri, "Theologie und Philosophie," *Theologische Zeitschrift,* Vol. 8, 1952, pp. 116–134; Buri, "Entmythologisierung oder Entkerygmatisierung der Theologie," in Bartsch, ed., *Kerygma und Mythos* II. Buri's position is summarized by Ogden in *Christ Without Myth,* pp. 105–110, and in "The Debate on Demythologizing," p. 24.

we die to our old selves and rise to new life in faith, an act of God?

Bultmann's answer is that as Christians we do in fact apprehend it as an act of God. What is added thereby is the destruction of any claim, on our part, upon God or of any grounds of boasting in our achievement.[53] The self-understanding of faith is precisely the understanding of ourselves as living from God's grace; hence, it clearly cannot be attributed by us to our own decision except as that decision is at the same time understood precisely as an act of God.

Assuming that this is an adequate answer, we may press the argument a step further. Granting that the decision for Christian existence is understood by faith as the act of God, why should we claim that a necessary relation exists between this act of God and the act of God in Christ? We may grant that, factually, we have had the Christian self-understanding presented to us in conjunction with the message that God acted in Christ. We may further grant that, historically, Christian existence came into being in conjunction with the belief that God has acted in Christ. We may even recognize that the message of God's act in Christ adds efficacy to the challenge to decide for Christian existence. But should we not also recognize that God has acted and can act for men in bringing them into Christian existence (whether they call it by this name or not) quite apart from any belief about Christ? [54] Should we not be concerned primarily that this existence become more readily available as a live option to men everywhere regardless of whether they are willing to acknowledge a unique act of God in history? Is not, therefore, the scandal of the Christian claim to absolute uniqueness an unnecessary obstacle to the real work of preaching the gospel?

The issue here is that of the content of the gospel. Is the gospel essentially that God offers man a life of faith and love that he may freely choose, or is the gospel that God has acted in Jesus Christ for man's salvation? The two ways of understanding what the gospel fundamentally is overlap extensively. The former recognizes its historical rootage in the event Jesus Christ, but it regards the factual relationship as existentially inessential. The latter recognizes that God's act in Jesus Christ is nothing other than the offer to man of a life of faith and love that he may freely choose, but it holds that this offer is made in the Christ-event and nowhere else.

Bultmann as a historian seems to give much color to the liberal's argument. His reconstruction of Judaeo-Christian history traces the emergence

[53] Bultmann, " Grace and Freedom," *Essays,* p. 170.

[54] Even a relatively conservative interpreter like Macquarrie seeks for this openness in Bultmann. Macquarrie, *The Scope of Demythologizing,* p. 152.

of the Christian self-understanding as a phenomenon of history.[55] It shows how the eschatological message of Jesus and the early church precipitated a decision for radical faith in God in a way essentially similar to that in which the church's message about God's act in Jesus called for such faith. Historically speaking, it seems that the radical intensification of the prophetico-eschatological message is sufficient to account for the emergence of Christian existence.

But Bultmann as a theologian simply denies that faith can accept as final the picture that Bultmann as a historian has constructed. For faith, the historical explanation is essentially irrelevant. For faith, it is the act of God in Jesus Christ made newly effective for us in its repeated proclamation that alone places us in the position of deciding for or against faith. To the question why God should have arranged matters in this way there is no answer. But that this is the situation in which we find ourselves is believed by faith as the presupposition of faith. To decide for Christian existence is to decide for precisely this faith. And to decide for Christian existence apart from this faith is delusion.

The gulf here is simply unbridgeable. Bultmann can give no reasons for his position except by showing that this is the intention of the New Testament and the self-understanding of faith. From the point of view of his position, the requirement of reasons is a false demand. One must decide for or against the acceptance of God's gift, and man cannot determine the grounds on which it is to be accepted.

This does not mean that the leap of faith is itself arbitrary. In fact, an apologetic for making the leap lies on the surface of Bultmann's writings. Philosophical analysis can point to the ideal possibility of authentic existence, but man's effort to realize it on his own terms leads to despair. The kerygma offers man the only possibility of understanding his existence.[56] It offers him also the realization of that which he already, as a human being, somehow wants.[57] Hence, it seems clear that there is *reason* for acceptance of God's gift.

The point, however, is that man must respect the freedom of God to offer us life on any terms he chooses. Furthermore, Bultmann holds that what is offered is so different from what natural man supposes that he seeks, that the decision to accept cannot be motivated simply by his natural desire.[58] Decision is made in sheer freedom. It is a leap.

55 Bultmann, *The Presence of Eternity,* p. 149 and *passim;* also, *Primitive Christianity.*

56 *Kerygma and Myth,* p. 41.

57 *Ibid.,* p. 192.

58 "Grace and Freedom," *Essays,* esp. pp. 180–181.

The liberal may protest that if the offer of Christian existence is tied thus to a particular event in time, then men who have not heard of this event are not responsible for having failed to choose it.[59] This would seem to conflict with the emphasis on man's responsibility for himself that Bultmann shares with Heidegger. But this objection fails to recognize the nonidentity of Christian existence as defined by Bultmann and authentic existence as defined by Heidegger. Authentic existence in some form may be a real option for every man, but to Bultmann the choice of authentic existence apart from Christ is the choice of despair and even expresses that self-assertion which in faith is perceived as sin.[60] Man apart from Christ is guilt-ridden and responsible for his own existence. But in the eyes of faith, man's effort to save himself rather than surrender himself to God is visible as sin.[61]

Bultmann's theology is a remarkable combination of strict Lutheranism and absolute scholarly openness. On the one hand, faith can affirm nothing that enters into the sphere of consideration of science or history. On the other hand, science and history can say nothing that gives any evidence for or against faith. Therefore, the option of faith is absolutely open to modern man as it has been open to every generation. At the same time, any quest for support for the decision of faith, any argument for its plausibility, is strictly excluded. God confronts man in the message of God's act in Jesus Christ as an act for man that can be reactualized in him through his response. The decision is his. The scholar and the theologian clear away every obstacle to that decision not intrinsic to the decision itself. By the same token they clear away every pretense that there is any objective justification for making the decision extraneous to the decision itself. Thus, the absolute freedom of the decision is made inescapably clear.

In every other decision, even in decisions as to how one shall understand oneself, man's past is brought with him into the decision.[62] Hence, there is no real freedom from the past. But confronted by the kerygmatic demand and promise, man is offered freedom from his past. His decision cannot be motivated by his past hopes and fears. It is made absolutely in the now. It is an abandonment of every security and a total trust in God.[63]

Clearly, there is no self-evidence about all these affirmations, and clearly they can and must be disputed by many liberals. But it is also clear that the issues involved are purely ontic in character. Either Christian faith

[59] Ogden, *Christ Without Myth,* pp. 118–119.
[60] *Kerygma and Myth,* pp. 29–30.
[61] "The Historicity of Man and Faith," *Existence and Faith,* pp. 96–97.
[62] "Grace and Freedom," *Essays,* p. 180.
[63] *Kerygma and Myth,* pp. 19–20.

does understand itself as Bultmann says or it does not. The question might appear to be terminological in that Bultmann seems at times simply to define Christian faith in this way and thereby to deny to those who understand themselves in any other way the label "Christian." But Bultmann's appeal is to the preaching of primitive Christianity and to the self-understanding of the believer as evoked by that preaching. Hence, responsible historical inquiry is relevant to, if not decisive for, the resolution of this issue. In so far as this is the case, discussion of this problem lies outside the scope of this book.

However, what is found in primitive Christianity depends in part, as Bultmann is the first to recognize, on the preunderstanding that is brought to it. Hence, the issue is not simply historico-exegetical. The liberal may agree with Bultmann that the New Testament must be demythologized and yet reject Bultmann's way of carrying out the program. He may, for example, assert that the literal truth about the relation of the believer to God, expressed in the myths, is different from the relation of one who stands in a closed, this-worldly system to transcendence. If so, he will dispute with Bultmann, not so much in his capacity as a historian reconstructing the beliefs and self-understanding of primitive Christians, but in terms of the fundamental understanding of God and the world that determines Bultmann's definition of myth and hence also his whole exegetical method. Hence, this analysis of the liberal discussion with Bultmann leads to the same conclusion as the analysis of the orthodox critique, namely, that the fundamental understanding of the relation of God and the world is decisive for Bultmann's whole position.

◈ ◈

At this juncture I turn from a presentation of Bultmann's position in relation to typical orthodox and liberal critics to a statement of my own systematic criticism. The criticism has two major parts. First, we must ask what clear meaning can be given to Bultmann's crucial concept of an act of God. Second, we inquire as to whether any sort of natural theology is assumed or implied by Bultmann's theological method, or by his understanding of the fundamental relation of God and the world. The next few pages are devoted to a consideration of the former question.

Bultmann clearly affirms that every objectively observable event must be understood in scientific and historical investigations as a part of a causal nexus that makes no reference to God. Nevertheless, he insists that some events are properly understood in faith as acts of God. How can this be? Is this understanding possible with respect to objectively observable events that are apprehended by science? Or is it appropriate only to the unobjective, unobservable events of human existence as such?

When Bultmann gives examples of the kinds of events that may be seen in faith as acts of God, he cites as one the healing of a child.[64] This raises acute questions as to the intelligibility of the concept. He affirms that the healing process belongs to the natural world, from which he excludes freedom. Hence, an event that follows necessarily from the preceding natural situation is also seen as an act of God, that is, as being grounded in transcendence. This would pose no problem if Bultmann meant that the whole sequence of natural events expressed God's will or simply that in so far as they occur at all they are given their being by God. But Bultmann explicitly rejects these interpretations.[65] Specific events, not the course of nature as a whole, are seen in faith as acts of God.

Probably Bultmann does not mean that the child's recovery of health as such *is* an act of God but specifically that in the believer's apprehension of its meaning for him it becomes an act of God. Thereby it is differentiated from the act of God in Christ in its relation to the believer. Whereas in the relation of God's act in the believer's existence to his act in Christ the priority stands with the act in Christ, in the relation of the child's recovery to the believer, it stands with the believer.

The entire following analysis assumes this interpretation of Bultmann's meaning. If it is erroneous, if Bultmann means that God has specific causal efficacy for the healing of the child that is not identical with the natural processes that effect the healing, then I cannot see how he can avoid the conclusion that on its own terms the scientific-deterministic account is incomplete. It must omit essential factors in the actual healing process. But Bultmann's whole point is that God's act is not one force alongside others that with them effects a conclusion. God's act lies in a radically different dimension and leaves the objective account entirely unaffected at its own level. Faith does not perceive a causal factor in the objective event to which science is blind. Faith sees the events as a whole as an act of God, and that means as having for the believer the significance of an act of God. Nothing is said thereby about the causes of the objective event.

I am arguing that, with respect to such objective observable events as the healing of the child or a historical occurrence in the life of Israel, we can speak of an act of God only in terms of the existential meaning of the event for us.[66] If this were the basic meaning of "act of God" in Bult-

64 *Jesus Christ and Mythology,* p. 62.

65 *Kerygma and Myth,* pp. 197–198.

66 Bultmann asserts that Jesus is not to be understood after the analogy of men like Abraham or Moses, who were decisive for Israel's history. Their importance was mediated through a national history that functioned for Israel as a history of

mann's thought, he could hardly escape the charge of subjectivism. But the possibility of speaking this way at all depends upon the decisive act of God by which a man enters into the existence of faith. This event occurs in the unobjective, unobservable sphere of human existence. As a free act it is not necessitated by its past, and hence it seems to be a more hopeful arena in which to grasp what Bultmann means. But can we intelligibly speak of one event as simultaneously an act of radical freedom on the part of man and an act of God?

This leads us to an aspect of Bultmann's thought that he has inadequately clarified, namely, the relation of the human self to the closed system of the this-worldly and to the transcendence of God. Two basic patterns of thought are in some tension within Bultmann's theology. Sometimes he sets God as radically transcendent over against the whole of spatiotemporal phenomena and includes man in this latter category. Sometimes he stresses that the transcendence of God over the world is paralleled by the transcendence of the human self over the world. In this case, God and human selves belong together in the realm of the transcendent.[67]

The former position is implied by Bultmann when he stresses the complete incapacity of philosophy to speak of God. Clearly, philosophy is not incapable of speaking of the human self in its transcendence of the world, but it is just God's transcendence that precludes philosophy from speaking of him. Hence, God's transcendence must be of a radically different kind from man's transcendence.

This position also seems involved in the fundamental insistence that the acts of God do not have causal efficacy in the observable world. For example, it seems that a man's free decision to give up a life of social conformity in favor of basic convictions and purposes does have an effect upon both the inner and the outer course of events, and that the historian has the responsibility to explain certain aspects of these events in terms of the man's free decision. Bultmann insists, however, that the historian must interpret the course of events *without* reference to acts of God. Presumably then, these acts are essentially unlike human acts.

This second argument would not apply if we adopted a philosophical position that denied that events in the realm of human freedom have causal efficacy in the sphere of physical and psychological occurrences.

---

revelation. For us, this history is not revelation. "The Significance of the Old Testament for the Christian Faith," unpublished trans. by B. W. Anderson, pp. 20–21.

67 Ogden interprets Bultmann in this sense. "Introduction," in Bultmann, *Existence and Faith,* pp. 15–16.

Perhaps Bultmann has some such metaphysics in view in some of his utterances, but if so he must not only involve himself in some very dubious philosophical speculations but also encounter the firm objection of common sense. If we allow human freedom at all, we can deny that it has causal efficacy in the physical and psychological spheres only by an extreme a priori judgment entirely alien to most of Bultmann's thought.

Therefore, we must conclude that much of Bultmann's thought depends on a radical difference between the transcendence of the world by God and by human selves. At the same time, much of his thought equally depends upon the claim that there is a real analogy between these two relations. Frequently, he explains the Christian understanding of the man-God relation by analogous relations among men. And, decisively, he affirms that the language about the acts of God must be understood by analogy with human acts.[68]

This duality in Bultmann leads to a serious dilemma. If we take seriously the radical difference between God and the human self and so preserve the view that God's acts never operate as causes of events in either the inner or the outer sphere, we can hardly understand these acts by analogy with human acts. If, on the other hand, we take this analogy seriously, there seems no reason for denying either that philosophy can talk about God or that God's acts have observable, causal consequences.

A clue as to how Bultmann may partly escape this difficulty is provided in his use of the category of encounter. In the believing hearing of the kerygma we encounter God. Faith is equally a free decision and an act of his grace, because it is only in this encounter with God that we become radically free.[69] We may then see that the historian will attribute to free decision what the believer attributes to the act of God in encountering him. Thus the believer perceives a real efficacy in the act of God, but this is adequately explained for the nonbeliever by reference to freedom. Although not all of Bultmann's assertions about acts of God lend themselves readily to this interpretation, it does seem to be the clearest expression of his thought. Here we may see how God's encounter with us may be understood after the analogy of the encounter of persons without thereby allowing for independent causal efficacy or philosophical accessibility.

One difficulty remains, and this one is acute. Bultmann does not identify

[68] *Kerygma and Myth,* p. 197; *Jesus Christ and Mythology,* p. 68. To explain what he means by analogy he refers to Frank, *Philosophical Understanding and Religious Truth,* pp. 44, 161–164, 179, etc.

[69] "Grace and Freedom," *Essays,* p. 180.

God's act in Jesus Christ with an encounter relationship between God and Jesus. This act of God by which he brought in the new age was of a different order.

The affirmation that God acted in Jesus Christ can be understood analogically only if that action resembles either man's act in encountering another man or man's act upon the world. To press the former analogy is to make God's act in Jesus Christ an existential event in the life of the historical Jesus. This would lead Bultmann to follow some of his own students in a new quest of the historical Jesus.[70] To press the latter analogy is to affirm that the course of events in the world is causally modified by God's acting in such a way that the events are erroneously interpreted if other causality is assigned to them. This would lead Bultmann toward an orthodox supernaturalism and force him to abandon much of his argument against his conservative critics.

Since Bultmann rejects both sets of consequences, it seems that he must deny the analogy of God's act to human acts. But to deny this analogy would leave the central kerygmatic affirmation unintelligible except in its existential import. Then Bultmann's whole basis for rejecting the liberal criticism of his position collapses.

One escape from this difficulty appears to be open. Bultmann may affirm that God's act in Jesus Christ occurred actually in God's encounter with the disciples. Thereby he can locate God's act in the encounter relationship without locating it in Jesus' historical existence. The encounter then is understood as occurring on Easter Day.

The difficulty with this position is that it reduces even the crucifixion of Jesus to a historical condition of God's act in the disciples, whereas the New Testament places God's primary act in Jesus and regards the awakening of faith as a secondary act of God. Furthermore, it is difficult to see how God's encounter with a number of disciples could be, as such, the indispensable object of faith. Nevertheless, if we are to dare to identify any one position as that of Bultmann, we must choose this one. It is on this basis that he places the historical Jesus entirely within Judaism and begins Christianity with the rise of the Easter faith.[71]

We now turn to the second of the two major criticisms of Bultmann's theological method. Does Bultmann employ a natural theology? Bultmann's systematic theology develops from key concepts that he finds in the New Testament. He insists that the New Testament can be intelligently studied only if we approach it with a fruitful philosophical preun-

70 See James McConkey Robinson, *A New Quest of the Historical Jesus.*

71 See Bultmann's treatment of Jesus in relation to Christianity in *Theology of the New Testament* I and *Primitive Christianity.*

derstanding. To this degree he acknowledges an autonomous role of philosophy in theological work.

However, Bultmann can correctly distinguish the preunderstanding that he employs from a natural theology. He wishes to limit the preunderstanding to a phenomenological account of the universal structures of human existence. Furthermore, he does not intend to employ this preunderstanding as a basis for establishing particular articles of belief. Its use is only to make possible the clearer understanding of the New Testament.

In addition to the phenomenological analysis of human existence, Bultmann *seems* to employ a definite world view in his theological work. He believes that God is real and effective in relation to human existence, that the objective world is closed to God's causal efficacy, and that man has or can have real freedom. Such beliefs might well constitute a natural theology, but Bultmann does not intend to employ them in that way. Such beliefs might also be affirmed as a Christian natural theology, that is, as a philosophical account of the implications of distinctively Christian data, but this also seems contrary to Bultmann's intention. If we are to form a clear judgment of Bultmann's success in avoiding dependence upon natural theology, we must consider how each of these three elements in his thought is systematically justified. They are treated below in the order listed.

Bultmann can speak of a universal sense of relatedness to transcendence at the basis of all region and myth.[72] If, however, he intends to justify belief in the reality of God on this basis, a difficulty arises. Any important universal aspect of man's existence should be included in a phenomenological ontology of existence such as that of Heidegger, but in fact Heidegger knows nothing of a universal relatedness to God. If the reality of God is to be maintained on the basis of phenomenology, the argument might take two forms.

First, one might argue that Heidegger's phenomenology is incomplete, that there are additional categories of existence that he has failed to see. Such an argument would require, however, a kind of exposition that neither Bultmann nor his pupils have provided or proposed.[73]

[72] The awareness of the transcendent as the ground and limit of existence is the intention of all myth. (*Kerygma and Myth,* pp. 10–11.) The hunger for God is expressed in all religion. (Bultmann, "The Question of Natural Revelation," *Essays,* pp. 90–118.) All men consciously or unconsciously search for God. (*Jesus Christ and Mythology,* pp. 52–53.)

[73] Karl Jaspers would give much more support to Bultmann here than does Heidegger, but to follow Jaspers might lead to a quite different theological position, such as that of Fritz Buri.

Second, one might identify some aspect of what Heidegger does describe phenomenologically with man's relatedness to transcendence, or God. Specifically, one might identify authentic existence as Heidegger presents it with the universal quest for God.[74] The problem here is that this procedure presupposes what we are presently concerned to justify. If we have other grounds for affirming the reality of God, then we may see some aspect of Heidegger's phenomenological account of human existence as in fact determined by man's relatedness to God. But if we limit ourselves to a phenomenological approach, we must also limit ourselves to Heidegger's conclusions or supplement his account phenomenologically. In any case, Bultmann explicitly affirms that existential analysis as such should disregard man's relation to God as it disregards all concrete encounters.[75]

We will assume, therefore, that Bultmann does not affirm the reality of God on general phenomenological grounds. Rather, he holds that the event of faith is the basis of such affirmation.[76] Faith understands itself as given by God. Existence in faith is living out of transcendence. The reality of God, although presumably an ontological truth, is affirmed on ontic rather than on philosophical grounds.[77] Furthermore, since the only acceptable assertions about God are those which express the existential relation between God and man, no philosophical conclusions can be drawn from the belief in God's reality.[78]

From the perspective given in faith, one may see all religion as conditioned by relatedness to the transcendent and all myth as expressive of man's apprehension of it.[79] By this approach, Bultmann gains a principle of understanding the intention of all myth. Most important, he achieves the possibility of interpreting New Testament mythology in terms of its intention.

We see, therefore, that if Bultmann is willing to throw the whole weight upon faith, he can assert the reality of God independently of any philosophical preunderstanding. Since faith understands itself as a gift of God,

[74] Bultmann asserts that the questions about God and about one's self are identical. (*Jesus Christ and Mythology,* p. 53.)

[75] *Kerygma and Myth,* p. 195.

[76] Bultmann, "A Chapter in the Problem of Demythologizing," in McArthur, *op. cit.,* p. 6.

[77] The fact that God can be known only in faith and that we cannot speak of what he is in himself does not imply that he does not exist apart from faith. (*Jesus Christ and Mythology,* pp. 72–73.)

[78] *Ibid.,* p. 69. See also "What Sense Is There to Speak of God?" *The Christian Scholar,* Vol. 43, 1960, pp. 213–222.

[79] Christian faith illuminates the fact that the question of the meaning of existence is in fact the question about God. (*Kerygma and Myth,* pp. 195–196.)

theology must assume the reality of God, and the Christian student of religion can be guided by this principle.

Here it is important to note that this kind of weight can be placed upon faith only because faith is understood as given in an act of God. This means that its occurrence is not conditioned by prior readiness or decision on man's part. If it were so conditioned, some supposition of the reality of God would be necessary before the human contribution to the occurrence of faith could be made. Bultmann does not always eschew the support of humanly understandable reasons for a human decision for faith, but I assume that he is always prepared to abandon this support in the interest of maintaining methodological freedom from speculative philosophy.

Bultmann is able to deny not only that belief in God's reality rests on natural theology but also that what is known of God in faith can be the basis of speculative elaboration on the order of a Christian natural theology. However, the belief in the reality of transcendence does function for Bultmann as a principle of interpreting religion and myth in general. It seems, therefore, that at this one point the truth grasped in faith does affect the work of the scholar as a scholar and leads in a rudimentary way to a Christian natural theology.

Whether or not one factually agrees that belief in God is sustained by the act of God in and for us without supporting considerations, the claim that this is true is an intelligible one that can operate legitimately as a decisive theological principle. We turn, then, to the second and more difficult principle, namely, that the objective world is closed to God's causal efficacy. On what basis is this affirmed?

Although other answers are also suggested in Bultmann's writings, his central conviction seems to be that once again it is faith itself that is decisive.[80] Faith understands itself as pure risk grounded in God's act of grace. It does not understand itself as based upon any objective evidence or calculus of probabilities. Hence, any idea of a miraculous intervention by God in the world is alien to faith. Interest in such ideas reflects a desire to achieve objective security of belief that is antagonistic to the essence of faith.

Bultmann believes that this understanding of faith is found in the New Testament itself. In the writings of Paul and especially of John it functions to begin the process of demythologizing that he himself wishes to carry through to completion. This demythologizing consists of deobjecti-

[80] See, for example, his assertion that demythologizing follows from radical application of the principle of justification by faith. (*Jesus Christ and Mythology,* pp. 72–73.)

fying the acts of God in the interest of the pure freedom and risk of faith. This means that the world can be left to be understood in terms of its immanent causal order, whereas God's relationship to man in grace and faith is understood as present in an entirely different dimension.

Bultmann's interpretation of the thrust and intention of the New Testament writers may be disputed by other students. One may grant that faith as understood in the New Testament is independent of objective support without agreeing that it is antagonistic to such support.

Bultmann's view, of course, is not that Paul or John denied the occurrence of miracles or saw the need of doing so in the interest of faith. His conviction is that when the nature of faith as they grasped it is more thoroughly understood, a further development of their thought leads to these conclusions.[81] Hence, the debate must center around the nature of faith as such rather than around the conclusions explicitly drawn in the New Testament.

David Hume made an important distinction between the occurrence of miracles and the evidential value of miracles. Although he undoubtedly disbelieved in their occurrence, he recognized the impossibility of making negative assertions on this point. He did argue very convincingly against the evidential value of miracles.[82]

Bultmann's perspective is remote from Hume's, but the Humean distinction is relevant to a questioning of Bultmann. In Bultmann's terms, faith clearly refuses the support of a supposed causal efficacy of God for this-worldly events. But can we affirm also on the grounds of faith that God never exercises such causal efficacy? The rejection of the support of the miraculous, whether one agrees or not, is clearly defensible. But that faith itself provides adequate grounds for denying the occurrence of miracles is very doubtful indeed. Furthermore, to make this negative assertion on the grounds of faith is to make faith the basis of a particular world view. This would lead to the development of a Christian natural theology. We may safely assume this is not Bultmann's intention.

Faith knows itself as the gift of God's grace through free decision. What seems to follow from this is that faith understands itself as wholly unaffected by beliefs about the causality of objective, this-worldly events. In this case, faith can be the basis neither of affirming nor of denying that God has causal efficacy for such events.

The intention of the foregoing argument is to show that acceptance of

[81] *Ibid.* Bultmann urges that the principle of justification applied by Paul against seeking security in good works be applied also against seeking security in objective knowledge.

[82] See above, Ch. 1, pp. 22–23.

Bultmann's understanding may entail the consequence that world views are irrelevant to faith but does not entail the particular world view that sees the world as closed to transcendence. If this view is to be maintained, some other basis must be offered.

We are now prepared to understand what Bultmann means when he asserts that he takes the modern world view as a criterion.[83] He emphatically does not mean that this world view has any essential relation to faith. However, once we see the indifference of faith to such questions, we can be quite open to whatever world view the most reliable contemporary thinking offers. We do not demythologize in order to harmonize with that world view; our motivation is to do justice to faith itself. But in carrying out our demythologizing with respect to matters that are theologically indifferent, we can be guided by contemporary nontheological thought.

In this context the modern world view plays a role in Bultmann's work. It is this world view which demands the doctrine that the world is closed to transcendence. All scientific and philosophical thought, he affirms, agrees on this point. On the authority of modern thought, therefore, it is properly accepted by theology.

Against Bultmann, we may argue that no such unanimity exists among serious contemporary thinkers. Major philosophical traditions in the English-speaking world have found it necessary to attribute to God a causal role in natural and historical processes.

Bultmann is aware that some philosophers have regarded God as in interaction with the world and that this tradition cannot be rejected simply on the basis of a negative consensus among many modern thinkers. To do this would be to enter into a philosophic debate for the purpose of establishing a principle of his theology, and Bultmann wishes to avoid such a procedure. Hence, he states that the philosophical idea of God as *Archē* is irrelevant for theology and has no bearing on what he means when he affirms the closedness of the this-worldly to the transcendent.[84]

My criticism of Bultmann here is not that his doctrine of the closedness of the world is false but that it cannot be taken as axiomatic on the basis of philosophic consensus. Some philosophers do not understand God as limited, in his relations to the world, to the function of the Greek *Archē*. We saw in Chapter 3 that it is possible to argue that the idea of cosmic mind in personal interaction with its creatures is the best philosophical explanation of what we have learned from science and personal experience. Such a claim may be erroneous, but it is not self-evidently so. If it is

[83] *Jesus Christ and Mythology,* p. 35; "A Chapter in the Problem of Demythologizing," in McArthur, *op. cit.,* pp. 2–3.

[84] *Kerygma and Myth,* pp. 103–104.

to be rejected, philosophic arguments are necessary.

Even if one finds it possible simply to ignore the philosophical tradition of cosmic theism as anachronistic, one must still acknowledge serious philosophical difficulties with the doctrine of the closedness of the world. This doctrine assumes that the closedness is constituted by a system of causal relations that are impervious to causal influences from without. But the very idea of causality has been in difficulty since the time of Hume and has been abandoned by many leading physicists as well as philosophers. Although it is still commonly employed in the life sciences and by historians, to the extent that they take their conceptual models and world view from physics, they are having to learn to do without it. If the idea of causality is abandoned in favor of sheer phenomenal descriptions based upon statistical procedures, then assertions about the closedness, or about the openness, of the world to transcendence become simply meaningless.

The point of all this is that the doctrine that the world is closed to God cannot be vindicated apart from philosophical discussion and particular philosophical commitments. If the doctrine is crucial to Bultmann's theological method, then the conclusion must be that a philosophical conviction plays a role in his thought parallel to that which natural theology plays in the thought of the theologians treated in Part I. This would, of course, be diametrically in conflict with his intention.

Before judging Bultmann in this way, we must re-examine the importance of the doctrine of the closedness of the world for his whole procedure. We have assumed thus far that this doctrine is methodologically crucial to Bultmann's theology. However, it may be that most if not all of what follows from this philosophical doctrine can follow also from the theological doctrine that the world view is a matter of indifference to faith. If so, substantial reconstruction of Bultmann's argument would be required, but his basic position would remain intact.[85]

This possibility is so important that some exposition of its implications is needed. Demythologizing would be carried out in purely theological terms. That is, the expositor would make no judgment whatever with regard to the factual occurrence of New Testament miracles or even the existence of such spheres of reality as heaven and hell and the spirits that inhabit them. His private credulity or incredulity would be simply set aside. He would not deny that spirits may invade this world and that

85 Bultmann has moved away from emphasis on the modern world view toward emphasis on the indifference of faith to all world views. Hence, such a reconstruction of his argument might well be demanded by his present theological position. Note the last sentence of *Jesus Christ and Mythology,* p. 85. See also "The Problem of Miracle," *Religion in Life,* Vol. 27, 1957–1958, pp. 63–75.

objective events may be affected by God's acts. But all this would simply be affirmed as theologically irrelevant. Theologically, only existence in faith matters, and this would be so expounded as to show precisely the irrelevance of everything else.

Such a program would necessarily have a tone and content quite different from that of Bultmann's actual writings, and this difference would be a good measure of the extent to which his acceptance of what he regards as the modern world view actually affects his work. Still, if by this alteration Bultmann can carry out his intention of avoiding dependence on speculative philosophy, we must regard such a program as the fulfillment of his own purposes. The conclusion is that, although many of Bultmann's own statements presuppose a definite cosmology, world view, or philosophy that he cannot derive from faith, his basic program *could* be carried out apart from these presuppositions.

It is clear that Bultmann has been strengthened in his conviction of the irrelevance to faith of natural theology and divine activity in the world, as objectively known, by his confidence that these things do not exist. If this support to the doctrine of irrelevance is removed by the abandonment of commitment to the world view that is presupposed, then the doctrine may prove difficult to sustain. That it remains a systematic, if largely unexplored, possibility, however, this does not deny.

The theological method at which we have now arrived would make faith central in every sense. It would show that faith is the ground not only for the Christian's own self-understanding and Christology but also for his belief in the reality of God. Faith is also the basis for ruling out as irrelevant every world view, ancient and modern, and for accepting a phenomenology of human existence as a preunderstanding for its comprehension. Since the faith in question is that to which the New Testament witnesses, everything will depend on the accuracy of the apprehension of the deepest meaning of faith in the New Testament. If New Testament faith is, as it is claimed, neutral and indifferent with respect to all possible world views (e.g., materialism, idealism, personalism) and to all possible acts of God in the objective course of events (e.g., the visible appearance of the resurrected Jesus), then a theological method should be possible that is loyal to Christian faith and indifferent to all else that is not phenomenologically established.

Serious criticism of this procedure must await its embodiment, but a crucial test is apparent when we turn to the third of the elements of wider philosophic import that Bultmann includes in his theology, that is, human freedom. Presumably, no Christian theology that could be considered Bultmannian could dispense with the idea that man in faith is free.

In Bultmann's own work, the idea of freedom appears within the phenomenological preunderstanding and is confirmed and actualized in New Testament faith. This procedure acknowledges dependence upon philosophy but only provisionally and in its nonspeculative form. However, we must ask whether the provisional acceptance and confirmation of this preunderstanding does not involve the abandonment of neutrality with respect to speculative philosophies and world views. Can we say that the theologicophenomenological affirmation of freedom is neutral with respect to a reductionistic-deterministic philosophy that understands mind and spirit as epiphenomenal manifestations of matter in motion? I assume that here Christian faith is radically incompatible with some philosophies, that it does, therefore, have implications for the choice of philosophy.

A theology based on faith alone can avoid this conclusion only if it asserts that its affirmation about freedom is at a level of discourse wholly different from that at which speculative philosophy operates.[86] Then it must abandon the support or even the use of a phenomenological analysis of human existence or else assert that it, too, operates at a level alien to all speculative philosophy. But such assertions would not only involve extensive and highly disputable judgments about the whole history of philosophy but also imply a profound duality in being, which view could itself not escape speculative philosophical consequences.

If this is correct, then in a Bultmannian context it is possible to escape dependence on a natural theology in the sense of an autonomous world view or speculative philosophy only if some elements of such a philosophy are affirmed on the basis of faith. This would mean that a Christian natural theology, however circumscribed, would in principle be accepted.

The critical conclusion of this over-all analysis of Bultmann's theological method is twofold. First, we must raise serious questions as to the intelligibility of his central affirmation as to the act of God in Jesus Christ. We have attempted a variety of interpretations of this affirmation only to find that each, when consistently developed, leads to consequences that Bultmann has been unwilling to adopt. As a result we have been forced to understand him as saying that the decisive act of God took place in the disciples rather than in Jesus. Thereby Bultmann may attain to internal consistency but only at the sacrifice of full faithfulness to the New Testament kerygma.

Second, Bultmann himself makes use of the modern world view in a

[86] Bultmann sometimes expresses this sense of faith's transcending all world views and philosophical accounts of being. See, for example, *Jesus Christ and Mythology,* pp. 64–65.

way that causes it to function, albeit negatively, as a natural theology. This is a serious inconsistency in his position as it stands. However, his basic hermeneutical and theological program could be carried out without making such use of the modern world view. The only objection to this procedure is that it places a very heavy burden, both positively and negatively, upon the precise accuracy of a particular apprehension of the deepest New Testament meaning of faith. Furthermore, it cannot escape affirmations that are *not* neutral among speculative philosophies, and hence, it leads in principle to the formulation of a Christian natural theology.

It is not surprising that those who have been most influenced by Bultmann have moved in quite divergent directions. It is not surprising that so many of Bultmann's critics have agreed on the fundamental inconsistency of his kerygmatic affirmation of God's act in Jesus Christ and his basic existentialist commitments. But it is also not surprising that Bultmann's brilliant and daring theological proposals have become the focus for much of the most creative theological work of our time.

10: Paul Tillich

THE THEOLOGY OF PAUL TILLICH HAS MANY SIMILARITIES TO THAT OF Rudolf Bultmann, but at each of the critical points in Bultmann's thought, Tillich takes a different turn. We have seen that Bultmann has an understanding of the relation of God and the world that he rests upon faith itself in conjunction with what he takes to be the modern world view. He attempts systematically to avoid dependence on speculative philosophy. Tillich fully recognizes the role of philosophy in dealing with God and the world as well as with man's self-understanding. Bultmann clings to the language of the acts of God in such a way as to maintain, for faith, the absolute and unique decisiveness of the event Jesus Christ. Tillich sees all events as grounded in God but understands the uniqueness of the Christ-event in terms of its transparency to the ground of being rather than in terms of a unique act of God in relation to it. Bultmann holds that Christian faith is faith in God's act in Christ. Tillich is concerned primarily with the new mode of existence that has become effective through that event.

Bultmann's theology may be seen as a synthesis of elements from Kierkegaard and from Heidegger. Hence, his classification as an existentialist is clear. Tillich's thought shows the influence of both these men, but they are much less determinative for him than for Bultmann. Therefore, his classification as an existentialist is much less clear. Nevertheless, there seem to be good reasons for placing him under this heading, especially since he sometimes classifies himself in this way.[1] He has been a major channel through which existential categories have been introduced into this country; although his dependence on Kierkegaard and Heidegger is

[1] Paul Tillich, "Metaphysics and Theology," *Review of Metaphysics*, Vol. 10, 1956, p. 63.

limited, he draws heavily from a movement of thought that is in the wider sense existential [2] and like the modern existentialists makes extensive use of phenomenology; finally, he explicitly rejects both the natural theology of Part I and the kerygmatic theology of Part II of this book.[3]

Against this classification of Tillich's thought is his extensive use of speculative ontology,[4] which seriously raises the question as to whether his use of philosophy differs significantly from that of those who avowedly employ natural theology. But we have seen that even Bultmann has not succeeded altogether in avoiding natural theology. Indeed the classification " existentialist " is used in this volume in such a way as to leave open the question as to whether existentialism really offers a methodological alternative to the use of philosophy as a natural theology on the one hand and the outright rejection of all use of philosophy on the other.

Tillich has provided us with a systematic account of his own theological method [5] as well as with a systematic exposition of his theology as a whole. Hence, our task in presenting the structure of his thought in terms of its principles of justification is simplified. However, there is an important difference between his explicit account of his method and the kinds of questions with which we are primarily concerned here. Tillich is focusing on the method of organizing his material and the grounds of exclusion and inclusion of material, and he can rightly describe his method as that of correlation.[6] By this he means that he presents an analysis of the human situation as posing the existential questions and then presents the answers that are given in the Christian message.

By the " situation " Tillich does not refer to the given psychological and sociological conditions. He refers to the interpretation of those conditions or the expression of what human existence is understood to be in those conditions.[7] It is this interpretation which poses the existential question to which theology, if it is to be relevant, must give its answer. Thus an analysis of man's being as finite raises the question that the Christian answers by the affirmation of God; the question raised by an analysis of man's existence as estrangement from his essence is answered by Christ; the analysis of life as the dynamic unity of essence and existence raises

[2] Tillich describes this wider movement in " Existential Philosophy: Its Historical Meaning," *Theology of Culture*, pp. 76–111.

[3] Paul Tillich, *Systematic Theology* I, pp. 8, 30.

[4] Note the polemic against Tillich at this point by Zuurdeeg (*An Analytic Philosophy of Religion*, pp. 150 ff., esp. p. 165.)

[5] " Introduction," *Systematic Theology* I, pp. 3–68; Tillich, " The Problem of Theological Method," *The Journal of Religion*, Vol. 27, 1947, pp. 16–26.

[6] Paul Tillich, *The Protestant Era*, p. xlii; *Systematic Theology* I, pp. 8, 59–66.

[7] *Systematic Theology* I, pp. 3–4.

questions that are answered in terms of the Spirit. The discussion of history and the Kingdom of God is separated from the last of these for purposes of convenience; the epistemological question of reason, as answered by revelation, since it is involved in all the others, is treated first. This rounds out the five parts of the system.[8]

This organization of the material, Tillich believes, expresses the profound differences between his approach and those of both the traditional apologete and the purely kerygmatic theologian.[9] The theologian of the former type first presents a body of ideas that are supposed to be held in common by the Christian and the rational man generally. He then presents the additional teachings of Christian faith as supplementary to this common belief in such a way as to display the reasonableness of accepting these teachings as well. The purely kerygmatic approach in theory ignores the present situation and simply presents the unchanging truths given in and through God's revelation. Thus, in terms of the structure of the systematic theology, Tillich correctly differentiates his theology from the apologetic and kerygmatic theologies as an "answering" theology employing the method of correlation.

The question that must be raised, however, is that of the sources of norms that determine the answers to the questions implied by the analysis of the situation. Tillich explicitly asserts that these answers are given by the Christian faith and are affirmed only from within the theological circle determined by that faith.[10] But the question remains as to how they are found therein. Obviously, Tillich does not employ a proof-text approach. Neither does he ask the Biblical theologians to provide him with an account of major principles running through the Bible or specifically with the teaching of Jesus or Paul. No more does he appeal to the historic creeds and confessions or to the consensus of contemporary theologians or believers.

The difference between the material in the question sections and in the answer sections is that in the former the depth dimension of existence or the ground of being does not come explicitly to attention. Rather, we are led to see how man's situation, in so far as he neglects this dimension, leads to insoluble problems and desperate conditions. In the answer sections, we are presented with an analysis of how, when this dimension of existence and its ground is taken into full consideration, the problems are

[8] *Ibid.*, I, pp. 66–68.

[9] These are roughly identical with the positions treated in Parts I and II of this book, but the reader will recognize that few contemporary theologians could be categorized so simply.

[10] *Systematic Theology* I, pp. 8–11.

resolved in principle. We are also shown how Christian faith embodies the ideal grasp of this depth dimension and its ground.

Nevertheless, it is clear to the reader of *Systematic Theology* that the actual norms guiding the presentation do not differ radically between the sections dealing with the situation and those presenting the answers. Phenomenological analysis and ontological analysis are employed extensively in both sections, and the results of analyses in the sections on the situation are employed normatively in the sections in which the answers are presented.

Without disputing the utility of the organization that Tillich has imposed on his theology, we must consider the whole body of thought as a unity and ask the general question as to how its affirmations are derived and justified. When we do so, we must recognize three distinct sources that are conjointly determinative for Tillich's thought. These we shall call the phenomenological, the ontological, and the specifically Christian.

In view of the importance that this threefold distinction has for this whole analysis of Tillich's thought, it demands some initial explanation. It may be hoped that the analysis itself will constitute by its functional value a justification of the distinction.

First, the distinction of phenomenology and ontology as parallel sources requires explanation since it is foreign both to Tillich and to the philosophers treated in Chapter 8. For Heidegger and Sartre, phenomenology is a method by which ontologies can be formulated. Hence, the ontology is the account of the most general characteristics of a given field of investigation as given to immediate experience. Nothing is affirmed on the basis of *inference* from experience. Nothing can be said within its compass, therefore, about the reality of God or about the ground or cause of being.

Tillich also develops his ontological doctrines in close conjunction with his phenomenological descriptions.[11] But in his case, ontology has a dimension that cannot be warranted by phenomenology alone. It deals with God as the ground of being of finite entities as well as with characteristics of the nonhuman world that are not directly open to phenomenological investigation. Although the whole of his thought is closely integrated, we must recognize a movement beyond the phenomenological data that requires inference or speculative generalization of a kind that would not be allowed by the other phenomenologists mentioned above.

Tillich himself includes both phenomenological and inferential ele-

11 There is a brief discussion of phenomenology in *Systematic Theology* I, pp. 106–107. A much more extended discussion of the method is found in "Religionsphilosophie," written in 1925 and published in Tillich, *Frühe Haupt Werke*, pp. 309–313.

ments within ontology. Hence, any distinction of phenomenology and ontology must be imposed upon his work rather than derived from it. Nevertheless, a clear distinction exists, and a terminological distinction will help to make it visible.

The distinction between that which is accessible for direct description and that which is accessible only by inference or speculative generalization is understood by Heidegger and Sartre as the distinction between the phenomenological, including the ontological, and the metaphysical. In their view metaphysics is inadmissible, and their objection to it does apply in part to Tillich's position. But Tillich also finds the connotations of "metaphysics" objectionable in so far as they suggest another world alongside this one.[12] Hence, it seems less misleading to distinguish the phenomenological, as that which falls within the sphere of direct description, from the ontological, which can be warranted only by inference or speculative generalization. In this sense, man's awareness of his contingency is phenomenological, but the assertion that God as being-itself is the ground of being is ontological.

Phenomenology and ontology are not as such distinctively Christian activities; hence, we would not expect their results to constitute a Christian theology. No statement is theological except as it deals with its object as a matter of man's ultimate concern, that is, as a matter of man's being or notbeing.[13] Furthermore, a Christian theology is such by having in addition to this formal criterion of any theology a material norm that binds it to Jesus Christ. Tillich's own formulation of this norm is the "New Being in Jesus as the Christ."[14]

The reference to the specifically Christian determination of Tillich's system is the reference to this material norm. Presumably, general phenomenological and ontological considerations cannot explain those assertions warranted by the claim that Jesus as the Christ is the New Being. On the basis of his own statements we can say that Tillich's theology is *Christian* to that degree to which this third source, or at least concern for this third source, is decisive for its affirmations.

For the sake of completeness we might add as a fourth source of Tillich's thought our knowledge of contingent historical fact. Incidental reference will indeed be made to this, but it is not used as a principle or organization in this chapter.

The exposition of the structure of Tillich's theology now proceeds in terms of the three sources of his thought: the phenomenological, the ontological, and the specifically Christian principle that Jesus as the Christ is

[12] *Systematic Theology* I, pp. 20, 163. [13] *Ibid.*, I, pp. 12, 14. [14] *Ibid.*, I, p. 50.

the New Being. Further discussion of the relationships among these sources is postponed to the critical section with which the chapter concludes.

Two main aspects of Tillich's phenomenology, each of which leads to a corresponding aspect of his ontology, require exposition. They are the phenomenological accounts of faith and estrangement. We will consider both before turning to the ontological development.

When Tillich takes the concept of faith as central for his theological development, he is not conceiving faith in the first place as Bultmann does. Bultmann holds that faith is a distinctively Christian condition that occurs only as God's act in Christ is made effective in the believer. Tillich, by contrast, takes faith as a universal phenomenon central to man's personal life as such.[15] It is exhibited in all seriousness whether it takes the form of belief or doubt, of theism or atheism, of Christianity or paganism. Hence, the analysis of faith is a suitable topic for a phenomenology that does not presuppose Christian existence.

Tillich uses the term " faith " in two senses. In both senses faith means ultimate concern, but in the strictest sense it may be directed only to that which is in actuality a matter of ultimate concern, whereas in the looser sense any entity whatever may be its object.[16] This distinction can be made at the phenomenological level.

Ultimate concern involves both total surrender of one's self and all lesser claims to the object of the concern and the expectation of total fulfillment through that surrender. This concern may be directed to a nation or to success as well as to the God of the Bible. What the believer is concerned with makes an absolute difference to him, but it does not affect the dynamics of the faith as such.[17]

Nevertheless, the phenomenological analysis of faith points to the error of placing faith in any finite entity. The *concern* of ultimate concern may be directed toward objects or states of affairs in the spatiotemporal continuum of worldly events. But the *ultimacy* of ultimate concern points to a dimension of all existence that cannot be understood at that level. For example, the scientist who is driven by a concern for truth implicitly acknowledges an unconditional quality in truth itself that cannot be identified with any particular discovery or proposition. Rather, it remains the norm by which all approximations are measured. In a similar way, good-

[15] Paul Tillich, *Dynamics of Faith,* p. 126.

[16] Cf. the discussion in *ibid.,* pp. 1–4, and the suggestion on p. 62 that faith be defined as " the state of being ultimately concerned about the ultimate." See also *The Protestant Era,* p. 239, where faith is described as " the state of mind in which we are grasped by something unconditional."

[17] *Dynamics of Faith,* p. 4.

ness itself stands outside the level of space and time as a norm that judges every approximation to goodness.[18]

Truth itself and goodness itself must not be thought of as entities that can be set over against other entities either in nature or in a supernature. They constitute a dimension of being revealed by the analysis of existence that points to the contrast between every existent entity and the unconditional element that gives it its meaning. This analysis points, therefore, to the falsity of every identification of personal success or of any entity, idea, or institution with that which really concerns us ultimately.

In terms of the dimension of the unconditional revealed by the phenomenological analysis of existence, we may judge as idolatrous every faith that is directed to particular entities.[19] These entities may properly be viewed as bearers or mediators of the unconditional, but they must never be identified with the unconditional. The rejection of every claim of finite entities for ultimate concern, Tillich calls the Protestant principle or protest.[20]

Phenomenological analysis also reveals a quality of experience that we may call the holy.[21] This quality has often been taken as marking off the distinctively religious realm of experience. In one sense this is correct, but it may also be misleading. It is misleading if it is supposed that holiness resides in certain entities or situations that thereby become objects of religious devotion. Holiness is revealed in the phenomenological analysis of human experience, not in a description of its objects. Here it presents itself as an aspect of man's experience of faith. Whatever concerns one ultimately is experienced by him as holy.

But the experience of the holy reinforces further the view that the true object of faith is never a finite, conditioned entity. The mystery and the fascination of the holy point to the dimension that transcends the sphere of spatiotemporal subjects and objects. They point to the holy as that which both sustains and threatens our existence. The holy appears through objects, but its very nature contradicts its identification with objects.[22]

Phenomenologically, then, Tillich shows us that there is a quality of ultimate concern that characterizes all those who are serious about life, regardless of the end to which they may give themselves. He also shows

[18] *Systematic Theology* I, pp. 206–207.
[19] *Ibid.*, I, p. 13.
[20] *The Protestant Era,* pp. 226, 233, 239–240. See also "Author's Preface" and Chs. XII and XIII.
[21] Tillich cites Rudolf Otto's analysis with approval. (*Systematic Theology* I, p. 215; *Dynamics of Faith,* p. 13.)
[22] *Systematic Theology* I, pp. 215–216.

that implicit in all such concern is a relatedness to an unconditional dimension of existence that judges every final commitment to any conditioned or finite entity. Hence, we see that faith in the full and normative sense is ultimate concern about that which is really of ultimate concern to us. If we ask what *is* unconditional or what *is* really of ultimate concern to us, we cross the frontier into ontology. Before doing this we will consider a second area of phenomenological investigation — that of existence as estrangement.

When I examine my own given existence, I discover that in my total being I am deeply divided. On the one hand, I am aware of an ideal or normative possibility for my being. On the other hand, I am aware of an actualized being that falls far short of the normative possibility. I perceive the former as my true being, my essence. The latter is my empirical actuality, my existence. I become aware of the gulf between my existence and my essence when I emerge out of the dreaming innocence of infancy into full consciousness. I do not experience this gulf as produced by this development; instead, I recognize it as having always been there. This separation of my existence from my essence is an alienation, an estrangement, a fall.[23]

Still within the phenomenological approach I can go farther in analyzing the structures of existential and essential being. In each case these structures can best be seen as "polarities." By a polarity we mean a pair of terms that face in opposite directions but that at the same time demand each other.[24] For example, I experience myself as a self in a world. Self and world are set over against each other. Yet if I lose the sense of a world over against me, I cannot maintain my awareness of my self, or if I lose my self-awareness, my world disintegrates. Thus each polar term demands the other.

In the same way we find that personality and community are polar terms. Only a centered, responsible self can participate richly in community life, and only in such participation can one become such a self.[25] Again, vitality and intentionality illustrate this relationship. The sheer life force within us can express itself only in meanings and ends, and these meanings and ends can be realized only through vitality.[26] Finally, freedom and destiny can be identified also as polar terms. Man can be

[23] *Ibid.,* II, pp. 32–36. For the clarification of the key terms "essence" and "existence" see ibid., I, pp. 202–203; II, pp. 19–28.

[24] *Ibid.,* I, pp. 198–199. Tillich treats polarities under the heading of ontological elements. However, I am presenting them in their human expression, where they are open to phenomenological analysis.

[25] *Ibid.,* I, pp. 174–178.

[26] *Ibid.,* I, pp. 178–182.

free only on the basis of an existing selfhood formed by nature and history. But this existing selfhood can be destiny only in so far as it functions as the basis for freedom.[27]

Man can perceive the ideal balance of these polarities as characterizing his essential being, but in his actual existence he experiences tensions rather than harmony. He finds himself striving toward one of the polar terms rather than the other, and at this point a peculiar characteristic of polarities must be noted. A movement toward either of the polar terms does not actually strengthen that term and, hence, also the other polar term. On the contrary, it so transforms the character of the pole toward which it moves, that both terms of the polarity are weakened. This is hard to understand in abstraction, so let us consider concrete examples.

Take the case of personality and community. Each depends for its development on the other. But consider what happens if either becomes the object of special concern. A lonely and insecure man may strive hard to enter into community. To this end he accepts community patterns and values — in other words, he conforms fully to whatever the community seems to demand of him. But in so doing he weakens his own centeredness in himself. He becomes "other-directed" rather than "inner-directed." He becomes less of a person and more like a thing. Thus he sacrifices personhood for community. But in so far as his personhood declines he becomes in fact incapable of community, for community is such only as an intercourse, a sharing among persons. A low level of personhood permits only a low level of community. Man's existence moves farther and farther from his essential being.

The situation is no better if an individual determines to cultivate his personality in isolation from community. Actually, such a decision can occur only when a fairly high level of community exists, for the very self-understanding that permits of such decision is a product of community. But even then the partial withdrawal from community that is possible weakens not only community but also personhood. One may develop in relation to his memories, which constitute still his sharing in community, but apart from fresh human interaction one dries up as a person.

Existential being consists in an alternation between these poles in such a way as to maintain always a destructive tension. This tension threatens the very humanity of our being.[28] It constitutes our fallenness from our true or essential selfhood.

Our awareness of this situation, in which we are fallen from our essence and continuously threatened by loss of our human being, is anxiety. But

[27] *Ibid.*, I, pp. 182–186.

[28] *Ibid.*, I, p. 199.

this is not the only form of anxiety that phenomenological analysis can reveal to us. There is another anxiety, which is the awareness of our finitude as such.[29] That is, we are aware of our radical contingency. We find ourselves in a network of causal relations and threatened by the ultimate certainty of death. We experience our being as having no necessity, as not having in itself the ground of its being.[30]

In the face of the threat both of relative loss of human being and of absolute loss of being itself, man can still affirm himself. That is, he can find "the courage to be." [31] In courage one accepts one's finitude, one's alienation, and the lack of objective meaning in life. But to do this one must try to transcend oneself toward the ground and power of being.[32] Thus courage, too, points to a dimension of being that transcends the spatio-temporal sphere.

The phenomenological account of human existence, like the phenomenological account of faith, points to unconditioned reality which as phenomenological it cannot describe. Hence, it demands completion in an ontology to which we now turn.[33]

In his ontology, Tillich places himself in the main stream of Western thought from the pre-Socratics through the great Christian philosopher-theologians down to the German idealists and especially Schelling. His intention is not to develop speculatively a particular form of ontology and defend it against all others. He seeks rather to lift out certain basic features indispensable to philosophical thought. If certain philosophers choose to limit themselves to a study of purely formal relationships or the meaning of language, they have that privilege, but they should not call in question the much wider scope of the historic philosophic task.

Tillich must, however, engage in philosophy on the basis of at least one further major decision. Greek and medieval philosophy assumed the reality of a world and asked what it was like and how we do in fact have knowledge of it. Descartes initiated the very different approach of doubting the reality of the world and asking how we can decide whether it is real. This latter approach has dominated modern philosophy and has led to a serious impasse.

[29] *Ibid.*, I, p. 191.
[30] Paul Tillich, *The Courage to Be*, p. 44.
[31] *Ibid.*, Chs. 4, 5, and 6.
[32] *Ibid.*, p. 155.
[33] Once again we must recognize that Tillich does not in fact separate ontology from phenomenology in this way but rather passes back and forth repeatedly between them, employing ontological categories in the phenomenological expositions. However, when we ask how particular aspects of his thought are justified, we must make this distinction.

Tillich believes that the task of philosophy emerges from the situation in which man finds himself and that this situation is most inescapably characterized by the self-world polarity.[34] This implies that the self as subject is in relationship to the world as object or to the many entities encountered in the world as objects. This subject-object relationship is the basis for all thought. In this sense, whatever is thought is, by being thought, an object, whether it is a stone, another person, oneself, or God.[35] But the status of being object for thought does not imply a status of being merely an object, that is, of lacking subjectivity.[36]

Every finite being participates to some degree in the fundamental ontological structure of self and world.[37] That means also that every being shares in selfhood and subjectivity. Hence, the polarities that at the phenomenological level could be found in human existence must also be understood as characterizing being as such. The anthropological forms examined above are only special cases of ontological polarities that are present in every being. Personality and community are the expression at the human level of the ontological polarity of individualization and participation. Vitality and intentionality are the human manifestation of dynamics and form. In the same way freedom and destiny are the human analogues of the universal polar elements of spontaneity and law.[38]

Ontology complements phenomenology in much the same way with respect to the investigations of the tension between essence and existence. Phenomenologically this tension appeared in the recognition of a separation between a normative state of being and an actual state of being. Ontologically, it constitutes a major theme of philosophy from the time of Plato. The ontological considerations arose out of prior existential experience, but they sought to set this experience in a wider context of being. Tillich surveys the history of this attempt [39] to point out the ambiguities in it and to seek the basic ontological structure expressed in it. Essence is the power by which an actuality is, but it contains potentiality for much greater actuality. Hence, it judges as well as empowers. Existence " stands out " of essence, thereby actualizing essence but only in a fragmentary way. Hence, existence always involves separation or a " fall." [40] The actual as existent is always less than, and in tension with, its own essence. What

[34] *Systematic Theology* I, pp. 168–171.
[35] *Ibid.*, I, p. 172.
[36] *Ibid.*, I, pp. 171–173.
[37] *Ibid.*, I, p. 173.
[38] *Ibid.*, I, pp. 174–186.
[39] *Ibid.*, I, pp. 202–204.
[40] Tillich regards this ontological account of the fall as more fundamental than the psychological account that provides an analogy for it. (*Ibid.*, II, pp. 32–36.)

we grasped phenomenologically as our human situation is now seen as the universal characteristic of finite being as such, although only in man does it come to self-consciousness.[41]

Just as the phenomenological analysis of experience reveals an unconditional vertical dimension that gives meaning to the horizontal but cannot be understood in terms of it, so the ontological analysis of subjects and objects points to that which transcends these categories. The togetherness of self and world can be rooted only in that which is neither subject nor object but the ground of both. The togetherness of essence and existence can be rooted only in that which is beyond both essence and existence.

Furthermore, the world of finite objects cannot explain itself. Every entity participates in the power of being, else it would not be at all, but no entity has the power of being as its possession. Being is always a gift received from beyond itself, and we cannot understand this beyond in terms of other entities in endless temporal succession.

There is a causal relationship between finite entities such that the structure of one affects the form taken by another. The study of these causal relationships is the proper domain of science. But philosophy must raise another question — the question of the sheer being of each and all of these entities. Why does anything at all exist? Why, even if it exists now, does it perpetuate its existence into the next now? This is the supreme question, and it necessarily drives us beyond the categories of subject and object to that which is the power of the being of everything that is, the all-embracing ground of being, or being-itself.

It must be emphasized that being-itself is not an abstraction from the concrete, finite beings that exist. This nominalist error must be rejected, because such an abstraction could give no answer to the ultimate question of the ground of being. At the same time being-itself must not be understood as a being that exists, for no matter what superiority is attributed to such a being, it would remain one among many beings. As such it could not be the ground of the being of all beings. Being-itself is neither an abstraction nor a being. It is the ultimate reality that is the ground and power of being of everything that is.

This means that no language that receives its meaning by reference to finite entities can have literal application to being-itself. Even such terminology as "ground and power of being" is analogical in so far as ground and power receive their literal meaning in their application to relations between finite entities. These terms must appeal to the intuition of

[41] *Ibid.*, I, p. 108.

a radical dependence that lies in a dimension other than that of natural and historical causality. For the rest we can speak negatively of being-itself, denying to it every limitation that is determined by the dichotomy of subject and object, of essence and existence.[42]

When we now place our phenomenological analysis of the unconditional dimension of experience into the context of our ontological analysis, we see that the unconditional dimension of our experience is that in which we are related to being-itself rather than to particular beings, to the ground of our being rather than to particular influences upon it. This ground of our being is unconditional in its own nature and is unconditionally our concern. The unconditional character of being-itself is the source of the unconditional elements also in the true and the good.[43]

As the object of our unconditional concern, being-itself is God. Here not only phenomenology and ontology but also theology and ontology meet. Theology differs from phenomenology in that it presupposes the reality, indeed the supreme reality, of the correlate of the element of ultimacy in personal experience. In this it agrees with ontology. It differs from ontology in that it is concerned with the *meaning* of God for man, whereas ontology treats the structures of being generally in their relation to being-itself. Theology is possible only when one is consciously involved in the relationship that is to him a matter of ultimate concern. Ontology is possible only when one maintains a relative detachment from the objects treated. But every theologian presupposes and to some extent participates in ontology, and no ontologist can actually detach himself from his human concern with the ground of his being. Hence, ontology and theology interpenetrate each other.[44]

The theologian must use language when he speaks of God as the object of his ultimate concern, but since God as the power of being or being-itself transcends the sphere in which language can be used literally, he must employ symbols.[45] To understand what this means, we must distinguish symbols from signs.

A sign points to and stands for another entity without any necessary inner unity with its referent. A symbol, on the contrary, participates in the power of that to which it calls our attention.[46] To speak of God sym-

[42] *Ibid.,* I, pp. 235–236.
[43] *Ibid.,* I, pp. 206–207.
[44] *Ibid.,* I, pp. 22–28, 132, 221.
[45] *Ibid.,* I, p. 239.
[46] *Ibid.,* I, p. 239. See also Paul Tillich, "Religious Symbols and Our Knowledge of God," *The Christian Scholar,* Vol. 38, 1955, pp. 185–197. Tillich also discusses symbols in "The Religious Symbol," *The Journal of Liberal Religion,* Vol. 2, 1940, pp. 13–33; "Existential Analyses and Religious Symbols," *Contemporary*

bolically is to speak of being-itself as it manifests itself to us as our ultimate concern through finite entities.

Symbols are in constant danger of being taken literally. When this happens they become false and lead us away from God. But when symbols are taken as symbols they are true in so far as they mediate to us the object of our ultimate concern. At this point a brief statement of the relation of Tillich's position to that of Bultmann is appropriate. Bultmann has proposed that we should demythologize the Bible by translating its myths into literal accounts of their existential meaning. He retains the kerygmatic idea of the act of God as a nonmythological but analogical expression. Tillich opposes demythologizing in that he denies that the language of religion can be given literal statement. He proposes instead that we deliteralize, by which he means that we should reject every interpretation of religious language that treats it as if it were speaking of events or entities at the finite level. We should understand mythical language as symbolic, and so long as the symbols maintain their power, we should retain them.[47]

The difference between Bultmann and Tillich is partly verbal and partly real. Both equally oppose any understanding of sacred language that would cause us to regard divine reality or activity as objectively given in the finite sphere. But Bultmann takes myth to be an expression of man's existential self-understanding and therefore translatable into philosophical existential language. Tillich takes myth to be a symbolic way of speaking of God and therefore not translatable into any literal language. Bultmann recognizes that Scripture speaks of the acts of God and that this language is analogical rather than literal. Tillich is not concerned about the acts of God in this sense, but rather with the universal activity of God and his manifestation to man as the object of ultimate concern. Hence, he understands the myths as expressions of man's awareness of God rather than of his understanding of his own existence.

However, when Bultmann speaks of man's self-understanding he includes man's understanding of himself as he is in relation to God. And when Tillich thinks of man's awareness of God, it is always an awareness of God as that which is of ultimate significance for him. Hence, in practice the difference is minimized. Tillich actually gives explanations of

---

Problems in Religion, Basilius, ed., pp. 35–55, republished in *Four Existentialist Theologians,* Herberg, ed., pp. 306–322; "Theology and Symbolism," *Religious Symbolism,* Johnson, ed., pp. 107–116.

[47] *Systematic Theology* II, p. 152. Bultmann acknowledges that symbols may be needed, but he insists that we should be prepared to explain their meaning nonmythologically. (Bultmann, *Jesus Christ and Mythology,* pp. 67–78.)

myths that differ but little from Bultmann's demythologizing, and where the myth no longer functions effectively as a symbol, he recognizes the need to abandon it. However, he insists that one symbol can be replaced only by another, not by literal language. This is because, regardless of all similarities with Bultmann's Christian existentialism, Tillich's theology is centrally concerned with God rather than with the Christian's understanding of his own existence.

Thus far in this presentation of Tillich's theology nothing has been said that necessarily appeals to a specifically Christian starting point or perspective or, in Tillich's terms, to the material principle of theology. But theology as such cannot maintain this apparent neutrality. To ask the question of the meaning of God for me, the nature of the divine demand upon me, or how God is manifest to me always presupposes a particular encounter with God. This encounter occurs in a community and is part of the history of that community. Every theology is the theology of some religion, no matter how open it may be to the insights of other traditions. As a Christian theologian Tillich takes his stand within the circle of Christian faith. In this sense he joins the theologians of " the leap."

However, this by no means makes of theology an irrational discipline. Nor does it imply any lack of interest on the part of the theologian in justifying his taking the position within this circle. It excludes only the possibility that Christian theology can follow deductively from ontological principles or inductively from detached observation. The same could be said of almost every position that understands itself as a theology, no matter how extensively it makes use of natural theology.

Tillich, however, makes a further point that does separate him from some liberal theologies. He asserts that Christian theology includes the claim to its own finality.[48] One cannot speak of what God means for Christian faith except as one speaks of his *final* revelation in Jesus as the Christ. To speak of Jesus as one figure in the history of religions, however great, who has been or might be superseded by later developments is to speak from outside the circle of Christian faith — to speak in some other capacity than that of Christian theologian.

The claim to the finality of Jesus as the Christ seems to place Tillich close to the tradition of Kierkegaard and to the thought of Bultmann. But in fact it functions quite differently in his theology. For Kierkegaard and Bultmann this finality is a matter of faith, and faith is a belief to which factual considerations are irrelevant. Ultimately, faith is itself understandable only as an act of God. Tillich by contrast develops an elaborate

[48] *Systematic Theology* I, pp. 15, 16, 132.

explanation of what is meant by the claim to finality and an extensive apologetic justification for it. Before classifying Tillich with the Kierkegaardian tradition, therefore, Tillich's own interpretation of his position must be carefully examined.

First, it must be understood that the claim of the finality of Jesus as the Christ involves no assertion of a supranatural character about the man Jesus. Indeed Tillich's ontological views preclude any supernaturalism at any point in his theology. What is asserted has nothing to do with a preexistent entity, whether God or angelic creature, taking on human form. All such thinking is radically excluded. Furthermore, Tillich recognizes, as Bultmann does not, that in the context of his thought it would be meaningless to talk about a unique act of God in Christ.

What is affirmed is rather that the *principle* of God's self-revelation became manifest in this human person, Jesus.[49] The point is that whereas innumerable other media have functioned in revelatory ways, all of them have been fragmentary and distorting. They have all lacked both concreteness and universality. When particular objects serve as revelatory media, they lack, not only universality because of their conditioned particularity, but also concreteness, for by this latter term Tillich envisages a power to include the other without losing its own identity. This power, hence concreteness, can be possessed only by a person. When abstractions serve as revelatory media, they lack not only particularity because of their abstractness, but also universality, for they are by their nature abstracted from some range of phenomena and applicable only to them. Only a person can be absolutely universal by his power to grasp all abstractions. Thus only a personal life can be both concrete and universal.[50]

But, of course, not every life is such. On the contrary, persons are also both particular and abstract in Tillich's sense. One could in principle reveal God universally only by sacrificing everything contingent in oneself to him, by becoming transparent to him. At the same time one could reveal God concretely only if that which is made transparent to him is itself a perfectly centered self.[51] The prophetic pointing to God lacks universality because of the contingent historical factors that are retained. The mystic's pointing to God lacks concreteness in so far as selfhood is abandoned. But in Jesus as the Christ, centered selfhood surrenders itself to God as such without ceasing to be centered selfhood. Hence, perfect concreteness and perfect universality are combined in him.

If one raises the question of how we can know this to be true, we must acknowledge that we cannot, in the strict sense, know any such facts of

[49] *Ibid.*, I, p. 16; II, p. 112. [50] *Ibid.*, I, pp. 16–17. [51] *Ibid.*, I, pp. 133–136.

history. We can only know that the picture of Jesus recorded for us in the New Testament points us to such a personal life and that whether or not it is correct as to details — even as to the name of the person who inspired it — it points to the historical existence of a personal life capable of inspiring this picture.[52] In any case, that the ultimate, normative, or final revelation occurred in history and is witnessed to in the New Testament is the essence of the distinctive Christian belief. This claim is in no way irrational or arbitrary, although it is neither inductive nor deductive in its origin.

Christian theology in every age is the exposition of the significance of this essential affirmation in the context of the self-understanding of that age. If men perceive their problem as God's wrath upon them for their sins, Jesus as the Christ is preached as the forgiveness of sins. If men perceive their problem as the need of guidance and aid in the achievement of a nearer approximation to ideal life, Jesus as the Christ is preached as the ideal person. Today man perceives his problem in terms of alienation, despair, and meaninglessness. Jesus as the Christ must be proclaimed as the bearer of the New Being in which man is healed and enters a new level of life.[53]

Just as the message that Jesus as the Christ is the New Being is the answer to the question implicit in the situation of modern man, so what is meant by the New Being can be grasped only in terms of the analysis of modern man's experience of estrangement. This analysis, as it is phenomenologically and ontologically developed by Tillich, was sketched above. Man finds that in his existence he is separated from his essence, and that the polar elements in terms of which he exists are in endless tension with each other. He experiences this tension as a threat to his very humanity.

In such a situation the only message that can afford hope is the message that under the conditions of finite existence the estrangement of existence and essence can be overcome. This means also that the destructive tension between the polar elements in existence can be overcome. This new existence which remains finite, but which overcomes the destructive consequences of finitude, is the New Being.[54] The Christian proclamation is that this New Being was actualized in Jesus as the Christ and that it is in principle accessible to us for our participation.

That the New Being is accessible in principle does not mean that Christians fully participate in it now. Such full participation is the eschatological hope. Furthermore, the Christian conviction that Jesus as the Christ is the bearer of the New Being does not mean that the power of the New

[52] *Ibid.*, II, pp. 97–118, esp. 114–115. [53] *Ibid.*, I, p. 49. [54] *Ibid.*, II, pp. 118–120.

Being has been present only in him. Except as there has been some overcoming of the estrangement of existence from essence there could have been no humanity at all. Wherever there has been any wholeness in human life, it has been by the power of the New Being. But everywhere this health has been fragmentary and open to demonic distortion. In Jesus as the Christ we find the norm in terms of which every degree of healing is seen and judged.[55]

Tillich's distinctively Christian theological affirmation is that Jesus as the Christ is the final revelation and the bearer of the New Being. Beyond this Tillich does not bind himself by the specific teachings of Scripture or tradition. These are, of course, important and suggestive, and Tillich has shown himself a brilliant interpreter of their meaning. But neither in terminology nor in content do they limit the freedom of the theologian. His task is, therefore, not the defending of the tradition nor the exegesis of Scripture, but rather the answering of man's basic contemporary questions in terms of all that can be known historically, phenomenologically, and ontologically, guided by the conviction that ultimate reality is decisively manifest to us in Jesus as the Christ.

◈ ◈

The question we must now ask is whether Tillich's answers to the questions implicit in man's situation are in fact determined by the belief in Jesus as the Christ. This is not to ask whether Tillich's doctrine of God is that found in the Bible or in Christian orthodoxy. It is rather to ask the methodological question as to how this doctrine of God is presented and justified. Does it arise within the circle of Christian faith, as Tillich seems to affirm, or does it in fact derive from philosophical considerations that stand outside this circle? In this latter case it would seem to constitute a natural theology. This interpretation is suggested by the fact that in the foregoing exposition the doctrine of God was placed before the specifically Christian aspect of Tillich's teaching. This implies that it stands outside the circle of Christian faith. Is this an accurate implication?

To answer this question we must note first that the term " God " is not an ontological, but a theological, term. Therefore, to describe Tillich's doctrine of God as an aspect of his ontology would be erroneous. Ontology deals with being-itself. Theology deals with that which is of ultimate concern. When theology recognizes in being-itself that which is of ultimate concern, it properly designates it as God. This means that the doctrine of God is a theological doctrine, but it does not mean that it is specifically

[55] *Ibid.,* II, pp. 165–168.

Christian. Furthermore, when one calls being-itself "God," one does not thereby cease to recognize it as having all the properties that ontology recognizes in being-itself. Thus the theologian can say nothing about God that the ontologist has not said. He may add only his witness to what God means for man, or how God has manifested himself to man as his ultimate concern.

With respect to what is said about God, it is ontology and not a specific appeal to revelation in Jesus Christ that is decisive. Therefore, if we are not to consider Tillich's doctrine of God controlled in its essentials by a philosophy that stands outside the circle of Christian faith, we must argue that Tillich's ontology is itself within the circle of faith. Tillich suggests this when he points out how all of Western thought has been decisively influenced by Christianity.[56] In this sense his ontology also is a product of a vision that has become an actual historical possibility because of Christianity. If we press this point, we may be able to answer that the use of ontology in formulating the answer to man's question is still a way of answering the question from within the circle of faith.

But Tillich himself does not allow us to rest in such an answer. Although ontologies are historically conditioned and therefore in the West are conditioned by Christianity, the philosopher does not stand within the Christian circle. To do so would be to construct a Christian philosophy in the sense that Tillich explicitly opposes.[57] Hence, we must regard the work of the philosopher in so far as it conditions the work of the theologian as a kind of natural theology.

It may properly be objected that Tillich's explicit rejection of Christian philosophy is not sufficient reason to deny that his ontology is ultimately based upon revelation. This whole presentation and criticism of his thought is based upon his actual performance rather than upon his assertions about his methodology. It remains open to us to affirm that Tillich in fact constructs a Christian philosophy and that hence the philosophic determination of his doctrine of God is not an intrusion from outside the circle of faith. To follow this line of thought would involve an extensive restructuring of Tillich's theology, but the proponents of this procedure may counter that no more violence is done to Tillich's position by this interpretation than by that adopted in this chapter.

The weakness of this line of argument is that it leaves Tillich highly vulnerable to the objection that in fact his philosophy does not do justice

[56] *Ibid.*, I, pp. 27–28.

[57] *Ibid.*, I, p. 28. Cf. Thomas, "The Method and Structure of Tillich's Theology," *The Theology of Paul Tillich,* Charles W. Kegley and Robert W. Bretall, eds., p. 101.

to the specifically Christian vision of reality as embodied in Scripture or Christian tradition. It forces us at point after point to abandon Biblical and traditional beliefs. This tension of Tillich's thought with historic Christianity is a point that will be made below, but there it must be recognized as indecisive. If we have autonomous philosophical grounds for believing certain things to be true about God and man, then as theologians we must come to terms with these truths, whatever the cost. But if the philosophy is claimed to be warranted by Christian revelation, then its disharmony with that historic faith becomes a decisive objection against it.

We will be both fairer and more accurate in our exposition of Tillich if we understand his ontological doctrines as claiming warrant in autonomous philosophical thinking outside the circle of faith. We must then recognize both that no specifically Christian act is involved in recognizing being-itself as God and that this means that Tillich's idea of God is largely determined by independent philosophical considerations. We must now ask whether there are not specifically Christian modifications or additions to the doctrine of God. For example, is Tillich's affirmation of monotheism, and specifically of its Trinitarian form, derived from Christian revelation?

According to Tillich two norms operate in the investigation of alternative doctrines of God — ultimacy and concreteness. God is necessarily the ultimate, else he cannot be the object of ultimate concern. Hence, every image of God that presents him as less than ultimate must give way. At the same time God can only be apprehended concretely. Hence, every image of God that conceives him abstractly must give way. Therefore, we are driven to an exclusive monotheism that, on the one hand, places God radically beyond all categories of finitude and, on the other hand, sees him as manifesting himself in everything finite. When the living unity of these two aspects of God is added to them as a third aspect we have a Trinity.[58]

Tillich goes on to say that the Christian affirmation of Jesus as the Christ as the manifestation of God makes the problem of Trinitarianism a radically important one for the Christian. Further, he declares that the Trinitarian dogma of the church is not identical with the Trinitarian principles sketched above.[59] Nevertheless, it is clear that Trinitarianism as such is systematically derivable apart from any specific appeal to the revelation in Jesus as the Christ. Tillich's ontological doctrines combined with his phenomenology of religion are sufficient to demand a Trinitarian consummation.

The foregoing argument is not to be taken as disparaging Tillich's doc-

[58] *Systematic Theology* I, pp. 228–229. Cf. also pp. 250–251

[59] *Ibid.*, I, p. 229.

trine of God or as arguing that it is unfaithful to Christianity. Historically, most theological doctrines of God have been based upon philosophical analysis. Furthermore, historians have suggested that the Christian doctrine of the Trinity has been profoundly influenced if not determined by considerations of the sort which Tillich introduces. Tillich is to be criticized only in so far as he has sought to deny the derivation of his theological answers from sources outside the circle of faith. The relation of his doctrine of God to his specifically Christian affirmations seems to be much the same as that found in theologians who avowedly make use of natural theology.

We must turn now to consider the specifically Christian affirmations. One of the criticisms of the use of natural theology has been that it provides in effect norms by which Christian revelation is judged. Does Tillich avoid this situation by deriving his norms for revelation within the circle of faith?

Tillich explicitly affirms that this is what he does.[60] He takes the Christian revelation as the basis of determining the norms of revelation in general. He then presents the phenomenology of the history of revelation in terms of these norms. Thereby the demonstration that Jesus is the final revelation is predetermined by the selection of Jesus as the source of norms for revelation. Surely one might say, "If this is to be criticized, it is in terms of the circularity and not in terms of the failure to take the circle seriously!"

Yet we must ask whether in fact the norms in terms of which Tillich judges revelations are systematically derivable from his ontology and his general phenomenology independently of the appeal to Jesus as the Christ as final revelation.

We have already considered the argument that the final revelation must be both concrete and universal. This argument seems to be dependent upon the phenomenology of religion as developed within an ontological context and not upon the Biblical picture of Jesus. Tillich went on to judge that the Biblical picture measured up to these norms. Or consider the related demand that final revelation must be transparent to its ground. This seems to follow from the general analysis of the relation of being-itself to any finite being. Any finite being that mediates the unconditional to us also distorts it to the degree that it identifies its finite characteristics with the ultimate. Hence, the complete sacrifice of all finite characteristics to the ultimate alone makes possible final revelation.

Indeed it seems quite clear that whatever the origins of Tillich's judg-

[60] *Ibid.*, I, pp. 106–107, 132, 135.

ments may have been in his own life history, they are systematically derivable from his philosophy. Hence, the meaning of the claim that Jesus is the final revelation is understood philosophically. Only the claim itself as a historical assertion is nonphilosophical.

Even this claim is not based upon a leap of faith in any ordinary sense. Given the criteria by which revelation is to be judged, and given the Biblical records, the factual judgment follows that Jesus as pictured in the witness of these records meets the specifications for final revelation. The entry into the circle of faith seems to follow from a philosophical and historical argument as an indicated next step. However, this would falsify the real existential element in Tillich's understanding of faith.

To enter the Christian circle is not simply to accept certain judgments about Jesus as historically probable. It is to risk living in terms of the new existence that he embodied. Hence, it is at the point of the New Being that Tillich's theology breaks away from its foundations in ontology, phenomenology, and historical judgment and points to the character of Christian existence in its particularity and its risk.

Even in the doctrine of the New Being, Tillich's general phenomenological analysis of the situation has a profound influence upon the form and content of the Christian doctrine. This was pointed out above where the doctrine was presented. This phenomenological analysis, Tillich recognizes, like his ontology, is already informed by the perspective of Christian faith, and in some respects he wishes to regard it as falling within the circle of faith.[61] Nevertheless, we must recognize its essential independence from faith. Furthermore, the affirmation that the New Being is pictured in the New Testament seems to be a historical judgment that is essentially independent of faith.

However, Christian faith affirms also that there has been a personal life in which the New Being was actually manifest. This affirmation arises decisively, Tillich asserts, only through Christian existence, that is, from experienced participation in the power of the New Being. Thus Christian faith is itself the ground of the affirmation that the New Being became effective in history through a personal life.[62] This means that at least at this one point a major theological affirmation can be made only from within the circle of Christian faith. Presumably also there may be other assertions about the character of the life of faith that can be warranted only by Christian existence itself.

The analysis thus far has indicated that the affirmations that comprise Tillich's theology rest upon three kinds of primitive assertions. The first

[61] *Ibid.*, II, pp. 14, 15. [62] *Ibid.*, II, p. 114.

is universal and objective in character, comprising the basic ontological and phenomenological assertions from which follow most of what is said about God and the formal character of revelation. The second is particular and objective in character, operating within the categories derived from the objective and universal assertions but making in this context specific historical judgments, including many of those about the finality of Jesus as the Christ. The third is particular and existential in character, comprising a limited but significant part of the whole. This includes some account of the distinctive character of Christian existence as participation in the New Being and the implications of this for Christology.

In and of itself this analysis is no criticism of Tillich's work, but it does point up the striking difference between what seems to be implied by some of his statements about method and his actual performance. The most natural interpretation of Tillich's account of theological method is as follows. Christianity consists in the commitment to the finality of Jesus as the Christ. From this perspective the questions of ultimate importance to man are asked and answered in the form that seems most relevant to our present situation. In this process ontological concepts and phenomenological descriptions are used for clarification and precision.

The most natural interpretation of Tillich's performance is as follows. Phenomenological and ontological analyses taken conjointly provide us with an understanding of God and man in terms of which the history of religions can be understood and judged. The criteria of judgment derived from these disciplines indicate that the Biblical picture of Jesus as the Christ fulfills the universal quest for revelation and the New Being. The self-experience of those who have committed themselves to this judgment in faith includes a participation in the New Being that confirms the essential validity of the New Testament picture.

Granting the oversimplificaton of this summary, it remains that we should ask why the program and the performance differ so drastically. The answer seems to lie in the recalcitrant character of Tillich's ontology. His doctrine of being cannot be simply an instrument employed by the theologian or a part of the question that theology answers.[63] By its very nature it is an affirmation about ultimate reality that is normative for all thought. Since Tillich treats his ontology as the necessary ontology,[64] and since it is an ontology that has very definite consequences as to the possibilities of interaction between God and the world, the distinctively Christian source of understanding this relationship is inevitably subordinated.

[63] Although apparently Tillich explicitly places it here. (*Ibid.*, I, p. 30.)

[64] *Ibid.*, I, p. 230. At least, being-itself is a necessary principle of any ontology, in Tillich's view.

We can ask now whether this methodological subordination of distinctively Christian elements to philosophical ones affects the content of Tillich's thought in such a way as to prevent it from embodying the historic Christian faith. Clearly, it does not do so in every respect. Tillich's doctrine of God has many affinities with those of Augustine and the Scholastics. The doctrine that Jesus as the Christ is both the final revelation of God and the bearer of the New Being surely belongs in the main stream of historic Christianity.

However, it must also be recognized that profound tensions are introduced. Tillich himself acknowledges with commendable frankness that many Biblical categories of thought cannot be taken at face value in his system.[65] Biblical personalistic theism must be transcended in the God above God.[66] Reinhold Niebuhr has pointed out that Tillich's conception of the Fall and its accompanying guilt as ontological in character robs them of their moral significance.[67] The centrality of the Biblical concept of sin is replaced by the categories of alienation and estrangement.

Tillich's actual methodology differs markedly from his own account of what is appropriate; and the content of his religious thought differs markedly from that of the Bible. However, neither of these statements taken in itself indicates that Tillich fails to offer a clear and adequate alternative for contemporary theology. The method that he in fact follows is ably and consistently employed. The doctrines that he affirms follow with remarkable unity and intelligibility from his fundamental vision of the relations of God and the world. His affirmations are profoundly meaningful and moving to modern man. Only if we have decided in advance upon a particular kind of faithfulness to the Scriptural records, will Tillich's departure from them be a reason for rejecting his position.

However, it must be said that formally speaking, Tillich is vulnerable to some of the basic objections that were leveled at theologians in Part I. The whole system depends upon basic philosophical judgments which obviously are not shared by most philosophers today. Hence, we can follow Tillich's theology only if we first believe that he has made his case as a philosopher. This question is likely to remain permanently in doubt. We cannot reasonably solve it by the risk of faith, for faith is not the basis for judging among philosophical positions.

If speculative philosophy is an inescapable precursor to theological

[65] *Ibid.*, II, pp. 10–12. See also Tillich, *Biblical Religion and the Search for Ultimate Reality*.

[66] *The Courage to Be*, pp. 186–190.

[67] Reinhold Niebuhr, "Biblical Thought and Ontological Speculation in Tillich's Theology," *The Theology of Paul Tillich*, Kegley and Bretall, eds., pp. 216–227.

thought, must we not give more explicit consideration to the way in which one should choose a philosophy? Of course, if one is convinced like Tillich of the truth of one philosophic position, there is really no choice. But for readers of Tillich it may not be apparent that his philosophy is necessarily superior to that of Thomas Aquinas, of Kant, of Heidegger, or of Whitehead. It is not the case, as he sometimes seems to imply, that his ontological judgments and their religious implications are really found in all great philosophies. Hence, if we are to accept his theology, we must accept his philosophy and thereby reject these others. To structure virtually the whole of theology in such a way that its acceptance depends upon an independent philosophic decision of this sort may be to create obstacles to faith that are not ingredient in the demands of faith itself.

11: H. Richard and Reinhold Niebuhr

THE TWO MEN WHO DID MOST TO INTRODUCE NEO-REFORMATION AND EXISTENTIALIST themes into the American scene are the Niebuhr brothers, H. Richard and Reinhold. One major contribution to this end lay in bringing Paul Tillich to this country.[1] Other contributions lay in mediating ideas that had been developed in Europe in the twenties in such a way that they became relevant to the American situation of the thirties. But neither man is to be understood primarily as a mediator of the ideas of others. Each has developed his own quite distinctive point of view deserving of independent attention.

One of the difficulties of treating the Niebuhrs in this book is that neither claims to be a systematic theologian. Both have given their professional lives to the field of Christian social ethics.[2] The larger part of the publications of both men face away from the more technical questions of theological method toward the application of Christian insights to social issues.

Nevertheless, both men have made suggestions with respect to the basic questions that have guided our presentation of other theologians, and these suggestions have been widely influential in America. Furthermore, they are systematically distinctive and intrinsically of great interest. Hence, abstracting even more drastically than elsewhere in this book from the larger corpus of the writings of each, this chapter presents systematically

[1] Reinhold Niebuhr invited Tillich to Union in 1933. (Charles W. Kegley and Robert W. Bretall, eds., *The Theology of Paul Tillich,* p. 16.) H. Richard Niebuhr published a translation of Tillich's *The Religious Situation* in 1932.

[2] Cf. Charles W. Kegley and Robert W. Bretall eds., *Reinhold Niebuhr, His Religious, Social, and Political Thought,* p. xii. Among others treated in this book, Bultmann is the only one whose central professional interest is not systematic theology or philosophy of religion.

and critically two interpretations of theological method within the existentialist camp that may reasonably be associated respectively with the names of H. Richard and Reinhold Niebuhr.[3] In neither case is the positive suggestion of theological method made in such a way as to rule out other supplementary approaches.

In simplest essence, these two alternatives are as follows. H. Richard Niebuhr has proposed that Christian affirmations should be understood as the confession of how that which is in itself absolute has been experienced from a conditioned and relative perspective. No apologetic is required or possible, since there is no claim that what is given for one community is the truth for others as well. The following presentation will be guided by the question as to how far Niebuhr himself carries this confessional and relative principle and whether it can be used as a basis for establishing the independence of Christian faith from speculative reasoning.

The suggestion of Reinhold Niebuhr is that the distinctive prophetico-Christian faith as found in the Bible provides an illumination of the socio-historical situation that other faiths and philosophies distort and obscure. If so, theologians would do well to articulate the Christian understanding of man in his relations to God and fellow man in such a way as to display its correspondence with the facts of history and its capacity to give guidance to wise action. We will examine some aspects of Reinhold Niebuhr's own performance of this task and will give special attention to his understanding of the relation of Biblical and philosophical categories of thought.

Since the presentation of the thought of the two brothers will be focused on distinctive methodological proposals, it will exaggerate the differences between them. Much of what is said in the exposition of each would be acceptable also to the other. The difference appears most clearly at just the

[3] I wish to stress that in this chapter, to a greater extent than elsewhere in this book, I am concerned with exploring systematic possibilities rather than with describing the total position of the men treated. To carry out the latter goal responsibly a full-length chapter would be required on each man. In the case of H. Richard Niebuhr, the confessionalist and antiapologetic approach advocated in *The Meaning of Revelation,* which I have emphasized for its systematic interest, represents a suggestion made twenty years ago. Although he has not repudiated this work or supplanted it with a later work on the subject of theological method, its emphases are not now central to his thinking. In the case of Reinhold Niebuhr, the approach that he has in fact affirmed and applied is here pressed farther than he has affirmed or applied it. He has stated, for example, that one does not prove the gospel by showing its relevance, but one accepts it in repentance and faith. (*Faith and History, A Comparison of Christian and Modern Views of History,* p. viii; *Christian Realism and Political Problems,* pp. 201–203.) In the body of this chapter, I attempt to avoid attributing to either man ideas he has not affirmed, but I have not attempted to introduce into the presentation the complexities that these qualifications might require.

point of our special interest, namely, on what basis the reader is asked to accept the ideas that are presented as Christian teaching.

A characteristic common to many existentialist philosophers and theologians is a new kind of individualism. Man's cultural milieu is recognized as important in the formation of his personality and thought, but authentic existence brings the absolute individual into relation with being-itself, thus transcending history and culture. Christian faith can be interpreted as this freedom from society and its history as it is attained in the encounter with the Word of God.

However, a Christian theology may relate itself positively to existentialism and yet take a radically different view of the nature of Christian faith. It may distinguish between the authentic existentialist encounter of the human individual with God, which does transcend all cultural differences, and the way in which in that existential encounter God is apprehended. This latter is largely a function of the history of the individual and his community. Christian faith, then, is sociohistorical at the same time that it is necessarily existential.[4]

Such in baldest outline is the theological approach of H. Richard Niebuhr. In his writings, he has stressed the sociohistorical relativity of faith, but equally he has insisted that what is apprehended in faith is not itself relative. It is our apprehensions of the absolute that are relative, not the absolute itself.[5] Hence, this exposition will distinguish sharply between the grounds for affirming the sheer being of God and the grounds for affirming his meaning for man. Parallels with the thought of Tillich will be apparent, but divergences of a decisive sort also emerge.

Man is a being who by nature must have some commitment, some object of loyalty and devotion.[6] This object may be his country, his family, some ideal, or simply his own self. Usually several of such objects function alternately and competitively in giving meaning to his life. Hence, we may say that man is naturally polytheistic. The god of conventional religion functions at best as one among the real gods even of the typical churchgoer.

However, despite the natural pervasiveness of polytheism, it remains an unstable and self-defeating way of life. Man can have no integrity of self-

[4] H. Richard Niebuhr, *Christ and Culture,* pp. 241–249.

[5] *Ibid.,* p. 238.

[6] The line of thought sketched in the following paragraphs is developed by H. Richard Niebuhr in, among other places, "The Nature and Existence of God," *Motive,* Dec., 1943, reprinted as "Faith in Gods and in God," *Radical Monotheism and Western Culture.* (See, especially, pp. 119–124.) What Niebuhr there calls the void and being, in the title essay of the volume he calls being itself, the principle of being, and Being. (See pp. 32, 33, and 38.)

hood while he is torn among competing loyalties that contain no inner order. What is demanded by one loyalty is forbidden by another, and there is no single principle in terms of which this struggle can be settled. Integrity can be achieved only if a single loyalty supersedes all others and allows them only such secondary status as they may have within an integrated life.[7] The need for such a unity of focus is the secret of the power of all totalitarianism. In our day it is the state that seems most prone to make itself into the one god of its citizens, but a cause or a party or pure selfish ambition may give men the peculiar power of an integrated life.

The unifying of all life around a single object of devotion may still remain an unstable and self-defeating way of life. Indeed, it must remain so if the object of devotion lacks the worthiness of devotion that is attributed to it. If, for example, the object of devotion is subject to destruction or even to change in those respects in which it is deemed worthy of devotion, the life built around it may collapse. Not only so, but the sheer possibility of its decay in principle makes complete devotion a lie. If the object of devotion is relative, only a provisional loyalty can belong to it. To escape their inner turmoil, men may attempt to absolutize this relative object, but they cannot wholly conceal to themselves the self-deceit that is involved in absolutizing what is by its nature relative. Hence, the fanaticism of all such idolatries.

Conventional institutional religion, including Christianity, does not escape these strictures.[8] For some of its devotees it does offer a basis for achieving a unity of focus and thus overcoming the internal turmoil of polytheism. A man may simply give himself to the church and its faith and allow it wholly to direct his life and give it meaning. But the church and its faith share in the relativity of all things human and finite.[9] To absolutize them is in principle no different from absolutizing the secular state or a utopian dream. The lie is only more skillfully concealed by the identification of the institution and its teaching with the absolute. The fanaticism of the churches has been through history no less an evil than the fanaticism of any other form of totalitarianism.

Some dim awareness of the falseness of all idolatry (that is, the absolutizing of the relative) [10] is present to man as man apart from the particular cultural and religious history in which he is nurtured. This realization ex-

[7] H. Richard Niebuhr, *The Meaning of Revelation,* p. 78.

[8] A discussion of two forms of henotheism characteristic of Christianity is found in *Radical Monotheism and Western Culture,* pp. 58–60.

[9] H. Richard Niebuhr (with D. D. Williams and J. M. Gustafson), *The Purpose of the Church and Its Ministry: Reflections on the Aims of Theological Education,* pp. 41–42.

[10] *Ibid.,* p. 36.

presses itself sometimes in the fanaticism that we have already noted and sometimes in the nihilism and skepticism of consistent relativism.[11] But in the end and in principle it must lead to a profound despair. Without unity of purpose, life is meaningless, and idolatry is self-deceit. Authentic meaning is possible only if man encounters a reality that is in its own nature absolute.

For a reality to be absolute means that it must have its own being in itself and at the same time be the one ground of man's being. It must be that upon which we are in fact absolutely dependent. In Tillich's terms, it must be the ground of being, its own and ours as well.

It is not enough that we should form a concept of such a reality and recognize in some detached way its worthiness of our devotion. If life is to achieve authentic integrity, man must come through his despair with all other ways of life to the existential encounter with Being as the ground of his being. Such an encounter, and only this, breaks through from polytheism and henotheism to monotheism itself.[12]

Thus far in the account of the grounds of theological affirmations, we are making statements that are in intention descriptive of man's universal situation. We must grant, of course, that they are made from the point of view of the existential encounter with Being. But what is said should have recognizable truth even for those who have not come to this encounter. Men of all cultural and religious traditions may be led, in principle, to a recognition of the human inadequacy both of polytheism and of henotheism. Hence, they may be led to an openness to the existential encounter with Being. The occurrence of this encounter in history and its consequences in the lives of men and nations may be pointed out quite objectively.

This means that Niebuhr's apologetic for radical monotheism is not decisively conditioned by the historical relativism that plays so large a role in his thought. For him, too, the existential experience as such is suprahistorical or supracultural, at least in principle. One does not simply confess that he has apprehended Being as one while acknowledging that objectively there is no criterion for preferring monotheism to polytheism. In *this* respect there are grounds for preferring one faith to another in terms of its adequacy to the way reality — human and divine — is.

But in this objective context little more can be said. We must recognize objectively that the significance of Being for those who have entered into

[11] H. Richard Niebuhr, *Christ and Culture,* p. 238. See, however, Niebuhr's expression of doubts that this is really possible. (*Radical Monotheism and Western Culture,* pp. 24–25.)

[12] *Radical Monotheism and Western Culture,* pp. 123–124.

the existential encounter varies almost limitlessly. One may experience Being as the evil threat to all human values and prefer a nihilistic meaninglessness or a worship of humanity and its ideals to the worship of God.[18] Or one may experience Being as love and enter joyously into a life of monotheistic devotion. There can be no objective criteria for deciding which apprehension of God is more adequate or more accurate.

The acknowledgment of this situation is the acceptance of revelation as our only avenue for knowledge of God. Beyond the sheer being of Being we can know nothing of Being except in the existential encounter. But what we learn in the existential encounter is not additional information about Being, but rather its meaning for us. First of all, this is, for some at least, the knowledge that Being is our God, that is, that Being is that to which we owe all and which rightfully claims from us our whole devotion.

Revelation is thus God's self-disclosure to us as our God. We cannot generalize this into universal objective terms and say that we thereby know that others ought to acknowledge Being as God. We can only confess that for us there is no other choice, for it is as our God and only as our God that we have encountered Being at all. Revelation is not some inferior order of knowing which can and should be superseded by clearer and more reliable sources of information. He who experiences Being as his enemy does not have some other, more objective, grounds for his apprehension of Being. All apprehension of Being is equally an apprehension of that which in its own being is absolute but which can be apprehended only by man in his relativity. From this relativity there is no escape whatsoever, and even the desire to escape it is a manifestation of refusal to let God be God.

The affirmation that God has revealed himself to man has often been regarded as justifying those who acknowledge the revelation in absolutizing their beliefs based upon the revelation. But to do this is tragically to misunderstand the nature of revelation. Revelation is not a body of propositions handed over to the keeping of a human institution. It is always God's revealing of himself to us as God. This means that God, and not our grasp of his self-revelation, is always and alone absolute. Our faith based on this revelation always points to the absolute. But it can do so only when it fully acknowledges that it does not participate in that absoluteness.

18 For H. Richard Niebuhr, "god" means object of faith, and for radical monotheism, Being is God. (*Radical Monotheism and Western Culture,* pp. 24, 38.) Hence, "God" in this chapter means Being as apprehended in faith. In conversation, Niebuhr mentioned Bertrand Russell's position in "A Free Man's Worship" as an example of this negative response to Being. Russell may be understood as authentically encountering Being, but as denying its claim to be "God."

The only response that acknowledges revelation as revelation is the confession of faith that recognizes itself as precisely and only a confession.

This means that among monotheistic faiths all claims to superiority, to fuller participation in truth, or to greater adequacy in any other way are wholly excluded.[14] One may, of course, point out the failure of every embodiment of monotheism to purify itself from elements that are not monotheistic. And one may give an account of how one faith in its human and relative embodiment appears to one who stands in another faith. But this must not be allowed to become a matter of claiming for one's own faith a status of security or finality that presupposes some kind of possession of a truth derived from a higher revelation. Here one can only confess how God has given himself to oneself and listen humbly to the confessions of others.

The relativity of revelation has individualistic elements, but it is to be understood primarily as communal.[15] We have not individually apprehended God (or been apprehended by him) in any way except as persons with a history and persons formed by that history. The history itself does not cause us to encounter God, but every encounter with God is an encounter by a historically conditioned person. And we are conditioned historically only as we share in the history of a communal existence.

It is in and through the community that I have become what I am, and it is in and through the community that I apprehend God. But in the great monotheistic communities, in so far as they remain loyal to the principle of revelation, this does not mean that the community points to itself as the medium of revelation. The community exists as the subject that apprehends God as its object.[16] In testimony to that object it tells the story of its life in history.[17] It constitutes itself as a community by its openness to the meaning of this history, and its present teaching is always subject to renewal and correction in terms of each fresh apprehension of that history.

For the Christian community, God is always apprehended as the God who revealed himself decisively in Jesus Christ. In every fresh encounter with God it is the event Jesus Christ that determines how he is apprehended as God. This does not mean that particular beliefs about Jesus are the norm for Christian faith. It does not mean that Christian faith derives from the encounter with the historical Jesus or with the Christ of faith or with the early church's proclamation of the good news. Christian faith is

[14] See, for example, the powerful formulation of this characteristic point in *The Meaning of Revelation,* pp. 39–41.

[15] *Ibid.,* pp. 20–21, 36, 141–142.

[16] *The Purpose of the Church and Its Ministry,* p. 19.

[17] *The Meaning of Revelation,* pp. 43 ff., 148–149.

always directed to God and arises in the renewed encounter with God as the Principle of Being. But Christian faith always acknowledges itself to be formed in its apprehension of the meaning of God by certain extraordinary events that occurred once long ago in Palestine. Just because Jesus Christ is for Christians *the* revelatory event, *the* clue for all understanding of God, Christian faith is always theocentric and not Christocentric.[18]

But how can any historical events reveal God for those who do not personally share in them? This question has disturbed the church of every century, and in one way or another it has attempted to substitute metaphysics or ecclesiastical authority or present faith for history. But every substitution has been an impoverishment and a corruption. The dynamic of the community lies in its memory and remembrance of its history.[19]

The problem is especially acute in our own day. On the one hand we face radical historical skepticism that calls our attention to how very little we can know about what really occurred in the past. On the other hand the techniques used for the study of outer history are designed to give us the picture of how events would have appeared to a detached observer and specifically to a detached observer who was conditioned by our present world view. When the event Jesus Christ is reconstructed in this way, it loses every possibility of functioning for us as revelation. It becomes one event among many, all equally meaningless to us except in terms of their influence in determining the course of future events that in turn can be judged only in similar terms. If history is to be understood only in these terms, the Christian community can no longer live by its memories.

But there is another dimension to history, that is, the inner history of selves. This history is not, of course, unrelated to the other, but it is different in kind and employs different modes of evaluation. The account by a scientific observer of an operation that restores sight to a blind man and the account by the blind man himself both have their truth.[20] They are both accounts of what from some point of view is the same event. Yet they are and should be radically different in kind. The memories of the Christian community are like those of the man who recalls the recovery of his sight and not like those of the observing scientist. The man may acknowledge that his memories in some respects require correcting in the light of the scientist's account, but he certainly does not regard the scientist's account as superseding his own.

The point is that what is supremely important to men in their inner lives as selves, as worshipers, as questers for meaning, may well be un-

[18] *The Purpose of the Church and Its Ministry,* p. 31.
[19] *The Meaning of Revelation,* pp. 56–59.
[20] *Ibid.,* pp. 59–60.

observable by the detached observer. He may note some changes in behavior, but he cannot do more than describe them and relate them to previous and subsequent observable events. On the other hand, the observable expressions of the inner event may appear to the man in question as pitifully inadequate expressions of what has really and decisively occurred in his life. The Christian community recalls such decisive inner events in the lives of a small group of men in Palestine and sees how inadequate even the vast institutions that have given external expression to those inner events have been as witnesses to them.

Again, this inner history is not an inferior form of history which we may hope will someday achieve the precision of outer history. As long as men are men, they must raise the question of the meaning of their existence. No account of all that has transpired as it is visible to the observer can ever come to terms with this question. At the same time, this question can be asked and answered only in terms of some memory of the past. The scientific account of man and nature in their enduring structures will not answer it. Hence, men will always be involved with their inner history.[21]

The two histories interpenetrate in many ways. Christians learn much about themselves from outer histories.[22] If they are faithful to their inner history, they will be humbly grateful for this light upon their own faithlessness and failure. At the same time, they may protest that the norms that govern the admissibility of evidence in the study of outer history do not escape the relativity of all norms but only absolutize norms derived from the relativities of secular skepticism.

If one presupposes that it is impossible for one who has died to rise from the grave, then one must assume that an objective observer would never see such an event occur.[23] If one then identifies what such an observer would see with what " really " transpired, one can affirm without question that no such resurrection has ever occurred. But such conclusions follow from the secular presuppositions with which the historian begins and not from some ideally impartial and open-minded evaluation of the historical data.

Here the interactions of inner history and outer history come sharply to focus. One cannot on the basis of the inner history of the community simply affirm that certain events actually took place in a particular way open to public verification. The sharer in the inner history must not at-

[21] *Ibid.*, pp. 82–84.
[22] *Ibid.*, pp. 84–85.
[23] H. Richard Niebuhr has not discussed the resurrection in these terms in print. However, in conversation he has said that he finds himself in basic agreement with the work of his son. See Richard Reinhold Niebuhr, *Resurrection and Historical Reason: A Study of Theological Method.*

tempt to dictate to the student of outer history what he shall or shall not find as a result of his investigations. He must be receptive and appreciative of the fruits of the painstaking labor of the historian and aware that these may introduce needed correctives to his memory.

Thus far we have noted that the possibility of the encounter with Being is an existential fact, but that the form taken by that encounter and the meaning that it has for the human person are relative to his personhood as it is formed in community. Hence, we have noted some affirmations that point to a universal human situation and others that are self-acknowledgedly confessions of a relative situation. But there are further complexities to be seen.

The recognition of the relativity of all knowledge of God is itself not a confession but an assertion of the inescapable situation of all men. Further, consequences of great religious importance follow from this situation, and these may be pointed out universally and not confessionally. For example, any claim that a human institution or doctrine grasps and holds revealed truth about God and so escapes from human relativity is condemned not confessionally but by the objective need for the confessional spirit. This provides some criteria for evaluating expressions of monotheistic faith and even, perhaps, the events that function for them as decisively revelatory. Hence, the confessional theologian is not simply shut in to the confession of the particularities of his communal apprehension of God's revelation.

Furthermore, there are criteria operating within the confessing community by which the confession validates itself, and these criteria have a self-evident relevance not limited to the community. An important criterion, for example, is adequacy. One function of revelation is to reveal meaning. A revelation is adequate to the extent that it casts light upon the whole range of human experience. Revelation validates itself in so far as it illuminates each experience in human life and relates it to a meaningful whole. If life brings experiences that remain opaque to its center of meaning, that center proves inadequate. The Christian community not only confesses that the event Jesus Christ is decisive for the way in which it apprehends God; it also confesses its conviction that the clue to the meaning of life given through that event is adequate to illuminate and integrate the whole range of human experience.[24]

A second important criterion is that of the scope of the past that a revelation allows one to encompass. When the clue to the meaning of life is found in the state and its worthiness, many events must be forgotten. More crucially, when life is built around the conviction of one's own

[24] *The Meaning of Revelation,* pp. 109–113.

worth, much that one is and has been must be denied. Revelation fulfills its function most fully when it permits and encourages the total recall of all the past. But it can do this only as it enables us to accept our own sinfulness without despair.[25] In a similar way, a revelatory event relevant to only one community makes impossible the appropriation of the whole of world history, whereas Christians see in Jesus Christ an event that binds the whole of history together. Through this event God's action can be traced in all the events of human history.[26]

A third criterion may be characterized as a pragmatic one.[27] The way in which one interprets the events and persons in one's environment determines the adequacy of one's response to them. If one attempts to use the categories of outer history to understand these events, he seeks to find the causes and consequences in other events and conditions of that outer history. Personal difficulties are interpreted in terms of inadequate adjustment of organism to environment. Impersonal and quantitative concepts are employed. But this approach necessarily leaves much of life uninterpreted, and when one moves from description to action, one is forced to make a judgment for which these categories do not allow. The result is not that personal factors are omitted but that they are included without adequate control and criticism.[28]

When these categories are abandoned and personal ones are used for the interpretation of internal history, they are usually corrupted by egotism. Each event is understood in terms of its impact on the interpreter, and vicious motives are attributed to those held to be responsible for suffering. The poor blame their woes on the willful selfishness of the capitalists; the rich, on foreign agitators; a nation, on some scapegoat race—now Jewish, now German, now Negro. Nations regard themselves as a chosen people and see the destiny of the world as centered in themselves. Religious individuals refer their joys and sorrows to God as immediate expressions of his pleasure or displeasure in them. All these imaginings lead to the isolation of man from man.[29]

Christian revelation, on the other hand, enables us to escape from these alternatives.[30] It provides us with categories for interpreting internal history that are properly personal. At the same time it checks radically the egocentric distortion of all our subjective interpretations. God, and not ourselves, becomes the decisive point of reference through which persons can be seen as such and not merely as they appear to us or impinge upon our lives.

[25] *Ibid.*, pp. 113–114.
[26] *Ibid.*, p. 116.
[27] *Ibid.*, p. 99.
[28] *Ibid.*, pp. 102–108.
[29] *Ibid.*, pp. 99–102.
[30] *Ibid.*, p. 109.

Criteria such as these have real objectivity in the sense that they are capable of functioning within a community and of validating and invalidating its faith. One function of theology is to criticize the faith in which the theologian shares.[31] But Niebuhr does not believe that criteria of this type can be used by a member of one community as grounds for asserting the superiority of his faith in respect to others. One can confess that much that he had been unable to acknowledge about himself, God's revelation has now enabled him to recognize. But he cannot catalog these discoveries about himself as universal truths and then judge other revelations by their inability to bring them to light. He can only testify to what God has done for him. Whether that testimony does or does not have revelatory value for those who hear it is beyond his power to control. He must guard himself constantly against the desire to use the fruits of revelation in his own life as a weapon of self-aggrandizement in subjugating the minds and wills of others to think and act as he does.

There is no conflict between reason and faith. In the sphere of practical reason there is no reasoning that does not presuppose some direction or commitment which gives meaning to action.[32] One may reason well or badly about means and ends, but if the man of faith reasons badly it is because he is a bad reasoner and not because he begins with revelation. Indeed, in so far as revelation has enabled him to know himself better and to escape the inner turmoil of polytheism and the fanaticism of henotheism, he should be able to reason more clearly and dispassionately than others.[33]

But there is another sense of reason in which it does conflict with revelation. We may mean by reason the sum of the apparently natural aspirations and expectations of man. We may then state what these are with respect to the source of meaning and the status of the self. We will then find that in every case revelation both fulfills and contradicts this reason.

Niebuhr develops this point in many ways, but for brief illustration we will here consider only the single idea of the power of God.[34] Man's universal religious aspirations are directed toward a reality that has power. A powerless being, reason insists, however admirable or adorable it may be, is not God. Revelation fulfills this demand in that the God who is revealed in Jesus Christ has power. But the kind of power, or the mode of the exercise of the power, is just the reverse of natural expectation. Reason

[31] *Radical Monotheism and Western Culture,* p. 15.
[32] *Christ and Culture,* p. 252.
[33] *Radical Monotheism and Western Culture,* p. 125.
[34] *The Meaning of Revelation,* pp. 185–187.

expects that power will express itself in the destruction of enemies and in compelling obedience. In Jesus Christ, power expresses itself in meekness and in obedient suffering.

This means that apart from any special revelation man's thought even about God has some validity. But it means equally that revelation does not simply supplement or correct that thought. It radically transforms it in such a way that its consequences for human life are largely reversed.[35] The validity of thought apart from revelation does not provide a common ground with revelatory faith. It provides only a partly common vocabulary in which that which reveals itself to us in Jesus Christ is recognized as God.

◈ ◈

In order that we may now move from exposition of Niebuhr's view to criticism, one central point must be brought to the fore, which thus far has been only vaguely suggested. According to Niebuhr, the Christian apprehends God through Jesus Christ as an infinite Self or Person.[36] God is person in such a sense that we must confess him as One who knows us and loves us and acts for us.[37] Niebuhr shows no disposition to slur over the personalistic categories characteristic of Biblical writings and of much Christian piety through the ages.

But if these categories are introduced seriously, and this is surely the case with Niebuhr, they raise special problems that his published writings do not adequately face. Clearly we must begin by saying that these assertions about God are confessional, that Christians affirm that it is only thus that they can confess the way in which Being has disclosed itself to them. They must recognize that others have apprehended Being in impersonal terms.

With regard to relational terms we can understand that different encounters with the same entity give rise to different ways of speaking about it and that no contradiction is involved in such differences. One pupil may describe a course as easy and another as difficult, and both may be quite accurate because what is easy to one may still be difficult to another. It would be meaningless to ask whether the course were in itself really easy or difficult. If terms like " self " and " person " and " love " are relational in this sense, we will have no difficulty in confessing God in these categories while not thereby affirming that he who calls Being impersonal is in error. But I do not see how this can be the case.

[35] *Ibid.,* p. 183.
[36] *Ibid.,* pp. 154–155, 164, 165, 166, 171, 176. See also *Radical Monotheism and Western Culture,* pp. 44–47.
[37] *The Meaning of Revelation,* pp. 88, 152–153.

One must suppose, for example, that God is either a subject of experience or not. If he is not, my confession of him as Self or Person would seem to be at least confusing if not strictly erroneous. If he is, then the assertion that Being is wholly impersonal would seem to be in error. I must, of course, recognize the conditionedness of my opinion either way and be prepared to grant to others the full freedom of their opinions. But this does not mean that when as a Christian I confess God as one who knows me better than I know myself and prior to my knowledge of myself (as Niebuhr does), I intend this only as an affirmation about a relationship and not about God's own being for himself.[38]

Niebuhr's reply is that what is seen from a limited and therefore relative standpoint need not itself be relative.[39] It is a limited and partial aspect of what is really there to be seen. Hence, the Christian who confesses what he has received from God confesses it as true of God as well as of his apprehension of God. However, as long as he remembers that God is apprehended from many other limited and relative standpoints, he will not claim superior truth for his own knowledge of God.

There is great wisdom here and a needed check upon the almost universal tendency to absolutize our partial knowledge and judge other claims to knowledge by it. Niebuhr cites with approval the saying of Maurice, derived in turn from J. S. Mill, that men are generally right in what they affirm and wrong in what they deny.[40] I, too, would wish to subscribe to this principle.

Nevertheless, I believe there are limits to the mutual compatibility of views, even when the object viewed is being-itself. There seem to be some "either-or's" that cannot be dealt with as partial aspects of one reality. Either being-itself refers only to the most abstract character of all particular beings or it has reality and efficacy in itself. In the former case, the apprehension of being-itself as God must be an illusion. Further, in spite of the dangers involved in attributing any conceptual categories to God, I would renew my insistence that between the apprehensions of being-itself as a personal self and as wholly impersonal there is an opposition that cannot be settled in terms of each being partially true. It might be

38 Of course, knowledge is a relational term. However, if A (God) knows B (a man), this knowledge qualifies A as A as well as describing the relation. That is, knowledge is a relation internal to the knower. Niebuhr says that B apprehends A as knowing B. If this is not an illusory apprehension, surely the knowledge must qualify A before the relation A knowing B qualifies B's apprehension of A.

39 *The Meaning of Revelation,* pp. 18–19. This point was further stressed in conversation.

40 *Christ and Culture,* p. 238.

that both are false, that is, that God's essence is so different from our human categories of personal and impersonal that the effort to think him either way is pure illusion. But I would insist that if Niebuhr is warranted in speaking seriously of God as a Self who knows us and loves us, then an apprehension of God as wholly impersonal is inferior if not illusory.

Once we accept the position that what is seen from a relative perspective is not therefore true *only* for that perspective, the purely confessional character of theology is challenged. What we learn through Christian revelation, we now believe, is in principle true for all persons and not only for those who share in that revelation. However tolerant we may be toward those who have not experienced God in this way, we must frankly believe that they are failing to see something that is really there for them to see and that their statements to the contrary are erroneous.

If we move in this direction, not only is the confessional principle greatly reduced in scope, but we will be forced to reopen the question of the relation of Christian affirmations to metaphysics. Is there a Christian philosophy that takes revelation as grounds for affirming God as Person? Or does metaphysics, as the Boston Personalists argue, provide independent support for this affirmation. Tillich, in his somewhat similar approach, avoids such problems by denying all literal meaning to the personalistic language about God. But Niebuhr seems to mean quite seriously that the Christian apprehends God as an infinite and primal Self.

We must also ask whether the criteria by which a revelation authenticates itself do not also function, more than Niebuhr allows, to discriminate among faiths. If we can point to specific aspects of experience that one revelation illuminates and another cannot illuminate, have we not given objective grounds for preferring one revelation to another? We must be open to the possibility that another range of experience may be pointed out with respect to which the other revelation has the advantage. But is this not in principle *a* basis for objectively judging the relative merits of revelations? [41]

The confessional orientation in theology may also be criticized in terms of the New Testament, to which it often appeals. There is certainly a strong confessional element in the New Testament in that men are directly testifying to their apprehension of God in Jesus Christ and not attempting to demonstrate his existence or his presence. But we must also recognize that the New Testament writers do not understand their faith as one among several ways in which God may be encountered. Neither do they understand their theological utterances as having validity only in

[41] Just this type of vindication of Christian faith is characteristic of Reinhold Niebuhr. See below, pp. 301–302, 307–308.

the community of shared revelation. They seem to be saying that the events that took place have altered the human situation as such in a way relevant for all men. They seem to think that those who do not believe in Christ are objectively rejecting truth and barring themselves from the one salvation.

The appeal to the New Testament against confessionalism, even if it demonstrated a profound difference, would not prove that confessionalism is in error. It may quite well be the New Testament writers who are to be criticized. However, the recognition of the difference does seem to warrant more attention than Niebuhr gives it. It accentuates the divergence of his position from that of the Christian community through most of its history. Christians have generally thought that the church or the Bible had an objective truth guaranteed by God. When some liberals began to give up this position in favor of a larger emphasis on Christian experience, they argued instead that Christianity as a teaching, an experience, or a way of life is the finest and final religion. Now Niebuhr sharply asserts that any such claim either for objective truth or for superiority is in flat contradiction to our status as those who have faith in the revealed God.[42] Until we have grasped all that this implies for our common habits of mind in justifying our adherence to the Christian faith and our encouragement of the adherence of others, we have not understood the profoundly radical character of Niebuhr's confessionalism.

In the light of this radical divergence from traditional theology, we must raise the question of the ground of Niebuhr's critique. When we do so, we see that there is a dual argument. First, it is based upon his view as to the relativity of all thought and experience and the understanding of revelation to which this leads him. Secondly, it is based on the specific judgment that Being can be known only as God as it is apprehended in faith. In his own eyes the recognition of sociohistorical relativism in general and of religious relativism in particular does not itself seem to be relative, or at least not in the same way as the specific valuations to whose relativity it calls attention. It seems, furthermore, not to have been achieved primarily in the inner history of Christians but rather from the work of historians and social scientists. In other words, methodologically speaking, Niebuhr seems to take principles of a more or less nonrelative type derived outside of Christian confession and in terms of them to advocate that the testimony and apologetics of the Christian community take on a quite new form.

The criticism that is made here is not against this procedure as such.

[42] Niebuhr, *The Meaning of Revelation*, pp. 39–41.

It may be that, at least in our day, we must approach the Christian faith from outside in order to select those expressions of it which we can support. The criticism is only that the emphasis on the confessional approach can be misleading if it is taken to be primary and normative for Niebuhr's own thought. It is in terms of nonconfessional principles that confessionalism is held to be the only legitimate expression for Christian faith. Confessional affirmations, therefore, should not be used to support the principles in terms of which confessionalism is vindicated. Hence, the relativity of knowledge and experience as an objective fact must be affirmed on empirical and phenomenological grounds. We may question whether our knowledge of the relativity of knowledge transcends that relativity sufficiently to warrant us in dismissing all counterclaims that revelation communicates in some way information that transcends historical relativity.

The point is not that Niebuhr is mistaken in his perception of the relativity of knowledge. The point is rather that he seems at times to ignore the fact that this means that his own support for the confessional approach to theology is caught in this relativity along with every other theological methodology. Theological scholarship is profoundly indebted to Niebuhr for calling attention to the relativity of all historical knowledge and for working out the implications of this relativity for theological work. But it seems that Niebuhr must either go still farther or else draw back from some of his own relativistic assertions.

One systematic possibility is to spell out carefully the boundaries that divide relative from objective knowledge or to distinguish the degrees of objective reliability in knowledge claims and then to work out the implications of this distinction. The results of such a procedure would probably introduce a larger claim to objectivity within the sphere of theological work than Niebuhr explicitly allows. Something like a natural theology might emerge.

Another possibility is to take so seriously the total relativity of all human knowledge that we accord it no authority at all with respect to our theological affirmations. This would lead to a thoroughgoing theological positivism. It is not clear that Niebuhr's confessional principle, developed within the context of his social existentialism, offers a definite alternative to these possibilities as they were explored in Parts I and II.

In the first half of this chapter we have examined a suggestion, made in an earlier book of H. Richard Niebuhr, *The Meaning of Revelation,* that theology should understand itself as confessional and eschew all criticism of other faiths and all other forms of apologetic. Even in that book, much is said that could be used for apologetic purposes, and in subsequent writings the specifically confessional and antiapologetic emphases are much less in evidence. Hence, we should not assume that the criticisms directed toward the confessional position as formulated by H. Richard Niebuhr apply to his present thought without extensive qualification.

In the case of Reinhold Niebuhr there has never been any embarrassment about writing apologetically. His work has had two focuses. The first is the interpretation of the history of our times as a guide to concrete action. The second is the demonstration that the most illuminating perspective for the understanding of this history is given in Biblical faith. In answer to our question as to the grounds on which Christian affirmations are to be accepted, the confessionalist appeals to conditioned communal experience; Reinhold Niebuhr appeals to the unique adequacy of Christian ideas for the understanding of the actual events of human history.

In demonstrating the unique adequacy of the Biblical perspective, Niebuhr contrasts it not only with perspectives of other religions but also with philosophy as a whole. Philosophy he understands as by nature committed to the investigation of the structures of being in such a way that things are ultimately displayed as determined by universal principles. Biblical faith, on the other hand, understands man and history in dramatic categories of freedom and dialogue that cannot be reduced to unchanging structures of being.[43]

The appropriateness of treating Reinhold Niebuhr under the general heading of existentialism lies in the similarity between what he identifies as Biblical faith and major themes in contemporary existentialism. His concern that man cannot be understood in terms of structures by which being is objectively grasped and his insistence on the radical freedom of man point to his close relations with existentialism. That he points to the Bible rather than to twentieth-century philosophical existentialism as his source lends color to the view that modern existentialism is itself a secularized version of elements of the Christian faith. In all this he has much in common with Martin Buber, to whom he freely acknowledges his debt.[44]

Even more emphatically than other existentialists, Niebuhr stresses that his denial of universal adequacy to Greek rationality in no way minimizes the greatness of its achievements or the indispensability of its continuing contribution. Rational philosophy and science are of indubitable value.[45]

[43] Kegley and Bretall, eds., *Reinhold Niebuhr, His Religious, Social, and Political Thought,* pp. 432–433.
[44] Reinhold Niebuhr, *The Self and the Dramas of History,* p. ix.
[45] *Ibid.,* p. 77.

Even with respect to man there are many respects in which they are profoundly illuminating.

Niebuhr's point is only that when this way of apprehending the world is understood to be the only way that is needed, it imposes upon its data distorted forms that conceal and confuse the realities of life. Specifically, they inevitably deny man's radical freedom and reduce history to a natural process. But whenever this is done, false expectations are aroused and false goals are posited. Since human history is the area of man's ultimate concern, these distortions are of no slight importance.

Niebuhr argues brilliantly that only the dramatic categories of Biblical thought can illuminate history and show its meaning. He has shown their power in this respect in volume after volume of social and theological criticism. The categories themselves are most clearly developed in *The Self and the Dramas of History*. Here he presents his intricate analysis in terms of a threefold dialogue of the self with its self, with others, and with God. It is, above all, in the first of these that he expounds his understanding of man's radical freedom.

We should recall that Sartre argued for man's radical freedom by denying any transcendental subject or ego. Man is free because as consciousness he is a lack, a nothing, a want. As such, consciousness determines its own becoming absolutely and, hence, must accept responsibility for itself. But man's freedom is at the same time his absurdity, in that it is always a wanting of that which cannot be — a wanting of being-in-itself.

Niebuhr's analysis is quite different. Whereas Sartre and Heidegger deny selfhood as the seat of responsible freedom, Niebuhr affirms it. Despite his fundamental disagreement with the leading existentialist philosophers on this crucial point, Niebuhr's doctrine deserves equally with theirs the label "existentialist."[46] What he affirms is not the transcendental ego of Kant or of Husserl, and it is not the mental substance of Descartes or Locke. Niebuhr's approach is fundamentally phenomenological although quite independent of training in the methods of Husserl.[47] As a phenomenologically impressive existentialist account of man as responsible self, Niebuhr's analysis has great intrinsic importance for Christian existentialists and indeed for Christian thought generally.

The self cannot be defined, for to do so would be to subsume it under some more general conception, but what the term means is evident to the unsophisticated mind. The learned, on the other hand, have been condi-

[46] Reinhold Niebuhr does not care about the label and is indeed highly critical of contemporary existentialism as a quasi-idolatrous extension of nineteenth-century romanticism. (*Ibid.*, pp. 67–68.)

[47] Reinhold Niebuhr is more likely to use the term "empirical," e.g., *ibid.*, pp. 4, 5.

tioned by their education and culture to regard the self as something quite different from what it appears to itself to be. They can regain the intuitive knowledge of the self only if they are willing in this instance to give up the principles of interpretation that are so fruitful in philosophy and science.

The difficulty of recovering self-knowledge is increased by the elusiveness of the self to objectification.[48] We can objectify ourselves, but when we do so, the self that objectifies is not identical with the self that is objectified. We can then objectify the self that objectifies, but still the objectifying self, the ultimate subject of the experience, is wholly and immediately itself objectified.

This does not mean for Niebuhr that what is objectified is not really the self. On the contrary, the capacity to objectify oneself is of the utmost significance for the human self. But it does mean that the objectification is never complete — that the whole self is never simply given in experience — that the self is always to some degree a mystery.

The self is then what common sense must always mean by " I," but it is far more complex than common sense realizes. Like all common-sense ideas, its ordinary vagueness leaves it subject to being explained away by intellectual systems if it is not defended by clarification and development. Such clarification inevitably goes far beyond common sense, though it intends to be faithful to the universal experience of human selves that gives to common sense its unity. Therefore, though we cannot define the self, we must discuss its activities and relations.

The self is not simply will, but it includes will. Niebuhr defines the will as the self organized for the attainment of a purpose.[49] Presumably, the self may also be the passive subject of experiences of pleasure or pain, hate or love, or may merely entertain ideas virtually without purpose. But though Niebuhr does not say so, it does seem that most of the distinctive characteristics of the human self depend upon will. Neither self-objectification or serious thought is ever wholly purposeless, though the purpose may be vague or unobtrusive in consciousness. Even in relatively passive sense experience the distinctively human features seem to depend on man's purposiveness.

The relation of self to its mind may come next in order of intimacy, but here genuine separateness is introduced.[50] My reason is not my self in the same sense that my will is my self. It is my possession, my instrument. Without it I would indeed be impotent, but though it gives me power it does not possess power itself. My reason is my capacity to think conceptu-

[48] *Ibid.*, pp. 6, 7. [49] *Ibid.*, p. 12. [50] *Ibid.*, pp. 17–18, 24, 29.

ally, to perceive, and to analyze logical relationships. It enables me to judge goals and to determine the means of pursuing them. It enables me to perceive inconsistencies between my opinions and my behavior. But it does not determine which goal I shall pursue or compel me to be consistent. Having made full use of reason, the self may still choose to act inconsistently or select an inferior purpose.

Finally, the relation of the self to its body must be noted.[51] This relation is essentially the same as that of the self to its mind, although it is probable that the separateness is more generally apparent here and in some respects greater. My body also is my instrument. Without it I would be powerless — indeed, would not be at all — but it is still my instrument to use as I will.

This emphasis on the instrumental character of body and mind is not intended to minimize the influence that they have on the self. Obviously, the character of the self is extensively influenced by its body and mind and by their relatively autonomous development. But influence is not determination, and it is the self that ultimately chooses within the limits of possibility imposed by the total situation, which includes body and mind.

Niebuhr stresses that a one-dimensional view of self is inevitably misleading.[52] By this he means that any view that lists the functions or faculties of the person or organism and identifies the self either with the whole or with any part of this list is fallacious. The self is not one faculty or function among others but rather is related to all of them in a way essentially different from that in which they are related to each other. As such it remains a mystery to reason.

The self identifies itself partially but never finally with one or another of its functions. Thus the dialogue of the self with itself may shift its point of reference from reason to impulse to conscience. One self takes many sides in the same discussion, while still remaining in its depth dimension transcendent to each of its special self-identifications.[53] The mystery of the self centers in its responsible freedom and in the corruption of that freedom.[54]

The idea of freedom is affirmed in so many different senses and at so many different levels that it is of the greatest importance not merely to state that Niebuhr affirms the radical freedom of man but also to explain in what sense and at what level he locates this freedom.[55] Freedom has

[51] *Ibid.*, pp. 26–29.
[52] *Ibid.*, p. 13.
[53] *Ibid.*, pp. 7, 8, 16, 29.
[54] Reinhold Niebuhr, *Pious and Secular America*, pp. 126 ff.
[55] Cf. Gordon Harland, *The Thought of Reinhold Niebuhr*, pp. 67–69.

been used in Western history sometimes in the sense of real capacity to do or to achieve some good, sometimes in the sense of absence of external impediments to the achievement of what one desires, and sometimes in the sense of self-determination. All three meanings are useful in characterizing Niebuhr's views, and all three can be shown to have important interrelatedness, but it is the third with which we will be concerned in relation to Niebuhr's doctrine of the self.

The assertion that man is free in the sense of self-determined is still very indefinite. It may mean simply that he shares with all living things the character of spontaneity and unpredictability. It may mean that through sharing in rationality man possesses a principle of thought and action not determined by the natural laws that govern animate as well as inanimate objects. Niebuhr is not primarily interested in freedom at either of these levels.

The freedom that seems important to Niebuhr is distinctive of man, not because he is rational, but because he is a self that transcends both his body and his reason.[56] If the self *is* its reason, then obviously the only freedom there can be is freedom to be rationally, rather than naturally, determined. But if the self is in command of both its reason and its body, then there appears a far more significant level of freedom — a freedom incomprehensible alike to scientist and philosopher but nevertheless the common assumption of Everyman. The self determines how it will use reason and whether it will accept its guidance. The self determines when it will resist and how strongly it will resist the cravings of the body as well as how and when it will satisfy these cravings.

But even this level of freedom is not the most significant for Niebuhr. Indeed it may still be compatible with a modified naturalistic determinism. For if the self determines how it will think and act in accordance with habit and purpose, and if habit and purpose are products of the self's past experiences — and presumably all this is largely true — then self-determination may be ultimately illusory. For past experiences would in turn be products of habit and purpose, but also of hereditary and environmental factors, and ultimately habit and purpose would appear as functions of the latter. Thus what appears to be self-determination would be simply one stage in a causal chain of rigid determinism. At best it would have only the same kind of freedom, creativity, or spontaneity that might be accorded to all nature.

If this result is to be avoided, self-determination must not be simply determination of thought and action by the self but also determination of

[56] *Pious and Secular America,* p. 127.

the self by the self — not of the future self by the present self, but of the present self by itself. Niebuhr sees not only that the self is beyond reason and body but also that it can objectify itself. We have already noted that such objectification is never complete, but at the same time no limit can be set to it. To objectify anything is to achieve the power to criticize and evaluate it.[57] When that which is objectified is also subject to modification, its objectification renders possible its alteration as well. Hence, the self can determine not only its thought and action but itself as well.[58]

To the liberal mind it may appear strange that in Niebuhr (as so often in the Christian tradition) a doctrine of radical freedom is coupled with a doctrine of the bondage of the will. However, the two doctrines belong together inextricably.

The liberal is likely to mean by freedom more than spontaneity but less than pure self-determination. He may identify the self and the good with reason and hold that reason can and sometimes does control behavior over against bodily impulse. Or he may recognize that the self is something more than mind and body and define good and evil in terms of how it uses these faculties. In this case he will define the good in terms of attainable ideals or at least the nearest approach to ideals to which body and mind can actually attain. On this view it is virtually incomprehensible that any man should fail to will what appears to him good. Hence, from the time of Socrates to the present the vast majority of philosophers have sought in ignorance, habit, or a corrupt environment the sources of the apparently bad will.

At this level of freedom these conclusions appear inescapable; hence, the importance of understanding Niebuhr's concept of freedom before approaching his doctrine of sin. At the level of the self, by its will determining thought and action in abstraction from the level of the self objectifying and judging itself, there may be actions judged better and worse in terms of consequences or even of motives, but there is no possibility of radical concepts of sin and guilt.

When man makes himself the object of his own thought, two tendencies appear simultaneously. One tendency is to perceive that he is one among many selves each of which objectively has the same rights to success and happiness. The other tendency is to focus his concern disproportionately

57 *The Self and the Dramas of History*, pp. 6, 12–13.

58 Reinhold Niebuhr speaks specifically of the self-transcending itself: *The Structure of Nations and Empires: A Study of the Recurring Patterns and Problems of the Political Order in Relation to the Unique Problems of the Nuclear Age*, p. 288; and of the self's freedom over itself: *The Self and the Dramas of History*, p. 18.

upon himself as if his own success and happiness were supremely important. This universal human tendency, rooted in the radical nature of human freedom, is "original sin." [59] The "bondage of the will" is to the interests of the self. Thus the bondage of the will is the bondage of a radically free will.[60]

Through these analyses Niebuhr suggests that a phenomenological description of experience guided and enlightened by the distinctive elements in the Hebraic-Christian tradition may constitute a theological method free from speculative philosophy. The results of this description may further be tested by their value in preventing distortion in the understanding of history and illusion with respect to future possibilities.[61] As such, despite Niebuhr's frequent disclaiming of the role of systematic theologian, he offers an alternative of utmost interest and importance. His suggestion indicates the possibility of an extensive existentialist theological development independent of speculative philosophy.

The crucial test of the adequacy of this approach arises with respect to the doctrine of God. Niebuhr touches briefly on the dialogue with God and notes that all those philosophies which deny the selfhood of God deny also, implicitly at least, the selfhood of man.[62] The question remains, however, as to the possibility of doing justice to the doctrine of God through phenomenology. Unless we can affirm this possibility, as Niebuhr does not,[63] a phenomenological theology must remain truncated.

Niebuhr does provide daring and original arguments for the Biblical understanding of God. First, he shows the inevitability of the religious quest once man recognizes his mysterious freedom.[64] Secondly, he offers a typology of religious responses.[65] Thirdly, he argues that the tests of internal coherence and consistency with other facts demonstrate the weakness of the alternatives to Biblical faith.[66] This means that Niebuhr supplements the phenomenological account of the self and its dialogues with an argument for the empirical superiority of the Biblical understanding

[59] *The Self and the Dramas of History,* p. 18. See also Reinhold Niebuhr, "Biblical Thought and Ontological Speculation in Tillich's Theology," *The Theology of Paul Tillich,* p. 219.

[60] For a well-rounded presentation of Niebuhr's doctrine of sin, see Harland, *op. cit.,* pp. 76–82.

[61] *The Self and the Dramas of History,* Chs. 11, 17, 18.

[62] *Ibid.,* pp. 64–65.

[63] *Ibid.,* p. 5. Here again we must stress that in this chapter the emphasis is on possible methods suggested in the writings of the Niebuhrs rather than on a rounded presentation of their total positions.

[64] *Ibid.,* p. 61.

[65] *Ibid.,* pp. 63–64.

[66] *Ibid.,* pp. 66–71.

of God in comparison with other possible understandings. He does this without engaging in philosophical discussion as such.

◈ ◈

The most decisive criticism of Niebuhr's position would focus on his account of the self and history. Is this account phenomenologically accurate? Is it as illuminating of the human situation as Niebuhr claims? And is it really found, as Niebuhr affirms, in the Bible? However, here, as elsewhere in this book, I am avoiding substantive questions of this sort and focusing upon formal and methodological issues.

Niebuhr's whole approach, in common with most other existentialism, assumes a deep duality between nature and history.[67] Niebuhr wishes to pair with this duality that of Greek and Hebrew modes of thought. When we think of nature we are concerned with enduring and recurring structures to the study of which science and philosophy are appropriate. But when we think of man as a historical being, we need the categories of drama, dialogue, and freedom that are characteristic of Biblical ways of thinking. Niebuhr's thesis is not that one or another of these approaches is better in general but that each is required in its own sphere. If Niebuhr's theological method is to be criticized, we should focus on this fundamental duality which it presupposes.

In the first place, we may note that the clear duality of history and nature itself emerged in the history of philosophy. It is because of the vast influence of Kant on the modern mentality that one may now abstract this principle from its philosophical setting. This suggests that philosophy has a capacity to transcend its commitment to the study of structures sufficiently to define a realm to which this kind of study is inappropriate, a realm of spirit and freedom. If so, the simple classification of philosophy with science as appropriate only to the study of nature seems unfair.

Furthermore, Niebuhr seems to leave us with a problem that can be treated only philosophically. If nature and history do exist as two orders of reality to which two types of thinking are appropriate, how are they related to each other? However distinct they may be, they jointly constitute one world.[68] And surely, also, if they do constitute one world, there must be some way of understanding the relations of the two kinds of thinking that are needed in this one world other than the way of pure disjunction. Again it would seem to be the task of philosophy to study the relations of the two modes of thought.

Niebuhr's objection to assigning a role like this to philosophy is that in

[67] Reinhold Niebuhr, *Christian Realism and Political Problems,* p. 199.
[68] *Ibid.,* p. 175.

the process of developing its inclusive view, philosophy will fail to do justice to the personal and dramatic modes of thought. Since these are of such great importance to mankind, we do better to leave an unresolved duality than to replace it with an inadequate synthesis. Adequacy to the facts is more important than a unified and consistent system.

If we must indeed choose between adequacy and consistency, I agree with Niebuhr that adequacy is more important. Furthermore, I find his elaborate discussion of how philosophies have distorted and obscured essential aspects of human history very persuasive. Hence, the theoretical objection that the task of synthesis belongs to philosophy has little relevance to the criticism of Niebuhr unless one can show how a synthesis can be developed that does full justice to the important Biblical insights about man and history.[69]

The central problem is that of freedom. Many philosophies affirm human freedom in some sense, but Niebuhr's analysis shows that their understanding of freedom is less radical than that of the Bible and is inadequate to account for the realities of history. Systematically, the philosophical difficulty is as follows.[70] It seems that any event must either have an antecedent cause or be uncaused. If it is uncaused, it is free only in the sense of being random. But to the degree that an event is to be understood as the result of an antecedent cause or nexus of causes it is determined, and to the degree that it is random it is a matter of pure chance. In neither case can we see grounds for imputing responsibility, in any radical sense, to the person acting. That is, we may establish rules for legal purposes as to when rewards or punishments are to be distributed, but the Biblical idea of sin is lost.

If this idea is to be maintained, we must understand a man as determining himself and set the idea of self-determination over against those of determinacy and indeterminacy. But even this does not seem to help. Self-determinacy is usually understood as simply one type of determinacy in general — that type in which the antecedent cause is located in the agent of the subsequent act. Since that cause also had a cause, and since tracing this sequence of causes eventually leads us outside the will and consciousness of the agent, radical freedom and responsibility are not established.

These consequences can be avoided philosophically only if self-determination occurs in an indivisible moment, that is, if the cause and effect

[69] Tillich also points out that it is not ontology as such but specific ontologies that disallow freedom. (*The Theology of Paul Tillich,* p. 339.)

[70] I worked out this line of thought somewhat more fully in "The Philosophic Grounds of Moral Responsibility; A Comment on Matson and Niebuhr," *The Journal of Philosophy,* Vol. 16, 1959, pp. 619–621.

are simultaneous. In this case, the cause of the occurrence is internal to the occurrence, and self-determination receives its strictest meaning. The difficulty is that time is generally conceived as a continuum, and, hence, as infinitely divisible. In a temporal continuum there could be no real units of time within which self-determination in this strict sense could occur. The cause must always be understood as antecedent to its effect. I believe it is for this reason that Niebuhr can correctly point out that during the whole course of the history of philosophy until quite recent times man's radical freedom remained a mystery all too often denied by philosophy because it was rationally unintelligible.[71]

However, in this century another conception of time has emerged that does allow for self-determination in the strictest sense. As rigorously developed by Whitehead, it displays time as a succession of actual occasions rather than as a continuum within which events occur. These occasions are profoundly affected by their past, but their selective inclusion of elements from the past as well as of novel possibilities depends on their momentary self-determination.

Further exposition of Whitehead's complex and profound analysis of freedom and causality is out of place here, and in any case the application of Whitehead's ontological doctrine of freedom to distinctively human freedom remains to be worked out. I wish simply to argue that it is no longer impossible for a philosophy to deal with radical freedom and that the possibility is now offered to achieve both adequacy and consistency in the account of human and natural events. If so, we must regard Niebuhr's dualism as a provisional one.

Very little of Niebuhr's constructive work is affected by the foregoing criticisms. They do suggest, however, that an interdependence exists between philosophy and theology that Niebuhr has neglected, if not denied. If Niebuhr's phenomenological account of self and freedom is correct, a philosophy that cannot encompass these categories without distorting them is inadequate as philosophy. On the other hand, Niebuhr's discussion of the relation of history to nature owes much to particular philosophical traditions that are philosophically debatable.

Granted some qualifications of Niebuhr's position with respect to the relation of nature and history, his apologetic for Christian faith remains extremely impressive and persuasive. Few if any men have illuminated the human situation more brilliantly than Niebuhr, and his success in using the Biblical perspective to this end powerfully displays both its relevance and its claim to credence.

[71] *Pious and Secular America,* p. 128.

In closing, however, I wish to raise a final question. Niebuhr's approach suggests that in the human situation the role of freedom is relatively constant.[72] Different perspectives are judged according as they are able to perceive, take account of, and give meaning to, this freedom. Biblical faith is judged best in these terms.

An alternative possibility, however, is that the freedom that Biblical faith illuminates has entered into history only through that faith. Perhaps it did not exist among primitive men or even within those high cultures which have understood themselves in terms of cyclic patterns of nature. If so, certain further limitations of Niebuhr's apologetic must be noted.

If the data are constant, then different perspectives may fairly be judged by their adequacy to the data. But if the data and the perspective arise together, then diverse perspectives will be suited to diverse modes of human existence. We would then be returned to a thoroughgoing relativism.

This criticism does not apply to Niebuhr's apologetic vis-à-vis other Western interpretations of history. Here diverse perspectives are focused on a single set of data. Furthermore, now that the whole world is being drawn into essentially Western history, the nonhistorical perspectives of the East must lose what warrant they may once have had. However, the fundamental fact that Biblical faith has largely created the history that it illuminates appears to me to be more important than Niebuhr recognizes, if indeed he would accept this idea at all.[73]

[72] *The Structure of Nations and Empires,* p. 287.
[73] For a discussion of the growth of freedom, see *ibid.*, pp. 288 ff.

Personal Conclusions

THROUGHOUT THIS BOOK, CRITICISM OF THEOLOGICAL DOCTRINE AS SUCH has been avoided. The effort has been to ask on what basis the position adopted is affirmed. Criticism has consisted in questioning the consistency with which any principle of justification is applied and in pointing to its fundamental presuppositions.

My assumption is that every system of thought has some starting point and some procedure for moving from that starting point to its conclusions. This does not mean, however, that most positions factually developed in this way. On the contrary, the systematic starting point and procedure are usually affirmed in large part to justify judgments that have arisen in the life history of the thinker largely independently of his argument for them.

For this reason, it is not surprising that a critic can often find inconsistencies between the avowed starting point and procedure and the actual performance. These inconsistencies do not invalidate the theological doctrines that are affirmed, but they do indicate inadequacies in the bases on which they are affirmed. Furthermore, since some of the most important theological doctrines are directly or indirectly doctrines about the character of the starting point and procedure, methodological criticism does have extensive implication for content.

Methodological criticism cannot in itself direct us to some one " correct " method for theological work. However, it is my belief that it can indicate that the number of living options is fewer than the bewildering array of contemporary theologies suggests. I believe that criticisms in the preceding chapters should have helped to distinguish real options from pseudo-options, and I want now to attempt to indicate my own conclusions based on this distinction.

First, I suggest that natural theology in its simplest and classical sense is a pseudo-option. That is, there is no satisfactory procedure whereby one can move from a universally given starting point to conclusions that are both theologically important and rationally probable or certain. Every natural theology begins with some vision of the world, some mode of perceiving the ultimate character of things and proceeds to conclusions that presuppose that starting point. Both Mascall and DeWolf recognize this fact to some degree, and I do not regard it as a serious criticism of their thought. However, unqualified acknowledgment on all sides of the impossibility of a purely neutral starting point would do much to clear the air in contemporary theological discussion.

Secondly, the impossibility of fulfilling the simple ideal of natural theology points to the real option of a Christian natural theology or a Christian philosophy. Given the necessity of starting with *some* vision of the nature of things, it may be assumed that those who have been deeply permeated by the Christian faith will, in fact, consciously or unconsciously, start with a vision that is to some degree distinctively Christian. To that degree to which it is Christian, carefully reasoned conclusions from this starting point will constitute a Christian philosophy. Since many who are not consciously committed to Christian faith may share in essential aspects of this starting point, those aspects of this philosophy relevant to specific Christian affirmations can constitute a Christian natural theology. I have argued in Part I that this is in fact what is occurring in the work of both Thomists and Personalists.

It must be stressed that I do *not* mean by Christian philosophy a kind of thinking that begins with specific Christian doctrines. For example, I do not mean that one might begin with the doctrine of bodily resurrection and then develop systematically the assumptions about nature, man, and supernature entailed in such a doctrine. I mean rather that one begins with what seems to him, quite apart from self-conscious acts of faith, most indisputably true. For example, Mascall begins with the finiteness of all the entities of experience; the Personalists begin with the conviction that reason properly demands an explanation of all phenomenal occurrences. Such starting points are not experienced as leaps of faith or even as distinctively Christian. It is only in our century that their historical conditionedness is clearly recognized, and there are many who still fail to see the decisiveness of the religious tradition in this conditioning process.

The men treated in Parts II and III were distinguished from those treated in Part I by their rejection of natural theology. But once we recognize that what is at issue is *Christian* natural theology, the distinction blurs in many cases. This is especially clear in the case of Brunner, who at one time specifically affirmed Christian natural theology. Later he shifted his terminology to speak of a Christian doctrine of creation, but no substantive alteration was involved.

It is true that Brunner speaks in opposition to any philosophical contribution to the formulation of a doctrine of God and that he apparently means that God cannot be discussed in his Christian natural theology. But we noted also considerable wavering and inconsistency on this point. There seems to be no systematic reason in Brunner that something cannot be said of God in the context of Christian natural theology. His objections seem to be based on his sensitivity to the tensions that have, in fact, existed between philosophical and Biblical thinking about God. If so, these objections might not apply to a more carefully formulated Christian philosophy. In any case, Brunner does not seem to afford a consistent option differing from this one.

With Tillich, again, the situation is not greatly different. Although he explicitly opposes natural theology, a philosophical ontology plays a role in his theological formulations. Although he stresses the autonomy of philosophy from specific religious faith, he knows that Western philosophies are affected by their Christian background and context. He seems to want to exempt some aspects of his ontology from this historical conditionedness, but in the face of the obvious possibility of alternative ontologies, this exemption appears unwarranted. If I am correct in these points, Tillich seems not to afford a genuine option to the use of a Christian philosophy and Christian natural theology.

The discussion of H. Richard Niebuhr focused on the systematic possibility that a confessional theology might be free of any kind of natural theology. However, the critical analysis suggested that this is not a genuine option. No less than in the case of Tillich, the reality of being-itself or a principle of being is presupposed by confessional theology. Furthermore, what is confessed about being-itself on the basis of existential encounter is held to be a real, if partial, truth about being-itself. If so, the total convictions of the believer must take account of this truth, however fragmentary he may acknowledge it to be. Although a variety of interpretations of this situation may be possible, the use of something like a Christian natural theology appears quite compatible with, if not demanded by, the confessional approach.

Reinhold Niebuhr avoids the use of a Christian natural theology by radically separating history from nature. His defense of Christian teaching by an objective analysis of history parallels and supplants the usual natural theology. I would suggest that the degree of its objectivity is also parallel to that of natural theology, that is, that ultimately its data, too, are conditioned by Christianity. Even so, it would seem to offer a live option to what I have been calling Christian philosophy and Christian natural theology.

However, if my criticisms of Reinhold Niebuhr are correct, his thought, too, needs the context of a view encompassing both history and nature. If an encompassing view is possible that does not distort history, then Niebuhr seems to offer no adequate objections to its employment. I have suggested that once again the philosophy of Whitehead, although undeveloped in this respect, affords the basis for such an inclusive view.

My own conclusion from this study is, therefore, that a *Christian* natural theology (and philosophy) is compatible with (or demanded by) the theologies of Brunner, Tillich, and the Niebuhrs as well as Thomists and Personalists. Hence, the widespread rejection of natural theology in our time is misleading if it is taken as a rejection of Christian natural theology. Contemporary theological discussion will make a major advance if, on the one hand, the ideal of a pure, neutral theology is universally and consistently abandoned and if, on the other hand, the widespread relevance of and need for a Christian natural theology is acknowledged.

There are two acute problems to which those who practice Christian natural theology should give extended attention. First, among competing claimants, what is in fact the Christian starting point? Second, is there any way of transcending to any degree the circularity and relativity that are involved in the recognition of the Christian condition of the starting point for natural theology?

In dealing with the first of these problems I suggest that we must beware of an either-or approach. For example, both the vision of the world as finite and the vision of the world as purposed (hence, requiring explanation) seem to have come into existence historically under the influence of Biblical faith. There seems to be no necessity of conflict in the conclusions drawn from these two visions. Since conflict in fact exists between Thomist and Personalist, we should examine very carefully the procedure by which each arrives at his conclusions. The key point of the conflict lies in the Thomist denial that there can be any change or passibility in God. I have tried to indicate in my analysis that this negative doctrine is not required by the essential starting point in the Thomist vision and that even within Thomism, it is a source of unresolved difficulties. If my analysis is correct, the two major ingredients in a Christian vision (finiteness and purposedness) are mutually compatible, and a Christian philosophy should begin with them both together. It is my conviction that the philosophy of Alfred North Whitehead as interpreted and developed by Charles Hartshorne can be of inestimable aid in the formulation of an adequate Christian philosophy.

It is my earnest hope that what I am suggesting here is not an *ad hoc* syncretism. This is far from my intention. I share with H. Richard Niebuhr the conviction that men are usually right in their basic affirmative convictions but often wrong in their negations. I do not believe that the impassibility of God is really as such a central conviction of Thomists, although I recognize that its antiquity and its sanctioning by the church may have made it very precious. At least, I believe, the justification for claiming a distinctively Christian status for this doctrine is derived from its supposedly necessary connection with the doctrine of God's necessary being. This vision of God and his world, central to Thomism, has spiritual and existential consequences neglected by Personalism but not flatly contradictory to its teaching. I am deeply convinced that genuine synthesis is possible.

I see no reason why the Christian natural theology formed by a synthesis of Thomism and Personalism should not provide a context in which the positive insights of Brunner, Tillich, and the Niebuhrs could be expressed. The point of greatest conflict would be Tillich's doctrine that God is Being in such a way that he is in no sense *a* being, even the Supreme Being. I would argue, however, that the radical uniqueness of God's being, which is Tillich's major positive insight here, is preserved when the radical contrast of necessary and contingent being is maintained, whereas the latter distinction need not have the depersonalizing implications with respect to God's being entailed in Tillich's doctrine.

My thesis is that if each of these theologians recognizes that part of his starting point should be found in the Christian vision of the world, the diversity of emphases within this vision can be reconciled and synthesized. The formulation of such a synthesis can never be completed once for all, but I am convinced that a much more satisfactory achievement is open to us than any now obtaining.

The second question that must be frankly faced is the relativism or circularity that is made apparent in the expression "*Christian* natural theology." Natural theology had once been thought of as a positive basis on which to approach reasonable people of other faiths. But we are forced to recognize now that our natural theology is no less alien to the reason of men outside our tradition than are other affirmations of faith. Furthermore, these other traditions exist no longer only in other parts of the world. In the post-Christian West an ever increasing portion of the population is profoundly estranged from that vision of the world that Christian faith had long made the basis of our cultural common sense. Even among those who self-consciously cling to the Christian faith, many find that the basic vision is fading and that the beliefs associated with it are increasingly problematic.

In this situation, the existing relativism or circularity constitute an acute problem not only for evangelistic method but existentially for sensitive Christians. There is a profound need to believe that the vision to which we cling is warranted by something more than its fading existence. Such a need demands that we try in principle to transcend our cultural conditioning in order to justify it — to break out of the circle in which we find ourselves and touch the bedrock of objective truth.

Such a demand must appear doomed to frustration, and if it were not so urgent it could simply be ridiculed and dismissed. If we enjoyed subjective certitude, a recognition of objective uncertainty would not be serious. But when subjective certitude crumbles, the question of objective warrant can no longer be pushed aside.

The task to which we are pointed cannot be a new natural theology in the classical sense. We cannot start somewhere else than in the circle in which we stand. But if we stand there, torn between belief and unbelief, we can imaginatively participate in other worlds than the world of faith. That is, in our new situation of self-conscious relativism we can objectify the visions that for centuries or milleniums have been the unsurpassable starting points for thought. Undoubtedly, there remains beyond all the starting points that we can objectify a more ultimate one of which we cannot become conscious, but since at this point the historical relativism is transcended, we need not be disturbed. Our problem is that we are newly conscious of a freedom to choose at a level that has through most of world history been closed to choice, and that lacking criteria for choosing, we also lack confidence in the vision into which we drift. Our fading Christian vision will not be restored until it regains our wholehearted confidence. Once the vision itself has entered consciousness as an object, confidence can be restored only at the level of conscious persuasion. That means, again, that we need criteria for choosing among visions.

The problems raised here are too difficult to be discussed in a few paragraphs of this concluding chapter. I am concerned here only to stress the urgency of the problem and the new form that it is assuming for our generation. I am convinced that both of the older solutions are rapidly becoming irrelevant. That is, we can neither appeal to neutral reason to support our faith nor show the independence of faith from all the conclusions of reason. We can neither deny the conditioned circularity of any point of view nor rest complacent in that circularity. Those who would support the

Christian vision in our time must develop new approaches to meet a genuinely new situation fraught with profound peril to the human spirit but *possibly* offering also hope for reversing the long decline of faith.

In dealing with the two crucial problems faced by natural theology I have suggested that the first can be progressively solved by hard work with tools now at hand; but the second, in its radical implications, is so new for us that we have hardly conceived of a direction in which to look for a solution. The emerging self-consciousness about our starting point in diverse visions of the world is responsible alike for what I take to be the possibility of progress on the first problem and the acute heightening of the second problem.

We must turn now to the question: Given a starting point in Christian natural theology, how is a transition made to Christian theology proper? Surveying those we have been considering, we see that Mascall appeals to participation in the life of the church that prepares for the acceptance of its authority; DeWolf and H. Richard Niebuhr appeal to the distinctive experience of the Hebrew-Christian community; Brunner appeals to a personal encounter with Jesus Christ; Tillich appeals to the existential experience of participation in the New Being. Reinhold Niebuhr has relatively little to say on this question since he hardly distinguishes Christian theology proper from what he defends on empirical or phenomenological grounds. In so far as he is to be treated here, he may be placed with DeWolf and H. Richard Niebuhr.

There is in fact little basic difference in these answers. No one supposes that one enters into faith by objective rational persuasion that faith is entailed in historical and philosophical beliefs. The individual experiences faith in the church as he enters into the peculiar mode of Christian existence. Differences emerge in the understanding of this existence and, hence, in the understanding of the content of Christian doctrine, and I would by no means belittle these differences. Adequate discussion of the problems involved would require several books.

The differences in the understanding of Christian existence, along with the accompanying differences in the whole range of Christian doctrine, have two major types of sources. First, there is a real diversity of human experience that entails a real diversity of understanding of the meaning and means of salvation. This diversity ought not in principle to lead to contradiction, but, in fact, it often seems to do so. Perhaps with great labor we might apply here, too, the principle that the central positive affirmations of serious Christians are usually sound, whereas negations are unreliable, and thereby move toward a more inclusive view. I have tried to clarify this problem in *Varieties of Protestantism* and can only mention it here in passing. Second, the diversity in understanding of Christian existence also reflects the diversity in understanding of Christian natural theology. No matter how much one of these theologians stresses that his understanding of God arises directly in his Christian experience, we will suspect also that that experience as he understands it is conditioned by his total understanding of himself and his world. Hence, I suggest that *if* the diversity of Christian natural theologies could be reduced, some reduction of the confusion with respect to Christian theology proper could also be effected.

Even within the circle of thinkers who, I believe, point us toward the use of a Christian natural theology as well as a Christian theology proper, considerable differences of emphasis are possible. One may hold that Christian natural theology contains much of what is most important to believers and treat theology proper as a minor supplement. Another may hold that the acknowledgment of the legitimacy of Christian natural theology does not imply its theological importance and may concentrate almost entirely on questions of theology proper. However, such differences of emphasis are relative to different purposes and situations. It is my personal judgment that in the situation into which we are now moving a great deal of attention must be devoted to Christian natural theology, but at the same time we must hope that many will give central and intensive attention to theology proper.

What I have called the Augustinian position offers still another variant here. Perhaps we should stress the homogeneity and continuity of Christian natural theology and theology proper in such a way that no line of distinction would be made. Christian theology and Christian philosophy would be understood as the one act of thinking under the guidance of divine grace. I see no serious objection to this course as long as it is a matter of emphasis rather than of principle.

However, there remains within the starting point given in faith a distinction between the fundamental vision of the world and the specifically Christian affirmations consciously referred to God's revelation in Jesus Christ as their warrant. Some conclusions can be drawn from the starting point in the general vision. Others require avowed commitment and quite specific experience as their warrant. The two should prove coherent and mutually supportive, but their distinction is not unimportant.

We must turn now to consider the two men in the analysis of whose thought it seemed most likely that genuine alternatives to Christian natural theology might be found. These are Barth and Bultmann. In the criticism of both, I have indicated that even in their cases there seems to be no complete escape from natural theology, but in both cases the issues become so refined and so intricate that it will be better not to pass a negative judgment.

In the analysis of Bultmann's many-faceted thought, we traced interpretations of his meaning that would lead us into a Christian natural theology, but there seemed to remain one interpretation faithful to some of his major emphases that almost wholly escaped this end. That is, if we set aside radically all concern for what is credible or incredible in the modern world, we may take as our one Christian principle justification by faith alone. We may then understand the occurrence of faith in an individual as an event in full discontinuity with both physical and psychological events. Theology may then be understood as the account of the occurring of faith and of the existence that ensues. No beliefs about the nature of the world or history are entailed in such an account. It may be possible to say also that the event of faith in our lives gives itself to us as dependent on a once-for-all event in the death and resurrection of Jesus Christ. But that event must be understood as wholly beyond the sphere of general investigation and as irrelevant to that sphere.

Barth's success in freeing theology from all involvement in natural theology depends upon the possibility of seeing the Bible as a unity and of finding within it the governing principle that its one function is to witness to Jesus Christ as God's presence to man. We have considered some of the internal difficulties involved in accepting Barth's view, but we cannot exclude the possibility that he is correct. If so, then, while Bultmann points to the possibility of a purely existential theology of Christian self-understanding, Barth points to a purely positive Biblical theology of testimony to Jesus Christ. Methodological criticism can deny to neither the claim to be living options in Protestant theology. The vast influence of both men suggests that these options are very vital indeed, even though they are usually impurely adopted.

We can see, then, that there are genuine alternatives to the acceptance of a Christian natural theology. These alternatives entail three major features. First, one must affirm a strictly supernatural occurrence as the basis for Christian existence. Christian existence must not be understood as a psychologically understandable modification of existence generally. Second, one must affirm nothing about the cause of Christian existence that either presupposes or implies anything about nature or history as they are visible from any other vantage point. Third, one must so formulate Christian faith that it has no implications that are in principle relevant to any perspective other than that of faith.

That theology is possible in these terms is an important fact. Once both its possibility and its inherent limitations are recognized, there is little more than can be said for or against it. If one has experienced the supernatural event in such a way that he can begin with it in his thinking, and if he further experiences his faith as in fact in total discontinuity with the world as seen from every other perspective, then he may be expected to reject Christian natural theology with full consistency and integrity. Since my own experience meets neither of these conditions, I must regard that which is systematically a living option as existentially closed to me. Further, I personally believe that the faith of which we read in the New Testament did not have the total discontinuity in question.

Thus far in this chapter I have made no mention of Wieman. I omitted him from the consideration of Christian natural theologies because I do not believe that the basic vision within which he operates is distinctively Christian. On the contrary, I regard it as definitely post-Christian. One may trace its gradual emergence through the decline of substance thinking, and some indication of this has been given in Chapter 1. However, philosophical reasons for the emergence of Wieman's type of process philosophy must be given the most serious attention in the formulation of a Christian natural theology. If a Christian natural theology entails that kind of thinking about substances which was philosophically undermined in modern philosophy, it is in very serious difficulty indeed.

I am convinced, however, that another type of process philosophy is possible that does not dissolve persons into strands with less ontological reality than the events in which they participate. I refer again to the philosophy of Whitehead. In his thought there is a thorough acceptance of the legitimate aspects of Hume's critique of earlier modern philosophy without the acceptance of the conclusions that Wieman in common with much modern philosophy has drawn from them. If so, then there is no philosophical necessity of adopting Wieman's basic ontology.

Here as elsewhere in this chapter, I have made dogmatic comments on highly disputable topics. A philosophy of events of the sort Wieman employs is often defended as more Biblical than the substance philosophy that is taken as its only alternative. The Bible, it is held, deals with occurrences rather than with entities. Within limits this is certainly true. However, I would argue that the Bible deals with selves acting, rather than with actions as such. Niebuhr's understanding of selves in dialogue seems much truer to the Bible than the modern view of a flow of phenomenal events. Indeed, in the latter, the depth dimension of existence, so essential to Biblical faith, is obscured if not lost.

Neither from Wieman's point of view nor from mine is the rejection of his ontology a basic attack upon his positive contribution. This contribution consists in the remarkable analysis of the processes in which human growth occurs. This analysis, in Wieman's view and in mine, is compatible with many different ontologies. Indeed, I argue that although these processes may be described within the modern post-Christian vision, they are not facilitated by that vision. On the contrary, it is the Christian vision of the world that has through the centuries provided the context within which these processes have had their fullest encouragement and support.

Once again, therefore, I believe that genuine synthesis is possible when we limit ourselves to that which is the central positive insight of a great thinker and do not try to incorporate also all his peripheral and negative judgments. There is no inconsistency between a synthesis of Thomism with Personalism in terms of their basic visions of the world and Wieman's careful description of the processes in which human good emerges. Indeed, a very large part of the theological task must consist in empirical and phenomenological accounts that, in so far as they attain their own ideal of objectivity, will conflict neither with each other nor with the Christian vision of the world.

For example, Reinhold Niebuhr's extensive and penetrating analyses of human existence and historical interrelationships are a solid permanent contribution to Christian thought. The same must be said with emphasis of Bultmann's brilliant account of Christian existence, which may be accepted quite independently of his attempted rejection of Christian natural theology. Tillich and H. Richard Niebuhr have also added invaluably to our understanding of our situation through phenomenological description.

We cannot, of course, simply add together all that these men have said on the basis of empirical and phenomenological work. The objectivity of these methods and their goals is ideal rather than actual. In the brief study of the thought of Husserl, Sartre, and Heidegger, we saw that these great philosophical practitioners of phenomenology had not succeeded in separating their phenomenological findings from the ontological positions they maintained. We may assume that the theologians likewise are affected in their phenomenological work by relativizing factors. Nevertheless, empirical and phenomenological research does afford us some possibility of transcending the pure relativity of personal opinion, and this possibility needs to be explored with increasing vigor and self-consciousness.

Where phenomenology is employed for the study of the structures of human existence, greater attention should be paid to the possibility that these structures themselves are partly historical. As one reads the phenomenological accounts of human existence in both Sartre and Heidegger, for example, one wonders whether the same structures are to be found in the same way among primitive peoples or in nonhistorical cultures. I believe that one of the major tasks that confronts our generation is the development of a phenomenological-existential history of man's emergence into various dimensions of consciousness and self-consciousness. To this end much material is already at hand, but the great work of synthesis has hardly been begun.

A further area for future exploration is that of the relation of the development of consciousness on the one hand to the emergence of diverse visions of the world on the other. It is my opinion that these operate in closest interconnection and that finally the level of consciousness that can be sustained by man is largely a function of his vision of the world. But the testing of such a hypothesis alone is more than one lifetime's work.

The tasks that lie before us are vast, the laborers are few, and the confusion in our ranks is great. The spiritual and intellectual climate in which we work is changing rapidly, and for the most part our tools are still geared to the situation that prevailed thirty or forty years ago — during the formative period in the lives of that great generation of theologians with whom this volume primarily deals. In our day we must run fast if we would stand still, and faster still if we would catch up. We can only hope that we will be granted both time and courage.

Bibliography

Anderson, Gerald H., ed., *The Theology of the Christian Mission.* McGraw-Hill Book Co., Inc., 1961.

Baillie, John, ed., *Natural Theology,* comprising "Nature and Grace" by Emil Brunner and the reply "No!" by Karl Barth; tr. by Peter Fraenkel. Geoffrey Bles, Ltd.; The Centenary Press, London, 1946.

Barth, Karl, *Against the Stream: Shorter Post-War Writings, 1946–52,* ed. by Ronald Gregor Smith. Philosophical Library, Inc., 1954.

——— *Christ and Adam: Man and Humanity in Romans 5,* tr. by T. A. Smail. Harper & Brothers, 1956.

——— *Church Dogmatics,* Vols. I–IV, ed. and tr. by G. T. Thomson, G. W. Bromiley, T. F. Torrance, *et al.,* T. & T. Clark, Edinburgh, 1936–1960.

——— *The Epistle to the Romans,* tr. from 6th ed. by Edwyn C. Hoskyns. Oxford University Press, London, 1933.

——— *The Humanity of God.* John Knox Press, 1960.

Bartsch, Hans Werner, ed., *Kerygma und Mythos: ein theologisches Gespräch,* II Band. Herbert Reich, Hamburg, 1952.

——— ed., *Kerygma and Myth: A Theological Debate,* with contributions by Rudolf Bultmann, *et al.,* tr. by Reginald H. Fuller. S. P. C. K., London, 1953.

Basilius, Harold A., ed., *Contemporary Problems in Religion.* Wayne University Press, 1956.

Berkouwer, Gerrit Cornelis, *Divine Election,* tr. by Hugo Bekker. Wm. B. Eerdmans Publishing Company, 1960.

——— *Modern Uncertainty and Christian Faith.* Wm. B. Eerdmans Publishing Company, 1953.

——— *The Person of Christ,* tr. by John Vriend. Wm. B. Eerdmans Publishing Company, 1954.

——— *The Triumph of Grace in the Theology of Karl Barth,* tr. by Harry R. Boer. Wm. B. Eerdmans Publishing Company, 1956.

Bertocci, Peter Anthony, *Introduction to the Philosophy of Religion.* Prentice-Hall, Inc., 1951.

Brandt, Richard B., *The Philosophy of Schleiermacher: The Development of His Theory of Scientific and Religious Knowledge.* Harper & Brothers, 1941.

Brightman, Edgar S., *Person and Reality: An Introduction to Metaphysics,* ed. by P. A. Bertocci. The Ronald Press Company, 1958.

Brunner, Emil, *The Christian Doctrine of Creation and Redemption,* Dogmatics: Vol. II, tr. by Olive Wyon. The Westminster Press, 1950.

——— *The Christian Doctrine of God,* Dogmatics: Vol. I, tr. by Olive Wyon. The Westminster Press, 1950.

——— *The Divine-Human Encounter,* tr. by Amandus W. Loos. The Westminster Press, 1943.

——— *Die christliche Lehre. Von der Kirche. Vom Glauben und von der Vollendung.* Dogmatik: III Band. Zwingli-Verlag, Zürich, 1960.

——— *Man in Revolt: A Christian Anthropology,* tr. by Olive Wyon. The Westminster Press, 1947.

——— *Revelation and Reason: The Christian Doctrine of Faith and Knowledge,* tr. by Olive Wyon. The Westminster Press, 1946.

——— *The Theology of Crisis.* Charles Scribner's Sons, 1929.

——— *The Word and the World.* Student Christian Movement Press, Ltd., London, 1931.

Buber, Martin, *Between Man and Man,* tr. by Ronald Gregor Smith. The Macmillan Company, 1948.

——— *Eclipse of God: Studies in the Relation Between Religion and Philosophy.* Harper & Brothers, 1952.

——— *I and Thou,* 2d ed. with Postscript, tr. by Ronald Gregor Smith. Charles Scribner's Sons, 1958.

Bultmann, Rudolf, *Essays: Philosophical and Theological,* tr. by J. C. G. Grieg. Student Christian Movement Press, Ltd., London, 1955.

——— *Existence and Faith: Shorter Writings of Rudolf Bultmann,* selected, translated, and introduced by Schubert M. Ogden. Meridian Books, Inc., 1960.

——— *Glauben und Verstehen: Gesammelte Aufsätze,* I Band. Mohr, Tübingen, 1954.

——— *Jesus and the Word,* tr. by Louise Pettibone Smith and Erminie Huntress Lantero, Student's edition. Charles Scribner's Sons, 1958.

——— *Jesus Christ and Mythology.* Charles Scribner's Sons, 1958.

——— *The Presence of Eternity: History and Eschatology.* Harper & Brothers, 1957.

——— *Primitive Christianity in Its Contemporary Setting,* tr. by Reginald H. Fuller. Meridian Books, Inc., 1956.

——— "The Problem of Miracle," tr. by Fred D. Gealy, *Religion in Life,* Vol. 27, 1957–1958, pp. 63–75.

——— *Theology of the New Testament,* Vols. I and II, tr. by Kendrick Grovel. Charles Scribner's Sons, 1951–1955.

——— "What Sense Is There to Speak of God?" tr. by Franklin H. Littell, *The Christian Scholar,* Vol. 43, 1960, pp. 213–222.

Buri, Fritz, "Theologie und Philosophie," *Theologische Zeitschrift,* Vol. 8, 1952, pp. 116–134.

Burtt, Edwin Arthur, ed., *The English Philosophers from Bacon to Mill.* Modern Library edition. Random House, Inc., 1939.

Butler, Joseph, *The Analogy of Religion, Natural and Revealed, to the Constitution and Course of Nature,* 23d ed. J. B. Lippincott Company, 1885.

Carnell, Edward John, *The Case for Orthodox Theology.* The Westminster Press, 1959.

——— *The Theology of Reinhold Niebuhr.* Wm. B. Eerdmans Publishing Company, 1951.

Carus, Paul, ed., *Kant's Prolegomena to Any Future Metaphysics.* The Open Court Publishing Company, 1933.

Cobb, John B., Jr., "The Philosophic Grounds of Moral Responsibility: A Comment on Matson and Niebuhr," *The Journal of Philosophy,* Vol. 16, 1959, pp. 619–621.

——— *Varieties of Protestantism.* The Westminster Press, 1960.

Collins, James Daniel, *God in Modern Philosophy.* Henry Regnery Company, 1959.

Davies, Rupert E., *The Problem of Authority in the Continental Reformers: A Study in Luther, Zwingli, and Calvin.* The Epworth Press, London, 1946.

Desan, Wilfred, *The Tragic Finale.* Revised Torchbook edition. Harper & Brothers, 1960.

DeWolf, L. Harold, *Acknowledgement of Non-Christian Contributions to Christian Faith,* Boston University Lecture for 1960. Boston University Press, 1960.

——— "Biblical, Liberal, Catholic," Article X in series How My Mind Has Changed, *The Christian Century,* Vol. 77, 1960, pp. 1303–1307.

——— *The Case for Theology in Liberal Perspective.* The Westminster Press, 1959.

——— *The Enduring Message of the Bible.* Harper & Brothers, 1960.

——— *The Religious Revolt Against Reason.* Harper & Brothers, 1949.

——— *A Theology of the Living Church.* Harper & Brothers, 1953.

Diamond, Malcolm Luria, *Martin Buber, Jewish Existentialist.* Oxford University Press, 1960.

Diem, Hermann, *Dogmatics,* tr. by Harold Knight. The Westminster Press, 1959.

——— *Kierkegaard's Dialectic of Existence,* tr. by Harold Knight. Oliver & Boyd, Ltd., Edinburgh, 1959.

Farley, Edward, *The Transcendence of God: A Study in Contemporary Philosophical Theology*. The Westminster Press, 1960.

Flew, Antony, and Macintyre, Alasdair, eds., *New Essays in Philosophical Theology*. The Macmillan Company, 1955.

Frank, Erich, *Philosophical Understanding and Religious Truth*. Oxford University Press, London, 1945.

Friedman, Maurice S., *Martin Buber: The Life of Dialogue*. Revised Torchbook edition. Harper & Brothers, 1960.

Fuchs, Ernst, *Hermeneutik*, 2 Auflage. R. Müllerschön, Bad Cannstatt, 1958.

Gilson, Etienne, *The Christian Philosophy of St. Thomas Aquinas,* tr. by L. K. Shook. Random House, Inc., 1956.

——— *God and Philosophy*. Yale University Press, 1941.

——— *Reason and Revelation in the Middle Ages*. Charles Scribner's Sons, 1938.

Greene, Norman N., *Jean-Paul Sartre: The Existentialist Ethic*. University of Michigan Press, 1960.

Harland, Gordon, *The Thought of Reinhold Niebuhr*. Oxford University Press, 1960.

Hartshorne, Charles, *Man's Vision of God, and the Logic of Theism*. Willett, Clark & Company, 1941.

Hartshorne, Charles, and Reese, William L., eds., *Philosophers Speak of God*. University of Chicago Press, 1953.

Heidegger, Martin, *Aus der Erfahrung des Denkens*. G. Neske, Pfullingen, 1954.

——— *Existence and Being,* Introduction by Werner Brock. Henry Regnery Company, 1949.

——— *Holzwege*. Vittorio Klostermann, Frankfurt am Main, 1950.

——— *Identität und Differenz*. G. Neske, Pfullingen, 1957.

——— *An Introduction to Metaphysics,* tr. by Ralph Manheim. Yale University Press, 1959.

——— *The Question of Being,* tr. with Introduction by William Kluback and Jean T. Wilde. Twayne Publishers Inc., 1958.

——— *Sein und Zeit,* Erste Hälfte, 6 unveränderte Auflage. Neomarius, Tübingen, 1949.

——— *What Is Philosophy?,* tr. with Introduction by William Kluback and Jean T. Wilde. Twayne Publishers Inc., 1958.

Henry, Carl F. H., *Fifty Years of Protestant Theology*. W. A. Wilde Company, 1950.

Herberg, Will, ed., *Four Existentialist Theologians*. Doubleday & Co., Inc., 1958.

Hick, John, *Faith and Knowledge: A Modern Introduction to the Problem of Religious Knowledge*. Cornell University Press, 1957.

Huber, Gerhard, ed., *Philosophie und Christliche Existenz, Festschrift* for Heinrich Barth. Verlag Helbing & Lichtenhahn, Basel and Stuttgart, 1960.

Hunt, George L., ed., *Ten Makers of Modern Protestant Thought.* Reflection Book. Association Press, 1958.

Husserl, Edmund, *Cartesian Meditations,* tr. by Dorion Cairns. Nijhoff, The Hague, 1960.

——— *Ideas: General Introduction to Pure Phenomenology,* tr. by W. R. Boyce Gibson. George Allen & Unwin, Ltd., London, and The Macmillan Company, New York, 1931.

Jaspers, Karl, and Bultmann, Rudolf, *Myth and Christianity: An Inquiry Into the Possibility of Religion Without Myth.* The Noonday Press, 1958.

Johnson, Frederick Ernest, ed., *Religious Symbolism.* Institute for Religious and Social Studies. Distributed by Harper & Brothers, 1955.

Johnson, Robert Clyde, *Authority in Protestant Theology.* The Westminster Press, 1959.

Jung, Carl Gustav, *Psychology and Religion.* Yale University Press, 1938.

Kant, Immanuel, *Religion Within the Limits of Reason Alone,* tr. with Introduction and notes by Theodore M. Greene and Hoyt H. Hudson. The Open Court Publishing Company, 1934.

Kegley, Charles W., and Bretall, Robert W., eds., *Reinhold Niebuhr, His Religious, Social, and Political Thought.* The Macmillan Company, 1956.

——— *The Theology of Paul Tillich.* The Macmillan Company, 1952.

Kierkegaard, Sören, *Concluding Unscientific Postscript,* tr. by David F. Swenson and Walter Lowrie. Princeton University Press, 1941.

Lowrie, Walter, *Kierkegaard.* Oxford University Press, 1938.

McArthur, Harvey K., ed., *New Testament Sidelights: Essays in Honor of Alexander Converse Purdy.* The Hartford Seminary Foundation Press, 1960.

McGiffert, Arthur Cushman, *Protestant Thought Before Kant.* Charles Scribner's Sons, 1951.

Machen, J. Gresham, *Christianity and Liberalism.* The Macmillan Company, 1923.

Mackintosh, Hugh Ross, *Types of Modern Theology.* James Nisbet & Co., Ltd., London, 1937.

Macquarrie, John, *An Existentialist Theology: A Comparison of Heidegger and Bultmann.* Student Christian Movement Press, Ltd., London, 1955.

——— *The Scope of Demythologizing: Bultmann and His Critics.* Harper & Brothers, 1961.

Mascall, E. L., *Christ, the Christian and the Church.* Longmans, Green & Co., Inc., 1955.

——— *Existence and Analogy.* Longmans, Green & Co., Inc., 1949.

——— *He Who Is: A Study in Traditional Theism.* Longmans, Green & Co., Inc., 1943.

——— *The Importance of Being Human: Some Aspects of the Christian Doctrine of Man.* Columbia University Press, 1958.

——— *Via Media.* The Seabury Press, Inc., 1957.

——— *Words and Images: A Study in Theological Discourse*. The Ronald Press Company, 1957.

Melanchthon, Philip, *The Loci Communes of Philip Melanchthon,* tr. by Charles Leander Hill. Meador Publishing Company, 1944.

Moore, E. Caldwell, *The History of Christian Thought Since Kant*. Gerald Duckworth & Co., Ltd., London, 1912.

Mounier, Emmanuel, *Existentialist Philosophies,* tr. by Eric Blow. Rockliff Pub. Corp., London, 1948.

Neve, Juergen Ludwig, *A History of Christian Thought,* Vol. II. Muhlenberg Press, 1946.

Niebuhr, H. Richard, *Christ and Culture*. Harper & Brothers, 1951.

——— *The Meaning of Revelation*. The Macmillan Company, 1941.

——— et al., *The Purpose of the Church and Its Ministry: Reflections on the Aims of Theological Education*. Harper & Brothers, 1956.

——— *Radical Monotheism and Western Culture*. Harper & Brothers, 1960.

Niebuhr, Reinhold, *Christian Realism and Political Problems*. Charles Scribner's Sons, 1953.

——— *Faith and History: A Comparison of Christian and Modern Views of History*. Charles Scribner's Sons, 1949.

——— *Pious and Secular America*. Charles Scribner's Sons, 1958.

——— *The Self and the Dramas of History*. Charles Scribner's Sons, 1955.

——— *The Structure of Nations and Empires: A Study of the Recurring Patterns and Problems of the Political Order in Relation to the Unique Problems of the Nuclear Age*. Charles Scribner's Sons, 1959.

Niebuhr, Richard R., *Resurrection and Historical Reason: A Study of Theological Method*. Charles Scribner's Sons, 1957.

Ogden, Schubert M., "Bultmann's Project of Demythologizing," *The Journal of Religion,* Vol. 37, 1957, pp. 156–173.

——— *Christ Without Myth*. Harper & Brothers, 1961.

——— "The Debate on Demythologizing," *The Journal of Bible and Religion,* Vol. 27, 1959, pp. 17–27.

Ott, Heinrich, *Denken und Sein*. Evangelischer Verlag, A.-G., Zollikon, Switzerland, 1959.

Pelikan, Jaroslav, *From Luther to Kierkegaard: A Study in the History of Theology*. Concordia Publishing House, 1950.

Robinson, James McConkey, *A New Quest of the Historical Jesus* (Studies in Biblical Theology, No. 25). Alec E. Allenson, Inc., 1959.

Sartre, Jean-Paul, *Being and Nothingness: An Essay on Phenomenological Ontology,* tr. by Hazel E. Barnes. Philosophical Library, Inc., 1956.

——— *The Transcendence of the Ego,* tr. by Forrest Williams and Robert Kirkpatrick. The Noonday Press, 1957.

Schleiermacher, Friedrich, *The Christian Faith,* tr. of second German ed. by H. R. Mackintosh and J. S. Stewart. T. & T. Clark, Edinburgh, 1928.

——— *On Religion: Speeches to Its Cultured Despisers,* tr. by John Oman, Introduction by Rudolf Otto. Torchbook edition. Harper & Brothers, 1958.

Schutz, Alfred, "Edmund Husserl's Ideas Volume II," *Philosophy and Phenomenological Research,* Vol. 13, 1953, pp. 406–411.

——— "Edmund Husserl's Ideas Volume III," *Philosophy and Phenomenological Research,* Vol. 13, 1953, pp. 506–514.

Smith, Ronald Gregor, *J. G. Hamann, 1730–1788.* Harper & Brothers, 1960.

Swing, Albert Temple, *The Theology of Albrecht Ritschl,* together with Albrecht Ritschl, *Instruction in the Christian Religion,* tr. by Alice Mead Swing. Longmans, Green & Co., Inc., 1901.

Tavard, George H., *Holy Writ or Holy Church: The Crisis of the Protestant Reformation.* Harper & Brothers, 1960.

Thomas, J. Heywood, *Subjectivity and Paradox.* Basil Blackwell & Mott, Ltd., Oxford, 1957.

Tillich, Paul, *Biblical Religion and the Search for Ultimate Reality.* University of Chicago Press, 1955.

——— *The Courage to Be.* Yale University Press, 1952.

——— *Dynamics of Faith.* Harper & Brothers, 1957.

——— *Frühe Haupt Werke,* Gesammelte Werke, I Band. Evangelisches Verlagswerk, Stuttgart, 1959.

——— "Metaphysics and Theology," *Review of Metaphysics,* Vol. 10, 1956, pp. 57–63.

——— "The Problem of Theological Method," *The Journal of Religion,* Vol. 27, 1947, pp. 16–26.

——— *The Protestant Era,* tr. by James Luther Adams. University of Chicago Press, 1948.

——— *The Religious Situation,* tr. by H. Richard Niebuhr. Henry Holt & Co., Inc., 1932. Reprinted in 1956 by Meridian Books, Inc.

——— "The Religious Symbol," *The Journal of Liberal Religion,* Vol. 2, 1940, pp. 13–33.

——— "Religious Symbols and Our Knowledge of God," *The Christian Scholar,* Vol. 38, 1955, pp. 189–197.

——— *Systematic Theology.* University of Chicago Press, Vol. I, 1951; Vol. II, 1957.

——— *Theology of Culture.* Oxford University Press, 1959.

Van Til, Cornelius, *The New Modernism: An Appraisal of the Theology of Barth and Brunner.* Presbyterian and Reformed Pub. Co., 1946.

Weber, Otto, *Karl Barth's Church Dogmatics: An Introductory Report on Volumes I:1 to III:4,* tr. by Arthur C. Cochrane. The Westminster Press, 1953.

Wieman, Henry Nelson, *The Directive in History.* The Beacon Press, Inc., 1949.

——— *Intellectual Foundation of Faith.* Philosophical Library, Inc., 1961.

——— *Man's Ultimate Commitment.* Southern Illinois University Press, 1958.

——— *The Source of Human Good.* University of Chicago Press, 1946.

——— *The Wrestle of Religion with Truth.* The Macmillan Company, 1929.

Williams, Daniel Day, *God's Grace and Man's Hope.* Harper & Brothers, 1949.

Wolfson, Harry Austryn, *The Philosophy of the Church Fathers.* Harvard University Press, 1956.

Zuurdeeg, Willem Frederik, *An Analytic Philosophy of Religion.* Abingdon Press, 1958.

Index

Names

Subjects